ALSO BY PETER PAGNAMENTA

Sword and Blossom
(with Momoko Williams)

PRAIRIE FEVER

British Aristocrats in the American West 1830–1890

PETER PAGNAMENTA

DUCKWORTH OVERLOOK

This paperback edition 2013
First published in the UK in 2012 by
Duckworth Overlook
30 Calvin Street
London E1 6NW
T: 020 7490 7300
E: info@duckworth-publishers.co.uk
www.ducknet.co.uk

First published in the USA in 2012 by
W.W. Norton & Company Inc., New York

A catalogue record for this book is available
from the British Library

ISBNs
Paperback: 9780715645338
Mobipocket: 9780715644430
ePub: 9780715644423
Library PDF: 9780715644416

Text design by JAM Design
Manufactured in the UK by
CPI Group (UK) Ltd, Croydon CR0 4YY

Contents

Introduction ix

Maps xviii

Prologue: 1887—Frontier Days 1

PART I   FREEDOM FOR THE SPIRIT

1. Encircling Vastness 11
2. Beyond the Mississippi 28
3. Red Men and Blue Bloods 56
4. Buffalo Dreams 83
5. "Who Would Not Go A'Pleasuring!" 113

PART II   STAKING A CLAIM

6. Private Paradise 147
7. A Place for the Boys 175
8. "Hail Britannia!" 195
9. Cattle Lords 230
10. "Land Grabbers" 265

Epilogue: 1887 282

Acknowledgments 295
Notes 299
Credits 317
Index 321

The prairie fever! I feel it now! While I am penning these memories, my fingers twitch to grasp the reins—my knees quiver to press the sides of my noble horse, and wildly wander over the verdant billows of the prairie sea."

—CAPTAIN MAYNE REID, *The Scalp Hunters*, 1851

Introduction

In the spring of 2010 I met a prairie farmer with 1600 acres of flat and fertile land in Kansas, almost in the centre of the United States. He told me how, on hot summer nights, as he roared across the huge fields ploughing in the wheat stubble after the harvest, his tractor spotlights picked out a myriad of dazzling sparkles from the newly turned furrows. The reflections were thrown back by splinters and shards of glass, from the old beer and spirits bottles cast aside by what he referred to as "the British boys".

In the spring of 2010 I met a prairie farmer with 1600 acres of flat and fertile land in Kansas, almost in the centre of the United States. He told me how, on hot summer nights, as he roared across the huge fields ploughing in the wheat stubble after the harvest, his tractor spotlights picked out a myriad of dazzling sparkles from the newly turned furrows. The reflections were thrown back by splinters and shards of glass, from the old beer and spirits bottles cast aside by what he referred to as "the British boys".

The broken glass is all that remains of Runnymede, a rakish community that existed for a few years in the 1880s and '90s, failed to flourish, and was then pulled down. The former township plays a vivid part in the history of Harper County. Local folklore goes back to a time when well-to-do Englishmen bought farm land in this part of southern Kansas, put on scarlet coats to chase after coyote, laid out a steeplechase course, played tennis on the prairie, and spent much of their time drinking and carousing.

Other traces of the upper-class British involvement with the American West are more uplifting. In Wyoming one of the noblest peaks in Yellowstone National Park is named after the 4th Earl of Dunraven, who came through these parts on an extended shooting foray, killing scores of bear, elk and mountain sheep. Every summer, the cars and camper vans of hundreds of thousands of park tourists grind up over a high mountain pass named after the same peer. Colorado has a lake first christened after a Scottish aristocrat who made repeated visits to fish and hunt. Western art galleries hold paintings of the Rockies and prairies, commissioned during the Nineteenth Century by wealthy British patrons. Out on the range, some of the most valued breeds of cattle and sheep can be traced back to blooded animals shipped over by the British owners, as they tried to improve the livestock on their American acres.

A few British farm buildings can still be found. In northwest Iowa, in the small settlement of Brunsville, another farmer showed me his double-level cattle shed and hay barn, constructed to the high specifications of an admiral in the Royal Navy, which has held out against 130 years of storms and tornadoes, and his equally well built Victorian farmhouse. He pointed to where the line of stables for the polo ponies once stood, and the paddock by the creek where the British boys played practice games.

In nearby Le Mars, the small wooden Episcopal church on 1st Avenue, is another survival from the same era. Built in the 1880s, when the prairie town became the headquarters of a large British community, St George's held Anglican services, led by a specially imported British clergyman. With its wooden pews, brass fittings, hymn board and lectern sent out from home, it still suggests the chapel of one of the English public schools through which most of the young, fit and ruddy faced congregation would have passed so recently.

The handful of British "colonies" that sprung up in the Mid-West and West of the United States in the 1870s and 80s was one of the later manifestations of a passion which began as Queen Victoria came to the throne, and which was to take several different forms over the following fifty years. Mass migration across the Atlantic was building up during the same period, and over the course of Victoria's reign nearly two million left as emigrants from England and Scotland, and nearly four million from Ireland. However this is not a story of the huddled masses who had to cross the ocean in steerage, but of the well-off classes who travelled in the comfort of the saloon deck, often with return tickets. It tracks a strange and, at times, controversial encounter as a class of people, who were quite unlike other new arrivals, and had no equivalent in the United States, were drawn to a landscape and opportunities with no match in Europe.

The influx of aristocrats and well-born Britons was just a small eddy in the great tide of incoming settlers and emigrants that washed across the country in those years, but their money, energy and self-confidence gave them a significance far beyond their number. They began to make the journey in the 1830s, taking their dogs, and sometimes their valets and servants, and making their way to the prairies. Some saw trekking across the Far West as a more challenging alternative to taking the Grand Tour in Europe. As the frontier advanced, their reasons for going began to alter. There was less emphasis on seeing the wilderness and the Indians for their own sake, and more on the unparalleled scope for hunting. The blue-blooded grandees were joined by members of the gentry, whose resources were still considerable by American standards, if smaller than those of the nobility who had preceded them.

A frenzy of buffalo killing was followed by attempts at settlement, when it was thought a country gentleman's lifestyle could be established in Kansas or Colorado. In the final round of this engagement, during the prairie cattle boom, British aristocrats joined in the beef business, stepping down from the Pullman cars of the transcontinental trains in Wyoming or Nebraska, to buy herds of animals, and then millions of acres of land. But the beef bonanza collapsed quickly, through a combination of overgrazing and unusually savage winters. At the same time American popular opinion hardened against the incomers and they were drawn into the political crossfire that raged over the use and misuse of government-held land in the West, and between cattlemen, sheepmen and small settlers.

Though the British presence has become part of local mythology in much of the prairies, a colourful aside in the epic narrative of westward expansion, this is part of British social history as well. It demonstrates the lengths to which the aristocracy would go to indulge their historic need for hunting and country sports, and reflects their private insecurities, as the Nineteenth Century advanced. In great family seats and country houses, they worried about the rise of a middle class who seemed to be usurping their old political power, about farm prices at a time of agricultural depression, and about the worsening political situation in Ireland, with the possibility of land reform to relieve their tenants. They fretted about the prospects for younger members of their families, who would not acquire landed estates because of the custom of primogeniture inheritance, but who found openings in the army or the civil service more difficult to secure because of new government reforms.

For a while the United States seemed to offer an outlet and greater immediate potential than any of the alternatives then available in the British Empire itself. It also seemed healthier, less dangerous and easier to reach. Yet the wisest heads knew that the Atlantic Ocean divided two social and political systems, and two sets of manners and attitudes, and these had to be recognized and allowed for. These were years when the idea of America, and what it might achieve, became the subject of a stream of books, articles, sermons and lectures. Liberals envied the Americans for their entrenched freedoms and wider voting rights, though they condemned the evils of slavery. Conservatives were horrified by the clamour and crudeness of populist politics, and portrayed democracy as little more than the rule of the mob.

As the early travellers made their way from the east coast to the setting-off points for Indian territory along the Missouri, they had their first experience of the brash new United States, which figured so largely in the British mind, with a mixture of fascination and fear.

Along with so many visitors, and Mrs Trollope, the list of their complaints was often trivial. They decried the ill-kept state of the New York streets and the poorly laid pavements, the rudeness of American railway staff, the excessive handshaking that preceded any meeting, the torrential amount of spitting, and the "over-familiarity" of their fellow passengers on the steamboats.

Once they reached the west they faced a more fundamental challenge to their own beliefs and sense of identity. Men brought up under a monarchical system, with a privileged position in a rigid social hierarchy, found themselves in the rawest, most democratic and robustly egalitarian part of the new republic. Inevitably, this led to clashes and misunderstandings. This was a place where no-one cared who your father was, with no tradition of deference, and where the principle of equality, often aggressively asserted, was part of everyday dealing.

In 1850 the fourth son of Earl Fitzwilliam, one of the wealthiest men in Britain, began a trip which would keep him in the Far West for over two years and take him down to Mexico and up to Oregon. His first impression was of how different American society was. "It does not matter what trade or profession a man is here..." he wrote to the Earl. "Everybody is equal."[1] British visitors who failed to acknowledge this, and who were haughty or imperious, like Henry Coke, a younger son of the Earl of Leicester, found their way made ever more difficult. Later, on the cattle ranches, it was a mistake to refer to the hired hands who worked the ranch as the "cow-servants".

Americans had their own engrained attitudes and expectations about this class, in the reverse direction. Most had a historic aversion to the idea of aristocracy, going back to the revolution. As the transatlantic journey became easier, Americans with the time and money to visit the former mother country for tourism or business found their preconceptions confirmed. Nineteenth-century American travellers to Britain complained of a dulling complacency and adherence to convention in society, and were shocked at the gap between rich and poor. In 1834 Henry McLellan, a young man from Boston who had come to study after graduating from Harvard, reported "In England, condition, title and wealth are everything; character, person, humanity comparatively nothing. All yields to the dazzle of wealth and hereditary influence. This aristocracy predominates everywhere".

The historic British pre-occupation with class and fine social gradations provides one of the major themes in this story. Americans referred to the first blue-blood visitors as "top shelfers", and from the beginning they mocked their social pretensions and sense of entitlement, even if they respected their pluck. The British remained quietly convinced of their national superiority. In the later years they stuck to each other's company when they could, establishing private clubs and revealing their true feelings about "the yankees" in letters home. The most frequent charge was that the Americans were not gentlemen, with the code of behaviour that term implied, and were only interested in "the almighty dollar".

Neither the obsession with hunting and sport, nor changing economic circumstances, are enough to explain the great enthusiasm for the West on their own. This was the era when Britons became the most enterprising and tireless travellers the world had ever seen, striking out to distant parts of Africa, Asia and the Pacific in search of adventure or trade, or to bring British rule to native people they regarded as less talented and fortunate than themselves. There were other places where the grandees could shoot, or send their sons, or buy land, so why did so many come to the Far West, and what explains the strength of their passion?

Underlying the appeal were emotional strands that sprang from the European Romantic movement and the popular literature of the time. The world had other wildernesses, and other savages, but in the early Nineteenth Century the American Indian had a special status, and seemed specially noble. The first accounts of the pristine scenery and the great variety of fauna suggested that the Far West was a lost Eden, with a uniquely invigorating climate. Returning travellers described a sense of extreme physical well-being. For younger members of the aristocracy, in particular, no part of the British Empire seemed to catch their imaginations in the same way, at least at that stage. Western Canada opened up later, because the railways crossed the country more slowly.

In 1852 Charles Wentworth-Fitwilliam wrote to his father from Indian territory: "We are all very well and in capital spirits, but none more than myself. It is delicious to get out into a wild country."[2] By the 1850s there was already a term for the condition. Captain Mayne Reed, the popular novelist, acknowledged it in a best-selling Western story, and returning visitors tried to define it. "In the prairie territories of America there is experienced by the traveller and the hunter, a strange sensation which has been called the prairie fever...", wrote Francis Duncan. "It is a sweet and exhilarating feeling, absorbing for a time all recollection of the past, and killing all anxiety about the future. It is a maddening enjoyment of the present, arising from lightened spirits, and the grandeur of surrounding nature."[3] Duncan, a young British army officer, speculated that this lightness came not just from the exposure to sublime and beautiful scenery, but had a metaphysical aspect. Out on the open prairie, God's work was closer. "Is it rash to say, that away in the great solitudes, fresh from the creator's hand... the mental faculties may acquire a higher power over the body, and somewhat loosen his faculties?"[4]

The one notable gainsayer to all this rapture was the young Charles Dickens. When the author made his first visit to the United States, in 1842, he wanted to see the prairies, forests and wilderness he had read so much about. Already famous after the success of *The Pickwick Papers*, *Oliver Twist* and *Nicholas Nickleby*, Dickens travelled as far west as St Louis, where he was received warmly and journalists reported his every word. His hosts arranged a special trip to show off the prairies and a party of local worthies took Dickens and his wife Catherine, in a procession of three carriages, on a thirty-mile excursion to a section of country near Lebanon. But Dickens was not at all impressed, except by the scale of the picnic. He did not succumb to the prairie fever. "The widely famed Far West is not to be compared with even the tamest portions of Scotland or Wales..." he wrote to a friend afterwards. He thought it was too flat, dreary and tame. "The prairie fell, by far, short of my preconceived idea. I felt no such emotions as I do in crossing the Salisbury Plain". It was later pointed out that Dickens could not claim to have been to the Far West at all, but had been taken east of St Louis, back into Illinois.

Dickens, an urban type without the privileged background that most travellers shared, was the exception. Other visitors continued to pay tribute to the special quality of the landscape, the light and the air. In 1862 Sir Richard Burton, one of the most intrepid and uninhibited of Victorian explorers, set out to see the American West, after his travels in Africa and Arabia. When he left by stage coach on the road to Oregon in 1860 he carried two pistols tucked into his belt and looked forward to "enjoying a little skirmishing with the savages."[5] Though disappointed when the journey proved boringly safe, he was grateful for the tonic air, the like of which he had never breathed before. He found it "brisk as a bottle of *veuve Clicquot* – it is this that gives one the 'prairie fever'..."[6] William Baillie-Grohman, one of the most well-connected big game hunters, who spent many months tramping through the backwoods, was still paying tribute to the same atmosphere twenty years later. "Dry and sparkling as perhaps none other on the globe, it seems to be composed not of one-fifth, but of five-fifths of oxygen. As your city-worn lungs inhale it, fresh life is infused into your whole being, and you feel that it is air which has never before been breathed."[7]

Some who came most frequently, or stayed on longest, never lost that sense of extreme exhilaration and well-being. For others the romantic and emotional charge was, in the end, damped down by the loneliness that went with the empty spaces, or by financial setbacks, or the particular hostility that some encountered. The other factor was that while the entrancement was playing out, the west was already changing very fast. In the space of a few decades, the native Americans were displaced or eliminated, and much of the wilderness was transformed into corn and wheat fields, cattle ranges and new cities. In his conjectures, Francis Duncan had referred to the unblemished natural realm, still in the state that the creator had delivered it, "where man's toil has not defaced, nor his dullness polluted." But the defacement and pollution were well under way at the time he was writing, with the British aristocracy contributing to it. They helped to slaughter the buffalo, invested in railways and mines, speculated in land and cattle, and strung barbed wire fences over tracts of country they did not own. In the process they helped to destroy the paradise that had first cast such a spell over them.

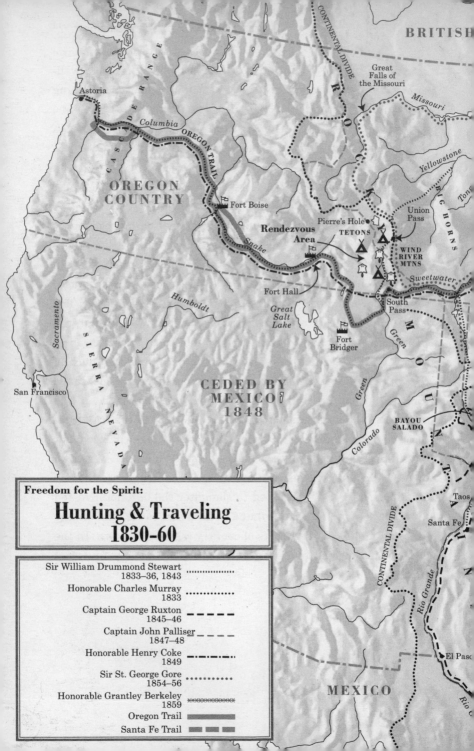

BRITISH

CONTINENTAL DIVIDE

Great Falls
of the Missouri

Missouri

Astoria

Columbia

CASCADE RANGE

OREGON TRAIL

ROC

Yellowstone

Tons

OREGON
COUNTRY

Fort Boise

**Rendezvous
Area**

Pierre's Hole
TETONS

Union
Pass

BIG HORNS

WIND
RIVER
MTNS

Snake

Fort Hall

Sweetwater

South
Pass

Humboldt

Great
Salt
Lake

Fort
Bridger

M

O

Sacramento

SIERRA

NEVADA

CEDED BY
MEXICO
1848

Green

Green

U

N

San Francisco

Colorado

BAYOU
SALADO

T

A

CONTINENTAL DIVIDE

Taos

Santa Fe

Freedom for the Spirit:

Hunting & Traveling
1830-60

Sir William Drummond Stewart 1833–36, 1843	··············
Honorable Charles Murray 1833	··········
Captain George Ruxton 1845–46	─ ─ ─
Captain John Palliser 1847–48	── ──
Honorable Henry Coke 1849	·─·─·─
Sir St. George Gore 1854–56	············
Honorable Grantley Berkeley 1859	xxxxxxxxxxxx
Oregon Trail	
Santa Fe Trail	▬ ▬ ▬

Rio Grande

MEXICO

El Paso

Rio

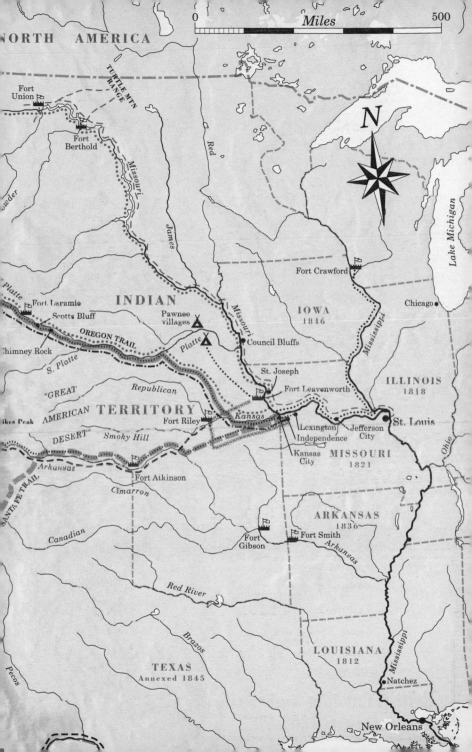

Staking a claim:
British Colonies and Cattle
Interests 1860-90

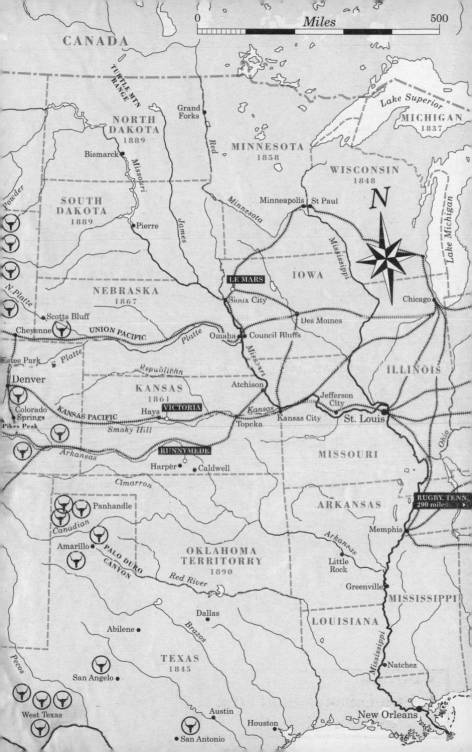

PRAIRIE
FEVER

Prologue:
1887—Frontier Days

All the different people, wild, painted Red Indians from
America, on their wild barebacked horses, of different
tribes, cowboys, Mexicans etc., all came tearing round at
full speed, shrieking and screaming. . . .[1]

—QUEEN VICTORIA'S JOURNAL, 1887

When they first took their seats on the tiered wooden benches
and saw the American prairies stretched before them, the
sweep of the Great Plains, the sagebrush, and the Rocky Mountains rising in the distance, audiences were struck by the sheer
boldness of the effect, and moved by the associations and spirit it
evoked. Painted on a band of canvas forty feet high, the backdrop
had taken a team of stage artists several weeks to complete. The
re-creation of the Far West ran in a half circle, directly across
from the crescent-shaped grandstand, on the far side of a dirt
arena one third of a mile in circumference.

In the summer of 1887, when it might have been expected that
the British would be entirely preoccupied with the Golden Jubilee
celebrations for Queen Victoria's fifty years on the throne, with all
their imperial pomp, tens of thousand of Londoners were making
their way to a different kind of celebration, projecting the bois-
terous history of American frontier conquest. They found Buffalo

Bill's "Wild West" encamped on the fringe of the residential district of Kensington, next to a trade exhibition intended to show the manufacturing achievements of the United States. The American Exhibition itself, with its displays of machine tools and coffee mills, typewriters and false teeth, was quickly overshadowed by the popular entertainment placed alongside it to draw visitors.

The "Wild West" was allocated an awkward triangle of wasteland surrounded by three railway cuttings. Once the crowds had crossed temporary bridges over the tracks, they reached a brash American outpost of six acres, with popcorn and peanut sellers, bars, refreshment rooms, a throbbing electricity plant, and a temporary grandstand built on a scale London had not seen before. The amphitheater could house 20,000 under cover, with standing room on the exposed terraces for another 15,000. They came to see Indians in feathered war bonnets, Mexican *vaqueros* in sombreros, and cowboys in boots and spurs. They were awed by feats of marksmanship and rough riding. The sound of battle whoops, thundering hooves, intermittent gunfire, and the roars of the crowd spilled into the streets of Kensington. Under overcast skies powerful electric lamps, brought from the United States, lit up the arena. The performances continued through all weathers for a six-month run, and on rainy evenings, when the arc lights fizzled, the horses kicked up mud, spattering the spectators in the cheaper standing terraces at the front.

Afterwards, Londoners could walk behind the prairie cyclorama and stroll through the "Indian Village" where the party of over ninety Native Americans, with squaws, young children, and babies in papooses, were living in a cluster of conical tepees. They could see Buffalo Bill's canvas headquarters, where animal skins were tossed across the floor, and pass through the lines of tents which housed the cowboys, Mexicans, and staff. After viewing the stables and pens where the horses, mules, buffalo, elk, and longhorn steers were corraled, it was only a short walk back to the modernity of Earls Court or West Kensington stations, on London's new underground lines, the first in the world.

With his shaggy mustache, strikingly shaped white beard, long ringlets of hair flowing over his shoulders, and fringed buckskins, William Cody had earned the name "Buffalo Bill" after killing 4,862 bison in one year, when he was hired to bring in meat for the laborers constructing the transcontinental railway. He had built on his experience as an Indian fighter and hunting guide to create a bankable legend around himself. His exploits were fictionalized in cheap novels, and portrayed on the stage, and then he turned promoter and director himself and toured the United States for four years with his "Wild West."

Cody avoided referring to his creation as a "show," maintaining this was not idle fiction, but a truthful replay of genuine historical scenes by real participants, a genuine picture of life on the frontier. The program stated that "The Wild West is designed . . . to graphically illustrate the methods by which the United States has been civilized, from the Atlantic to the Pacific Coast."[2] A stampede of eighteen lumbering buffalo was unleashed into the arena, and hunters raced after them firing blank ammunition. A train of emigrant wagons trundled through, and were set upon by tomahawk-wielding Indian warriors until rescued by a posse of cowboys led by Buffalo Bill. Settlers built a log cabin which was then attacked, and the terrified family rescued, by now predictably, by Buffalo Bill. Other acts showed frontier skills and tricks. The diminutive Annie Oakley tripped in, bowing, waving, and wafting kisses to the crowd, raised her rifle, and shot the lighted tip off the end of a cigar clenched between the teeth of her partner, standing 20 yards away. Cowboys galloped in through openings in the prairie backdrop, stooping low from the saddle to pick up handkerchiefs and hats from the ground. Only the hoots of railway engines passing through the cuttings beside the arena, and the coal smoke billowing from the serried ranks of chimneys on the apartment buildings beyond the cyclorama, brought audiences back to urban reality.

This was robust popular entertainment, staged by a man born in a log hut in Iowa, with a firm belief in the "manifest destiny" of the United States and his own role in assisting it. If the "Wild West" was conceived as a tribute to American vitality, it carried a more general underlying message, in the high era of European empires. The display at Earl's Court was a celebration of what seemed, in 1887, a self-evident and unstoppable trend—the inexorable advance of the white, Anglo-Saxon races even in the most distant parts of the world, the drama of civilization, and the rollback of savagery.

In the first few weeks a succession of distinguished visitors came to see the spectacle for themselves, including William Gladstone, the Liberal elder statesman. He was followed by Edward, Prince of Wales, who brought his children, and the Duke of Cambridge. Complete royal endorsement was confirmed when Queen Victoria found time to drive to Earl's Court for a private performance only a few days before her Jubilee service in Westminster Abbey, watching from an improvised royal box decked in velvet, on a gray evening. Afterwards she was introduced to Cody and members of his cast, including Annie Oakley, and to Ogila-sa, or "Red Shirt," the Sioux who had been on the winning side at the Battle of the Little Bighorn eleven years earlier, when he had helped slaughter General Custer's 7th Cavalry.

Writing in her private journal, Victoria described the extraordinary cast of characters, and the thrilling scenes she had just seen. "An attack on a coach and on a ranch, with an immense deal of firing, was most exciting, so was the buffalo hunt and the bucking ponies, that were almost impossible to sit. The cowboys are fine looking people, but the painted Indians, with their feathers, and wild dress (very little of it) were rather alarming looking and they have cruel faces." The Queen found Cody himself "a splendid man, handsome and gentlemanlike in manner. He has had many encounters and hand to hand fights with the Red Indians."[3]

The impact of Buffalo Bill as a character and a presence on the London social scene that summer was almost as great as that of his prairie extravaganza itself. The former army scout and self-made impresario was accorded the privileges and respect due to a visiting hero. "Buffalo Bill continues to be the great social lion of London . . . ," wrote a correspondent for the *Chicago Daily Tribune*. "Mr. Cody is seen at all the best London houses and the ladies are all anxious to attract his notice."[4] He was received by the Lord Mayor in the Mansion House, and Henry Irving and Ellen Terry took him to the theaters. The aristocracy were particularly welcoming. The first to come on board the *State of Nebraska*, which had brought the troupe across the Atlantic, was Lord Ronald Gower. Cody was entertained by the Duke of Beaufort, the Duke of Teck, Lord Bruce, Lord Randolph Churchill, and plied with more invitations from titled hostesses than he could accept. Lord Charles Beresford took him through Hyde Park in his coach. He dined with the Marquis of Lorne, a former Governor-General of Canada, and played poker with the Prince of Wales, the future King Edward VII. When reports of all this reached the United States, Buffalo Bill was criticized for "flunkyism," and betraying his rough diamond republican past, by so much hobnobbing with royalty, dukes, and earls.

The troupe's senior Indian, "Red Shirt," an imposing and dignified figure in war paint and a headdress of porcupine quills and eagle feathers, was also fêted beyond Earl's Court. He was given honorary membership of the smartly idiosyncratic Savage Club, and taken to see the House of Commons. The man who had taken so many scalps in an earlier phase of his life now became the pet of duchesses.

The extraordinary success of the "Wild West," which was seen by over 2 million people in London before moving on to the provinces, could not be explained by the novelty value alone. This was not just another visiting circus. Though Buffalo Bill may have thought little about Europe until his chartered Noah's Ark of selected westerners and livestock arrived in the Thames that May, the British had been visiting the American frontier, at least in their imaginations, for five decades. When a journalist watched the company coming down the gangplank in the Albert Docks, it was with a sense of familiarity. He thought he knew these faces, from the books of James Fenimore Cooper that he had read as a boy: "Looking upon the chiefs, braves and squaws, one could not help recalling the delightful sensations of youth— the first acquaintance with the Last of the Mohicans, the Great Spirit, Firewater, Laughing Water and the dark Huron warrior. Here were their counterparts—moccasins, feathers, beaver skins, beads and a fine show of war paint; ugly faces made uglier by rude art, dignified countenances which retained a stamp of high breeding. . . ."5

Fed by novels and travelers' accounts, the fascination with the Indians, and the curiosity about the immense wilderness west of the Mississippi, could be dated back to the 1820s. British readers had followed the crossing of the continent, the settlement of the prairies, and the Indian wars with almost as much attention as they had given to Britain's imperial adventures in Africa or Asia. The Queen herself had read frontier stories in her girlhood, and seen paintings and sketches of the Far West.

For most ordinary Britons who joined the crowds on the open terraces where the ticket cost 1 shilling, or sat in the covered seats for 2 shillings, the "Wild West" was a chance to see an enthralling, distant world they knew they would never visit themselves. But the show appealed to all classes, and what accounted for the particular warmth of Buffalo Bill's reception by the upper crust was the much more informed interest of the aristocracy, whose elegantly dressed parties filled the boxes (25 shillings) that ran along the front level of the grandstand at each performance.

Many of Queen Victoria's most privileged subjects knew the American West at firsthand. Wellborn Britons had been exploring the prairies since the beginning of her reign, traveling over them, hunting across them, and putting money into them. Her own son, the Prince of Wales, had spent a few days shooting in the Midwest in the course of an American tour in 1860, and many in her own circle, including her son-in-law, the Marquis of Lorne, had made excursions to the plains. By 1887, the stuffed heads of buffalo and bears from the prairies and the Rockies glared down from the walls of many of the great houses in the British countryside. For some grandees the western landscape had provided a formative experience, and for them Buffalo Bill's arrival in London allowed a reunion. At a dinner given by Lord Ronald Gower and the Duke of Sutherland, at Stafford House, the grandest private palace in London, Cody was reunited with some of those he had guided in the 1870s. He met the Earl of Dunraven again, whom he had first encountered waiting on a Nebraska railway platform, and had taken buffalo hunting from Fort McPherson.

British aristocrats collected Indian dress and weapons, and western pictures. Aristocrats had sent their younger sons to settle in the West, even if some had already returned. More recently, members of the nobility had invested fortunes in American cattle operations and land, and were able to appreciate the steer roping at Earl's Court because they had employed cowboys on their own cattle ranches in Texas and Nebraska, Wyoming and Colorado.

What made Buffalo Bill's 1887 visit particularly poignant, at least when seen in retrospect, was the timing. Though William Cody built on his popularity, and returned to make another three British tours, the era of direct upper-class involvement in the Far West, which had started just as Victoria was coming to the throne, was almost over. Social and economic links with the prairies were being abandoned. After fifty years, a long and improbable chapter had ended, and the blue bloods were withdrawing, under a fusillade of highly charged polemic, and a hail of political arrows.

PART I

Freedom for the Spirit

1

Encircling Vastness

These are the gardens of the desert, these
The unshorn fields, boundless and beautiful,
For which the speech of England has no name—
The Prairies. I behold them for the first,
And my heart swells, while the dilated sight
Takes in the encircling vastness. . . .[1]

—WILLIAM CULLEN BRYANT,
"The Prairies," 1833

The journey lasted many days, as the steamboat pulsed past
the tangled, heavily wooded banks of the Ohio, from Pittsburgh or Cincinnati, or pushed up against the Mississippi current
from New Orleans. Passengers knew they were near their destination when they first caught sight of the chimneys of flour mills and
breweries, spewing smoke into the blue prairie sky. As the boat
drew closer they saw church spires, and then the city itself, three
parallel streets of pink brick stores and houses, on a limestone
bluff on the left bank. St. Louis was halfway across the continent,
and by the 1830s the former French trading post had a population
approaching 10,000. With its warehouses, provision merchants,
gunsmiths, saddlers, horse dealers, and wagon makers, this was

the marketplace of the frontier, and the city dominated western trade and commerce.

Most passengers were arriving to do business: insurance agents and corn dealers, salesmen from the East bringing samples of hardware or fabrics, soldiers and government officials headed to new postings. But in the early 1830s a new type of traveler was to be encountered on the boats, wealthy Europeans coming out of curiosity, not need, in search of adventure, sport, or personal fulfillment. American passengers were intrigued by their different dress, their manners, and what they were coming for. William Fairholme, a British army lieutenant who kept a daily journal, wrote: "None of our fellow passengers could understand our motives in leaving our comfortable homes to go on such an expedition as we were engaged in, and what puzzled them most was our disclaiming any idea of profit accruing to us there from."[2]

What drew them was not the bustling city of St. Louis itself, with its diverse mix of English and French speakers, Creoles, Indians, Spaniards, and Negro slaves, but what lay to the west. Missouri, newest of the twenty-four states, marked the very edge of the United States as it then was. Beyond lay the great swath of territory acquired through the Louisiana Purchase in 1803, when the size of the country had been doubled at a stroke. To visionaries like President Jefferson, the new lands could provide the space for future expansion, "room enough for our descendants to the thousandth and ten thousandth generation."[3] Between 1804 and 1806, Lewis and Clark had traveled up the Missouri by keelboat, and portage, struggled across the Continental Divide and the Bitterroot Mountains on horseback, and descended the Columbia to reach the Pacific coast. Other explorers had made long journeys to establish the pattern and rough coordinates of the river systems and mountain ranges; but there were still great areas that had not been entered by the white man at all.

The Native American tribes, who hunted across the plains and through the valleys and forests of the Rockies and considered them their own, were suspicious of intruders, and reacted to them unpredictably and sometimes lethally. A small number of white men ventured in to trade with the Indians, or trap beaver for the furs that were so sought after in the eastern states and Europe. A few scientists made expeditions to study the topography and the abundant wildlife, but most Americans were awed by the Indian Territory, and the difficulties of crossing it. At best it was a challenge, full of potential; at worst a dangerous obstacle that had to be overcome as the country pursued the drive west. For the early European visitors, who could be more detached, the appeal was broader, harder to articulate, and involved the whole concept of the unspoiled wilderness, and all its human and animal inhabitants.

For anyone wanting to go into the Indian Territory, for whatever reason, St. Louis was the place to make preparations and buy supplies, where the prime route into the great wilderness began. Only ten miles up the Mississippi, the river was joined by its greatest tributary, the Missouri, whose yellowish, muddy, debris-carrying waters could be followed west as far as the setting-off points that offered the most direct heading across the prairies. If travelers stayed on the river as it turned north, they could continue up the Missouri for hundreds of miles further, all the way to the Great Falls, the North and South forks, and the Rocky Mountains, as Lewis and Clark had done.

Once passengers came down the gangplanks onto the wide sloping levee, the first impression of St. Louis could be overwhelming. The age of the steamboat had arrived, with as many as eighty vessels in the river. As each boat nosed in, tying up at a diagonal, a throng of porters, carters, and runners for hotels and rooming houses rushed toward it. The air was filled with a cacophony of sound: the roar from the boats releasing steam from their high-pressure boilers, the shouting from the crowds of vendors and touts, and the clattering of wheels on cobbles. The Englishman whose motives for coming had puzzled fellow passengers confided to his diary that the tumult "formed a disagreeable contrast to the silence and solitude of the prairies and the forests we had for some days been traversing."[4]

Among the first wealthy foreigners to run this gauntlet, and be driven up to Front Street, weaving their way round the waiting cargo and the huge heaps of wood to fuel the boats, were two German princes with an interest in plant collecting, and several French dilettanti. The best known, and the visitor who made the greatest impression in the early days, was William Stewart, a peppery, red-faced captain on the British Army's retired list, who arrived from the East in the autumn of 1832.

Stewart was the first of a long line of wellborn Britons who were drawn to the West, and the fact that he could find the time was explained by his background. His father, the 17th Laird and 5th Baronet of Grandtully, owned 50,000 acres of forest, moors, and rich farmland in Scotland, near Dunkeld in Perthshire, where the river Tay swept out of the hills into the agricultural plain and toward Perth city. His family had produced diplomats and soldiers, and he was accustomed to deference and respect from the servants at Murthly Castle and the tenants on the estate farms. After fighting in Wellington's army at the Battle of Waterloo, he had spent his time drinking and gambling in London clubs, following the horse races at Epsom and Newmarket, and shooting on his father's moors and hillsides. With no employment or responsibilities to detain him, he had made several hunting expeditions to the eastern Mediterranean and Turkey.

Determined, self-confident, Captain Stewart arrived in St. Louis with a clear goal. He wanted to travel over the Great Plains he had read about, see the Indians in their natural home, and reach the Rocky Mountains. While passing through New York he had met the newspaper publisher James Watson Webb, who had given him letters of introduction to use in St. Louis. One of his earliest calls was on General William Clark, the veteran of western exploration, who had crossed the prairies and the Rockies with Meriwether Lewis, on the government-funded Corps of Discovery expedition for President Jefferson. Later Clark had become Superintendent of Indian Affairs and Governor of the Missouri Territory. As St. Louis's most illustrious citizen, he received visitors at his house at Vine and Main streets, and liked to show them the museum he had built to hold his collection of Indian dress and weapons, his animal skins and his trophies. The sixty-two-year-old Clark gave the thirty-eight-year-old Captain Stewart advice, and passed him on to others who could help.

The letters that reached Stewart from home brought news of the friends he had left behind, and showed their preoccupations, and the views of America that then prevailed. The thirty-year-old Earl of Ashburnham, who lived with his brother in a Palladian country house in Sussex, wrote to Stewart: "You are often remembered in the smoking room and at beer time, and Percy and I always conclude with the very sincere wish that we may see you in your old place before the end of October." By the time Stewart read this, it was already December. Most of Ashburnham's letter was about the season's shooting and fishing. "The Front Water has been stocked with trout, 470 fish have been turned in since May and I am convinced that some of them have already increased in size. Partridges are abundant, pheasants, it is supposed, have not been quite so well. . . ."[5] The Front Water was one of three lakes in the Ashburnham park, laid out by Capability Brown.

A few months later the earl's younger brother Percy showed his feelings about the United States, his prejudices having been confirmed by a series of scornful books by recent British visitors. "I should hope to hear of you being on your way back to England . . . ," he wrote, "not that affairs here have any favourable aspect. On the contrary we are going down as fast as we can, but it is always a consolation to see one's friends no better off than oneself. . . . I cannot help thinking that this country is not yet quite as so horrible as America, judging from all the accounts I have heard or read of late, and I hope that by this time you have come to the

same conclusion. I should be glad to hear that you have had good
sport in fishing and shooting for it will be the only recompense
you are likely to meet with for a long voyage. . . . I do hope that you
will not find anything so very charming as to induce you to stay
away longer than you at first intended." He closed by "wishing you
well out of the land of Indians you have got into." Lord Ashburnham then scrawled on the back of his brother's envelope: "Again,
we long to see you back when good folks are so scarce. Why give
up your real friends for the Yankees? Yours in haste, Ash."[6]

Some of Stewart's friends were more open-minded. Lord Ormalie, son of the Earl of Breadalbane, wrote from Taymouth Castle
in Scotland: "I should have liked very much to have been with
you . . . and to have viewed the Americans and their government
really as they are, and not as Captain Hall and Mrs. Trollope and
such visitors would endeavour to make us believe. . . . I trust you
will escape all the dangers of your American trip and that I shall
see you here next season in robust health."[7] Stewart's circle, made
up of fellow army officers, schoolfriends, and the scions of great
families, was to be disappointed. Though the captain survived
intact, he was so taken by the western landscape and life that
he stayed away for seven years, and the occasional reports of his
adventures provided a new topic in the clubs and officers' messes,
and around the billiard tables, even if he was absent himself. For
the British of his background he helped set a fashion, passing on
his enthusiasm for a distant landscape and the limitless horizons
to others. For western Americans he was the prototype upper-
class British visitor, against whom the behavior of those who followed would be measured.

THE UNITED STATES had no equivalent of Captain Stewart, Lord
Ashburnham, Lord Ormalie, or the British aristocratic, landowning class of which they were a small but typical part. If the term

"aristocracy" was sometimes applied to the old ruling families of Virginia and the South, their transatlantic cousins were in a different league of wealth and privilege. The plantation owners were never so rich, or so apparently idle, for such a long period. These aristocrats were people who, at least to the eyes of republican Americans, had no need to earn a living in any sense that could be recognized, took their social position for granted, and seemed free to indulge their whims as they chose. With wealth entrenched in the great castles, country houses, and estates their families had owned for generations, a stream of income from their tenants allowed them to live secure and cosseted lives. In a country in which the ownership of land conferred status and position, they had an unshakable sense of their own importance in the national structure, and many had a place in the House of Lords as a right of birth, or seats in the House of Commons in their gift.

For those who did not wish to play a part in Parliament or public service, one of the perpetual dilemmas was how they should spend their time. The most energetic traveled, taking menservants and maids and sometimes their own carriages, on lengthy visits to continental Europe. Captain Stewart, like his father, spent many months in Italy, and had traveled in the Balkans and Turkey. He probably regretted that he lacked the funds to mount anything as ambitious as his friend Lord Ashburnham, who had diverted himself for over a year with a private expedition across Asia Minor, wearing Turkish dress, with his own dragoman and an armed escort to see off Anatolian bandits. Ashburnham had been hospitably received by local Turkish officials, and went as far as Beirut and Damascus. On his return from the Pashas, he came to shoot grouse and snipe with Stewart in Perthshire, and had visited Murthly again in August 1831. Some blue bloods kept themselves busy making grand improvements to their mansions, or landscaping their parks. While Stewart was in St. Louis, his older brother John, the 18th Laird of Grandtully, was spending hundreds of thousands of pounds to complete a monumental new house at Murthly, with turrets and domes, in front of the original seventeenth-century castle. Other peers concentrated on the acquisition of pictures and sculpture, sending back crates of art from Rome and Florence. The 4th Earl of Ashburnham was building up a library of rare books. The Earl of Breadalbane and Lord Ormalie, like Lord Mansfield at Scone Palace, were keen collectors of foreign plants, commissioning botanists to bring specimens back from distant corners of the world.

The activity that preoccupied the British aristocracy most of all, and helped define them, was field sports. The passion seemed to be genetically implanted, and the calendar of the sporting year, taking in foxhunting, grouse, pheasant and partridge shooting, trout fishing, salmon fishing, shooting deer and stalking stags, steeplechasing and flat racing, determined their schedule and their progress around the British Isles. The piece of domestic business they took most seriously was the running of their estates for the maximum production of birds, and the legal principle they clung to most aggressively was the right to stop anyone but themselves from shooting over their ancestral acres or fishing their waters.

For a class who conceived of themselves as the upper section of a God-given social pyramid, with the landowning gentry, the middle classes, and the toiling masses supporting the perfectly tapered edifice from below, and only the monarchy above them, the early 1830s were an alarming time. Whig reformers were trying to end the peers' control of "pocket" seats in the House of Commons, and widen the franchise, but any change had to be passed first by the House of Lords. There had been riots, and attacks on the country houses of the most reactionary peers. The third attempt at a reform bill was reaching a crucial stage in the House of Lords in the week that William Stewart left Liverpool, in a sailing packet for New York, in April 1832.

In many respects, American society represented what the British die-hards opposing the reform bill most wanted to avoid, at least politically. After traveling in the United States and visiting the U.S. Congress and state assemblies, Captain Basil Hall had pronounced himself appalled by the results of short-term sessions, the rotation of office, and universal suffrage. "The moment of re-election is always close at hand; and if the members fail to conform strictly to the wishes of the electors, they are ousted as a matter of course." The constant turnover mitigated against good government, which required experience and judgment built up over the years, and it was perverse to include in the definition of public opinion "the crude ideas of persons whose knowledge is confined to the objects of mere manual labor."[8] Hall's book *Travels in North America* supported Conservative aristocrats who were convinced the concept of "democracy" could only lead to rule by the mob. They were appalled by the idea of a society with no tradition of deference, where people did not know their place. Many of the same Tories had still not forgiven the "disloyal" Yankees for turning on their king. Less than sixty years had passed since the American Revolution, and less than twenty years since the "second war of independence," when the United States fought the British again, over interference with their shipping. It would take the American public some time to recover from the burning of Washington in 1814, and the shelling of Baltimore's Fort McHenry, when the volley of British bombs and rockets inspired the patriotic imagery of "The Star-Spangled Banner."

While the grand political idea of "the land of the free and the home of the brave" was anathema to the British upper class, it was nevertheless true that their geographical and scientific awareness of the North American continent was growing all the time. In part this reflected a general interest in discovery and exploration all over the world, after the end of the Napoleonic wars. With foreign travel possible again, European adventurers journeyed across deserts and into remote mountain ranges, and learned societies met in candlelit assembly rooms to hear accounts of Tartary, Mongolia, or Arabia. Though most of the world's coastlines were charted by now, vast areas of the interiors were still blank voids, waiting to be filled in.

The great stretch of territory that lay on the western fringe of the United States, between the Mississippi River and the Pacific, and its exotic native inhabitants, seemed particularly intriguing. British atlases showed the coast of California, with whales spouting along the coast, a chain of Spanish missions running up to San Francisco, and the old city of Santa Fe, seat of the Spanish governor until Mexican independence in 1821, but an empty void for half the continent, apart from a vaguely placed smear of hatching to indicate mountains. The first book based on the journal of the expedition of Lewis and Clark, edited by Nicholas Biddle, was printed in London within months of its American publication, in 1814, and read with almost as much attention as it was in New York or Boston. When the U.S. government sent Major Stephen Long to investigate the region south of the Lewis and Clark route, and he followed the Platte River to reach Colorado and the future site of Denver, the record of his trip was also published in London, in 1823.

Accounts of American flora and fauna proved just as popular. The artist naturalist John James Audubon had to come to England in 1826 to raise financial backing for the rigorously comprehensive, exquisitely drawn and colored depiction of 435 American birds he had been working on for so long. He wrote home that "I have been received here in a manner not to be expected during my highest enthusiastic hopes."[9] Audubon's pictures were exhibited in Liverpool, Manchester, Edinburgh, and other cities. He was made a member of the Royal Society, and wealthy British patrons paid the advance subscriptions he needed to complete the five-volume set of engravings, on the giant paper size known as double elephant folio, allowing a trimmed page height of 39 inches, which then found their way into private libraries.

Alongside the detailed botanical, geological, and ethnological studies was a growing intellectual interest in what the American

wilderness might represent and the questions it raised about
man's status in nature, and the philosophical debate about savagery versus civilization. When the journal of Lewis and Clark
was published, a British reviewer noted that the account seemed
plain and workaday, a record of interminable marches and river
journeys, sightings and measurements. He regretted that the
extraordinary country had been seen only by "rough boatmen
and hunters" instead of "gentlemen of a more refined cast," poets
or natural philosophers, who might have been able to interpret
and reflect a vast region that "no reflective being had looked upon
since the beginning of time" in more elegiac terms. The writer
hoped that when travel was easier and safer, and "all the Indian
tribes shall have been intimidated or diminished into a state to
make them obsequious to the masters of the Continent," it would
be possible for an artist to go along and record what he saw.
"European curiosity may then be gratified with accurate repre-
sentations of the various physiognomy of the Aborigines, of the
shapes of the subordinate wild animals, of the vegetable singu-
larities, and of those sublime spectacles beheld by the American
party at the falls of the Missouri and in the passes of the Rocky
Mountains."[10]

For the moment, in the absence of such illustration from artists, or more vivid reporting, readers had to rely on fiction for
their sense of what the primitive North American wilderness was
like, and for some reflection of its significance. One author more
than any other helped to raise this consciousness, both among
American readers in the Atlantic states and abroad. James Fenimore Cooper was hailed as America's answer to the great Scottish
writer of historical romances Sir Walter Scott, and British readers bought his books almost from the start of his writing career,
in the early 1820s. *The Spy*, set in the Revolutionary War, made
his reputation, but it was when Cooper began a series of grip-
ping stories based in the backwoods of New York State, where
his family had property, that sales soared. His strong narratives

involved settlers, trappers, Indians, bears, wolves, and maidens
in distress.

With his eye for fine detail, and ability to set characters into
huge, slowly rendered landscapes of woods, lakes, and vivid skies,
Cooper presented an inspiring, tantalizing account of the country beyond the eastern seaboard. *The Pioneers* was published in
New York and London almost simultaneously in 1823. Set several decades earlier, when the sound of axes echoed across the
forests and hills of northern New York as settlers cleared farms
and townships from virgin country, the central figure was Natty
Bumppo, a hunter, woodsman, and rugged loner. Also known as
"Leatherstocking," he is a friend of the Indians who are being
displaced, and bemoans the damage that the march of progress is
doing to "God's wilderness." The prolific and fast-working Cooper
produced a total of five "Leatherstocking" tales, in the course of
which the saga of Bumppo's entire life unfolded, though the epi-
sodes did not appear in chronological order.

British readers began to buy *The Last of the Mohicans*, which
found Bumppo in an earlier period, as a scout during the French
and Indian War, when the book was published in London in early
1826. A few months later the writer crossed the Atlantic himself,
to take advantage of his rising foreign earnings and spend time in
Europe with his family. He acknowledged a tenuous link between
his most popular novel so far and the British aristocracy. Before
he left the United States he had got to know a group of young
Englishmen, all the sons of peers, including Edward Stanley, soon
to be Earl of Derby, and the future Lords Taunton and Ossington.
The patrician tourists met him in New York after the publication
of *The Pioneers*, and he accompanied them on a sightseeing excursion to Cooperstown, Lake Champlain, Lake George, and Saratoga. While they were visiting Glens Falls, the Honorable Edward
Stanley suggested to Cooper that he use the mist- and spray-
shrouded caves behind the cataracts on the Hudson River as the

scene for a novel, and Cooper said that was where he decided to write *The Last of the Mohicans*.

He stayed in London only briefly before moving on to France, where he rented a house in Paris and continued writing. By the time he returned to England for a longer visit, his fame had increased further, and the fact that he was a liberal American, who decried the idea of aristocracy and institutions such as the House of Lords, had no effect on the company he kept. The earlier friendship with Stanley gave him an immediate entrée to fashionable circles. Lord Holland asked him to parties at Holland House; the Duke of Devonshire brought him to Devonshire House on Piccadilly; and Lord Lansdowne invited him to dinner in Berkeley Square. Cooper was a frequent guest at the breakfast salon of the wealthy poet Samuel Rogers. In letters home, he wrote about the London scene with some acidity. He described a formal dinner with Lord and Lady Spencer, their son Lord Althorpe, a handful of other peers, and a bishop, where he was puzzled and amused by the fine calibration of ranks, and the fact that it mattered greatly in which order guests went up a staircase: "To a certain point there is a great delicacy and propriety in high English society, but there are things on which nearly all fail. I never knew an Englishman who could joke on etiquette! It is part of their natures: they see in it a necessary ingredient of order, morals, and almost of religion."[11]

The great nabobs of London took Cooper up because they were always partial to a celebrity and he was regarded as the finest American novelist, but also because they had themselves been gripped by his frontier adventures, as had their families. Though he took their hospitality, for the most part he did not like them. "Lords Grey, Holland, Lansdowne and Normanby excepted, I can positively affirm that I never had communion with an Englishman of high rank, who knew how to be civil." He found wellborn Frenchmen and Italians more charming and less stuffy, and did his best not to be over-impressed. At a dinner in Park Lane, a

seventeen-year-old youth was ushered in, having asked to meet
the famous author. "I was told that he had come expressly to see
me, so I said a few civil things to him, but as a man would address
a boy." Although his host told him, in a hushed and solemn tone,
that the boy carried the title Lord Kerry for the moment, but
would inherit three earldoms on the death of his father, Cooper
was unimpressed. "I had a boy at home that I would not change
for him and six Earldoms."[12]

. When Cooper left New York he had brought the half-completed
manuscript of a third Leatherstocking novel, and he completed it
in Paris. In *The Prairie*, published in London and Philadelphia
almost simultaneously, he acknowledged how rapidly his country
was changing, and shifted his canvas 1,000 miles west, to the new
territory beyond the Mississippi. Cooper's readers, who included
so many of the British upper classes, were now introduced to the
Great Plains and a different type of Indian, and the book captured
imaginations and raised awareness just as *Last of the Mohicans*
had done. Since he wanted to keep Natty Bumppo as a central
character, he could not set the story in the present day, or readers
might work out that the former scout and backwoodsman would
be over a hundred years old. So, though the scenes and process
the book described were contemporary to the 1820s, he wrenched
the story back to 1804, and rediscovered Bumppo as a weary and
ancient trapper who had trekked west from New York State in
his final years to recapture the freedoms he had known in his
youth, on the new frontier. The Leatherstocking meets an inept
and partly criminal settler family coming out from Kentucky to
find a homestead, and helps them survive Indian attacks and capture, in a narrative whose twists and turns were as exciting as
they were far-fetched.

Cooper's *The Prairie* was the first account to give readers
a sense of the look of the Great Plains, the buffalo who grazed
them, the deer and antelope, and the Indians, in a more vivid
form than the clipped, factual journals of the early travelers. In

an introduction, Cooper tried to describe the scenery and climate of the prairies, maintaining that "They resemble the steppes of Tartary more than any other known portion of the world,"[13] thus accepting Lieutenant Zebulon Pike's gloomy assessment that the region had no agricultural future.

"From the summits of the swells, the eye became fatigued with the sameness and chilling dreariness of the landscape. The earth was not unlike the ocean . . . there was the same waving and regular surface followed, the same absence of foreign objects, and the same boundless extent to the view."[14] If this sounded forbidding, he was more lyrical in his accounts of shallow river courses, groves of cottonwoods, circling buzzards and eagles, and wispy white clouds scudding across enormous skies. Readers accustomed to the stealthy tracking skills of the moccasined warriors of the eastern forests were now introduced to the Plains Indian, who led a more nomadic life, rode fast horses, chased buffalo on the open range, and bore down on his enemy firing arrows from the saddle.

After a murderous fight between the Pawnees and the Sioux, which left hundreds of corpses decapitated, mutilated, or scalped in the rank grass around a shallow river crossing, Cooper described the tranquil and idyllic dawn that followed: "The work of blood had entirely ceased, and as the sun arose its light was shed on a broad expanse of quiet and solitude. . . . The river was to be traced far through the endless meadows by its serpentine and smoking bed, and the little silvery clouds of vapour which hung above the pools and springs were beginning to melt in air, as they felt the quickening warmth, which, pouring out from the glowing sky, shed its bland and subtle influence on every object of the vast and unshadowed region."[15] The notion of this vast space, as yet unmarked by "civilized" man, fascinated Cooper. His New York friend, William Cullen Bryant, who shared the same enthralment, wrote a lengthy poem which was included in a collection of his verses that appeared in 1834:

> *. . . My heart swells, while the dilated sight*
> *Takes in the encircling vastness. Lo! they stretch,*
> *In airy undulations, far away,*
> *As if the ocean, in his gentlest swell,*
> *Stood still, with all his rounded billows fixed,*
> *And motionless forever.*

All of this was helping to increase public curiosity, but as yet very few had set eyes on these scenes, and the encircling vastness was still very hard to reach. The journey, even as far as St. Louis, was time-consuming and costly and not undertaken lightly. When *The Prairie* was published, James Fenimore Cooper had never been west of Niagara Falls, and had little firsthand knowledge of the Indians. When he was writing about the primitive wilderness he was in Paris, staying in an elegant apartment on the rue St. Maur, where his desk looked out over a city garden. He garnered the background information he needed from books. For descriptions of waving grass, unusual rock formations, buffalo herds, prairie fires, tornados, and the making of canoes, Cooper used the record of the Lewis and Clark Expedition, the account of Stephen Long's journey to the Rockies, and the earlier journal of Alexander Mackenzie, who had crossed Canada to the Pacific coast. Much of his Indian detail came from a missionary, John Heckenwelder, who had published *An Account of the History, Manners and Customs of the Indian Nations*, about Indians in a quite different part of the country, in 1819. Cooper's sense of geography was sometimes vague, and the courtly, metaphor-laden language he gave his Native Americans to speak was ridiculed in subsequent years, though by then it had been taken up and imitated by other writers. But his powers of invention, and his ability to transmit his idealistic, romantic vision, made him the main influence and inspiration for most of the British gentlemen who were to travel west in the following decades.

THE LAST OF THE MOHICANS and *The Prairie* both appeared in
the two years before William Stewart left for America. Cooper's
narrative and prairie images had a particular appeal for Stewart,
who had a Byronic streak and an unconventional, almost mystical
turn of mind, but his departure had as much to do with a desperate wish to leave Scotland quickly as the call of the wild.

The main disadvantage Captain Stewart had to live with came
from being a younger son, in a class where the principle of primogeniture dictated how property was passed on. Elder sons inherited their father's estates and the bulk of their financial capital,
to keep them together. In 1827 he saw his older brother take the
family title and become the 18th Laird of Grandtully. Inevitable
as this was, it would have been more tolerable if Sir John, the new
master of Murthly, had not been a pious and intolerant character,
who took a disapproving attitude to his younger brother's style of
life, and tried to hold back money William believed he was due. In
the sort of family row that was typical of landed families, involving social convention and money, the final rift came after Captain
Stewart had an affair with a Perthshire farmer's daughter, and
made her pregnant. He agreed to marry her, in haste, but his new
wife Christina was judged to be not of his class, and the rest of the
family would not acknowledge her. Stewart may not have seen her
as a lifetime companion either. Having done the decent thing, he
installed her and his baby son George in a house in Edinburgh,
and made arrangements to leave the country. Others might have
gone to Europe; but Stewart, who was naturally contrary, headed
west for America.

2

Beyond the Mississippi

Above all this, there is an inexpressible charm in the life I
was about to begin: there is something in the air, there is
something in the rich woodland, and in the silent waste,
that is of inexplicable interest.

—SIR WILLIAM DRUMMOND STEWART,
Edward Warren, 1854[1]

During the winter, when snow was on the ground for many weeks, Captain Stewart soon realized that the only way to get to the Rockies was with one of the St. Louis fur companies, whose secure limestone warehouses lined the river, the heavy smell of musk wafting out of barred windows. They knew the West better than anyone else. From the 1820s onward, the city's fortunes had risen with the fur trade, at a time when the most stylish fashion for men in New York and Philadelphia, Paris, and London was to wear a tall black hat with a velvety sheen. To make it, workshops needed the skin of the beaver, whose soft underhair could be converted into a fine and waterproof felt. Almost all the beaver were already gone from Europe and the eastern and central United States, and the main source had become the valleys of the Rockies and their approaches. Even there, mountain men were having to work ever deeper into the backwoods. Each pelt, once scraped

stretched and dried, could be worth $6, but the fur country was
so far away that it required capital, and exceptional organization,
to reap the profits.

Each year, pack trains from the competing companies took
supplies hundreds of miles across country to the trappers, and
brought back the skins. The fur trade caravans knew the routes,
and were large enough to cope with difficult river crossings and
the risk of Indian attacks. Stewart persuaded Robert Campbell
and William Sublette to let him join the brigade they were sending out for the Rocky Mountain Fur Company in the spring of
1833, and staked $500, most of his remaining funds at that stage,
to buy a place with them.

He left with high hopes. He wanted to see the wilderness,
study the Indians in their home territory, and hunt. He would
collect specimens of plants and trees, while keeping an eye open
for animals that could be captured alive and sent back across the
Atlantic. Before leaving St. Louis he made a suggestion to Lord
Ormalie, who replied: "I have to thank you for your kind offer of
sending me beasts and other animals . . . anything of the deer
tribe would be most acceptable or if you think that the huge animal the byson would agree with our climate and food he would
be highly acceptable more particularly as you say he is so very
good to eat. I would willingly go to some expense in obtaining and
getting over anything in this way you think may turn out to be
useful or curious or handsome—especially what would suit our
woods at Taymouth to give variety to the sports." [2]

When the thaw began, in April 1833, Stewart was ready
to leave. He packed his baggage, including a powerful double-
barrel rifle firing a 1-ounce ball, and a lighter fowling piece or
shotgun, both from Joseph Manton, London's finest gunsmith,
and took a steamboat 320 miles west along the Missouri. The
river passed through the center of the state, where farmers were
already coming in to clear the trees beside the river, and open up
fields. He disembarked at Lexington, a small settlement east of

present-day Kansas City, which was then the forming-up point for
parties going west, where animals and supplies could be bought,
and where Campbell and Sublette's fur company pack train was
assembling.

The Rocky Mountain caravan, of 44 men and 150 horses and
mules, left the campground at the end of April. For the first two
days the long column followed a rutted trail, marked by blazes
on the trees, through tall oak woods which had not yet leafed up,
with wild pigs dashing across the path. William Campbell, Stewart, and the voyageurs were on horseback, and the packers rode
mules, each leading two more animals behind them. Wrapped
in black oilcloth, the bulky loads balanced across the mules contained guns and powder, flints and knives, shirts and blankets.
They carried corn meal, sugar and salt, beaver traps, and goods
that could be traded with the Indians: beads, mirrors, bells,
knives, pipes, and blankets. A flock of twenty sheep brought up
the rear, herded along to provide meat until they reached buffalo
country. Only a few miles after passing the more recent settlement at Independence, they reached the Great Bend, where the
Missouri turned northward. The column struck due west, leaving
the river behind them, and crossed the Missouri State border into
Indian Territory, where the woods stopped and Stewart had his
first sight of the rolling open prairie. He would now be out of touch
for at least six months, depending on when he decided to return.

Though Charles Larpenteur, one of the young packers, kept
a daily log as the party moved westward, Stewart did not keep
a diary of his own. He left it until much later to distill his experiences in two novels. *Edward Warren*, which he described as a
"fictitious autobiography," follows a young man making a similar
journey to the Rockies. Though the plot was opaque, the background and scenery, and the viewpoint of his central character,
were undoubtedly his own. Early in the book Stewart, through his
character Edward Warren, remembers the first night on the prairies. "My heart bounded under the feeling that I was not beholden

to the trashy twaddle of law manufactories for my freedom, but to space, to a fair field in which to win my way . . . never have I felt the enjoyment of travel but there, where I could dwell upon its pleasures, and enjoy its troubles and mishaps."[3]

After crossing the Kansas River, in mid-May, the caravan fell into a steady routine that they would keep up for eight weeks until they reached the site agreed for the rendezvous. They rose at dawn, turning the horses out to graze while they ate breakfast, then loaded the pack animals and moved off. At noon they halted for half an hour. In the late afternoon they stopped and set up the night's camp in the shape of a hollow square, with a fourth side against a river or creek where possible, hobbling the horses and leaving them to forage. After lighting fires, and eating the evening meal, the last task was to bring the animals into the square and picket them to stakes. They had tents, but unless it was raining they slept in the open, on top of their buffalo-skin saddle blankets or "epishemores," with a saddle as a pillow, by the piled-up baggage. Campbell divided the party into "messes" who ate together, and imposed almost military discipline, with a rota of men to gather fuel, and guard the camp and horses at night.

For the first few days the weather was vile, with spring rains, hailstorms, and the ground sodden underfoot. After eight days, they came to the crest of a low sandy hillside and saw the Platte River below them, running almost straight to the west in a shallow valley, the slow muddy water widening out into shallows, with islands and stands of cottonwood and poplars. The Platte had become the fur traders' main route west. For the most part they rode along the flatland beside the water, or up on the bluffs keeping the river below them on their right, making between twenty and thirty miles each day. Up to then they had seen only antelope, hard to shoot because they moved so fast. Spirits improved when they saw the specks in the distance that were grazing buffalo. Men selected as hunters rode off from the main caravan and returned by evening with the tongues, the hump ribs, and the side ribs, butchered from bulls where they had fallen, though this was still early in the season and the meat was poor and stringy.

In *Edward Warren*, Stewart describes the journey along the Platte in almost Arcadian terms, as the travelers rode through thickets of ash and wild cherry, festooned with grapevines, passing ravines lively with antelope and deer. Herds of wild horses gambolled beside them, with flowing manes and long tails, "rearing up and striking out with their forefeet"[4] and eagles and hawks soared overhead. The lower Platte was Pawnee country, and the Rocky Mountain Fur Company caravan passed Indian villages but had no contact with them. When the Platte split into two, they had to cross over the southern stream to get up to the North Fork. At a point that was normally fordable the water was too deep, and they spent a day building a raft from driftwood logs and ferrying the packs, while the mules were roped and tugged across. When they reached the North Platte there was no timber for a raft, so they improvised a boat, using scraped buffalo hides that had to be dried in front of a fire, then stitched together with animal sinews and bound onto a willow frame. The prairie was greener by now, and covered with flowers. As they picked up the course of the Sweetwater, and followed it, the mountain ranges came into view. William Anderson, a member of another caravan, described the wonder of that first sighting in his journal: "This morning I saw the distant snow clad summits of the Wind-river mountains. This indeed was a lovely scene. I have heard of the ice castles of the north; I doubt not, in the least that this equals or surpasses it. It is like the most pure and most fantastic white clouds of heaven, but more brilliant, not one dark spot to mar the charms and loveliness of the scene."[5]

For many hours they made their way up a long, exposed slope of stonier ground, with clumps of sagebrush agitated by the constant wind. They were approaching the wide gap in the Rocky Mountain range known as the South Pass, where a twenty-mile saddle, at a lower altitude, connects the snow-topped Wind River

range to the Antelope Hills to the south. As they came over the
ridge, so wide that it hardly seemed to justify its description as a
pass, they were crossing the spine of the continent, and from now
on the streams and rivers they followed were draining into the
Pacific.

Stewart was aware of his unique situation, as observer and
supernumerary rather than hired hand or investor, but he proved
his competence and was accepted by the brigade. He rode alongside Campbell and ate with the other "officers" in the same mess.
He took his turn standing guard, a duty which came up for three
hours every third night, and the mule drivers and packers were
willing to take their orders from the greenhorn. He saw how
dangers could arise quite unexpectedly, from a missed step on a
slope, or a vicious kick from a mule. Waking one morning, he felt
a throbbing movement under the pile of foliage on which he had
put his head for the night, and found he had been sleeping on a
rattlesnake, which scuttled off quickly.

Two days after crossing the divide, they reached the valley
of the Green River, or the Susquadee, in the mountain men version of the Indian name. "How lovely are the nights! The moon
and stars shine with a purer and brighter light than I ever saw
them before,"[6] wrote Anderson. They were entering the heart
of the fur country, and the filigree of streams and creeks that
fed into the upper reaches of the Green, intricately dammed and
interfered with by the unremitting beaver, provided some of the
richest trapping waters known. Though the Green ran out from
the Wind River Mountains to the east, high trails linked the valley to the Tetons, the Snake River, and the Yellowstone country
to the north. Hundreds of trappers had spent the previous eleven
months on their own, trekking through the forests, wading in ice-
cold water to set the heavy traps, baiting them with a mix of beaver castor and urine, and returning days or weeks later, hoping to
find a drowned animal caught in the vicious iron jaws.

The mountain men were confined to camp during the months

of deep snow, but emerged for the spring trapping, which produced the best pelts, with the thickest fur. By early July they were making their way toward that year's rendezvous, at Horse Creek, close to what is now Pinedale in southwest Wyoming, where the Green loops across a flat plain of open grassland, with willow, poplar, and cottonwood along its banks. Indians from at least five tribes trekked in the same direction, some dragging lodgepoles behind their horses, so they could join the bartering, sell their horses, and acquire the blankets and calico cloth, vermilion paint, guns, and knives they needed, and share in the spectacle and carousing.

As the caravan approached the rendezvous site, trappers who were waiting for the arrival of supplies and news from St. Louis came out to meet them, pulling their horses up short, shouting and firing guns into the air. The line of tents, lodges, and encampments stretched for several miles, and the business of the rendezvous ran on for three weeks. Campbell's party and the rival companies based themselves in tents and log compounds, took in the bundles of dried and stretched skins from their own trappers and from freelances, and packed them for transport back to the East. The mountain men acquired the powder, lead, gun flints, and trap springs they needed for the following season; but the rendezvous was also a chance for release and entertainment after months of isolation. Whiskey, rum, and raw alcohol, brought across the plains, were sold at exorbitant prices, though officially alcohol could not be taken into the Indian country. Indian women were available, like everything else, for a price, a tryst in exchange for a bucket or pail, a mirror or buttons. Some trappers entered into marriages with Indian girls.

From the start, Stewart was fascinated by the intense interactions and spirit of the rendezvous, by the trade conducted, the deals cut, the roistering with old friends and the drunken brawls, the games of poker and dice, and the bets placed. For a sporting man, who as a young gallant had spent much of his time on the soft turf of English racecourses, the horse racing across the open pasture was specially thrilling, as Indian took on white, whites competed with each other, and Stewart took part on the horse he had ridden from the Missouri landing. Up above them, cradling the valley on three sides, were the snow-covered mountaintops, tinged with red at the end of the day, as the valley fell into shade and the sun set.

The Scottish aristocrat had little contact with Indians on the long cross-country journey, and the rendezvous offered the first chance to see the Plains tribes close up. The Snakes, or Shoshone, the Nez Perce, Flatheads, and Bannocks were all present, with tepee lodges beside the Green. Chiefs paraded in feathered war bonnets, a fringe of human scalps decorating their leggings. Stewart visited the separate villages and was asked to a meal with the Shoshone. Drums throbbed, Indians and trappers galloped through the camps, wheeling and turning, dogs barked. The rendezvous was a mix of country market, carnival, and saturnalia. Stewart was captivated by the extraordinary gathering and was to return again and again in the years that followed.

Though they often heard them howling, wolves usually kept their distance from humans unless they were starving for food; but during the weeks at Horse Creek several camps were bothered by a mangy and deranged wolf that came in at night and attacked sleeping men. Twelve were bitten. Stewart incorporated the story of the rabid wolf into *Edward Warren*, and in a footnote to the novel, he gave a tantalizing account of his own real-life role, taking the blame for another man's death. "I was with Campbell's camp, we had moved to the spot a day or two before, and George Holmes, a young mountaineer, had aided me in constructing a bower of birch and willow, over which to throw a blanket in case of rain, and in which to contain our couch. . . ." The laird and the young trapper sat in the shade, and received visitors. "The best looking of the young squaws of the neighbouring camp came over in groups to wonder at the riches of the white man, as well as to tempt him to dispense them." Though his account left out

important details, Stewart seems to have responded, and made
an arrangement for later with one of the Indian girls. "On an evening of one of these days, I had for some cause . . . begged of my
friend Holmes to take his blanket, and make himself a welcome
in some other hut, as I wished to have our shanty for the night at
my own disposal; he consented, but as I afterwards found he had
laid himself down on the grounds to sleep by a brake of fragrant
roses close by."[7]

Holmes knew of the wolf's nocturnal forays, and Stewart
sensed he was worried.

> The night came, and deepened toward the middle watch, when
> I was roused by confused sounds, shouts, and the discharge of
> firearms, as well as the deep roar of a bull, such as he emits
> in terror rage. There could be no Indian attack, and I still
> hesitated about getting up when there came a sharp cry close
> to the bower and a voice I well knew, and no longer hesitating,
> I belted a blanket round me and rushed out. Poor Holmes was
> seated on the ground, the side of his head and his ear bleeding
> and torn; a mad wolf was ravaging the camp. We did not get
> her, she had other lives to sacrifice elsewhere. Poor Holmes
> changed from that hour, instead of alertness and joy, melan-
> choly and despondency grew upon him day by day. . . . I felt
> I was linked in a death struggle with one who whatever he
> might do to help a friend, considered his own fate as sealed.[8]

Having succumbed to rabies, Holmes was dead within three
months, and Stewart took some time to recover from his sense of
guilt.

At the rendezvous Stewart met many of the legendary characters in the fur trade, including Joe Meek, Jim Bridger, Moses
"Black" Harris, and Kit Carson, and he in turn began to acquire
a certain curiosity value. The presence of the British grandee,
and the almost incomprehensible fact that he was traveling "for

pleasure," was noted in the diaries of several other western travelers of the time, including missionaries and traders, as the distinctive figure was encountered on the Green River, on the Yellowstone, and in Oregon. Charles Larpenteur described a return visit by the wolf, when Stewart's strong sense of discipline got in the way:

> The next night at nearly the same time there was a loud screaming and the cry of "Mad Wolf" was heard all through the camp. All hands arose with their rifles in their hands and were posted in different places in order to kill him. During the time we was posted I heard him about the cattle, and would have shot him but I was hindered by Captain Stewart who was officer of the guard at the time, for it was dangerous to shoot in the midst of the camp. After all our care and good watching, our enemy got away from us.[9]

Nathaniel Wyeth, a Massachusetts man trying to break into the fur trade, rode alongside Stewart in the days after the rendezvous. "Last night Captain Stewart had some sport with a bear near our camp in the willows, which he wounded but did not kill. He represented him as large as a mule."[10] Now that they were away from the open plains, in the forested approaches to the mountains, the danger of a sudden meeting with a grizzly was greater. Stewart incorporated several impromptu meetings with bears into his novels, and in another note in his own voice he admitted that on one occasion he was confronted by a large bruin, reached for his rifle, aimed at its head and pulled the trigger, to hear nothing but a metallic click. Making an elementary tenderfoot's mistake, he had ridden into the woods with an unloaded gun. The bear was diverted for a moment, giving him just enough time to load a percussion cap and ball, and he managed to kill the beast and survive to tell the tale. These were skills less of hunting, more of self-defense.

In the heart of the fur country the threat from Indian attack was also greater, because trappers moved on their own or in small groups, whereas on the prairies protection came from the size of the caravans. Indian numbers were greater and relations between the Native Americans and the white men who had moved into their territory over the previous twenty years were volatile. Grievances emerged suddenly, and alliances were subject to the manipulations of rival fur companies. The whites complained of trickery and dishonesty, and sometimes individual Indians saw targets of opportunity, stealing horses or picking off a lonely trapper for his gun and furs, despite the best promises of their chiefs. Beside the Green that July there was much talk of the bloody skirmish after the previous year's rendezvous, held to the north, in the Teton basin, at Pierre's Hole. Robert Campbell, whom Stewart had come out with, was among those caught up in an all-day fight with the Gros Ventre, in which six trappers were killed by bullets, arrows, and hatchets, and bodies were left mutilated. A greater number of Gros Ventre, who had arguably been provoked, lost their lives.

Lord Ashburnham had written that he hoped Stewart would soon be out of "Injun country," for the sake of his own safety. Five weeks after the 1833 rendezvous, he was deeper into it than ever. The Rocky Mountain Fur Company split its forces, and while Robert Campbell took that year's pelts back to St. Louis by a different route, via the Big Horn Valley, and eventually down the Missouri, his partner Thomas Fitzpatrick stayed to direct the autumn trapping. Captain Stewart went with him, and they headed east into Absaroka, the Crow lands. Stewart had a chance to see how the trapping was done, as small groups of men went out for short sorties to clean out the beaver from the streams that led into the Powder and Tongue rivers, and the hunting was the best yet. The summer heat was over, the light had a crisp golden clarity, and there was more time to pursue game, without the relentless pressure to keep up the necessary twenty-five miles a day of the prairie crossing. Fitzpatrick was hoping to build a trading alliance with the Crows. He did not know that his opposition, the American Fur Company, was ahead of him and had already made an agreement for protection, in exchange for goods, tying things up insofar as this was ever possible with the Crows.

As Thomas Fitzpatrick, Stewart, and their brigade of about thirty men, with pack animals and spare horses, made their way across the desolate low hills and badlands into what is now southwest Montana, they were conscious of Indians trailing them at a distance. On September 5, when they reached the Tongue, the Crows caught up with them and the chief, with an effusive speech of peace and friendship, proposed they camp alongside each other on the gray sandstone bank of the river. Fitzpatrick was suspicious, and declined the offer. He set up camp separately, but then rode back with two or three others to see the chief, who received him cordially and gave more assurances of his good intentions.

Meanwhile Captain Stewart, the Waterloo veteran, now accepted as Fitzpatrick's deputy, was left in charge of twenty-five men, including poor Holmes who was still sickening from his wolf bite, back at their camp by the Tongue. He was no longer a detached observer but an active participant in the tensions of frontier life, and he had to work out the best way of handling matters when a party of young Crow braves, outnumbering them by at least four to one, galloped into the camp, on what they maintained was just a fraternal call. In the course of the shouts, exaggerated embraces, enforced camaraderie, effusive admiration of blankets and hats, and much pushing and jostling, Stewart lost control. The feigned good humor was abandoned as knives and hatchets came out, and the Indians shook the whites down, grabbing guns, watches, and anything of value, and making off with all the furs, traps, trade goods, and horses. As they rode away with the booty they met Fitzpatrick returning, and for good measure plundered him too.

Though they were now totally at the Crows' mercy, and feared for their lives, in the next few days Stewart saw Fitzpatrick's skills at Indian handling. He prevailed on the chief to at least give them back enough horses, rifles, and rounds of ammunition to enable them to get out of the Crow country. They turned west again, in the direction they had come from, trying to intercept another party of trappers, who would help them rearm and re-equip. Stewart was not blamed for the debacle, and Washington Irving, who researched and wrote about the Crow robbery in the course of a book about the fur trade, judged that he had "behaved with great spirit."[11] In *Altowan* and *Edward Warren* Stewart always presented the Crows as a specially treacherous lot.

Stewart was lucky to have escaped, and managed to regain his own horse. All he lost were personal possessions, including his watch, and he was in no way put off. There was still half a continent he wanted to see, and if he ever had any intention of returning to Scotland and his wife and son after one trip, he soon forgot it. He spent all that winter in the West with another Rocky Mountain Fur Company party, going down through Colorado to New Mexico with the trapper and guide Kit Carson. Near Taos he was robbed again, this time in an inside job, by a young Iowa Indian who had been hired as a camp helper. In another of his factual footnotes to his novels, Stewart told how he discovered that the man had gone off with a favorite rifle, and his two horses. "I was in great trouble, and rushed out of my lodge; the greatest part of the camp were assembled to examine the pickets, no rope had been cut, and the rifle had been taken from beside the fire, and I exclaimed in my wrath 'I'd give five hundred dollars for his scalp.' . . ." One of the party, a grizzled trapper called Markhead, took this as a challenge and went out on a search, soon finding the Indian, beside the carcass of a buffalo he had just shot with the stolen weapon. Stewart continued, "In the evening, between us and the sun, the loiterers of the camp saw two men leading two horses making their way toward camp, and on a rifle was displayed the scalp of the horse-thief. This was a little more than I looked for, and I tore the bloody trophy from the gun and flung it away."[12]

The recovery of his horse Otholoho, which he had raced at the rendezvous and claimed was "the swiftest in the west," was only temporary. A year later it was taken by the Blackfoot. Stewart was back for his second rendezvous on the Green River in the summer of 1834. From there he went past the Salt Lake and over the Cascades to Oregon and the Pacific, making a brief return to the British Empire when he stopped at the Hudson's Bay Company's tidy outpost at Fort Vancouver on the Columbia. He crossed east again in time for his third fur trade rendezvous in 1835, and did not return to St. Louis until that October.

Captain Stewart had been in the backwoods and out of contact for two and a half years. On his return to the city he wrote his first letter to his friend James Watson Webb, the New York newspaper editor whose introductions to St. Louis had been so valuable. "It is now a long time since I have seen or heard from you . . . the life I have led since my Indian pilgrimage commenced in April 1833 has been one of very varied but never failing interest, sleeping under the canopy of the night was the only moment of inactivity, and often danger and pleasure divided its watches in an almost dreamy succession . . . the Rocky mountains were capable of producing but few pleasures I have not tasted and few dangers I have not tried." But he found it hard to set down all he had seen. "I cannot willingly devote any little power of writing that remains unforgotten to a description of some of these scenes which I know must interest you—but it really is a matter of such difficulty to write well, to one long dead to such things, that you must allow me to defer it until I am somewhat familiarized with literature and orthography." He paid generous tribute to the men he had been living beside. "The American trappers in the mountains have all been so kind to me that I feel the instincts of a brother in all of them. . . ."[13]

Mail was waiting with news of his family in Edinburgh. He also found another Scottish aristocrat in the city, and with the serendipity that accompanied many meetings between one such British traveler and another, they were related. The Honorable

Charles Murray, who had arrived on the boat from Louisville that summer, was another second son of a great family, brought up at Dunmore Park in Stirlingshire, and was Stewart's cousin through his mother's side. He had just come back from his own adventure with the Pawnee Indians, further up the Missouri. The urbane Murray was going on to Havana, since the island of Cuba was part of many American grand tours.

After such a long time on the trail, spending hours a day in the saddle, eating round campfires, sleeping under the stars or in bivouacs of branches, Stewart may have wanted some recreation, and to find pleasures St. Louis could not provide. He and Charles Murray boarded the steamer *The Far West*, and twelve days later, after an alarming downriver journey marked by a series of accidents and near disasters, they reached the softer climate of Louisiana. Staying in New Orleans that winter, Stewart went to the theater, gambled, and probably dallied with women. He was sought after by hostesses, and attended dinners and balls, but this was just a sybaritic interlude. The Far West still had him in its thrall. He had no plans to return to Scotland, and in the spring of 1836 he went upriver to St. Louis again for another return to the prairies.

So far Stewart had been accepted—insofar as was possible for any outsider—by the fur traders as an equal. He had jogged across the plains with them under the beating sun, throat parched, saddle leather creaking, dust rising, sharing the same discomforts and living from day to day in the same frugal manner. All he had with him was what survived of the kit he had left St. Louis with, in April 1833, and most of the time he wore buckskins and moccasins made by Indian squaws at the rendezvous. But in his travels from 1836 onward Stewart started to equip and conduct himself in a different way, and the contrasts in social background and financial resources were more obvious. He had two years of experience of roughing it behind him, and as he approached his fortieth birthday, he was ready for more comfort. He had more

money, either from the Perth remittances that had built up while
he was away, or from shrewd speculation on the New Orleans cotton exchange during his winter in the South.

At the same time the nature of prairie travel was altering.
Though Stewart's first cross-prairie caravan, with Robert Campbell in 1833, had been made up exclusively of horses and pack animals, others had started to take the first wheeled vehicles along
the Platte route and over the South Pass, at a high cost in broken axles, upset loads, and wagons swept away in perilous river
crossings. When Thomas Fitzpatrick led a new trading caravan
out from Bellevue on the Missouri in 1836, with Captain Stewart
along once again, they had mules pulling nineteen two-wheeled
carts loaded with trade goods and supplies, in addition to a string
of pack animals. As a separate presence in the column that
creaked along beside the muddy Platte, Captain Stewart had two
wagons of his own, carrying the personal supplies he wanted to
bring for his second journey to the mountains, to ease any depri-
vations he may have felt during the first.

As well as guns, lead, and powder, his baggage now included
hams, cases of tinned sardines, coffee and sugar, jams and pre-
serves, wines, brandy, whiskey, tobacco, and presents he was tak
ing to the rendezvous. He was no longer traveling on his own,
but recruited Herr Sillen, a wealthy German adventurer he had
met in New Orleans, to share the hunting and his delicacies. As
well as the horses and two mules to pull his wagons, he brought
two riding horses, and a black thoroughbred stallion chosen for
its speed, which he planned to use in that summer's races at the
rendezvous beside the Green.

While the two tourists rode near the head of the train, which
totaled more than seventy men and four hundred animals, a new
sort of traveler followed at the back, going in search of souls rather
than pelts. The first missionaries hoping to convert the Indians
had crossed the country two years earlier, when the Methodist
minister Jason Lee had looked on the red men at the rendezvous

in 1834 and prayed, "Oh that these sons of nature may soon be children of Grace."[14] The Presbyterians were not far behind, also bearing the news of salvation, and Fitzpatrick had agreed to take a group of missionaries, despatched by the New England–based American Board of Commissioners for Foreign Missions, under his wing. Led by the resilient and determined Dr. Marcus Whitman, they had equipped themselves with two wagons, much impedimenta, reams of Christian literature, a plow, seeds, and sixteen cattle. From this nucleus they planned to establish a mission in Oregon. Adding special interest for the rough American hunters and the French-Canadian *engagés* on the journey, the missionaries had two females among them. Narcissa, the wife of Dr. Whitman, and Eliza Spalding, another spouse, would become the first white women to cross the continent. Some days they rode sidesaddle; on others they allowed themselves to be carried along in the carts.

Keeping up the civilities of their life in New England, the ladies would ask Stewart to take tea with them at the end of the day, in tin cups, but with fresh milk and freshly baked bread. Stewart liked the Whitmans, and was rather smitten by Narcissa. A few years later the couple would be massacred, Marcus brained with a pipe-tomahawk, Narcissa shot three times in the chest, when Cayuse Indians they had been preaching to concluded they were sorcerers.

Stuart had now been in America for four years, in which time he had met almost no other Englishmen, and received very little news of home. For the Americans he was traveling with, he remained a puzzle. One account of him came from William Gray, the lay member of the 1836 missionary party in charge of the livestock and wagon driving.

He was about five feet nine inches high. His face had become thin from the free use of New Orleans brandy, rendering his nose rather prominent, showing indications of internal heat in bright red spots, and inclining a little to the rum blossom, that would make its appearance from the sting of a mosquito or sand-fly, which to his lordship was quite annoying. Though his lordship was quite advanced in years, and, according to his own account, had traveled extensively in the oriental countries, he did not show in his conversation extensive mental improvement; his general conversation and appearance was that of a man with strong prejudices, and equally strong appetites, which he had freely indulged with only pecuniary restraint.[15]

Gray's portrayal said as much about the writer's own preconceptions as it does about Stewart himself, and showed the natural abhorrence that many Americans, particularly those from the Atlantic states where the sense of the colonial past was keener, felt for the British nation as a whole, as the old tyrant. "This Englishman with his party consisted of himself and a young English blood. I did not learn whether he was one of the first, second, third or fourth grade in the scale of English nobility; be that as it may, Sir William D., K.B. messed and slept in the same tent with this traveling companion of his, who between them had three servants, two dogs, and four extra fine horses." Gray was incorrect in identifying Sillen as English, and was also wrong when he called Stewart a knight. At that time he had no title, but Americans were not inclined to be technical about the British upper classes, and they knew one when they saw one.

As a teetotal Presbyterian, Gray found the very concept of Captain Stewart offensive, and thought his fellow countrymen were servile and too easily impressed.

Occasionally they would give chase to that swiftest of mountain animals the antelope, which in most instances, would, especially where the grass was short, leave them in the distance, when Sir William and his companion would come charging back to the train swearing that the antelope could outrun a streak of lightning, and offering to bet a thousand pounds that if he had one of his English 'orses he could catch 'em. The English nobleman, as a matter of course was treated with great respect by all in the caravan; while in the presence of the ladies he assumed quite a dignified carriage, being a man (excuse me, your honour), a Lord of the British realm. . . .[16]

Gray's portrayal of Stewart as a limited, anti-intellectual, hunting-obsessed national stereotype was unfair, or ahead of its time, for plenty of these would cross the Atlantic in the years to come. Though he had the surface manners and bearing of his class, he did not carry their standard set of prejudices. He seems to have liked the fact that on the frontier you were judged on your actions and your stamina rather than your pedigree, at least by most people. He became a close friend of Robert Campbell, William Sublette, and Jim Bridger, who found him generous and a useful man to have in a tight spot. Writing later, Kit Carson, the trapper he had spent a winter with, paid him fulsome tribute: "For the goodness of his heart and numerous rare qualities of mind, he will always be remembered by those of the mountaineers who had the honor of his acquaintance."[17]

If Stewart liked to drink and gamble, he was also thoughtful. He had had a classical schooling. He spoke French and some Italian, and took Shakespeare and Byron on his travels. His novels, whatever they lacked in construction and plot, showed he could be a good, if wordy, descriptive writer. He was no James Fenimore Cooper, but he knew more at firsthand than the master, and had a sensitive understanding of the mixed cast of Indians and half-breeds, backwoodsmen from Kentucky and Tennessee, traders from the Atlantic states, French-speaking whites and Creoles, who peopled the West in the 1830s. His principal character in *Edward Warren* displays mysterious longings and a melancholy restlessness that were probably true of the author himself.

Since he left the army at such an early age, he had been without a clear role at home, and the West had provided a substitute for the adventure and fulfillment he had found in military service. In one passage he describes the sort of simple pleasure he enjoyed in the Wind River Mountains. "The fire burnt clear, and the stream ran by on its rocky bed, sparkling and pure, retaining still the cold of the snows from which it came. I cannot tell you how that evening passed, or how the next; all I can tell is that I never tired, and that no period of my varied life calls up the memory of such perfect joy."[18]

In America, William Stewart discovered a rough open-air way of life that suited him, and a passion that stayed with him for the rest of his life. At the same time he knew more of the modern nineteenth-century world than many of the people he was moving among, and had a different perspective. After four years he could see how fast the West was changing, and that the untouched landscape, the original native population, as well as the woodsmanship, craft, and rituals of the fur trade, were under threat. By the time of the 1836 rendezvous, the richest trapping areas had been worked out, and thanks to the fickleness of fashion, the price of pelts was falling. In the East and in Britain and on the continent the silk hat was the coming thing, and the fur companies feared their best days were over.

While the missionaries, including Narcissa Whitman, Eliza, and William Gray, decamped from the rendezvous and headed for Oregon, Stewart hunted for a few weeks in the forests of great trees that started where the flat plain of the Green met the foothills of the Wind River Mountains. Then he went back to St. Louis, where he received news, from his younger brother Archibald, that changed all his assumptions and prospects. Their brother John, who had continued to burn up the Stewart fortunes with his building project at Murthly Castle, was in Paris, where he had become seriously ill and was not expected to survive. John still had no children, and William Stewart now knew the succession to the family title and estates might after all be his. When he went down to New Orleans for another winter stay, he had this possibility in mind.

Stewart may have thought his next journey would be his final one, and he wanted to record the scenes he had known while he still could. He started to search for an artist who had the time and stamina to travel with him, and the talent to paint the Indians, the trappers, and the landscape he was so taken by. The idea may have come from Prince Maximilian of Wied-Neuwied, the fellow tourist he had met early on in St. Louis, who had brought a Swiss artist, Karl Bodmer, with him, in the way that later visitors might have brought a camera. But neither Bodmer, who had been up the Missouri, nor George Catlin, who painted the Plains Indians, had been to the mountains, and no artist had been over South Pass or to the fur trade rendezvous.

After taking advice Stewart approached Alfred Jacob Miller, a slightly precious young man from Baltimore who had studied painting in Europe, and had recently arrived to produce pictures and portrait commissions to order for the wealthy families of the Delta city. Stewart went to Miller's studio, over a dry goods store on Chartres Street, to sound him out. He liked the work the painter was able to show him, including a view of Baltimore, and a few weeks later a fee was agreed, and the twenty-six-year-old artist was writing to a friend, "I am at present under engagement to proceed with Capt. W. Stewart, (an affluent gentleman,) on an expedition to the Rocky Mountains, (professionally) the tour to occupy six months. . . ."[19]

The steady flow of sketches and paintings that sprang from the journey would provide the only visual record of the mountain fur trade, make Miller's reputation, and eventually put his work into museums and galleries all over the United States. The hiring of Miller would be Stewart's greatest act of patronage and most long-lasting legacy. If the British aristocrat had not had the money, taste, and conceit to take an artist all the way to the

Rockies with him when he did, it is unlikely anyone else would have done so before most of the encounters and characters the artist recorded had gone.

Miller had his first real sense of his British patron's temperament as he watched the outfitting in St. Louis and Westport, and then set off in a caravan led once again by Thomas Fitzpatrick. Stewart, by now a veteran, quickly initiated Miller into the disciplines of prairie travel. The captain "was somewhat of a martinet, and would not tolerate for a moment any neglect of orders by a subordinate,"[20] Miller noted. "He seemed to be composed of the same iron as 'the Grand Duke' himself." As a concession, and to allow more sketching time, Stewart let Miller off guard duty, and ordered one of the packers to erect and take down his tent for him, but he refused to relieve the artist from having to catch, bring in, and picket his own horse. Miller complained that "The government of our band . . . is somewhat despotic."[21]

One morning, the artist had perched himself on a rock and was sketching intently, when he felt a hand come up from behind and take hold of his neck and head so tightly that he could not move. He assumed his hour had come, and a stealthy savage was about to slice his throat and scalp him. Only after five minutes of silent suspense was the fierce grip finally loosened. It was Stewart, who lectured him for getting so absorbed in drawing that he was neglecting to keep a lookout for Indians. When Stewart thought Miller was becoming unnecessarily depressed after days of constant rain as they slogged across the prairies, he would "banter" with him about his feebleness. "Your early training, he would say, has been faulty—on such days I am more exhilarated, if possible, than if the day is clear. There is something to contend against."[22] With this chide, Stewart was only confirming what most of his class were certain of, that their stiff upper lip approach gave them a unique advantage over other ranks, let alone nationalities.

For the moment Miller used only pencil and watercolors, planning to produce oils from some of his field sketches once he had returned to the civilized comfort of his studio. He drew the daily routines of breakfast, the striking of camp, and picketing the horses, and less predictable events—a mule throwing off its pack, an encounter with a party of Oglala, carts being dragged up a steep riverbank. He sketched buffalo and elk hunts, a carcass being butchered, and landmarks along the route: Fort Laramie, Chimney Rock, Scotts Bluff. Once they had crossed the South Pass and reached the Green River, Miller was captivated by the sights of the 1837 rendezvous, just as Stewart hoped he would be. When the Snake Indians mounted a grand entry in the Scotsman's honor, Miller sketched what he called the "cavalcade," with the Snake chief Ma-wo-ma riding in front, in full war bonnet, and about 2,000 magnificently dressed and mounted warriors following behind, while Stewart watched the ride past from his white horse. He drew the galloping, the gambling, the carousing, and the trappers with Indian women. He produced a series of portraits of individual Native Americans, including Ma-wo-ma. After drawing the Crow chief, Shim-a-co-che, the artist wrote that "his behavior . . . was full of dignity, and such as you might look for in a well-bred civilized gentleman."[23]

Stewart had brought a special box across the prairies in his baggage, so he could fulfill some kind of private joke. Over the winter the former army officer had arranged for a polished steel cuirass and helmet, as worn for ceremonial dress by the British monarch's most elite troop, the Household Cavalry, to be sent out to him in St. Louis. When he was reunited with Jim Bridger at the rendezvous, he produced the heavy Life Guards breastplate, and gave it to the guide and trapper as a present. Alfred Jacob Miller then drew one of his more culturally complicated sketches, showing Bridger, the nineteenth-century mountain man, wearing British armor of the sixteenth century, advancing across a broad plain dotted with tepees, while Indian braves and French Canadian mule handlers look on in puzzlement. Henceforth, Miller explained in his notes, Bridger "donned it on all special occasions and rode so accoutred at the head of his men."[24]

During the rendezvous, Stewart met the self-righteous missionary William Gray once more, this time making his way back from Oregon, and the daily journal the missionary was keeping offered a counterpoint to the bucolic memories of others: "This evening I have heard the reports of several guns . . . and from their noise I should think they were mad or intoxicated with liquors. . . . No tongue can tell the extent that blasphemy is carried at this place. There seems to be no thought of God but to blaspheme his name." He was appalled by the whoring and debauchery: "Today I was told . . . that Indian women are a lawful commerce among the men that resort to these mountains from the states and elsewhere . . . the buying and selling of Indian women is a common occurrence at this rendezvous, especially among those having a white face."[25]

William Stewart's sense of himself had inevitably changed in the time he had been in America, and from the greenhorn on the trail he had become an old hand, increasingly aware of his unique, privileged position in the western firmament. For the 1837 rendezvous he brought a green-striped tent, and spread rugs out in front, to mark an almost imperial presence. Miller sketched his patron constantly, making him the central figure of many pictures, and giving him a place on the sidelines, as a detached observer, on others. Stewart was always recognizable, with his hook nose and large mustache, the only figure in white buckskins, on a white horse, wearing the same large black hat with a jaunty bird's feather he would have worn on the Scottish moors. Miller drew him riding beside his personal hunter, Antoine Clement, or trying to resolve a dispute between Delaware and Snake Indians.

Sketches he made during the rendezvous showed Stewart reclining round the fire with the trappers, as they exchanged stories of hairbreadth escapes, and comical incidents such as the time a bear neatly scalped a trapper with his claw. In notes which Miller put together to accompany some of his pictures, he wrote that

our leader would entertain them with his adventures in foreign lands, the curious cities and monuments of antiquity he
had visited. It was edifying to see the patience with which
he answered their simple questions as if they were matters of
course and full importance, all the while maintaining a gravity that was most amusing. It is not to be wondered at that he
became immensely popular amongst them. No doubt all of the
men would have followed him into any danger regardless of
consequences. One of them told us that he had a "h'ar of the
Grizzly" in him, meaning bulldog courage.[26]

Though Captain Stewart had known, from the winter of 1836,
that he had a good chance of inheriting the title and moving into
Murthly, it was always possible that his brother might defy the
terminal diagnosis and recover, or that his wife might turn out
to be pregnant and produce an heir at a late stage. So, until he
received definite news, he wasted no time and headed off to the
mountains again, but not before he and Miller had looked at the
field sketches and agreed on a first list of pictures to be worked
up into oils. The fact that he was ordering large and expensive
pictures suggests his confidence that he would, at some point,
have somewhere to hang them. When he returned to St. Louis
in October 1838, a letter was waiting from Lord Breadalbane,
along with others from his family, telling him that his brother
Sir John had died on May 20. Captain Stewart was now the 19th
Laird of Grandtully and 7th Baronet, the owner of the estates of
Murthly and Grandtully. He also added the name of Drummond,
as he inherited a third Scottish estate, his mother's property at
Logiealmond, and for the rest of his life would be Sir William
Drummond Stewart.

Though his relatives expected him to hurry back by the first
ship to take charge, Stewart found it hard to leave, and there
were still arrangements to make. He had collected a selection
of native plants and trees, including western hemlock, Lawson

cypresses, Sitka spruce, and the most magnificent western tree
of all, the Rocky Mountain Douglas fir. He had these wrapped
in hessian and sent off to Scotland. He packed up his collection
of Indian souvenirs, weapons, and clothing. He had already sent
home several live buffalo, as offered, to Lord Breadalbane, and
he wanted to ship some beasts for himself. After recruiting two
Indians to look after them, he sent animals and keepers down the
river from St. Louis on the steamboat *Vandalia*.

Miller, now back in his New Orleans studio, took a sympathetic
interest in the welfare of the animals and went to the wharves to
check on them as they were landed. He wrote to Stewart, "Yesterday arrived two of your buffalo and a Grizzly bear. The male
of the former giving already an assurance of a goodly sized hump
rib and a proportionate body. The female looked thin and possibly worried while traveling. But the bear is a most noble fellow.
. . . When I was there a piece of meat was handed to him, which
censed him and I could perceive a plentiful supply of Savage while
he was engaged in feeding."[27] The British consul, John Crawford,
arranged for them to be transferred to a ship sailing for England.
He paid $100 for the passage, another $25 for the erection of a
temporary buffalo house on the deck, and $7.50 for hay, and sent
the bill to Sir William.

In May 1839, eighteen of Alfred Jacob Miller's completed pictures from the plains and the Rockies were put on show at the
Apollo Gallery in New York, James Watson Webb helping with
the arrangements. To city dwellers who crowded to view them,
the exhibition offered a chance to see a fabled part of their country never illustrated before, and scenes of the western fur trade,
camping, and hunting they had only read about. The pictures on
show included *The Hunting of the Buffalo*, *Portrait of an Arikara
Squaw*, *Portrait of a Chief of the Snake Nation*, *General View of
the Indian Camp*, *Trappers Camp*, and *One of the Sources of the
Colorado*, and they had an extraordinary impact. Critics paid
tribute to both Miller and his patron. "Of Sir William himself,

the originator, the traveler and the subject of the picturesque
and the grand, we hardly know how to speak. The romance of
his taste, and the enthusiasm of his character, in spending seven
years around and about the Rocky Mountains, are without parallel in these days of steamboats and railways."[28] It was made clear
that the paintings would not be in the United States for long, and
the number of daily visitors to the gallery doubled. The run was
extended, but at the end of the month they were crated up and
shipped to Scotland, where they were due to be hung on the walls
of Murthly Castle. It would be many years before New Yorkers, or
any other Americans, would see the canvases back in their home
country.

Sir William presided over the New York exhibition, and then
left at the end of May, on the Collins Line packet *Sheridan*. By
that time his buffalo and bear had already made the crossing, and
the animals reached Perth before their owner. His private artist
worked on, producing more paintings from the field sketches, that
were to follow those already on their way. One of the most spectacular was the still uncompleted grand rendezvous scene, showing the welcome cavalcade of the Snakes.

At the end of his seven-year sojourn, the contribution of this
pioneer British aristocrat was viewed entirely positively, at least
by the New York papers, and those who had had dealings with
him in St. Louis. A journalist went to visit Miller, to see work in
progress on the big rendezvous picture, and conduct an interview.
The artist paid another handsome tribute to his patron:

Captain Stewart is an extraordinary man! He understands
the variations of human character at a glance and is rarely
if ever deceived; at the same time his own character is perfectly undisguised. He is brave, self possessed, prompt and
generous beyond any man I ever met with . . . the Indians
soon learned his character and esteemed him very highly. If

he were disposed to undertake any enterprise in that country which required a force of ten thousand warriors, it would be raised without difficulty at his bidding. . . . He departed from this country with regret and will probably return to it at some future time.[29]

3

Red Men
and Blue Bloods

Every one of these red sons of the forest (or rather of the prairie) is a knight and a lord. . . .[1]

—GEORGE CATLIN, *Letters and Notes . . .* , 1841

When Sir William Stewart returned to Perthshire in the summer of 1839, he found his American buffalo grazing in a pasture by the Tay and their two Indian minders installed in one of the outbuildings. The bear had a cage by the stables. His tenant farmers gave him a welcome-home dinner at the Birnham Hotel, paying respectful tributes to his bravery in America. He started to put the home farm and the estate in order after a period of neglect during the last years of his brother's control and his own delayed return. What gave him most satisfaction was the planting out of his rhododendrons, azaleas, and western trees. Estate workers set out the spruce and the cypresses, and prepared a large area of bare hillside south of the house for the hundreds of Rocky Mountain Douglas firs, which were also planted in terraces further along the river. He was soon shooting on his own moors again, and joining the stalking parties at the Breadalbanes and on other Highland estates. He found his friends much more aware of the American Far West than when he had left.

IN THE YEARS Stewart was away James Fenimore Cooper's novels had run through reprint after reprint, and more books had continued to appear. Washington Irving, the American author who had come to England before Cooper and been embraced and lionized earlier, had now produced his own account of the frontier. After living abroad for seventeen years, writing sketches and stories firmly rooted in the quainter aspects of old Europe, with English and Spanish themes, Irving went back to the United States in 1832 to reestablish his American credentials, and catch up on the changes that had occurred while he had been away.

James Fenimore Cooper had managed to write *The Prairie* without ever going beyond Buffalo and Niagara. Irving upstaged him by taking his own journey west, in search of insights and stories that could form the basis of a book. Traveling with an English gentleman and a wealthy Swiss count he had met on the boat from Europe, the writer reached St. Louis, crossed the Mississippi, and made a month-long excursion into Indian Territory between the Arkansas and Canadian rivers. After years of sedentary city existence, and just approaching his fiftieth birthday, Irving was refreshed and enchanted by the unbroken country, the outdoor life, and the bravado of the rough characters he was with. He rode a bay horse, and tried buffalo hunting, though the mild-mannered and stout author was not a natural sportsman. He carried two old pistols, provided by officers at Fort Gibson, but America's greatest living writer was never in real danger of Indian attack because he was traveling with a government official, and his party was accompanied by eighty armed U.S. Rangers. Each day began with a bugle call at dawn.

A Tour on the Prairies, the first of three books Irving produced about western life and recent history, was the most literary and evocative description of the country based on firsthand knowledge

yet to appear. Just as American readers were happy to have
Irving writing on an American theme again, his British readers
looked to someone who knew their tastes and interests, for the
more imaginative and philosophical approach they had been waiting for. "It is delightful," he wrote of a night bivouacking on the
plains, "to lie awake and gaze at the stars; it is like watching
them from the deck of a ship at sea, when at one view we have the
whole cope of heaven. . . . I felt this night unusually affected by
the solemn magnificence of the firmament, and seemed, as I lay
under the open vault of heaven, to inhale with the pure untainted
air, an exhilarating buoyancy of spirit, as it were an ecstasy of
the mind."[2] The book was published in London a month before it
appeared in the United States, and was an immediate success.
A London critic called it a work of striking beauty, to be read
by all who love nature in its grandest and most imposing proportions. "The literary wanderer really felt all the raptures that
scenes like this must fling into the bosom of one sensitively alive
to the profoundest emotions of poetry . . . his narration is animate
with energy, with grace and with beauty."[3] As well as providing a
new account of the landscape, Irving's slender *Tour* was sharply
focused on the Indians who hunted over these "desolate yet beautiful regions of unmitigated barbarism."[4]

Irving's well-guarded party was traveling with a government
commissioner, sent out to inspect territory set aside for the resettlement of tribes displaced from the East, and to see if more Indians could be dispatched there. In a letter to his sister from St.
Louis, Irving showed where his feelings lay: "I find it extremely
difficult, even when so near the scene of the action, to get at the
right story of these feuds between the White and Red man, and my
sympathies go strongly with the latter."[5] Yet in his book he chose
to avoid the controversial questions about forced removal, and the
catastrophic effects of the white man's alcohol and disease. Limit-
ing himself to the romantic and the picturesque, he was mainly
concerned with Indian aesthetics and physiognomy. He described

decoration and dress, elaborating on the embroidered kneebands and tassels some wore on their leggings, the multicolored hunting shirts of others, and the ornamentation of moccasins. He admired the "fine Roman countenances, and broad deep chests" of the Osages, and found the Creeks "a well-made race, muscular, and closely knit, with well turned thighs and legs." He was fascinated when a group of braves stretched themselves by the fire and began to make a low nasal noise. "Their chant seemed to consist of regular staves, every one terminating, not in a melodious cadence, but in the abrupt interjection, 'hah!' uttered almost like a hiccup."[6]

To the well-off, more adventurous reader, Irving's book acted as a powerful new advertisement for American travel. One reviewer, writing in 1835, said: "The excitement of the early scenes is so stirring that one absolutely wants to start up, and off to the Prairies of the Far West, crossing the Arkansas in a buffalo skin . . . and freshening the soul in all the wild transports of untrammeled nature."[7]

AFTER HIS RETURN to Murthly, Sir William Stewart, a bona fide veteran of the prairies with many stories to tell, seldom left Perthshire. His name was far better known in America than it was at home. He gave no lectures and wrote no articles. When the first of Alfred Jacob Miller's oil paintings arrived from New York and were unpacked and hung, the canvases were for his own private enjoyment, and little known beyond the county. *Greeting the Snake Indians* and *Portrait of an Arikara Squaw* were given pride of place in Murthly Castle, and *The Hunting of the Buffalo* was a constant reminder of Stewart's promise to return as soon as he could. He began his first novel, which was to contain his stories of the prairies and the Indians. But writing did not come easily to him, and *Altowan* would not appear until 1846.

Stewart's relative and companion on the Mississippi River

journey, the Honorable Charles Murray, second son of the Earl of
Dunmore, was faster off the mark. Though he had spent only a
small fraction of time in the West compared with Stewart, it was
Murray who, building on Cooper and Washington Irving, went
into print first and did most to propagate interest in the red men
in particular. By the time he returned he had a unique story to
tell, and his specially privileged position allowed him to make the
most of it. As a result, the aristocracy were soon identifying more
closely with the Red Indians than any other section of British
society.

Murray had set out on his wilderness adventure in 1835 with
a sense of eager expectation. After traveling for some time on the
east coast and through the South, the prairie expedition was to
be the high point. He had met Washington Irving several times
in London. When his mother heard he had reached St. Louis, she
wrote to a friend, "Poor Charles himself is now as happy as possible with his bearskin bed, his guns and pistols and dirks among
the Wild Indians on a Buffalo hunt expedition!" The Countess of
Dunmore could only pray for him. "I wish I could enjoy the idea
as much as he does—however I know the kind protection of his
Heavenly Father need not be confined to civilized places, so to his
mercy I commend him, and endeavor in the meantime to feel as
comfortable as I can. . . ."[8] Had his mother known what he was up
to, she would have worried more.

At Fort Leavenworth, twenty miles into Indian Territory from
the Missouri frontier, he met a group of Pawnee chiefs who came
into the remote U.S. Army post for a dinner, escorted by the Indian
Agent who dealt with the tribe on behalf of the government. Murray was impressed by their grave demeanor and self-possession,
in totally strange surroundings. Few had been in a white man's
settlement before, yet "they entered the room with considerable
ease and dignity, shook hands with us all, and sat down comfortably to cigars and Madeira."[9] Their impeccable behavior seemed
to bear up the European notion, based largely on Cooper, that

the red men were natural aristocrats, with a sense of honor and decorum predating the frippery and conceits of "civilization." The Scottish nobleman got on so well with them that a scheme formed in his mind. He asked the senior chief, Sanitsarish, if he could return to his tribe with him and study their language and customs at close quarters, living as a native. Sanitsarish agreed that Murray could come as his guest, and gave assurances he would protect him, though the Indian Agent, and the army officers, gave dire warnings of the risk involved. Sanitsarish could guard Murray's life and possessions while he was in his care, but other Indians might not be bound by the same inhibitions.

The twenty-eight-year-old Murray was undeterred and set off for his host's temporary village, 100 miles away, with Indian guides, conceding that it was a "strange and wild experiment." He was alone except for a German he had met in Kentucky, a half-breed interpreter who spoke Pawnee and some French but no English, and his Scottish valet. Bounding beside the horses was his faithful hunting dog Peevish, also brought from Scotland. After a difficult journey, in temperatures well over 100° F., Murray caught up with the main body of the Pawnees. "A more interesting and picturesque scene I never beheld. Upon an extensive prairie gently sloping down to a creek, the winding course of which was marked by a broken line of wood here and there interspersed with a fine clump of trees, were about five thousand savages, inclusive of women and children; some were sitting under their buffalo skin lodges lazily smoking pipes; while the women were stooping over their fires busily employed in preparing meat and maize for these indolent lords of the creation."[10] Murray's Victorian biographer, writing later, suggested he had reached the happy state he was striving for: "At last he had achieved his desire. Civilization, as far as his own environment of many hundreds of miles was affected, was as though it had never been."[11]

Charles Murray, used to the comforts of his family's ancestral seat in Scotland and their London home in Mayfair, took some time to settle in to the routine of Indian domestic life. His personal servant laid out his bedding in Sanitsarish's tepee, an irregularly shaped tent whose dimly lit interior housed the chief's wives, grown-up son, younger children, and six dogs, packed in as tightly as "the horses in a stage-coach stable." Animal skins covered the earth floor, and mysterious medicine objects, including skulls and dried buffalo body parts, were suspended from the roof poles, with other relics of spiritual significance. The constant din and commotion, and the fetid air, made sleep almost impossible. Dogs yapped ceaselessly, the children were suffering from chronic whooping cough, and "the loquacity of the ladies knew no bounds."[12] Fleas ran riot in the furs, blankets, and clothes, battalions of lice colonized human hair, and the stench was overpowering.

After his first night, the fastidious young aristocrat left the tepee with soap, towel, and a clean shirt provided by his valet, looking for somewhere to wash. All he could find was a muddy streamlet, with children and dogs splashing, and horses trampling through in every direction. Trying to maintain his dignity, he bathed "by lying down and rolling where the water was about nine inches deep,"[13] while curious Indians watched him, going through his clothes and pockets and examining his toothbrush. Murray was challenged by the diet, and found the bowls of thick maize gruel, boiled prairie roots, and raw or semi-cooked meat hard to digest, the more taxing because the Indians would invite him to up to seven feasts a day, in different lodges.

As the weeks went on, Murray began to adjust some of the rosier notions he had arrived with. "Every hour I spent with the Indians impressed upon me the conviction that I had taken the only method of becoming acquainted with their domestic habits and their undisguised character. . . ." It seemed the Pawnees did not, after all, have the high sense of honor he had been led to expect. His disillusion grew after a string of incidents, when he felt he was cheated into buying horses that turned out to be uncontrollably wild or crippled by lameness, or threatened into making "swaps" of his clothing, pistols, or knives for Indian items he did not want. One brave tried to steal his rifle. Another took a fancy to his small folding telescope. He felt particularly upset when the Indians caught and ate his dog Peevish. But he never doubted the good faith or honesty of Sanitsarish himself. "Nature had made him a gentleman, and he remained so in spite of the corrupting examples around him."[14]

Murray relied on his own reserves of dignity and strict self-control to get through, much as the Native Americans had done at the Fort Leavenworth dinner where he had first met them. He tried to practice psychological oneupmanship, never allowing his hosts to see any weakness. The Indians referred to him as Neshada-ta-ka, or "White Chief." "I made it a rule to humour their prejudices, and to accommodate myself to their usages, however absurd. Moreover I endeavored to make them believe that I could surpass them in anything which I chose to attempt." He inveigled some of the strongest young men into a contest, lobbing heavy stones as far as they could across the prairie. There was no way they could pitch them as far as Murray, who had learned the "stone put" as practiced in the Highland Games. "I thought it essential to my estimation, if not to my safety among them, to keep up this belief in my superiority. . . ."[15]

The reliable performance of his heavy, double-barreled London built Purdey rifle allowed him to hit targets the Indians' own weapons could never reach. One day, while chewing his way though a meal of raw meat, he saw an animal moving beyond the line of tepees. He raised his gun and brought down an antelope, rather to his own amazement, at a distance of 200 yards. "Shouts of admiration and surprise were raised by the savages who ran to secure the little prize; but I pretended that it was a mere matter of course, said nothing, laid down my rifle, and continued my meal." Pursuing deer on foot, he found himself trying to keep pace with an Indian hunter who could carry on for miles at a time, up and down hill, through tangled brushwood and shrubs. "His wind seemed almost as inexhaustible as his appetite, and running quite as easy to him as sitting. I kept up, however, without giving him to understand that I was annoyed by the heat and cooled myself now and then by wading and dabbling in the creek."[16]

Murray, who had been schooled at Eton and Oxford, was measuring what he saw against the yardstick of British upper-class life, and the perspective led to comparisons that would not have sprung to the American mind. When leaving the Missouri and coming onto the open prairie for the first time, the undulating grassland, broken by stands of timber, reminded him of the skillfully planted open landscapes that surrounded the country houses of his friends. He thought in particular of Windsor Great Park, which stretched away from the royal family's castle in Berkshire. When he tried to follow an elk with an Indian hunter, he judged the man was not as good as the deer stalkers the Dunmores employed in the Highlands at taking advantage of wind direction and the lie of the land. He thought the stage at which young Indian men were first allowed to hunt might be compared with "the Oxonian's first appearance in London life after taking his B.A. degree."[17] The cries of "Hou! Hou!" with which the Pawnees responded to an excited orator at a feast reminded him of the "Hear, hear" used in the House of Commons.

Murray was a classicist and a Fellow of All Souls, the august Oxford college which considered itself the elite among intellectual elites. On the prairies he became an amateur ethnologist, watching the Pawnees closely, trying to make the most of his remarkable access. He smoked the medicine pipe with them, gambled, and joined a game in which small javelins were thrown into hoops placed on the ground. He shared the general alarm, and tried to calm his terrified valet, when the Pawnees thought their Cheyenne enemy were about to raid the camp, and worked themselves up with an exchange of hideous battle cries. He tried to learn the language, taking a daily lesson with Sanitsarish, and rendering words into his notebook with accents to show pronunciation, as with Něshâdă-tâ-kă for "White Chief." He studied the hierarchy, the etiquette at meals, and conventions of dress.

He tried to find out about courtship, and the brave's attitude to marriage. "The most extraordinary part of this matrimonial affair is that having married the older sister, he [Sanitsarish] has a right to marry all the younger ones, as they successively attain the age of puberty. . . ." Unlike Captain Stewart, who had fallen for Snake girls at the fur trade rendezvous, Murray was not attracted by Indian women himself. "I never saw one instance of beauty, either in face or figure—of neatness in dress—cleanliness in appearance, or any one of those grateful and attractive attributes which generally characterize the softer sex."[18] But he sympathized with the squaws, who carried huge bundles of firewood that would defy a London porter, and had to light the fires, pulverize the maize, cook, make the clothes, strike the tents, load the animals, in what Murray described as a round of perpetual degradation and slavery.

His insights into Pawnee life were waspish, and comparative. The earl's son described the routine he observed each morning, as his opposite number, the elder son of Chief Sanitsarish, prepared himself on days when there was no buffalo hunting:

> He began his toilet, about eight in the morning, by greasing and smoothing his whole person with fat, which he rubbed afterwards perfectly dry, only leaving the skin sleek and glossy; he then painted his face vermilion, with a stripe of red along the center of the crown of his head; he then proceeded to his coiffure, which received great attention, although the quantum of hair demanding such care was limited, inasmuch as his head was shaved close, except one tuft at the top. . . . He then filled his ears, which were bored in two or three places, with rings and wampum and hung several strings of beads around his neck; and then sometimes painting stripes

of vermilion and yellow upon his breast and shoulders, and placing armlets above his elbows and rings upon his fingers, he proceeded to adorn the nether man with a pair of moccasins, some scarlet cloth leggings fastened to his waist–belt, and bound round below the knee with garters of beads four inches broad.

Having got so far, he pulled out a small mirror to review progress. Murray suggested that no female, "from the time of Eve," ever studied her reflected self with more perseverance or satisfaction than his chief's son. "I have repeatedly seen him sit, for above an hour, examining his face in every possible position and expression." [19]

The young brave would expend more time decorating his horse, daubing stripes of crimson onto the animal's forehead, neck, and shoulders, twisting feathers into the tail, and stringing small bells on the reins. Then, "All things being now ready for the promenade, he threw a scarlet mantle over his shoulders; thrust his mirror in below his belt; took in one hand a large fan, of wild goose or turkey feathers . . . mounted his jingling palfrey, and ambled through the encampment, envied by all the youths less gay in attire." Murray knew the narcissism that London swells were capable of, dressing in the sharpest fashion for the afternoon ride in Rotten Row, but he maintained that the young Pawnee took the crown: "I have seen some dandies in my life—English, Scotch, French . . . but none of them can compare with the vanity and coxcombry of the Pawnee dandy."[20]

Many others, including the early explorers, fur traders, and missionaries, had described Indians in their full parade or battle dress, but the Honorable Charles Murray's account of the preliminaries was, in a small way, a first. He had managed to see all this from inside the tepee, from under an adjacent buffalo skin, and was in a unique position to compare it with the different and considerable vanities of his own world.

Murray had managed to spend a few weeks with a people who were already more beholden to the whites, and more compromised by them, than the so far less cowed tribes further west. While first steaming up the Missouri, on the way to the Indian Territory, he had a chance meeting with George Catlin, a Pennsylvania painter and author who had managed to visit forty-eight tribes, and had been studying the Indians for five years to the exclusion of almost everything else. The single-minded Catlin was ten years older than Murray, and had become so knowledgeable in the course of his travels in British, American, and Mexican territory that Murray must have felt like an amateur dabbler and been in some awe of him. The painter was about to return east with his extensive collection of Indian pictures, hoping to sell them to the government. By now a campaigner as well as an artist, he wanted to convince his white countrymen that the remaining Indian tribes needed to be safeguarded, and that his pictures offered a unique record of their culture.

The chance meeting on a riverboat was to prove very helpful to Catlin, after Washington rebuffed him, and he failed to get the support he needed in the United States. For Murray, it was the start of a friendship that allowed him to widen his knowledge of the Native Americans, and become a sympathetic, if realistic, advocate for them in Britain.

Murray returned home without Peevish, but bringing two jet black Indian ponies he had acquired during his American journey. His social connections proved as valuable as ever, and soon after his return from the buffalo-hide tent of the Pawnee chief, he was living in the grandeur of Windsor Castle, serving the Queen. Given a sinecure appointment by Lord Melbourne, the prime minister, Murray was sent to join the court of the young Victoria when she had been on the throne for only a few months. With the title "Groom in waiting," he accompanied her on daily rides in Windsor Park, which presumably reminded him of the prairies, and looked after the stablemen, grooms, coachmen, and postilions who were based in the Royal Mews.

Queen Victoria was interested in his small but fast American horses, and asked him to show off their paces. "We rode out at half-past three, and my pony 'Blackbird' excited much admiration by his speed and action. The Queen asked me his origin, history, name etc, and laughed very much when I told her that I had christened his black companion 'Jim Crow.' "[21] In the evening, under a gilt and painted ceiling, with powdered footmen hovering, he ate with the Queen, her inner circle, and the foreign royalty visiting Windsor. A witty raconteur, he entertained the eighteen-year-old Victoria with stories of life among the Pawnees. In his first months, after dinner, and a game of whist with the King of the Belgians, or draughts with the Duchess of Kent, he made his way down long passageways to his own rooms in the Round Tower. There Murray stayed up by candlelight, working on the book he was writing about his journey. Victoria agreed that he could dedicate it to her, and his *Travels in North America* appeared in 1839. In a preface he said he hoped that his work would interest the monarch and perhaps "beguile a leisure hour stolen from your Majesty's more grave and weighty occupations."[22] By that time Murray, known for his charm, had been promoted to Head of Household, in charge of all the royal palaces and the payroll.

Murray's *Travels* was a gallop around American society and institutions, from a member of the British ruling class whose family were closely identified with the old colonial regime. His grandfather had represented the King as Governor of Virginia, where the Dunmores still owned land. Though Americans found him less prejudiced than recent British visitors, including Mrs. Trollope and Captain Basil Hall, who were dismissed by one reviewer as "these little scribbling wretches,"[23] he remained the aristocrat, uneasy with the lack of respect for rank and station—"There is nothing that strikes a foreigner so much as the real republican equality existing in the Western states, which border on the wilderness. . . ." It worried him to see clerks or grocers drinking or playing cards with a member of Congress or a senior army officer, laughing together and calling each other by their first names. Murray, who insisted his valet take his meals separately on the steamboats, believed the notion of "equality" was incompatible with civilized life, because "it contravenes that advancement of and exaltation of superior power, or intellect, which Nature has for centuries proved to be part of her system."[24]

By far the greatest part of his book was devoted to his time with the Pawnees, and the other Indians he sought out. During a separate journey on the upper Mississippi, he visited the Fox or Outragami Indians, near Fort Crawford. He admired the Menomenee women, finding them far prettier than the "homely" Pawnees. He interrogated "a tolerably intelligent Delaware, from whom I got some information about his tribe and tongue."[25] He called on the Kickapoos and the Powtawatomies and took down some of their speech for a basic vocabulary. He went inside the Winnebago tents, finding them different from the Pawnee ones, circular, with better ventilation and more comforts, including cooking utensils. As he saw more of the tribes who had been shifted west, as well as Indians who had lingered behind in the white man's United States, he became more sensitive to the wider moral questions.

Passing through Natchez on his way down the Mississippi, he saw an Indian near the quay, rolling on the ground, completely incapacitated by alcohol. Murray abandoned his usual droll and supercilious style, and his response to the wretched Chickasaw was untypically straightforward and heartfelt:

. . . when I see him groveling in the dirt, with a helpless body and a reeling brain, and uttering thick and half choked sounds, which no ear near him can understand, I cannot help thinking—We have done this! We who boast of our civilization—we, who pretend to spread abroad the refinement of art and science, and the purity of the gospel among

nations,—we have reduced the eagle eye, the active limb, the
stately form of our red brother to the grovelling animal which
I now see before me.[26]

AT A TIME when overseas travel for leisure and learning was still
difficult and expensive, and before the days of photography, London impresarios tried to import scenes from the distant world to
show on their own home ground. In the 1830s the city offered a
series of static but spectacular panoramas, with grand views of
exotic foreign scenes, for a few pence admission. Calcutta could
be seen in the Strand, Canton in Leicester Square, Constan-
tinople in Regent Street. By the 1830s the Egyptian Hall, in
Piccadilly, had become one of the most sought after places for
temporary exhibitions and exotic displays. An architectural odd-
ity in itself, with a facade of inclined pilasters and two carved
Pharaohs supporting a transom of hieroglyphics, the design was
claimed to be loosely based on a Nile temple. It stood at the eastern and commercial end of the street, next to coaching offices
and print dealers, and across from the smart Burlington Arcade,
a glazed and glittering new gallery of small shops, milliners,
apothecaries, jewelers, and silversmiths, that catered to the
wealthiest district of London. As the fashionable axis continued
westward, Piccadilly passed through the heart of Mayfair and
St. James's to the park, lined with the substantial town houses
of the aristocracy.

Catering to the neighborhood, the Egyptian Hall advertised its
shows as being "for the Nobility and Gentry," and its frequently
changing attractions ranged from spectacular works of art to
remarkable plants and animals. A rare and active Gibbon ape
from the forests of Sumatra was followed by a notable new painting of Christ's entry into Jerusalem, then a re-creation of the
Battle of Waterloo, featuring 95,000 model soldiers. This would

be the place to see a pair of Siamese twins still linked at the hip, or a scale replica of the city of Venice. Nautch girls from a temple in Pondicherry were brought to perform Hindoo dances, though critics complained they moved in too sinuous and rubbery a style. A group of Laplanders were imported from the snowy wastes of northern Sweden, with several reindeer, and positioned in front of a painted backdrop, where they offered visitors short sleigh rides.

In the autumn of 1839, the Honorable Charles Augustus Murray was in active negotiation with the owners of the Egyptian Hall on behalf of an American friend. His groundwork led to the most successful and long-running exhibition ever mounted there, becoming a semi-permanent feature for over three years. It would raise British interest in the American frontier still further, providing what was, in effect, the first British "Wild West" show almost fifty years before Buffalo Bill came to Earl's Court. In the earlier version, the Native American tribes were the entire focus, interesting in themselves. It was too early for cowboys or sharpshooters, and the prairies were still thought to be a desert.

George Catlin arrived at Liverpool with 8 tons of baggage, including over six hundred paintings and drawings, several thousand Indian items that included weapons, jewelry, and clothing, a dismantled wigwam with thirty pine poles, and an immense iron cage holding two grizzly bears. Catlin had caught the bears as cubs in the Rockies four years earlier. They had now grown to maturity, weighed 900 pounds each, and had become, their master admitted, "troublesome pets."[27] Their presence on the steampacket *Roscius* from New York alarmed fellow passengers and crew. When a sailor tried to tease the animals through the bars, early in the voyage, the she bear put out a paw and swiped off his nose. When an Atlantic gale blew up, the cage was dislodged and shifted about on the deck, and as the ship tossed through mountainous seas, the bears bellowed in distress. Passengers, convinced the savage and soaked bears had escaped and were about to run amok in the saloon, became hysterical, and it was only after the storm calmed and the beasts were found to be still secure that the captain was able to restore order. Once in Liverpool the bears terrified lodging house keepers and railway officials, and local boys threw stones at them.

Catlin had shown his collection in Boston, New York, and Philadelphia, but without the acclaim he hoped for. Most worryingly, he had not managed to persuade the United States government that it should buy his collection, for a requested $60,000, and incorporate it into a national museum. When he left for London, it was a measure of last resort. He said he was crossing the Atlantic to tell the British people about the true character and condition of the North American Indians, and "to awaken a proper sympathy for them."[28] But he was also hoping he could still earn back some of his costs, get subscribers for the definitive book he was planning, and persuade the British to adopt and house the collection Congress had scorned. Catlin had a showman's instincts, and the bears would be an added attraction, justified on the grounds that they represented all the other inhabitants of the Rockies, besides the red men.

George Catlin was to give lectures all over the country, and would take his collection to Manchester, Dublin, and Edinburgh, but it was the warm reception he was given by the highest tier of society, and members of the royal family, that ensured the success of his stay, which was to last for more than four years. He had already been in correspondence with Charles Murray, and when he reached London he drove through the muddy streets of the metropolis, on a dark December day, to visit Murray in his office at Buckingham Palace. The senior courtier, whom he had last seen on the Missouri, was heavily occupied with arrangements for the Queen's wedding in a few weeks' time, but greeted him warmly, and recommended the Egyptian Hall as the place to be. Catlin agreed to pay £550 rent for a first year, with an option on a second and third. In the big assembly room on the upper floor, lit by candelabra, he lined the walls with 300 portraits of Indian men, women, and children, some of them full-length. He hung a further 200 pictures and sketches, some of them very roughly drawn, depicting landscapes, fights, hunts, canoe journeys, horse races, and games. On the central tables he laid out papooses, war clubs, and scalping knives. The Crow wigwam was erected at the far end of the room, and covered with dressed hides, ornamented with porcupine quills and scalp locks. The grizzly bears never reached Piccadilly. Their reputation was by then so bad that the landlord refused to have them in the building. They languished in a yard at Euston Station for a while, howling in the gloomy January fogs, and were then passed on to the Royal Zoological Society, where they pined away, and died of what Catlin identified as "despair" a few months later.

Before the official opening to the public, early in 1840, the Honorable Charles Murray arranged an extended viewing for his friends. Carriages and hansom cabs decanted the quality onto the paving stones outside the gallery, and Catlin, flattered by the interest, noted down the names of his patrons: "Among the most conspicuous . . . were H.R.H. the Duke of Cambridge, the Duke and Duchess of Sutherland, the Duke and Duchess of Buccleuch, Duke of Devonshire, Duke of Wellington . . . Lord Grosvenor, Lord Lennox, Duke of Richmond, Duke of Rutland, Duke of Buckingham, Countess of Ashburnham, Earl of Falmouth, Earl of Dunmore, Lord Monteagle, Lord Ashley, Earl of Burlington . . ."[29] and the list went on, through knights and barons, extending down to churchmen and newspaper editors.

Over a period of three days the cream of London society came in, peering at the portraits of the Indian chiefs, braves, and squaws who had posed in front of Catlin during his journeys up the Missouri to its headwaters. The artist showed them as composed, dignified, rather haughty, in dark colors or lean line drawings, and explained that he had been trying to convey their natural nobility. They included the Mandan chief Mah-to-toh-pa, "Four Bears," with a pair of fined-down buffalo horns soaring up from a headdress of eagle feathers, which continued down to his feet, and the Sioux chief Ha-won-je-tah, "One Horn," his hair tied into a turban filled with glue and red earth. Visitors could stare at the Nez Perce brave Hee-ohks-te-kin, "Rabbit Skin Leggings," and the medicine man Ko-man-i-kin-o-haw, with his wand, looking-glass, and scissors. The Sioux chief and magician Shon-ga-ton-ga-chesh-en-day, translated as "Horse Dung," was there, as was Pshan-shaw, "Sweet Scented Grass," the twelve-year-old daughter of Red Bloody Hand, in a dress of mountain-sheep skin.

The Queen's Head of Household took an almost proprietorial interest, spending hours at the Indian Gallery each day, and act-ing as a guide and interpreter beside Catlin. Murray showed the Duchess of Sutherland how the braided rawhide lasso was used to catch wild horses, and explained the horrific tortures of the Man-dan initiation ceremony, when young men were starved for four days and then suspended from wooden splints pierced through the flesh of their shoulders, to the bishops of London and Norwich. He was in his element, reliving his visit to the Pawnees for the bene-fit of those who had seldom ventured beyond the drawing rooms of Mayfair. Catlin described how his friend "led Duchesses, Count-esses, and Ladies in succession upon his arm, into the wigwam of buffalo-hides, where he descanted, to the great satisfaction and amusement of his friends, upon the curious modes of Indian life into which he had been initiated . . . on the vast plains and prai-ries of the wilds of America."[30]

The Duke of Sussex, a son of George III and a senior member of the royal family, asked if he could hold "an Indian council" with the American artist. The two sat inside the Crow wigwam for an hour and a half, smoking long Indian pipes filled with tobacco from the bark of red willow. The duke, Queen Victoria's favorite uncle, was deeply sympathetic to the Indians, referring to them as "good fellows." When he left Catlin to go back to Kensington Palace, "he took me by both hands and thanked me for the rich treat I had afforded him, and assured me that for the benefits I was rendering to society, and the justice I was doing to the poor Indians, I should be sure to meet my reward in the world to come. . . ."[31] Later, Catlin was invited to breakfast by the elderly duke, who received him in his white flannel morning gown, his head covered with a black velvet cap embroidered with gold. They smoked more Indian tobacco together, and Catlin thought the old man had formed a more correct idea of the Indians than any other person he met in Britain. "Thus passed my first interview with the English aristocracy. I was in the midst and the best of it; and by it, on all sides, was met with the kindliest feelings and condescension, while I received compliments from all . . . for the successful efforts I had thus made to perpetuate the records of an abused and dying race of human beings."[32]

Catlin hoped the young Queen would come to his gallery and bestow the final seal of approval, but Murray told him precedent forbade this. Nevertheless, when he began to raise subscriptions for the large book he planned on *The Manners, Customs and Condition of the North American Indians,* to have a full text and four hundred engravings taken from the original paintings, the list of advance subscribers was headed by Queen Victoria, Prince Albert, the Duchess of Kent, and a lineup of foreign royalty and British nobility. In part this was because the grandees were already convinced, under the influence of James Fenimore Cooper and Washington Irving, that Indians had an innate nobility they could recognize and identify with. They might be cruel but they were nevertheless stylish, dignified, self-controlled masters of the wilderness. Sir William Drummond Stewart would present them in this way in his two novels. Writing about the Crows, Catlin referred to them as natural aristocrats and described the typical brave in the language of the medieval court, as he mounted his snorting steed, "with his bow and quiver slung, his arrow shield upon his arm, and his long lance glistening."[33]

As the weeks went by, the artist gave daily talks in Piccadilly, and was invited to lecture at the Royal Geographical Society, the

Royal Geological Society, and the Royal Institution. He continued to add to what was on offer in the gallery. He dressed mannequin dummies with robes and headdresses collected from the Crows, the Blackhawks, the Blackfeet, and the Mandans. More ambitiously, he recruited a band of twenty Londoners to dress in his Indian clothes, smear on stage makeup, and try to perform Indian dances and songs. In a series of tableaux they played out a marriage ceremony, a visit from the medicine man, a game of Tchungkee played with sticks and rings, and a wrestling match. In the most striking scene, a war party was discovered at night, outside the wigwam, followed by an alarm, a pitched battle, and the smoking of a pipe of peace. Catlin's twenty-three-year-old nephew Burr was part of the troupe, dyeing his skin and shaving off his hair except for a central strip, so that at all other times, when out and about in the streets of London, he was obliged to wear a wig. In the evenings the faux Indians could be hired out to attend balls and dances.

At first Catlin was impressed by the attention, which far exceeded anything he had received in the United States, and by the invitations that were showered on him. But by 1842 it was clear that this was not going to lead to the outcome he was hoping for. His proposal for a "Museum of Mankind," built around his collection, was not to be taken up in London either. Growing disenchanted, he wrote to his father, "I am . . . sick of the insolence of wealth and the wretchedness of poverty which belongs to this great polished nation, with its boasted institutions—its wealth, its refinements, its luxuries."[34] Catlin's nephew Burr was also indignant about the inequalities he saw in London, with the destitute starving in the streets "while the Lords and Gentry are giving their Grand Balls and Soirees and spending thousands nightly."[35]

After three years at the Egyptian Hall, and a six-month tour of the provinces, just as Catlin thought the time had come to return home, his fortunes changed. While his traveling troupe may have been entertaining, they were never convincing. Discriminating Londoners could tell the genuine article they saw it. What they liked in particular was any chance to see the real thing, genuinely different and exotic specimens of *Homo sapiens*, that they could study as they might admire animals in a zoo. The "Hottentot Venus," a woman with unusual bodily proportions from the Namaqua tribe in southern Africa, had been put on display in the much older freak show tradition that took in albinos, dwarves, and giants. Since then, a series of more serious-minded "ethnological expositions" had brought over fellow humans with cultural rather than physical differences, and the Egyptian Hall had shown Mexicans from Mexico as well as the Laplanders.

What people now wanted to see were "real" Indians; but the Secretary of War in Washington had tried to stop the export of Native Americans "for exhibition" as degrading. At the end of 1843 an entrepreneur managed to get round the ban by bringing over nine members of the Ojibbeway tribe, whose territory straddled the American and Canadian border at the western end of the Great Lakes and who could therefore be considered beyond Washington's writ. On arrival, he asked Catlin if he would like to rent the Ojibbeways for £100 a month. Disapproving of this kind of trafficking, Catlin at first refused the terms offered, but it was too good an opportunity to miss. He met the manager and the Indians and came to a partnership agreement under which the six men and three women would join him and become his central attraction.

The nine Ojibbeways allowed Catlin to re-launch his gallery in London, and gave it a new lease of life. With two appearances daily, the Indians would make their way through the expectant audiences in the Egyptian Hall in single file, in full dress, with shields, bows, and quivers, and crouch on a central platform. On a cue from Catlin they sprang up, brandishing clubs and spears, beating a big drum, shaking rattles, and began a noisy war dance. The blood-curdling war whoops could be heard on the other side of

Piccadilly, in the Burlington Arcade. "With the exception of some two or three women (whose nerves were not quite firm enough for these excitements, and who screamed quite as loud as the Indians did, as they were making a rush for the door) the audience stood amazed and delighted with the wildness and newness of the scene that was passing before them," wrote Catlin. The Ojibbeways played a game, throwing and catching a ball between them with hooped rackets, and then broke into a victory scalp dance. Catlin provided the commentary, explaining that "the women, occupying the center, hold up the scalps attached to the tops of little poles, while men, who have come from war, dance around in a circle brandishing their weapons, gnashing their teeth, and yelling the war whoop at the highest key in their voices."[36]

The Indians received thunderous applause after each appearance, proving so popular that Catlin was able to raise the admission price to an extraordinary 2/6d. He was sensitive to any charge that he was exploiting them. At one lecture a questioner accused him of bringing in "poor ignorant people" to make money. Catlin replied that the Ojibbeways were men "with reasoning facilities and shrewdness like our own," who had knowingly entered into a written agreement. "I have undertaken to stand by them as their friend and advocate—not as wild beasts, but as men, laboring in an honest vocation amid a world of strangers . . . for the means of feeding their wives and little children."[37] When not on duty in the Hall, the Indians toured the sights of London. The "wild looking" figures, on the open top of a horse-drawn omnibus, caught the attention of curious crowds as they passed along Holborn and Cheapside. They visited St. Paul's, the new London Bridge, and the city's most recent engineering marvel, Brunel's tunnel under the Thames at Rotherhithe. On Sundays, Catlin arranged for them to be taken into the country for fresh air and a run.

The arrival of the Ojibbeways finally did the trick with Queen Victoria. In December 1843, thanks to backroom work by Charles Murray, Catlin received an invitation to take his protégés out to

Windsor Castle. The two worlds met in the vast Waterloo Chamber, on a December afternoon. The young Queen, a small figure in a plain black dress, was already in the room with Prince Albert, her ladies-in-waiting, and Charles Murray, when Catlin and the Indians were ushered in. The seventy-five-year-old Ah-Quee-weezaintz, the "Boy Chief," was presented to her, followed by the rest of the party, including the second in command, Pattana-quotto-weebe, "Swift Driving Cloud," and the young warrior Gish-e-gase-ghe, "Bright Moonlight Night." The Queen held the hands of the ten-year-old daughter of one of the braves, Nib-nab-be-qua, "Tobacco," and questioned her through an interpreter.

The Ojibbeways then performed their full war dance, cries and shouts echoing through the hall under the eyes of the generals and ministers who had defeated Napoleon, and whose portraits lined the walls in heavy gilt frames. After roast beef and beer, they returned to London, and the Queen sent them £20, and a length of plaid in the royal tartan that could be made into blankets, to thank them.

Several more groups of Indians were brought to England shortly afterwards, though none made the same impression as the Ojibbeways in their glory days at the Egyptian Hall. A party of Iowas appeared for a week at Lord's cricket ground, one of the shrines of upper-class British sport, where the squaws erected wigwams on the hallowed turf and crowds came up to St. John's Wood to see archery and demonstrations of a lacrosselike ball game. Catlin took a second group of Ojibbeways round the country for a while, and went on to Paris and Brussels, but the artist was never a good businessman and was brought low by a series of family misfortunes and growing debts. At one stage he rejected an offer from a titled English collector to buy his entire gallery for $35,000—or £7,000—on the grounds that he did not want it disappearing into "some Duke's castle" where the public would never see it again. Nevertheless, he was forced to sell off the collection in 1852, and the pictures and costumes were put into storage, until the Smithsonian Institution in Washington finally acquired them twenty years later.

By coming to Europe Catlin had succeeded in at least one of his aims, even if he had failed to have the collection taken over and underwritten. With the gallery's long run in Piccadilly, and the help of the Ojibbeways, he gave the British an intensive education in Indian manners and behavior and a better informed interest in their rights and plight. His most important book was published while he was in London. The two-volume *Letters and Notes on the Manners, Customs and Condition of the North American Indians* was crammed with information on every aspect of Indian life, from the way different tribes dealt with their dead, to the comparative merits of log versus birchbark canoes, rain-making methods, and the bedside manners of medicine men. With encyclopedic thoroughness Catlin explained how the Mandans suspended their corpses from high poles where they were left to dry in the air, and how a Comanche doctor would put on the head of a yellow bear, to make a horrifying mask, when calling on the sick. Though the intention was to scare off the evil spirits and effect a cure, the visit drove some patients over the edge.

It was thanks to Cooper, Irving, Murray, and Catlin that the British seemed far more excited by the customs and culture of the Native Americans, and the threat to them, than they ever were by the indigenous inhabitants of most of their own growing empire. The African tribes in the Cape Colony, the Aborigines in Australia, or the Maoris in New Zealand, with whom the British signed a treaty dealing with rights and land in 1841, received none of the same upper-class attention or emotional engagement.

Underscoring Catlin's detailed treatment of the ways and habits of nearly fifty tribes was his own conviction that all he had recorded was about to disappear. The traumatic process of resettlement, after their traditional land was "bought" by Washington, left many of the Indians beleaguered in unfamiliar territory with inferior food sources. White travelers and settlers exposed them to diseases they had no protection from. Already the Mandans, whose villages Catlin had visited beside the Missouri in 1832, had been completely wiped out by smallpox, and their portraits on the walls of the Egyptian Gallery were posthumous memorials. Charles Murray's Pawnees had also been decimated by disease, carried up the Missouri in the steamboats.

To the British the Indians of the United States represented no threat or danger, and the notion of the fierce warrior standing in the way of settlement was replaced by the melancholy, but equally compelling, idea of a vanishing race earlier than in the United States itself. The new sympathy for the red man as victim developed alongside the much more widespread agitation about the condition of black Americans in the southern states, and the mounting condemnation, from British pulpits and abolitionist campaigners, of slavery. Nevertheless, the aristocracy found it much easier to identify with the humanity of the original red men, apparently free spirits who liked hunting, horses, and open space as they did themselves, than they did with the oppressed and abused African-Americans who were toiling in the sugar and cotton fields.

If there was growing disagreement, it was not about the threat to the Indians, or their ethnographic and aesthetic qualities, but about the fundamental character of those who were thought to be vanishing. The Romantic era was ending. Many British visitors to America, influenced by the unsentimental and contemptuous view of most white Americans they were traveling among, found it hard to believe in the "noble savage" any longer. Even Charles Murray, whose book appeared before Catlin reached London, concluded of the Pawnees that "Truth and honesty are unknown, or despised by them. . . . I never met with liars so determined, universal, or audacious."[38] Catlin, who had known many more Indians and many more tribes than Murray, assured his audiences and readers in Great Britain that this kind of prejudice was unjustified. The idea that the Indians were dishonest, or cruel and

murderous, was misconceived, and if there were bad Indians they
were to be found only among those who had been corrupted and
degraded by contact with the white man. In his natural state the
Indian was an honest, honorable, and highly intellectual being,
hospitable and kind, faithful and brave. But if he was able to convince the likes of the Duke of Cambridge that these were "good
fellows," he was fighting against the tide.

Charles Dickens, who had made his first trip to America in
the early 1840s, took a dismissive line. In his weekly *Household
Words*, a few years later, the novelist wrote a vicious and satiri-
cal attack on the conceit of the "noble savage," and especially on
George Catlin's part in promoting it in England.

There was Mr. Catlin, some few years ago, with his Ojibbeway
Indians. Mr. Catlin was an energetic, earnest man, who had
lived among more tribes of Indians than I need reckon up
here, and who had written a picturesque and glowing book
about them. With his party of Indians squatting and spitting
on the table before him, or dancing their miserable jigs in their
own dreary manner, he called, in all good faith, upon his civilized audience to take notice of their symmetry and grace,
their perfect limbs, and the exquisite expressions of their pantomime, and his civilized audience, in all good faith, complied
and admired. Whereas, as animals, they were wretched creatures, very low in the scale and very poorly formed. . . .[39]

Though few were as harsh as Dickens, the era in which Catlin's view was the generally accepted one was over. Victorian Britons were still fascinated by the wilderness, and they still wanted
to come to the prairies, but they began to see the Indians through
different eyes, aware of the realpolitik that was to dictate their
fate.

4

Buffalo Dreams

*Buffalo-hunting is a noble sport, the animal being swift
enough to give a good horse enough to do to close with him;
wheeling round with such quickness as to baffle both horse
and rider for several turns before there is any certainty of
bringing him down.*

—JOHN PALLISER,
Solitary Rambles and Adventures . . . , 1853[1]

In Perthshire, Sir William Drummond Stewart was ordering up
still more paintings from Alfred Jacob Miller, to help keep his
memories of seven years spent in the Far West alive. The painter
crossed the Atlantic at his patron's expense, to produce further
pictures in the castle where they would be hung, in the same year
that Catlin was setting up his Indian Gallery in London. The
American had seen nothing to compare with the establishment he
found at Murthly, with a plethora of servants, footmen in livery,
and Monsieur Marque, Sir William's French chef, preparing elegant meals. Neighbors and guests admired Miller's paintings and
the leatherbound portfolio of prairie sketches that Stewart put out
on display. "At his table I met some of the most distinguished of
the nobility. The Staffords, Pagets, Athols, Breadalbanes etc some
of them giving me pressing invitations to visit them."[2] Asked to

paint Lady Breadalbane, he went over to Taymouth Castle to complete the portrait. He wrote to a friend in Baltimore, "I shall not
say anything about the manner in which I travel here or you will
begin to think that my republicanism is fast oozing away."[3]

Miller found one other American at Murthly, and a familiar
face. Antoine Clement, the exceptional shot and skilled if sometimes moody hunter who had served Sir William for so many years
on the prairies, had returned with him. "He has been metamor-
phosed into a Scottish valet, and waits on the table in a full suit
of black."[4] For special occasions Antoine, half French-Canadian,
half Cree Indian, was kitted out in Highland dress, with a kilt in
the Stewart tartan.

Miller enjoyed the setting of the house, the wooded hills that
rose up on each side of the valley, the large west-facing garden
with its parterres and fountain, the old yew trees by the chapel,
and the parkland, where a long drive of closely scythed grass ran
high above the swiftly flowing Tay. "I have a delicious little painting room which looks out upon the garden, and when I raise the
window in the morning the birds pour in a perfect flood of song."[5]
He spent more than a year in Scotland, working up another ten
oil paintings from his field sketches and watercolors. The new
canvases included *The Trapper's Bride*, showing a mountain man
and an Indian girl at the fur trade rendezvous on the Green, and
Attack of the Crows, a historical reconstruction of the 1833 shake-
down Stewart had described to the artist, with his patron surrounded by threatening Indians. Sir William took a close interest,
visiting "every day after luncheon to examine and perhaps to offer
a criticism [on] any point wherein he thinks I may be wrong, and
woe to the Indian who has not sufficient dignity in expression and
carriage, for *out* he must come."[6]

While Stewart's respect for the Indians was as great as ever,
Miller's hunting scenes gave him as much pleasure. The first
batch of paintings, shipped after the brief New York exhibition,
included *Hunting the Grizzly Bear*, *Fishing on the Grand River*,

and *Hunting the Argali*, and reminders of the buffalo were everywhere. A set of large pictures, *Approaching a Herd of Buffalo*,
Hunting of the Buffalo, through to *Butchering a Wounded Buffalo*, looked down onto the stone floors, over which softly tanned
buffalo skins were strewn. A set of heavy "buffalo chairs," commissioned by Sir William from an Edinburgh furniture maker,
stood in the entrance hall. The sitter leaned back against the
head and horns of a wild, snorting, buffalo with protruding glass
eyes, carved from mahogany, with the beast's foreshortened legs
doubling as the legs for the chair. Maintaining a habit he had
developed in the Far West, Stewart still slept on buffalo robes at
night, and his dreams were probably of buffalo as well, for he was
planning his return.

OF ALL THE animals that the British aristocracy were hearing about in the Far West, the bear, the deer and antelope, the
argali or mountain sheep, it was the thought of the American
buffalo, or bison, that excited them most. Though only a small
number of people had managed to make the journey out west
so far, many more savored the fantasy. Wherever sporting men
were gathered together, in shooting lodges and clubs, manly conversation invariably came round to the great sport buffalo were
said to offer, based on the word-of-mouth accounts of men like
Stewart and Murray. Buffalo were reputed to offer the supreme
hunting experience—exciting, fast, dangerous. Though there
were bison in Europe and Asia, they were smaller, with a different physique, and there were fewer of them. The American
bison was larger and heavier in the body, with huge shoulders
and forequarters, and light hindquarters. It was the size of the
animal, and its powerful, hunched attitude, that was so impressive. "The full-grown bull is immensely shaggy, especially about
the head, which is covered in a vast quantity of fur, wool and

long hair hanging down over his eyes and almost concealing his horns," reported a British hunter a little later; ". . . a long glossy black beard hanging from his chin like a deep fringe sweeps the ground; which with his savage-looking muzzle and prominent black eye flashing between the tangled locks of his hair, give him altogether a most ferocious appearance." [7]

Native Americans depended on the buffalo for the necessities of life, not only for meat, but clothing, bedding, skins to build tepees, sinews for bow strings and thread, bone for needles and tools. They carried water in buffalo bladders, and burned the dung as fuel. "I cannot convey any just impression of the total dependence of the remote western tribes on buffalo," wrote Charles Murray after his stay with the Pawnees, warning that ". . . where the buffalo is exterminated, the Indian of the prairies must perish."[8] To white Americans in the fur trade caravans, or travelers on the Santa Fe and Oregon trails in the early days, they were an essential source of food during the long overland journey. To the professional hunters who cut them down for the skins alone, they were a commodity, and a robe could be sold to the fur companies for around $4. But to a small class of determined British visitors, the herds of buffalo, with their size and bulk, and the thundering speed at which they could move, offered entertainment. The prospect of chasing and bringing them down epitomized the appeal of the prairies, along with the wilderness landscape itself.

By the 1840s the fur trade had collapsed, as the waterproof but heavier beaver-felt hat passed out of style in favor of the sleeker top hat made from silk. The last rendezvous of trappers and voyageurs was held in 1840. But though the fur caravans had ceased, the trails across the prairies were more traveled and better marked, with wagon trains going down to Santa Fe, soldiers proceeding to new military posts, missionaries, and a growing number of families setting out for California or Oregon. Each spring, emigrants assembled in camps beside the Missouri landings around Westport and Independence, where they equipped themselves, bought mules and horses, and waited for the grass to grow a little longer, to give fodder for the animals along the route. As the wagons began to move west, poor emigrants eking out their supplies for the long journey were sometimes overtaken by parties of British gentlemen of leisure, far better supplied, out for a prairie jaunt. Some launched assaults on American wildlife that were lethally effective, while others proved less of a threat. One aristocrat met some of his father's tenants, from the Wentworth estate in Yorkshire, on the Oregon Trail. They were surprised to see him.

AT THE AGE of forty-seven, in 1843, Sir William returned for one more leisure expedition, to revisit the high country, and hunt and fish in the Wind River Mountains. The laird was far wealthier now, having sold the Logiealmond estate, inherited from his mother, for £200,000. In a series of letters from Scotland to make the arrangements, he asked William Sublette, his old fur trade comrade, to purchase horses, mules, and wagons in advance. When he reached St. Louis, bringing Antoine as his hunter, his valet Corbie, and a young servant called Tom, he found the place more than doubled in size. There were more steamboats in the river, and the levee, with its noisy throng and stacks of cargo, had been paved with limestone blocks. The city had a new hotel, the Planter's House, built to the same design as the de luxe Astor House in New York.

Stewart's expedition was to be an extended and stately swan song, in agreeable company, comfortably equipped. For his own baggage and ammunition he took five wagons, as against the two he had fielded in 1836, with a crimson tent for himself, and two rubber boats for river crossings, to a design used by Colonel John Frémont's expedition the previous summer. His party of thirty included old friends from St. Louis, with William Sublette, and

Jefferson Clark, son of General Clark, as well as young bloods he had met in New Orleans who had never seen the prairies before. Several adventurers, and a botanist, came from England. A further sixty men were hired to drive the wagons and handle the stock, put up tents, and cook.

With Alfred Jacob Miller now back in Baltimore and busy with other commissions, Sir William looked for an artist who could record this trip in Miller's footsteps. He thought he had a substitute when he met John James Audubon, the naturalist and illustrator of *Birds of America*, and tried to persuade him to come along. Despite a generous financial offer, the earnest Audubon turned Sir William down, worried about the "sporting" character and unwieldy size of the expedition. So while Audubon continued up the Missouri, seeking specimens to draw for the follow-up book of "American Quadrupeds" he was working on, Stewart's party set out in grand style, to shoot as many quadrupeds, and feathered bipeds, as they could find. They were without an artist, but Matthew Field, a journalist from New Orleans, was in the party and sent dispatches which reached his paper, the *Daily Picayune*, months later.

In 1843, the shift westward that would come to be called the Great Migration was just beginning. That spring, nine hundred emigrants set out for Oregon from the Missouri, in four or five separate caravans, with two hundred heavy wagons, driving their cattle along beside them. The number going west would increase dramatically each year, with over five thousand in 1848, before the great rush of 1849. As Sir William's better-horsed, better-outfitted, and more carefree party moved along the Platte, overtaking what they called "the Oregon people," they scanned the prairie for the telltale black smudges that indicated groups of buffalo grazing in the far distance, but found none at all until they were nearly at Fort Laramie, after 650 miles and twenty-seven days of traveling. At night Sir William provided wine and punch, and they kept up spirits with concerts around the fires, singing ballads and popular songs. When they played excerpts from Shakespeare's *Romeo and Juliet*, they used the back of a wagon for the balcony scene, and a tin lamp for the moon. One man had brought along his flute. On a clear night they sang a chorus from Bellini's *La Sonnambula*, which had already been staged in St. Louis.

> *Here we'll rest in these green shady bowers,*
> *Where the streamlet is bordered with flowers,*
> *Yes, we'll rest for our footsteps are weary,*
> *And the road to the castle is dreary . . .*

"When our vocal entertainments were over . . . ," wrote Matthew Field, "we dropped off to sleep in our buffalo robes, and the still- ness of the wilderness was only broken at intervals by the guards calling and answering to each other 'All's well!' "[9]

After they had crossed the South Pass they went up into the belt of forest that clothed the lower spurs of the Wind River Moun- tains, with their spruce and pine, and small glades under the high canopy of Douglas firs, *Pseudotsuga menziesii,* with their immense girth. They spent ten days by the small lakes Sir Wil- liam had grown so fond of. Field wrote in his diary: "Found a most lovely encampment on the lake—everybody in ecstasies with the scene—I thanked God for the blessing of sight! Trout a foot long darting about in the glassy water—20 lines were in the water in as many minutes and as many fish were floundering in the grass immediately after." The next morning they were up at daybreak. "Grand sunrise over the snow peaks, grizzly bear tracks—now and then a duck flying over the still lake."[10] Sir William kept as tight a grip as ever. Annoyed by one of his decisions, Field referred to his commander, testily, as "*His Omnipotence.*"[11]

On their way back, they detoured to revisit the flat grass pastures by the Green River, near Horse Creek, the site of Cap- tain Stewart's 1833 rendezvous, where he had first seen the fur company camps, the lines of Indian lodges, and wild scenes of drinking and gambling. The meadows and groves of willow were eerily silent, with a few goats grazing. For old times' sake Sir William organized horse races between members of his party, taking part on his spotted bay Chieftain, but not winning.

They did not encounter buffalo in numbers large enough to live up to Sir William's memories until the return journey was under way. There were more and more of them from the time that they left the Sweetwater and turned back onto the North Platte, and in late September Field was part of a hunting frenzy: "Saw 50,000 buffalo through the day, and hunted them from morning till night. . . ."[12] Once they had struck the herds, there was no letup. On the following day, "Hunting still continued with great spirit—chasing large bands into the river and out of it, over hills and hollows . . . 3 bulls plunged headlong over a precipice of 15 feet, and ran on unhurt from the fall! A large band was cornered into Ash Hollow, where rare sport and a regular bull baiting took place."[13]

Another member of the party, William Kennerly, recalled that the buffalo "gladdened the heart of Sir William, who had come four thousand miles to shoot them." Even the horses "fell readily into the excitement of the chase and seemed to enjoy dashing along beside the shaggy monsters until we could reach over and put the muzzles of our guns almost to the buffalo's shoulders. When one was out of the running, the race was kept up and another singled out, and so on until the prairie was strewn for miles back with the bodies of the dead bison."[14]

On another day by the Platte the hairy multitude was so immense that hunting was impossible, and they feared for their lives. Kennerly wrote that "we descried coming toward us a herd, which I can state without any exaggeration must have numbered a million. The pounding of the hooves on the hard prairie sounded like the roaring of a mighty ocean, surging over the land and sweeping everything before it. Here was more game than we had bargained for, and the predicament in which we now found ourselves gave us much cause for alarm. On they came and we were directly in their path and on the bank of the river there was the great danger of our being swept over."[15] The herd took two days to pass, and for all that time Stewart had to post a line of men, shouting and gesticulating, with bonfires at night, to fend them off.

It added to the joy and mystique of buffalo hunting that the meat was so excellent to eat. While the flesh of the bull could be stringy and rank, the cow was tasty, gamey, tender and fiberless, and easy to digest. Lieutenant William Fairholme described it as "the most delicious we had ever eaten, very fat and tender."[16] Captain Ruxton, an intrepid solo traveler, called it "the most delicious of flesh."[17] John Palliser, hunter and explorer, found the fat peculiarly tasty, more like that of turtle than beef. Charles Murray rhapsodized over "buffalo gumbo" and Sir William Stewart described a blissful "buffalo haggis." The ribs and the hump were the most prized parts, along with the liver, heart, tenderloin, and the fat covered "fleece" that ran on both sides of the spine above the ribs. Dismembering and carving up the huge beast was almost as great a challenge as shooting it. Once brought back to camp, with long bloody strips of flesh draped over the back of a horse or mule, the meat could be boiled, sautéed in a pan, or cooked over the fire using a wooden stick as a spit. The guts, or *boudins*, were roasted over the flames, or stuffed with diced liver and other innards to form a sausage. The marrow bones, a favorite prairie delicacy, were thrust into the embers, and the marrow could be used as butter on biscuits or bread. The Honorable Grantley Berkeley found that "when hot . . . and, put on thin toast, it was perfection!"[18]

Buffalo meat was the main feature when Sir William presided over a special celebration on the Fourth of July to mark Independence Day. Two tents were put together to form a high canopy, and his guests sat cross-legged, with the feast laid out on the ground. "The viands displayed upon the oil cloth were buffalo hump ribs, buffalo side ribs, buffalo tongues, buffalo marrow bones, buffalo

'sweetbreads,' and buffalo *et ceteras*."[19] One of the British friends
that Stewart had invited, Major Long of Purley Park in Berkshire, made two plum puddings. Field did not like him, complaining that he "talked to us constantly of his large estate, hereditary
property and high connections."[20]

No one on Stewart's expedition ever claimed that they were
just hunting for the pot. Hundreds more buffalo were killed than
were needed by the cooks, and even when the beasts were butchered, they removed only the hump ribs and the best cuts, leaving
the rest for the wolves. A St. Louis man, not used to this British-
led profligacy, acknowledged the toll: "I must admit that a great
many more buffalo were destroyed than was necessary." But he
excused himself on grounds of general excitement and raised pas-
sions. "What man would resist the temptation when the whole
earth, it seemed, was a surging, tumbling, waving mass of these
animals?"[21] Matthew Field felt some remorse about the slaughter,
if only briefly. He recalled an evening when he stretched out on
the soft grass, looked up at the sky, and thought he saw a message from the creator. "The sun was still plunging lower in the
West, and the vapors we looked upon suddenly became enormous
masses of gore. A tumbling ocean of buffalo blood occupied the
evening sky, and with almost a serious sensation of repentance we
thought of the many murders we had committed among the poor
brutes of the prairie . . . the rolling masses in the vast expanse
grew still more fiery red, until they seemed to be tongues of flame
hissing down vengeance upon us from the sky."[22]

From the start, Stewart's return to the plains attracted public
attention and interest. St. Louis newspapers called the tour "a
party of pleasure." Field referred to it, in one of his despatches, as
"this extensive hunting frolic."[23] Field's newfound enthusiasm for
shooting for sport's sake, as against shooting for a useful purpose,
was mocked by another paper, which published a series of spoof
reports, as if from Stewart's prairie camps, recording improbable
shooting feats and heroically silly discomforts endured. "The other

night we sat out all night in the rain, as our baggage had taken
the wrong fork. . . . It would have done you good to see us enjoying
ourselves out here, sitting Indian fashion, in a ring, and soaked
through, and smoking all over like rotten straw upon a cold morning." The satire picked up on Sir William's sometimes tyrannical
style. "Sir William Stewart has put us all under 'martial law' and
some of the 'young 'uns' make wry faces at it." [24]

ANY SHOOTING EXPEDITION still required a major outlay of time,
money, and pluck. But as the trail along the Platte as far as Fort
Laramie improved, beaten down into something that almost
resembled a wide road by the creaking wheels of so many heavy
wagons, it became easier to travel with a smaller outfit than
that of Sir William Drummond Stewart. Two brothers, John and
William Chearnley, dedicated shots whose father owned 19,000
acres in County Waterford, Ireland, made a successful crossing to
Oregon in 1846 with only a small entourage. When the brothers
passed through the city on their way home, New York newspapers marveled at their baggage, which included so many antlers,
heads, skins, and other pieces of animal for onward shipment to
Liverpool.

In 1852 the twenty-five-year-old Honorable Charles Wentworth-
Fitzwilliam, fourth son of Earl Fitzwilliam, wrote to tell his father
about the preparations he had made in St. Louis, where he had
arranged traveling companions and bought "coffee, sugar, biscuits
and gunpowder."[25] Traveling with his valet and another servant,
he addressed his letters home to the earl at Wentworth Woodhouse, the vast Palladian family pile south of Sheffield, where the
east front was said to be the longest facade of any private house
in Europe, and twice the width of Buckingham Palace. Providing
Charles with the funds he needed to support his two-year adventure presented no problem, because Fitzwilliam's 20,000-acre

Yorkshire estate passed over some of the richest coal seams in the country. The income from farming tenants that had made previous earls so rich was now enhanced by the profits from his many collieries, in grimy new pit villages. From Wentworth, Charles's occasional letters were posted on to be read by his older brother, Lord Milton, and the rest of his family dispersed around the other Fitzwilliam properties, at Milton House in Northamptonshire, Coollatin in County Wicklow, or Grosvenor Square in London.

Once in Indian country, Charles Fitzwilliam managed to get another letter back from Fort Atkinson, describing the characteristics of the various tribes close by, and his losses from horse thieves, though he seemed to share Catlin's faith in the Indians. "The Arapaho chief, Yellow Bear, is one of the finest men I ever saw, and a perfect natural gentleman."[26] Though his letters were thin on detail, they confirmed that he was finding all he had hoped for on the prairies: "I can say that we are in good health, and as for myself I never remember to have felt better." Like so many others, he was delighted by the Rocky Mountain valleys around Pikes Peak. "This has always been considered by trappers and hunters as a paradise and certainly it is, for game would certainly be fools if they neglected this district. The bear can fill himself to his heart's content with currants, gooseberries, cherries of two descriptions and plums, and the herbivore may grow fat on grass that would enchant a Leicestershire farmer. What seemed to me a wild barley and oats grow luxuriantly, and the summer climate is I think as delicious as any I have ever felt."[27]

Apart from the occasional letter, which could take many months to get back even as far as St. Louis, few aristocrats felt any inclination to keep a careful account of what they were doing, preferring the outdoor life of action to onerous "penmanship," or too much reflection. Apart from Charles Murray in 1835, only one young blue blood, the Honorable Henry Coke, kept a complete record of his journey, and if Murray's charm, confidence, and intelligence had carried him safely across the prairies, Coke's ineptitude led to near disaster. A younger son of the 1st Earl of Leicester, he had been brought up at Holkham Hall, the largest estate in Norfolk, where his father was a pioneer of agricultural improvements. Coke and an Eton schoolfriend, the young Lord Durham, decided to cross the prairies to the Rockies, conceiving of the journey in the spirit of a picnic outing that would while away some time and combine a little adventure with plenty of scope for buffalo hunting. Coke was twenty-three.

Once in America, they met another schoolfriend, the eldest son of Lord Calthorpe, who had been in Texas and wanted to join them. Lord Durham became ill, and stayed with friends in New York, which proved a blessing from his point of view. In St. Louis it irked Coke that the growing numbers passing through on the way to the California gold fields had driven up the price of the standard rations, bacon and salt, flour and coffee. He and Calthorpe had to pay extortionate prices for the eight horses, nine mules, and two heavy wagons they purchased, and all their supplies.

The young noblemen reached the setting-off point three weeks later than planned, at the end of May, by which time most of the parties heading for California and Oregon had gone in front of them, their cattle grazing down a swath of grass many miles either side of the trail. The Englishmen complained that the emigrants, slowly making their way across their own country, were bothersome in a number of ways. Fodder and firewood were hard to find, and they found themselves *"pestered"*[28] by poor emigrants who begged supplies of flour or coffee from their own store. Despite these irritations, Coke's first sight of the true prairies was as uplifting as he had hoped. He wrote in his diary: "Grease the wheels and start again at two. Come immediately into the Prairies. What a sight it is! All the descriptions in the world fail to give one the slightest conception of its real magnificence. One might as well attempt to describe the sea to a person who had never seen it, as to paint in language the calm grandeur, and boundless extent, of the rolling prairie. . . ."[29]

Coke, like so many others still to come, acknowledged his debt to James Fenimore Cooper. "I had an hereditary love of sport, and had read and heard wonderful tales of bison and grisly bears. . . . No books had so fascinated me, when a boy, as 'The Deerslayer,' 'The Pathfinder' and the beloved 'Last of the Mohicans.' "[30] But the pair of Honorables posed little threat to the buffalo herds. When they saw the first bulls in the distance, through their spyglasses, the little party grew excited and "Masters and men all wanted to leave the mules and go after them."[31] Leaving the men, the two young masters galloped over a mile toward the animals, only to find that when they came up to them their horses were already blown and too tired for a run alongside. Between them, Coke and Calthorpe managed to get off seven shots at one particular animal, claiming hits in the side, neck, shoulder, and leg, but then ran out of ammunition as the beast staggered off defiantly.

Next day, Coke found another small herd. He knew he had to select an animal, and get close enough to shoot into the shoulder. "Separating one from the herd by firing my pistol into the midst of it, I devoted all my efforts to overtake him; once or twice he turned his unwieldy body and glared furiously with his small black eyes. At last I headed him and he stopped short. . . ." The buffalo did not appear to know the rules. "Instead of showing tail, he put his head down, and foaming with rage, came at me full tilt. My horse never stirred; I had no time for anything but to take aim, and having fired between the neck and the shoulders, I was next minute sprawling on my back, with the mare rolling over four or five yards beyond me."[32] The buffalo escaped, and Coke took several hours to recapture his horse.

Prairie tumbles apart, the excursion proved a disaster in almost every way. Heavy rainstorms turned the trail into impassable mud. Their wagons were overloaded with supplies of all kinds, including tarpaulins, 100 pounds of lead for shot, hams, cases of ginger beer, chocolate, and a stock of white kid gloves. Wheels splintered, axles broke, and wagons overturned and had to be

righted and repaired. The mules shed their packs and bolted. The
men were bombarded by mosquitos, and weakened by dysentery.
"I am convinced there is no severer trial of a man's temper than
such a journey . . . ," wrote Coke, who had looked forward to it
for so long. "In reality, every circumstance connected with it is
provoking and disagreeable, and it requires a constant and vigorous effort of the mind to delude oneself into the idea that one
is performing a romantic and heroic act."[33] After 400 miles they
abandoned the wagons altogether, threw out the superfluous supplies, and continued with horses and mules alone. They quarreled
irrevocably with the hired help, and finally with each other, split-
ting up after they reached Fort Laramie.

As they continued separately, Henry Coke, who was a member of the Garrick Club in London, nearly drowned in the Snake
River and was revived by a tribe of Panack Indians when he wandered into their camp half naked. He finally reached the Pacific at
the mouth of the Columbia after a 2,200-mile ordeal he wished he
had never embarked on. At one of the many crisis points he wrote
in his journal: "It really is very distressing, and I do wish that
people who write books, and inveigle one into this sort of tour,
would speak the truth, and tell of the common-place disagree-
ables as well as the amusements and hair-breadth escapes."[34] To
set the record straight, and describe all the rigors, Coke wrote
his own book, which appeared in 1852. One reviewer, after listing the misfortunes with some glee, thought it an encouraging
sign that young men of family and fortune were willing to aban-
don "the luxurious ease of home" for such breakneck expeditions.
"Whatever the faults of the nobles of Great Britain, effeminacy is
certainly not of the number. May the day be far distant when this
is otherwise, and when we cease to possess, in a bold and manly
aristocracy, one important guarantee of our national greatness."[35]

However manly the aristocrat, many of them still liked to
travel with personal servants to ease the daily bother of dressing, washing, and looking after baggage. The gradations of class

that governed these relationships were not always appreciated by
frontier Americans, and in Missouri, a slave state, this was further complicated by the question of race. "It is well known that in
America, especially in the west of it, a white servant is a being not
understood," wrote the Honorable Charles Murray. He ran into
this confusion when taking his Scottish valet on riverboats, where
it was assumed the person accompanying him must be a gentleman, traveling on an equal basis; "accordingly, before bringing
him on board, I explained to the Captain that, though a white
man, he was my domestic."[36] Difficulties followed, over whether
his employee could travel at the half fare Negro domestics would
be carried at, and where on the boat his man should eat, since it
would not be proper for Murray to dine with his own servant. His
valet ate with the white crew.

Affluent British visitors could also take direct advantage of
slave labor, for their trips into Indian Territory, however much
they might condemn the system of slavery when at home. Colonel
William Greenwood and a group of six fellow army officers took
a leave of absence to spend three months on a buffalo-hunting
adventure along the Arkansas River in 1840. They hired French-
Canadians, at $20 a month each, to provide for most of their
needs, but they rented a slave cook, Henry Johnson, from one of
the sons of William Clark in St. Louis, and took slaves to drive
the heavy wagons. When one of the drivers stole some sugar, his
slave status made him vulnerable. Lieutenant Fairholme wrote in
his journal that "the Negro was threatened with a severe flogging
if he transgressed again, which however was only a threat which
we of course never intended carrying into execution, although as
we had a perfect right to do so, having hired him from his master,
it answered as a check upon his propensities."[37]

For personal servants, most of the aristocratic visitors believed
the only way to maintain the standards they expected was to
bring their man, or men, with them. The downside was that their
own staff, used to the total security and below-stairs hierarchy of

the British country house, did not find it easy to adjust to open-air life on the prairies. Charles Murray's valet, John, had come from the family seat in Scotland. Though it is not clear if he had volunteered for western service or been press-ganged, his master grumbled about him constantly. "14th: . . . Endeavoured to start at daybreak; but my Scotch servant could not learn to balance or fasten a pack on a horse; and his slow awkwardness cost us repeated and vexatious delays."[38] Used to the backstairs corridors and pantries of Dunmore House, John was accident-prone. He was kicked by the mules, and had narrow escapes with rattlesnakes. After a night sleeping out on the plains, it took him too long to catch his hobbled horse in the morning. "It must be owned that two hours horse-hunting before breakfast is not good preparation for a day's march, but the man was extremely slow and sulky; had he been willing and active, I believe the horses might have been collected in half an hour."[39] Murray was forced to admit that he had made the wrong choice. "This man was a willing and well-conducted servant in civilized life, but Nature had not formed him for a prairie hunter."[40]

The Honorable Henry Coke did not bring a valet, but had constant trouble with locally hired staff on his ill-fated expedition. He complained that his American drivers and packers were over-familiar, surly, and helped themselves to supplies and liquor as they chose: "Nearly all our men have turned out to be totally use-less." After a series of disputes and near mutinies, Coke admitted that "Our manners as Englishmen are perhaps more authorita-tive and imperious than our Yankee servants have been used to, and I have more than once heard complaints that might have been interpreted as threats."[41]

In May 1854, another Englishman called on Colonel Alfred Cum-ming, the Superintendent of Indian Affairs based in St. Louis. The visitor was forty-three, bald-headed, with striking side whiskers, of medium height and described as "resolute looking."[42] Cumming must have grown accustomed to the type by then, because anyone wanting to leave the United States and cross into Indian Territory, whether it was to take goods down to Santa Fe and Mexico, embark on missionary work, or simply to hunt, had first to get a permit, and a succession of Britons had passed through the office on Fourth Street. The regulations were designed to stop the trading of arms and liquor, and Cumming issued a document saying that the bearer was traveling for "recreation or amusement," which could be shown to Indian agents or military posts that might be encountered. This particular passport would prove politically controversial, and Cumming was clearly unaware of the sheer scale of the assault the aristocrat had in mind.

Sir St. George Gore, unencumbered by any family or professional ties, owned 7,000 acres in Ireland. Following the classic model for an absentee landlord, he left the management of the estates in Galway, Donegal, and Offaly to his land agent, Charles Cage, who sent the rents to him in England. After leaving Oxford, he led the life of a wealthy sporting bachelor, basing himself in a series of rented country houses in Berkshire, Nottinghamshire, and Derbyshire. He spent his unearned income on horse racing, foxhunting, fishing, and shooting, and was particularly proud of his deerhounds and greyhounds. He was a leading breeder and trainer of dogs for hare coursing, most cathartic of English blood sports, in which two hounds raced to devour a fleeing and terrified hare, released as live bait from a sack some way down the course. Gore's champion greyhounds—including Shade and Dream, Lincoln and Pilgrim—raced after the hares at meetings all over the country, and his dogs won the Waterloo Cup, the preeminent coursing event, held on Lord Sefton's land near Liverpool, for two years running.

When not with his dogs, Gore worked his way steadily through the sporting year. In the winter he was on the Moray or Beauly

Firth, gliding over estuary waters in a punt, blasting ducks and wildfowl with a seven-foot-long gun of exceptionally large bore. In August, he joined the line of smart, well-turned-out private carriages, rolling through Perth on their way up into the Highlands, for the grouse shooting and deer stalking. The Scottish season was both a social ritual and a contest in culling, in which the titled and the wealthy vied with each other not just over the number of birds brought down or deer shot, but the weight of the stags and the span, length, and spur system of their antlers. Gore was a loner, and not particularly sociable, but he was one of the most competitive participants. Renting a succession of lodges—Flowerdale House, behind Gairloch; Inverbroom, near Ullapool; or Tulloch Castle—his addiction was supported by an extensive cast of gillies and gamekeepers, beaters and cart drivers. His shooting and fishing records were written up regularly in the "Moors and Forests" and "Sporting Intelligence" columns of the newspapers. In 1841, on the river Ewe, in Ross-shire, Gore caught 153 salmon in three weeks. The following year, in Inverness-shire, he was credited with eleven stags in a week, four of them on one day. He excelled himself in 1847: "In the forests near Strathvaich, Sir St. George Gore, Bart. has had three days of great success, as during that time 12 deer were stalked and shot, six of them in one day and at one stalking."[43]

The confident and conspicuous spending of men like Gore, based on the income that came from thousands of Irish peasant farmers, was threatened in 1847 and 1848 by the Great Famine. With his tenants starving after crop failures and unable to pay their rents, Gore's ever efficient agent began to evict the defaulters, clear their land, and hand out small sums to get the dispossessed out of the way and onto emigrant ships to America. With all the agitation, secret societies formed in the countryside, and arson and revenge attacks increased. Shooting was no longer restricted to the upper classes. At one of the busiest times in the English hare-coursing season, in November 1849, Gore had to leave his hounds and kennels and make a rare visit to Ireland, after two men hid behind a hedge near Ferbane, and shot and killed his agent. Charles Gage was on his way to church, and had ignored threats that if he carried on making evictions on behalf of his master, he would be assassinated.

Gore's response was not to spend more time repairing his estate affairs in Ireland, but to get further away from them. After a run of over fifteen seasons in the Scottish Highlands, he wanted a field with more scope, where he could shoot more animals, and find new targets, without distraction. He had met Sir William Drummond Stewart in Perthshire after his second trip, and heard his stories of the buffalo, the bears, and the mountain men at firsthand. He would almost certainly have read Francis Parkman's *The Oregon Trail*, the newest and most widely read account of a prairie adventure taken in the mid-1840s, when the tide of immigration over the plains was picking up speed. Parkman, a young Harvard graduate who devoted himself to the history of the frontier, and its national implications, spent three months on the plains and along the Rockies, traveling, and living with the Dakota Indians. For his upper-class British readers it was his description of buffalo hunting that was, inevitably, the most appealing. One passage seemed to catch the quintessence of the whole business, and the level of adrenaline-filled, primal excitement it could produce: "I could see nothing but a cloud of dust before me, but I knew that it concealed a band of many hundreds of buffalo. In a moment I was in the midst of the cloud, half suffocated by the dust and stunned by the trampling of the flying herd; but I was drunk with the chase and cared for nothing but the buffalo."[44]

Gore planned a foray that would be more ambitious than anything that had gone before, that would outshine and outgun Sir William Stewart's more leisurely swan song. Along with his steward, who handled all the luggage and equipment, he brought his valet and personal servants, his gunsmith, and Alexander

Mackenzie, the Inverness man who tied the flies and lures Gore believed essential for his fishing. His dog handler, and fifty of his finest hounds from the kennels at Beesthorpe Hall, made up the traveling party, the hounds barking and yapping their way across half a continent until they reached the Mississippi. Basing himself in the Planter's House, he cashed several large drafts drawn on Barings Bank in London, and he and his steward began to buy transport and provisions.

A writer for an Ohio paper saw the party just as they were preparing to set off west from the Missouri at Fort Leavenworth, coming upon a large encampment, with tents and wagons drawn up in an orderly fashion. "It turned out to be a grand hunting company for the plains. Sir George Gore, an English baronet, has taken it into his head that it will be fine sport to hunt buffalo, etc, on our great western prairies."[4b] The correspondent was impressed by the scale of Gore's outfit, with more than 40 men, 112 horses, 18 oxen, 40 mules, and three cows to provide milk for the baronial breakfast. His vehicles included six heavy wagons and twenty-one two-wheeled carts. Sir George, who dropped the "St." once in the United States, had a tent with striped green and white lining for himself, with a brass bed and a steel bathtub. One wagon carried his armory of seventy-five guns, including rifles of various bores, single- and double-barreled shotguns, revolvers and pistols. Another, pulled by a team of oxen, was loaded down with 3 tons of ammunition in the form of lead stock, shot of different calibers, percussion caps, and boxes of black powder. A smaller cart carried fishing rods, lines, nets and hooks, and Mackenzie's flies and materials.

The quality of Gore's thoroughbred hounds impressed the American journalist as much as anything else. He described them as "the most magnificent pack of dogs that were ever seen in this country. Between forty and fifty dogs, mostly greyhounds and staghounds, of the most beautiful breeds, compose this part of the expedition." The correspondent thought Gore looked a strong, forthright character, but feared he might not know what he was in for; "there are other things beside fun in such a trip, and it will try the manner of stuff of which he is made before he returns."[46] To act as his captain, Gore hired Henry Chatillon, the fur company guide who had accompanied Francis Parkman along the Oregon Trail, but Chatillon took a sharp disliking to the baronet, and left him when they reached Fort Laramie.

In the late summer and fall of 1854 Gore hunted and fished in what is now Colorado, and then came back to establish a winter camp near Fort Laramie. The following spring, he began to get into his stride. Now guided by Jim Bridger, Sir William Drummond Stewart's friend and recipient of the Life Guard cuirass, they headed up into the Powder River country in what is now Wyoming and southern Montana, and into the Big Horn range. Gore stayed on for another two years, wheeling about the high reaches of the Rockies on a horse called Steel Trap, fishing in mountain lakes and fast-running rivers, and shooting with the same intensity he had brought to the Scottish glens. For Gore, there was no time-wasting with play readings, campfire story-telling, or impromptu horse races. He was a loner, single-minded in his pursuit of what he had come for. He became a master at running down the buffalo, and shot birds as he had done in Scotland, with a gunbearer standing close by, to pass him a freshly loaded weapon. He was lethally accurate, often hunting on until ten o'clock at night, and recording all his kills in his game book at the end of each day.

Gore's first guide, Chatillon, later complained that "This Lord was a very disagreeable 'Jonney Bull' . . . he put on any amount of airs and had 18 Bloodhounds to chase the antelope, and play smash in general. . . ."[47] Other frontiersmen were less offended by his manner, and saw him with a mix of wonder and respect. William Cody, "Buffalo Bill," was a boy at Fort Laramie in the early 1850s, and may have seen Gore set out. "He was a sportsman among a thousand," Cody wrote, ". . . and he spent money with extraordinary freedom in the gratification of his passion."[48] General Randolph Marcy, the trailblazing frontier soldier and author of *The Prairie Traveller*, the standard guide for emigrant parties, met Gore in St. Louis. He found him "one of those enthusiastic, ardent sportsmen who derived more real satisfaction and pleasure from one day's successful hunting than can possibly be imagined by those who have never participated in this exhilarating and healthful amusement."[49] Nevertheless, Gore's zealous quest, which cost him at least $100,000, took such a toll on wildlife that protests were made on behalf of the Indians, and the favorite pastime of the British aristocracy became, for the first time, a political issue.

Once in the upper Missouri country, Gore was running into not only the Indians but also the Indian agents, working for the government's Department of Indian Affairs, who were meant to watch over the Indians and look after their interests. Though the agents out in the territory were answerable to Colonel Cumming in St. Louis, who had issued Gore his permit, they took against the baronet once he came into their country. They accused Gore of trading illegally with the Crows by selling them horses and gunpowder, and damaging the Indian food supply. One agent protested against the "killing and scattering of game vital to the sustenance of the red man, merely so that the nobility might enjoy itself."[50] A complaint on behalf of the Indians went up as far as Secretary of Interior Robert McClelland in Washington, flattering Gore with an even bigger kill than he had, in fact, been able to manage. Gore was accused of culling "at least 6,000 buffalo," and doing and acting as he pleased. "We punish an Indian for killing a settler's cow for food. . . . How can such destruction of their game be permitted by their friends in the Government of the United States?"[51]

An official suggested the government take legal action to recover all the skins, sets of antlers, and trophies that Gore had collected in the Indian hunting grounds, and sell them off.

Secretary McClelland advised restraint, since a foreigner was involved. Meanwhile Gore, still in the wilderness and unaware of the brouhaha he was causing, was having his own troubles with the Indians. When the same agent heard reports that Gore and twelve of his men had been killed in a raid by the Blackfeet and the Sioux, he may have thought the baronet had got his just deserts. But though raiders had attacked his camp, taken his horses, and plundered the wagons, Gore himself survived, returning safely to St. Louis in June 1857 after thirty-seven months in the wilds.

By the time he started back, Gore had beaten all records for what the Americans now referred to as "international Nimrods,"[52] though the figure of 6,000 buffalo was an overestimate. His own scorecard showed that he had killed a mere 2,000 buffalo, 1,600 deer and elk, 105 bears, and thousands more mountain sheep, coyotes, and timber wolves.

Gore was not so different from earlier gentlemen adventurers with buffalo on their mind, except in the scale of his odyssey, the time he was able to give to it, and the depth of his pocket. Though he hunted in Canada in later years, he returned to the United States only once more. This time the prairie buffalo escaped and he went south to Florida to slaughter birds and alligators. Because he played little part in London society, and never wrote an account of his long hunt, he was hardly known in Britain. He continued his dog breeding, and spent his later days in the Gore family's large town house in Brighton, on the coast in Sussex, surrounded by his trophies. But in the American West the stories of his trip were further embroidered as time went on.

Accounts of the haughty behavior and fabulous excess of British lords, often loosely classified as "royalty," circulated in bars and bunkhouses, among outfitters and guides. As well as bringing the finest hounds and horses, it was said that Sir George had been drawn across the prairies in a gilded carriage, that his camp blazed with light at night, when bewigged flunkies served dinners prepared by European chefs, from silver dishes. Later, when the American resentment of the British upper class had developed much more of an edge, a writer looked back on the early history of Colorado and Wyoming and placed Sir George Gore in the context of the land clearances that had been the cause of so much grief in Scotland and Ireland: "His only object in seeking the mighty solitudes of the heart of the American continent was the gratification of that savage instinct preserved with so much care by the landed aristocracy of Great Britain, the love of the chase, to secure themselves in the enjoyment of which the land is kept from the homeless poor."[53]

Though the first British visitors had been welcomed for the funds and employment they brought with them, they were always a puzzle. Around the time of Gore's trip, puzzlement turned to irritation. In 1854, a correspondent visiting Missouri reported to the *New York Times*:

From what I have been able to see, I should judge that St. Louis has been, and is yet, much bored and victimized by foreign noblemen and quasi-noblemen, who pass through, stopping for some time preparatory to a hunting tour through the Rocky Mountains. It would seem that the younger sons and illegitimate offspring of the scions of the English Aristocracy get tired, as too tame, of shooting quail and pheasants at home, and yearly come out here to shoot buffalo on the Plains. The Planter's House register frequently announces the arrival of my "Lord Fitz Snooks" and so many dogs and servants on route for the Plains, and the "Republican" and other city papers duly inform the public of their arrival in flourishing terms.[54]

BACK IN NEW YORK, among America's own wealthiest citizens, the influx of foreign noblemen was seen rather differently, and

over time their obsessive example helped to bring a slow cultural
change. When the first upper-class Britons came through on their
way west, their nearest social equivalents, the free republic's
already entrenched elite in Philadelphia, Boston, or New York,
were mystified by them. They themselves had no interest whatever in uncomfortable backwoods adventures. They did not share
the buffalo dreams, and they viewed the whole business of shooting, and tangling with the savages, with disdain. Sport, in the
sense that the British aristocracy subscribed to it, was not part
of their lives, and in the 1830s the term "sportsman" still suggested a card player or a riverboat gambler. There were plenty of
"hunters" in the Atlantic states, but the term was applied to farmers, laborers, and backwoodsmen, in egalitarian and unregulated
pursuit of deer, wild turkey, pigeons, possums, or squirrels for the
pot. "Hunting" was an indiscriminate and sometimes improvised
affair, much of it having to be conducted in dark, uncleared forests, with no equivalent of the open hillsides, covered in purple
heather or yellow gorse, of Scotland or northern England, and no
laws or seasons to protect wild game from annihilation.

In 1839, *The Sporting Review*, a British monthly entirely dedicated to the elegant pursuit of foxhunting, shooting, steeplechasing, and yachting, complained about the situation in the former
colony, where, as yet, "the people of America have neither leisure
nor taste for field or rural sports." The explanation lay in the fact
that "very few of her wealthiest citizens are as yet wholly untram-
melled by business of a professional or mercantile nature; so that
there is not even a nucleus of that class of person we style country gentlemen." There were plenty of foxes, for example, both red
and gray, but no one seemed to have the time or style to go after
them properly. As a result, "that heart-stirring sight—a full field
of 'belted and booted knights,' scarlet coated and mounted on gallant steeds, with a pack of thoroughbred foxhounds before them,
in full cry, is a sight that the present generation of Americans
may not hope to behold." [55]

Even if full-dress foxhunting was still some way off, a dedicated few were just beginning to dabble in sport for leisure. It started with shooting for snipe and wildfowl on the marshes of Long Island and New Jersey, and more interest in bird shooting in the northeastern woods. A new weekly paper, *Spirit of the Times*, aimed at an upper-class readership with a developing interest in outdoor pursuits. A few hunting clubs were set up, hiring men to drive birds or deer into the guns. The tyro sportsmen found themselves roundly condemned by older Puritan attitudes. "To what purpose do you hunt?" a New York preacher and pamphleteer demanded of them in 1835. It was clearly not to provide sustenance, or a means of life. "For what then do you take the trouble to break dogs; to hire carriages; to consume time; in order that you may shoot a few harmless snipe, woodcock or quail? It is with most of you from *foolish vanity*, or from *idle habit*."[56]

A young British aristocrat living in New York did most to lead the American rich further from their austere path, and toward idler pursuits. William Herbert was a member of one of Britain's noblest families, and counted the earls of Pembroke, going back to the twelfth century, as his ancestors. His grandfather was the Earl of Carnarvon, whose family seat was Highclere Castle in Hampshire. Brought up in the world of great country estates where shooting and field sports were the main focus, he had been at school at Eton, before university. But as the younger son of a younger son he found himself short of funds, and racing and gambling after Cambridge soon led him into debt. Avoiding his creditors, Herbert came to New York at the age of twenty-four, where his charm and pedigree gave him immediate access to the smartest circles. With his evenings booked for dinners and dances, he began to earn a daytime income from writing about what he knew most, for *Spirit of the Times* and the *American Turf Register*. Within a few years he became the most prolific sporting author in the United States, producing newspaper columns, books about horses, collections of sporting sketches, novels, and a series of comprehensive directories.

Herbert made it his mission to change attitudes and educate wealthy Americans in the sporting ethos of his friends and class in Britain. He wrote later that when he arrived in New York, the man who loved field sports was still taboo, and a social pariah. These were years when no man "was held altogether reputable as an associate, or entirely right in his mind, if he were not wholly and solely devoted to *business*; and the only business, which was esteemed business in the eyes of the wise men of Gotham, was that of making and hoarding money." Herbert believed this led to dissolution and physical degeneracy. Looking around at the company he was keeping in the private houses of Manhattan, he complained of "the bleared eyes, sallow half-valanced faces, dwindled limbs, undeveloped frames and rickety gait of the rising generation of those, who, by virtue of their natural advantages of wealth and position, ought to be the flower of the land. . . ." When not making money, Broadway dandies spent their time preening themselves at their tailors or barbers, or dancing the latest polkas. "Never was there more need that some measure of manliness be infused into the amusements of the youth of the so styled upper classes, the *jeunesse dorée* of the Atlantic cities. . . ."[57] They could be rescued through the fresh air and exercise that came from striding over the hills, spending long days in the saddle, or wading in fast rivers clasping a fishing rod. Hunting, Herbert suggested, could provide a positive moral benefit, which "would prevent the demoralization of luxury" and "the growth of effeminacy and sloth. . . ."[58]

Under the pseudonym "Frank Forester," Herbert wrote authoritatively about the natural history and habits of game birds and animals, how and where to find them, and the correct dress, rituals, and code of behavior to be followed when despatching them. Researched during his travels up and down the eastern seaboard, his guidebooks included *Field Sports of the United States*, *Fish and Fishing of the United States*, and the *Complete Manual for Young Sportsmen*, which dealt with buying guns and training dogs, and recommended tactics for every creature from bears and elk to woodcock and widgeon. His books pointed Americans toward all the possibilities that were available: the snipe and partridge on the ocean shore, hares and deer in the Catskills, bears in the Adirondacks, ducks and geese in the Chesapeake Bay. Though he never went to the Far West, he managed to include several paragraphs on buffalo shooting, though this still seemed a remote prospect.

The earl's grandson was fiercely chauvinistic, trying to shame the American upper crust with national comparisons: "It is worthy of remark that whatever faults, whatever weaknesses, follies, deficiencies or vices, may be justly laid to the charge of the English gentry and nobility, want of manliness, of pluck to do and endure, is not one of them." Herbert believed these qualities had a racial explanation and the sporting mania of British aristocracy went straight back to what he called the "hunter ardour of the Norse populations," naming the Huns, the Scandinavians, the Teutons, and the Saxons. "To this day," he told his readers, ". . . wherever a drop is to be found of that fierce Northern blood surviving in people's veins, there you will find, and in no other land, the passion for the chase alive and dominant."[59] Herbert's notion that the warrior races of northern Europe formed a vigorous elite was a foretaste of the "Anglo-Saxonism" that would become so common in the upper tiers of American society in the next thirty years.

The takeup of Herbert's books, the fact that many more of the rich were now visiting Britain and seeing the attractions of the Old World country life at firsthand, and the traffic of noblemen heading west, all had a transforming effect. A small number of Americans began to emulate their British contemporaries, buying expensive guns in London, and taking time off for shooting. Hunting for sport, instead of just for the pot, became fashionable. When the British traveler and explorer Sir Richard Burton

passed through on his way to the Rockies, he found well-off easterners discussing buffalo more seriously: "Every week the New
York papers convey to the New World the interesting information
that some distinguished Britisher has crossed the Atlantic and
half crossed the states to enjoy the society of the 'monarch of the
prairies.' Americans consequently have learnt to look upon this
Albionic eccentricity as 'the thing.' . . ."[60]

By the 1850s, the remote U.S. Army outposts in Indian
Territory—Fort Leavenworth, Fort Atkinson, and Fort Laramie—
which had until then extended help to a small handful of Albion's
hunters, began to receive American merchant princes, venturing
out from Cincinnati or Pittsburgh or from as far as New York, for
manly activities, even if none of them came with the panache or
style of Stewart or Gore. As this was happening, a few of the more
sophisticated and discerning British visitors started to say that
buffalo hunting was too crude a business, overrated as a sport,
though their delight in prairie camping was as great as ever.

5

"Who Would Not Go A'Pleasuring!"

I must confess that the very happiest moments of my life have been spent in the wilderness of the Far West. . . . With a plentiful supply of dry pine logs on the fire. . . . I would sit cross-legged, enjoying the genial warmth, and, pipe in mouth, watch the blue smoke as it curled upwards . . . scarcely did I ever wish to wish to change such hours of freedom for all the luxuries of civilized life.

—GEORGE RUXTON,
Life in the Far West, 1849[1]

Even after George Catlin's Indian Gallery had closed, shows that gave a sense of the American West, whether they involved live human beings, oil paintings, or even stuffed animals, continued to attract disproportionate interest. A new and remarkable attraction opened in Piccadilly in 1848, when it was possible to sit or stand in the central gallery of the Egyptian Hall and contemplate a twelve-foot-high depiction of the mouth of the Mississippi and the port of New Orleans in the early morning light. With a certain amount of backstage creaking, the huge picture would begin to jerk sideways, with a perspective that allowed visitors to imagine themselves on the deck of a steamer. Edging slowly along, the scene changed from the wharves and warehouses of the city, and moved up the river, passing high levees, luxuriant yellow-green sugar plantations, and impenetrable canebrakes.

The viewer was taken past fields of cotton, small settlements with gray, mildewy clapboard houses running down to the water, and dark stretches of uncleared forest. Subtle lighting changes suggested the shift from dawn to dusk and then the river under the full canopy of the night sky. Soon after Memphis, the Mississippi widened and broke into shifting channels separated by low sandbanks. The accompanying program continued: "Amidst these islands is seen by moonlight a magnificent steamer taking in wood; her rows of windows are all blazing with lights like some fairy palace; the sound of merriment rises from her decks. Strangely contrasting with the silence and solitude of this primeval scenery around."[2]

John Banvard, a jobbing frontier artist and onetime backdrop painter for itinerant theater companies, had spent nearly four years on the river, preparing his masterwork. Sailing his own skiff, he drew what he saw, and camped on the bank at night when between towns. Renting a barn in Louisville, the young painter then transferred his sketches of the river scene to a roll of canvas, to make an exceptionally long horizontal painting. When finished, it measured 900 yards in length, though Banvard's advertising improved on this, claiming the picture ran for three miles. It had already been shown in New York and Boston, but in London Banvard found his most receptive audience yet, just as Catlin had done. Using a system of two tall vertical spindles, the picture was unwound from a spool and taken up on the other side, with two operators behind draped curtains. The artist gave a running commentary while his wife, at the piano, filled any longueur with appropriate music.

For the Piccadilly audience, the most exciting passage came after St. Louis, when the panorama shifted onto the Missouri and tracked across the prairies for an accelerated 1,500 miles, to the mouth of the Yellowstone and the Rockies. As the spectator was carried further into the West, Indians appeared on the riverbank. "The bark-covered tents of the Shawnee Indians are pitched upon the shore; the feathered warriors recline indolently upon the grassy brink, while their squaws prepare their repast." Moving on, when the picture showed flames roaring across the landscape, Banvard gave a signal, and smoke billowed into the hall, as a special effect, before the full grandeur of the prairies returned. "As the clouds roll off, the fresh vivid grass expands in verdant wave upon wave, as far as the eye can reach; black herds of buffaloes are seen rushing madly over the boundless expanses, with the Indians in chase."[3] Royal courtiers, knowing the "three mile picture" to be just the sort of thing Queen Victoria was interested in, asked Banvard to bring it out to Windsor. He showed it to the monarch in the Waterloo Chamber, the same hall in which Catlin's Indians had stamped their way through the war dance.

More than half a million people followed Banvard's western journey, not just in London but at later unrollings in Manchester, Liverpool, Leeds, Glasgow, and Edinburgh. Because his expenses were lower, without so much to shift and display, or Indian mouths to feed, he made far more money than Catlin. Eyeing his profits, other promoters sent off artists to record the Nile, the Ganges, and the Rhine in a similar horizontal format. "We live, indeed, in an age of panoramas,"[4] sighed one newspaper. But the New World still generated the most excitement. At a gallery quickly renamed the Grand American Hall, in Leicester Square, another painter, John Rowson Smith, was soon offering a rival trip up the Mississippi and the Ohio to Cincinnati, claiming his version to be better painted and even longer. Banvard secured a testimonial from the American minister in London and henceforth advertised his as the "true original."

When the number of visitors began to drop, Banvard's journey along the Mississippi and Missouri was replaced by another, which, for 1 shilling, or 2 shillings for a reserved seat, took spectators across country from Independence, Missouri, to California.

The new panorama was based on sketches made by Colonel John
Frémont, on a government expedition of 1842, incorporating
scenes borrowed from some of Alfred Jacob Miller's pictures. "You
go along the prairie, a field of a million acres, ascend mountains,
dive into gorges, hunt the buffalo . . . ," wrote one visitor. "You see
hunting, shooting, fishing, fighting . . . and lastly, a land where
gold is scraped up in handfuls."[5] On tables beside the moving picture, the public could peer at lumps of quartz rock, brought from
the Sierras, and said to be seamed with gold.

THE BRITISH PERCEPTION of the far-off American West was growing more informed and sophisticated all the time. In the 1830s
it had been limited to a romantic fascination with the untrammeled wilderness and the Indians who roamed it, spiced with the
prospect of exceptional hunting. Twenty years after Captain William Stewart first ventured onto the plains, educated Britons had
a sense of the great process that was pushing back the frontier,
and were starting to accept the notion of "manifest destiny," the
phrase coined in 1845 to describe the inevitability of westward
expansion by the Anglo-Saxon race, at the expense of any others
that stood in their way, as a matter of moral right. They followed
the long-running quarrel about where the border between the
United States and Canada should be drawn in the Pacific Northwest, which finally led to the Oregon settlement in 1846. They
watched the annexation of Texas, and the U.S. attack on Mexico.
They learned about the new territories of Kansas and Nebraska,
and the further displacement of the Indian tribes. They were
intrigued by stories of the polygamous Brigham Young, and the
strange, shocking, but fascinating holy city the Mormons were
building for themselves beside the Great Salt Lake. They marveled at reports of the stately riverboats, with no equivalent in
Europe, and of a railway that would one day cross the continent.

They were awed by tales of the glinting wealth just starting to be extracted from diggings in the Rockies and the Sierras.

Catlin's pictures and Indians, and the rolling panoramas, supplemented a growing number of factual travelers' tales that were appearing in print. British publishers brought over books by American authors, including Francis Parkman's *The Oregon Trail*, in which he wrote approvingly of the way civilization was triumphing over savagery. A series of titles by dauntless Britons, from the same social background as most of their readers, showed the pluck and sangfroid of the upper-class gentleman being put under test. One reviewer for *The Athenaeum*, inundated with accounts of quick "prairie scampers" and "Rocky Mountain rambles," complained that accounts of American travels were now "as plentiful as blackberries."[6] Another, in the *Literary Gazette*, exclaimed, "Who would not go a'pleasuring to the Rocky Mountains!"[7]

The most successful accounts were those that best conveyed the double appeal of the prairies, as a liberating space where there was no "society," where the traveler coming from the increasingly urbanized and convention-ridden life of Victorian Britain could find a sublime sense of well-being, and as a playground for unmatched sport. Two young former army officers, Captain George Ruxton and Captain John Palliser, almost the same age and writing within a few years of each other, brought a firsthand veracity and a particular British perspective. Ruxton's *Adventures in Mexico and the Rocky Mountains* set the model when it appeared in 1847, a year before Banvard's panorama first rolled past Londoners. At age twenty-five, the former lieutenant, who had read *Last of the Mohicans* while at Sandhurst, had set out for the Southwest and the prairies in search of action and excitement. After seeing the war between the United States and Mexico, and the fighting on the Rio Grande, he rode north to the central Rockies on his horse Panchito, to explore and hunt around the headwaters of the Arkansas River. He reached the Bayou Salado—shortly to become known as the South Park—several years before Charles

Fitzwilliam, and the area had the same strong appeal. "I never recall but with pleasure the remembrance of my solitary camp in the Bayou Salado, with no friend near me more faithful than my rifle, and no companions more sociable than my good horse and mules, or the attendant coyote which nightly serenaded us."[8]

Though an excellent shot, and formidably competent, the thoughtful Ruxton was more interested in the Comanche and Apache Indians than he was in hunting for its own sake. He had mixed feelings about the pursuit that still aroused the greatest fervor back in England, and thought that buffalo shooting "soon degenerates into mere butchery." Having seen huge herds massing over the prairie, he declared that "setting aside the excitement of a chase on horseback, buffalo hunting is too wholesale a business to afford much sport."[9]

Drawing on what he had seen and learned in the Rockies, and the stories he had heard from veterans on his return journey via St. Louis, Ruxton followed up his firsthand *Adventures* with *Life in the Far West*, a broad and lightly fictionalized account of the fur trade days that were now gone. Though he had never witnessed the scenes himself, his stories of the cross-prairie treks, the rendezvous, the rivalries, the fortunes won and lost, and the fights with the Indians provided a clearer narrative than Sir William Drummond Stewart's and Charles Murray's long and impenetrable novels.

Ruxton told the recent history through the eyes of two fictional trappers, Killbuck and La Bonté, and because they were now part of the legend, he included the earlier British travelers in his story. At one point his pair of mountain men, hungry and down on their luck, moccasins worn through and greasy clothes in tatters, come across a party of English hunters, moving through the country with their wagons, on a trip of Sir George Gore–like ambition. Ruxton tries to see them through the American trappers' eyes, as aliens, unlike anything they had ever seen before. One was "clad in a white shooting jacket, of cut unknown in mountain tailoring, and a pair of trousers of the well known material called 'shepherd's plaid.' A broad brimmed panama shaded his face, which was ruddy with health and exercise." His companion wore a "wide-awake hat," a blue handkerchief knotted jauntily round his throat, fine English leather gloves and riding boots, and was armed with "a superb double rifle, glossy from the case, and bearing few marks of use or service."[10]

One of the Englishmen greets the weatherbeaten trappers with the patrician bonhomie he would have adopted when addressing tenants at home. " 'Well, my men, how are you . . . any game here?' Then he broke off. 'By Jove!' he suddenly exclaimed, seizing his rifle as at that moment a large buzzard, the most unclean of birds, flew into the topmost branch of a cottonwood." The Englishman approached the inedible bird, which the Americans would not have bothered with, "in the most approved manner of northern deerstalkers," throwing himself prostrate on the ground and remaining motionless so as not to alarm the buzzard. "It was worth while to look at the countenance of old Killbuck as he watched the antics of the 'bourgeois' hunter. . . ." When he saw the quarry the man was so carefully pursuing, "his mouth grinned from ear to ear, and turning to La Bonté, he said 'Wagh! He's some—he is!' "[11]

The trappers, unable to shoot for food because they were out of powder, had been reduced to toasting rattlesnakes over the embers. The grandee insisted on feeding them: "As soon as the animals were unhitched, and camp formed on the banks of the creek, a black cook set about preparing a meal. Our two trapping friends looked on with astonishment as the sable functionary drew from the wagon the different articles required to furnish forth a feed. Hams, tongues, tins of preserved meats, bottles of pickles, of porter, brandy, coffee, sugar, flour were tumbled promiscuously on the prairie. . . ."[12] Ruxton was adapting, for his readers, a moment from one of Stewart's trips, when he had rescued and re-equipped a party of trappers who had been robbed by Indians.

Life in the Far West had a special influence and impact because it was serialized in six instalments in the popular *Blackwood's Magazine* before appearing as a book. Ruxton pronounced it impossible that anyone visiting the prairie, once they had tasted "the sweets of its attendant liberty and freedom from every worldly care," would not continue to sigh for a return. "I must confess that the very happiest moments of my life have been spent in the wilderness of the Far West. . . ."[13] Still only twenty-seven, he decided to go back for another rejuvenating journey. "My route takes me via New York, the Lakes, and St. Louis, to Fort Leavenworth or Independence on the Indian frontier," he wrote to his publisher. "Thence, packing my 'possibles' on a mule, and mounting a buffalo horse, (Panchito if he is alive), I strike the Santa Fe trail to the Arkansas, away up that river to the mountains, winter in the Bayou Salado . . . cross the mountains next spring to Great Salt Lake—and that's far enough to look forward to—always supposing my hair is not lifted by Comanche or Pawnee."[14] Alas, it was too far. Ruxton never got beyond the Planter's House in St. Louis, where he died in September 1848 of an old back injury that had been with him since he was thrown from a mule and impaled on an Indian tent peg.

Further testimony to the joys of the prairie life came from Captain John Palliser, whose *Solitary Rambles and Adventures of a Hunter in the Prairies*, appearing in 1853, went into almost as many editions as *Life in the Far West*. Like Ruxton, Palliser was a young army officer with a country gentry background; he had grown up on his father's estate at Comeragh House, on the eastern slope of the Comeragh Mountains, looking out across the rich farmland of County Waterford. When his army friend William Fairholme returned from his hunting trip on the Arkansas, he gave such a compelling account that Palliser decided he had to follow him.

A giant of a man, standing six foot four, Palliser's spirits and energy seemed inexhaustible. Like Ruxton, he did not need to travel with the entourage that the true grandees fielded, and roughed it on his own for much of the time. Unlike Ruxton, who had a broader interest in the history and geography of the West, Palliser had time for little else but bringing down animals, but he wrote pithily and lucidly. He compared the improvisation and enterprise needed for prairie shooting with the smooth backup he was accustomed to in an English country house: "It is only when left to our own resources that we sportsmen feel how very helpless we are rendered by our civilization. Very delightful is the refinement of sport in England, rising not too early, shaving with hot water, and tea cream-softened waiting for you in the breakfast room, guns clean as if not used the day before; and you take them without the slightest compunction from that invaluable individual called the gamekeeper. . . ."[15]

After crossing the prairie during the summer of 1847, Palliser spent the winter months on the upper Missouri, where buffalo sheltered in stands of trees beside the frozen river. When the snow was too deep to hunt from horseback, he stalked them, crawling along on his hands and knees under a white blanket, to disguise himself as snow. As the cold increased, the wolves howled dolefully, until Palliser thought they were overplaying their part: ". . . the cadences of voices from a high key to a low one, and vice versa, were most extraordinary, and sometimes so extravagantly dismal as to be quite ludicrous." His lowest moment came after he left Fort Union on a solitary deer hunt, the weather so cold that icicles formed in his beard—and his whiskers "jingled like bells." He spent a bitter night under a heavy buffalo robe, locked in an embrace with his dog, trying to retain vital heat. "As soon as it was daylight we rose; Ishmah patiently submitted to be harnessed, and we resumed our march."[16]

It was an essential part of the genre to include hairbreadth escapes and the occasional spill, and Palliser offered many of both. He was left alone in the frozen woods when Ishmah deserted him, running off still dragging the sled that bore all his possessions, to gambol with wolves. He could not follow the tracks, and was lost without fire, blankets, food, or weapons, with darkness falling. After many hours the playful dog returned, the sled still attached, and Palliser was saved. As he climbed up mountainsides after bighorn sheep, they showered a bruising and near-fatal avalanche of scree and rocks down on top of him. Approaching a wounded but not quite dead elk with his knife, to deliver the coup de grâce, the animal kicked the knife out of his hand and nearly pawed him to the ground. When an enraged buffalo bore down and hit him amidships "with a shock like an earthquake," he was lucky to be caught between, rather than on, the horns. Though the impact was softened by the enormous mass of fur, wool, and hair that clothed the shaggy head, he was pitched into a snowdrift.

Palliser's most sublime period came with the arrival of spring, when he moved about 100 miles up the Yellowstone, camping near the mouth of one of its tributaries, the Big Horn. The woods were thickly stocked with evergreens and shrubs in flower, the river rolled majestically along, and for some distance luxuriant grass carpeted the alluvial deposits on each bank. "We lived like fighting-cocks in my little Yellow Stone camp; I used every day to sit down to several kinds of meat, besides fish. One day we actually supped on buffalo-beef, elk-meat, venison, antelope's liver, and wild mutton, besides the luxuries of catfish and marrow bones."[17] This proved to be his own equivalent of Ruxton's Bayou Salado, or Stewart's lakeside camp in the Wind River Mountains.

Everything Palliser could possibly want to kill was close by: "If I wished to shoot from horseback, a ride of a few miles afforded me most splendid runs; if I wished to hunt wapiti, the points on the river contained them in just sufficient abundance to afford that amount of toil and labor without which nothing is duly appreciated; of deer I had a considerable number; black tailed deer I could always obtain by going a few miles distance to look for them."[18] Bighorn sheep, antelope, duck, and pheasant were all to hand. Sometimes a serendipity set in, whereby one animal's execution facilitated another, producing glorious sanguinary riffs. He would shoot a buffalo, then watch over the carcass to fire at the wolf that came to eat the remains. Since the wolves were keen cannibals, the flesh of a dead one could in turn attract more of its brothers, and sometimes eagles circled overhead, eyeing the wolf offal, and could be shot down as well. Palliser's only grievance was that he could find no bears on the Yellowstone, so he headed back east of the Missouri to the small Turtle Mountain range, in what is now North Dakota, where the timbered slopes were almost overrun with them.

Though he wrote about the landscape, the hardships of travel, and the food, it was his steady concentration on the moment of despatch, and the death throes of his targets, that most aroused gentleman readers. Bullets cracked against bones and animals tumbled to the ground on almost every page. Spying a mountain sheep on a crag, he wrote: "I pointed my rifle downwards, and as the echo and smoke of the shot rolled away, I saw that my bullet had broken his back and sent him floundering below." Climbing down to it, he inspected the dead ram "with great delight." After shooting a bear at close quarters, the beast tumbled down "floundering like a great fish out of water, till at length he reluctantly expired." In pursuit of a running buffalo, "I got pretty close behind her, and raising myself in my stirrups, fired down upon her. The effect was grand. She dropped at the report, the bullet breaking her spine." Going after an elk, "I took a steady deliberate shot as he turned his flank toward me. I heard the bullet crack against his shoulder; he rushed a short distance back, and rolled over in the snow." When he hit a "splendid cream-coloured wolf" in the flanks, the animal turned with a guttural growl, snapped at the wound, "performed a brilliant somersault, and after rolling over twice or thrice, expired."[19] One London critic described Palliser's book as a succession of striking adventures, with animals being slaughtered so frequently that the reader "finds himself insensibly entertaining a half latent hope that the terrible destroyer of life will himself not get off without a good hugging by some resolute old grisly bear."[20]

After nine months of hunting, Palliser had accumulated so

many skins, horns, skulls, paws, and claws that he needed two buffalo-skin boats to take the trophies down to the stockaded American Fur Company post at Fort Berthold, where they could be loaded onto the annual steamer returning to St. Louis. As additional souvenirs he rounded up several live buffalo calves, and a bear, sending them back to his home via New Orleans and Cork. Later, Palliser would return to North America for several more expeditions, surveying the Canadian Prairies and Rockies for the Royal Geographical Society and the British government.

Thanks in part to Ruxton and Palliser, knowledge of the Far West now went well beyond the private memories, trophies, or oil paintings of the first generation of rich aristocrats. The geographical range had been extended too, with less of a focus on the strip of the prairies crossed by the Platte route to the Sweetwater, and over the South Pass. Equally enthralling experiences could be found in the upland valleys of what is now Colorado, down into the Southwest, or in the smaller ranges that could be reached from the upper reaches of the Missouri and the Yellowstone. Returning travelers continued to stress how invigorating the prairies were. "The atmosphere in these regions is extremely healthy, and its effect upon the constitution something wonderful," noted John Palliser; "so much so that persons never suffer from coughs or colds; the complaint is quite unknown."[21]

One commentator felt the Far West could provide a new sort of mental release for the country's blue bloods in far greater numbers. Vigorous sport was the one activity that allowed them to escape from "the feeble luxury of timid indolence" with which they were burdened, and until then stalking and shooting on the Scottish moors had provided this. "How gladly does even the gloved and booted *elegant,* after dissolving at the opera, doing duty at ball and dinner, and getting 'used up' at everything throughout the season, seek the more rugged life of the moors, and recruit his exhausted frame and languid energies upon the mountain heath!" Now the American prairies were available to soak up their energies. "Yield, ye recreant shooters of partridge and grouse; enlarge your notions of sport and danger; we offer you a new field of excitement—a new remedy for *ennui* and indigestion."[22]

This was more easily said than done. Ruxton and Palliser were an inspiration, but not all their readers were young men, or had as much time available, or shared their remarkable bravery and stamina. Palliser improvised shelters with branches, built buffalo-skin boats, and was infinitely resourceful, even to the point of shooting his own trousers. He described how, when his clothes were torn beyond repair in the wilderness, he sought out a black-tail deer, shot it, flayed, dressed, and smoked the skin, then cut out a pattern and sewed the parts together, to make what he described as "a new pair of inexpressibles."[23] Ruxton had traveled through Mexico with a small sack of silver dollars and an arsenal of weapons that included a double-barreled rifle, a shotgun, a short carbine, and four revolvers, fighting off desperadoes.

Not all the booted *elegants* were capable of this degree of physical toughness, and many practical hurdles remained to be overcome before those sublime moments, with the blue smoke curling up into the sky, could be achieved. Even getting to the starting point required a commitment of time, and a degree of advance knowledge and organization, that some were too listless to be capable of. What they needed was easier travel, and more guidance. Meanwhile, the Duke of Leeds became the first aristocrat to bring down a buffalo in Scotland, when the Marquis of Breadalbane allowed him to shoot one of his growing herd on the hillside at Taymouth Castle in 1854, though it was more an assassination than a sporting chase.

On a spring day in 1860 Londoners walking along the Strand—the broad commercial thoroughfare lined with theaters, publishing offices, and booksellers, where Catlin's Ojibbeways had provided a sensation when spotted on top of a horse-drawn omnibus—were jolted by another American sighting. Next door to the Gaiety Theatre, at number 346, a striking new feature had appeared in the window of a magazine office. A full-size buffalo bull, with wild eyes, a huge head of shaggy hair, and a squat powerful body, stared out over the pavement. The lifelike appearance was a tribute to the skills of Henry Ward, London's leading taxidermist, who had received the animal's head, fleece, ribs, legs, hooves, and tail from St. Louis in a packing case. Ward had reassembled the beast over a wooden frame in his studio, stuffed it, and then sent it round to the Strand. Once maneuvered into the broad front window, between two Corinthian pillars, the buffalo's role was to attract publicity for *The Field*, established seven years earlier as "The country gentleman's newspaper." It was also meant to inspire and energize readers, and show what they could hope to achieve if they followed the advice of the magazine's shooting correspondent, who had shot it. "The bull is drawn up . . . ," he wrote proudly, "as he stood when contemplating one of his numerous charges on his single-handed assailant on the plains, and therefore the spectator has the opportunity of seeing the powerful beast in a fighting attitude as opposed to man and horse."[24]

The Field had sent the Honorable Grantley Berkeley, a prolific and long-standing contributor, by then age sixty, to the prairies to show readers in the shires that western hunting need not be as challenging as they feared. The aim was to demonstrate how recent improvements in Atlantic shipping and the American railways made a quick trip easier than ever before. It was no longer necessary to have the family resources of the Earl of Leicester, or Lord Fitzwilliam, behind you. "I left England," Berkeley wrote, ". . . to be able to tell Englishmen in what way they should proceed on a visit to the Far West, what adventures they would most likely encounter, what would be the costs of their journey, and how they [can] best fit themselves out and at the least expense."[25]

His journey to New York on the steamship *Africa* took eleven days. He went on by train to Cincinnati, and then took the just-completed Ohio & Mississippi Railroad, which ran in an almost straight line, westward across Indiana and Illinois. After fifty-five hours of rail travel, Berkeley reached the new riverside station at East St. Louis on a Sunday morning in early September, where a steam ferry took him, his servant George Bromfield, and his five hunting dogs, across the Mississippi to St. Louis, now a burgeoning city of 100,000 people. Sir William Drummond Stewart's friend Robert Campbell helped to find housing for the dogs, and advised Berkeley on the purchase of a special vehicle, with springs and a double-lined covering, to an ambulance design, in which he could both travel and sleep.

The ambulance, and a wagon for the baggage, were craned onto the top deck of a steamer and taken up the Missouri to Kansas City, where Berkeley bought horses and mules, a dogcart, and hired a guide and nine men, with whom he headed out. He named his own horse Taymouth, in honor of Lord Breadalbane, whose Perthshire buffalo he had studied carefully before leaving. Keeping up a brisk pace from the start, he said he wanted to show the "adventurous and hardy sportsmen" of the present day that a hunting expedition in the West did not require the nine months it had taken Palliser, Ruxton's twenty months, or Gore's three years. Even if his readers were members of the House of Lords or the House of Commons, Berkeley asserted, it was quite possible to attend the parliamentary session, get out to America, make free with the buffalo, and be back in time for Christmas.

After following the Santa Fe Trail for a while, Berkeley turned north at Council Grove, taking the military road to Fort Riley, an imposing set of newly built stone barracks, stables, and officers' quarters on high ground, on the north bank of the Kansas River. Driving up to the camp, Berkeley presented a letter of introduction to the commanding officer, Major Wassells, who offered him all the help he needed.

Though he went at what was said to be the wrong time of the

year, never saw the Rockies, did not travel more than a few hundred miles onto the prairies, and failed to encounter the dense
buffalo herds he had read about, Berkeley was excited when Fort
Riley officers led him to small groups of grazing buffalo a little
way up the Smoky Hill fork of the Kansas: "Oh! It was so lovely,
that wild ride over the plains, the mighty game in view . . . both
Taymouth and myself were as hot as man and horse could be—he
was white with foam from head to foot. . . ."[26] He shot twenty or
thirty, depending on whose account was to be believed.

Having left Liverpool on August 20, Berkeley managed to keep
to his schedule and was back in London by early December, carrying buffalo steaks for his West End club. In addition to the carcass destined for the window in the Strand, he brought back an
assortment of buffalo tails. With his own ideas about decoration,
Berkeley had them adapted into bellpulls, to provide "a sporting
finish"[27] to the dining and drawing room of his house in Hampshire, and for tugging when he wanted to call his butler.

The Field had a record for sensing what its readers in the country were interested in. The editors advertised the series heavily, claiming their correspondent's success in hunting the buffalo
"has been unprecedented." Soon afterwards, the collected articles
appeared in book form. Engraved illustrations showed Berkeley
on the plains, as he fired his carbine at the gallop, or sat on the
corpse of a beast he had brought down, wearing a bowler hat. But
while Berkeley's account certainly added to British expectations
of the West, his own behavior during the trip seemed to reinforce
all the western American prejudices about what to expect from
the British aristocracy. Palliser and Ruxton had been modest and
civil, and wise enough not to pass judgment on the egalitarian
frontier society. Though they were well connected, and had private incomes, neither was an aristocrat from the top tier. Berkeley
was the real thing, and he was thick-skinned and perhaps dim-
witted enough to let Americans know exactly what he thought
about them.

Even to his own countrymen, the Honorable Grantley Berkeley seemed a caricature of a certain sort of blustering and blinkered type, a throwback to eighteenth-century England rather
than a mid-Victorian. The son of the Earl of Berkeley, he was
brought up at Berkeley Castle in Gloucestershire and Berkeley
House in London. From boyhood he took an almost houndlike
delight in the chase, and after a brief time in the Grenadier
Guards, when he helped defend George IV's court at St. James's
Palace and Windsor, he became a full-time huntsman. For a
while he kept his own pack of staghounds, hunting country
to the west of London with a field of dashing Guards officers
and friends who coached out from Mayfair. Then he became
Master of Foxhounds for the Oakley Hunt, galloping across
Buckinghamshire and Bedfordshire three days a week in his
family livery of yellow plush coat, black cap, and white cord
breeches. For variety he would send hounds splashing along
the riverbanks of Hampshire after otters, and when there were
no otters, arrange for them to be imported and released from
boxes in front of his dogs, for a riverine version of greyhound
coursing. He kept and bred hunting dogs of all kinds, moving
in the same circles as Sir St. George Gore. His famed English
bloodhound Druid was a lethal presence in the old royal hunting preserve of the New Forest, running and grabbing down the
deer with unfailing zest.

Berkeley, heavily whiskered, with a ruby complexion gained
from so much time in the wind and rain of the British countryside, seemed to be related to most of the greatest families of the
peerage, and the King had been his godfather. He was a Member
of Parliament for twenty years, though his Westminster interven-
tions were rare and eccentric. When a reviewer dismissed a novel
he had written as "about the stupidest it has ever been our misfor-
tune to read,"[28] Berkeley went round and lashed the editor with a
horsewhip. He had taken part in several duels. He was irascible,
opinionated, outspoken, and snobbish. In releasing him onto the

prairies, *The Field* must have known the effect he was likely to have on his American hosts.

From the moment he reached New York and saw how the many small craft in the harbor refused to give way to his incoming 2,500-ton steamship, tiny fishing boats tacking straight across the Cunarder's path, Berkeley was outraged by the lack of respect for authority and position in the republic. Though it was the American railways that were allowing him to pursue his quest, he found them "filthy and falsely democratic." Not only were the floors disgusting, and the drafts down the open corridor carriages so strong that "any man used to comfort is sure to catch the ear-ache," but many of the fellow passengers were an affront. Without the first-, second-, and third-class divisions he was accustomed to, and on routes where no special emigrant car was attached, the earl's son was obliged to share a carriage with people he identi-fied at once as rogues, thieves, and the diseased. "Oh! after I had experienced the travel of these boasted trains, how I longed for the cleanliness and privacy, and civility and choice of society, on the railways of Old England."[29]

He threatened to thrash "insolent" railway officials who han-dled his baggage roughly, and complained about the fares and accommodation for his much-loved dogs, who included the legend-ary Druid, his retrievers Brutus and Alice, a setter, Chance, and a lurcher called Bar. When hotel staff were slack, he admonished them briskly, concluding that "if the American gentlemen would be more particular in exacting attention, and bear themselves less on the equality system, dinners would be better waited on, and the serving men no worse." He was dismayed that Americans had no idea who he was, and that the fine distinctions of manners, dress, and vocabulary that allowed the British to recognize and place each other in a social pecking order meant nothing. But he was pleased that at least Robert Campbell gave him the treatment he expected on reaching St. Louis, because, "being an enlightened gentleman, he of course understood my station in society."[30]

Berkeley's confident self-belief allowed him to run the yardstick across every feature of American life. He criticized the slouching posture and tobacco chewing of the men. He found the mealtimes inconvenient and thought Americans did not hang their game birds for long enough. He knew that London-made guns could fire further and more accurately. He ridiculed the western saddle, with its low-hanging cloglike stirrups, and high crutch rising from the pommel. "Of all the unsightly, hideous and dangerous things on a saddle, this excrescence is the worst." His orders to functionaries and staff were crisp and emphatic. " 'Here,' I cried to the sable attendants of the stable of the hotel, 'take that horrible unicorn saddle off that horse, and put my English saddle on; take that gagging bridle out of his mouth, put mine in . . . and I'll throw myself across the horse and see what he will do with me.' "[31]

Based on his reception by Campbell, Sublette, and their friends in the upper echelons of St. Louis, Berkeley conceded that the best type of American could be as good as any in Europe, and found their ladies charming. It was the clerks and storekeepers, the blacksmiths and mechanics, who offended him. "The tradesmen are for the most part assuming, uncivil, and under a lamentable mistake in the supposition that rudeness to their betters proves there are no betters, but that a general equality pervades the land."[32]

Berkeley grumbled that his British title, "the Honorable," commanded no respect, because in America it was given to elected members of Congress, who might be anyone, regardless of birth. The problem of recognition solved itself, as newspapers reported the progress of "the celebrated English Nimrod"[33] in slightly mocking tones. By the time he reached Kansas City, his reputation had preceded him, and the horse dealers and provision merchants who wanted his custom generally addressed him as "Sir Grantley" or "Lord Berkeley."

Out on the plains, Berkeley was as much of a martinet as Sir William Drummond Stewart, but without the Perthshire laird's charisma and uncomplicated enthusiasm: "I endeavoured to impress on all my men that there ought to be, and with me, *could only be*, one head and one commander to the little force of which my small party consisted." When one of Berkeley's mule drivers slept on his watch, and proved truculent, he decided to send the man back across the prairies on his own, determined to be more resolute than George III in dealing with the breakaway colonials. The muleteer eventually kowtowed: "on finding that I would put up with no sort of American independence, he became more civil, and said that he did not wish to displease me."[34]

Berkeley believed that behind all these instances of challenge and insubordination, and the disrespectful attitude of salespeople and hotel staff, ticket inspectors and baggagemen, lay a broader malaise. The American lower classes had become "rudely intoxicated with liberty," and the granting of the vote for all white males in most states, and the politics of the common man as promoted by Andrew Jackson, was to blame. Unreconstructed aristocrats like Berkeley had resisted even the limited widening of the British franchise through the Great Reform Act of 1832. The idea that all adult men should get the vote regardless of the property they owned or their education, as now demanded by the Chartists who demonstrated in the streets of British cities in the 1840s, was anathema. While liberal reformers like Richard Cobden and John Bright cited the United States as the model Britain should follow, conservatives saw it as a warning lesson. Berkeley disliked the hail-fellow-well-met familiarity he ran up against, and the ordinary American's assumption that he was on an equal footing with his "betters." "A man has but to travel in the United States and to mix with all classes to see the errors in the system of what may be called the universal suffrage of an irresponsible people."[35]

Berkeley seemed happiest when he was in the generous care of the U.S. Army, in which many officers had the gracious manners of the South. Fort Riley was a place where position was respected, and afternoon tea was served on the small wooden verandas of the identical officers' houses, with the ladies sporting parasols. "I found the barracks a sort of heaven upon earth in regard to the habits of much of the society in which I had latterly been thrown, and had discovered that, with some exceptions, the army alone held the courtesies of English life. . . ."[36]

Many other visiting aristocrats may have been as critical as Berkeley in their private thoughts, but they had not published their views or dilated on politics. On his way back, Berkeley gave lectures in St. Joseph and St. Louis, regaling large audiences with his views on American manners and democracy, which he warned them could only lead to rule by the rabble. The press savaged him, or treated him as a figure of fun. "He has set himself up as a censor upon our national affairs, and upon the character of our government," complained *Spirit of the Times*. He had made it quite clear "that Hammerica is perfectly 'orrid, and not the thing at all." In a spat that ran over a number of months, the magazine jeered at Berkeley's pretensions and claims: "When he arrived in New York he was much surprised that there were no preparations for his official reception, and he was indignant 'all the way along,' that he received no more attention than any other well-behaved citizen, and that his deer dogs didn't receive any especial attention whatever. . . . One thing is certain, his ignorance of our geography was only paralleled by his want of knowledge of our people."[37]

Berkeley's self-glorifying account of his short hunting expedition irritated even those who had helped him, including Captain Randolph Marcy. The figures Berkeley gave for the total number of animals he had brought down, and the list of different game shot, were reckoned to be exaggerated. "Mr. Berkeley is exceedingly superficial; and imperfect in almost everything he touches; he is so especially in his knowledge of natural history. His contributions to the London 'Field' about American ducks, rabbits, deer and other 'varmints' are simply nonsense. . . . Most of the things he describes were 'out of season' or were never to be met with in the route he pursued."[38]

Berkeley made much of a heroic and climactic buffalo chase that had lasted for forty-five minutes, and taken Taymouth and himself across the open grassland, down into creeks and scrambling up steep hillocks, after a huge creature that turned and challenged him several times. He claimed no one had thought it possible to keep up this pace and ride down an animal. This drew a sharp response:

> He formally announced that he was the first man in the world who ever on horseback ran down a buffalo and shot him while at bay!! All this self-laudation was very amusing, and quite pardonable for a man who had never before pointed a deadly weapon, except at a deer raised in a nobleman's park: but there is something . . . sublimely impudent in Berkeley putting his *three weeks experience* on the frontier against Captain Marcy's twenty five years of actual campaigning, that it is worth an especial exclamation mark, for we have never met with any like it, used as we are to the self importance of "Greeneys" born in the hearing of Bow Bells.

If Berkeley was really as brave and ferocious as he claimed, and such a master at seeing off Indians and slaughtering game, then "Our frontiersmen must immediately go out to Old England and take lessons in their profession and business from this St. James Leather Stocking."[39]

Berkeley was impervious to sarcasm. Far from identifying himself with Cooper's Natty Bumppo and his backwoods, Leatherstocking dress and craft, he said he would like to see the introduction of a more elegant, and English, way of hunting. As he left Kansas City and came out onto the rolling plains, his first instinct was to compare the landscape to what he knew at home: "Oh! What a country for an English pack of foxhounds and a thoroughbred horse! A gigantic Leicestershire lay before me, without a thing to stop horse or hound but pace or the death of the hunted animal!" To make the most of it he would have needed to bring over his friends, to replace the motley band he had recruited: "How the sight of those prairies made me long for . . . the presence of my brother sportsmen of old, Lord Cardigan, Lord Clanricarde, Lord Rokeby."[40]

To lure lords of this caliber, Berkeley told Americans, they needed to do more to make them comfortable. He suggested making private railway cars available, in which the aristocrats could travel in the seclusion of their peer group, with the dogs and retainers following behind. "If the American railway companies would only concede fair accommodation for the hounds and dogs of English gentlemen in vans, and permit them, if four or five gentlemen were in company, to have a 'state carriage' to themselves, that would be perfect."[41]

Berkeley still expected that visitors would be coming on short excursions, and the possibility of buying property in the United States, let alone trying to live there in the style that a British gentleman would expect, horrified him. He had heard of American landowners who had attempted to establish parks and keep deer in them. But the rights of property were so little respected in the great democracy that local youths, "Rowdies and Boh-hoys," had come in and shot them all, and taken them away. With the lower class of inhabitants "so unrestrained and drunk with freedom," and the protection of the law so inadequate, it was impossible for landed gentlemen to have personal security. Berkeley strongly advised against putting money into America: "to invest English money in railways, or in land, or in any other permanent purchase in the United States would not, at this moment be attended with safety."[42]

THE TIMING OF Berkeley's attempt to further popularize American shooting and bring more British aristocrats to the prairies was poor. In the months that *The Field* buffalo was glowering in the Strand, the political news from the United States was becoming ever more alarming, and the prospect of the breakup of the Union made sporting tourism seem frivolous. The raid on a federal armory at Harpers Ferry, Virginia, led by the abolitionist John Brown to seize arms for a slave rebellion, had taken place while Berkeley was out in Kansas. Reports from Washington and New York, still eleven or twelve days out of date by the time they appeared because the transatlantic telegraph was not working yet, told of the escalating tensions between the North and South, the free states and slave states, and the moves toward secession.

All British visitors to the United States had to make their own personal judgment about whether to identify themselves openly with the abolitionists, as many did, or hold their council. Most of the early British aristocrats on their way to the Far West were so beguiled by the deep blue sky and boundless horizons that they took little interest in the moral and political debate. Nevertheless, no visitor passing through St. Louis could ignore the cruelties of the system, for Missouri was a slave state. When their luggage was unloaded from the steamboats, slaves carried it across the decks and down the gangplanks to the sloped levee, and drove the drays and carts up into the city streets. In the 1830s, when Captain Stewart first arrived, slaves were still being bought and sold in front of the white-pillared courthouse. When Britons made social calls on the city's leaders, they found slaves working as butlers, cooks, and valets. Sometimes the British parties setting out for the prairies hired Negroes from St. Louis masters.

The letters of the Honorable Charles Wentworth-Fitzwilliam, fourth son of Earl Fitzwilliam, charted one young aristocrat's reaction to what he saw. Soon after landing in New York, he wrote to his father, "Everybody, I believe, both in the North and the South, agrees that slavery is a curse, but nobody knows how to get rid it."[43] In the course of his journey out to St. Louis, by a touring route, he stayed at Colonel Wade Hampton's plantation at Columbia, North Carolina, where slaves were plowing the cotton fields before sowing the next year's crop. Influenced by his host, Wentworth-Fitzwilliam judged them "as contented and lazy a set of individuals" as any he had ever seen. In a swipe at those people British aristocrats traditionally judged the most slothful in Europe, he said that "even an Italian would be a hardworking man in comparison with a negro, if the latter had much liberty to be idle."[44] The full horror of the system only came to the twenty-five-year-old lordling when he saw a group of men who had been purchased at Richmond, Virginia, being taken south to Louisiana, shackled and fettered, in a carriage at the back of a train he was traveling on. A little while later some hunting dogs caught his eye: "At Montgomery I saw a pack of hounds and on asking what they were used for, found that runaway negroes were hunted with them. I think I was never more disgusted in my life."[45]

Such indignation was rare. Lieutenant William Fairholme described a meal served on a Missouri farm by "several clean, merry-looking slaves who seemed much amused with us because we were probably the first Britishers they had ever seen."[46] While the Honorable Grantley Berkeley said he "detested" slavery, he also hated the "anti-slavery humbugs" from his own country who painted the Negroes as "the most cruelly treated wretches in the world," exaggerating their plight and assisting in the political breakdown of the country. Supercilious as ever, Berkeley complained that he had not heard the beautiful but artless melodies the slaves were supposed to chant. "I told my friends that it was the general belief in England that the scenes on the banks of rivers in America were always deeply interesting, from the perpetual dancing and singing of black men, but that up to the time at which I was speaking I had met with nothing of the sort."[47] George Ruxton was more serious and more prescient, devoting a section of his *Adventures in Mexico and the Rocky Mountains* to slavery, and calling it "a foul blot upon humanity" in a nation that boasted of its liberty and equality. "That this question will

some day shake to its very centre, if it does not completely anni-
hilate, the union of the American States, is as palpable as the
result is certain."[48]

 The pace of advance toward the Pacific, and the calls to create
new states from the territories west of the Mississippi, were bringing Ruxton's shattering moment closer all the time. With settlers
from the East taking up land in the twin territories of Kansas
and Nebraska in growing numbers, the question of whether they
should become free states or slave states was the central issue in
the growing political storm. The level of violence between abolitionist free-staters, slavery backers, and anti-black groups earned
the territory a grim new tag: "Bleeding Kansas." St. Louis, and
Missouri, were divided between the slaveowning interests, who
wished to secede with the southern states, and those who wanted
to stay neutral. As the two sides slid toward war, Missouri saw
early clashes between secessionists and unionists. Over the next
four years Union and Confederate armies would wheel through
the woods and new corn fields of the Missouri Valley.

 Once the Civil War had started, in 1861, sentiment in Britain was divided, with the vociferous Christian anti-slavery
campaigners supporting the North, the government trying to
maintain neutrality, and many conservative aristocrats supporting the cause of "states' rights" and the Confederacy. For British
merchants and factory owners, America's self-destructive war
meant heavy financial losses, as the supply of slave-picked raw
cotton, shipped through Liverpool to feed the textile factories of
Lancashire, was interrupted. Tens of thousands of mill workers
were laid off. For the privileged few, it meant an end to prairie
hunting expeditions. Berkeley's book appeared just as the journey he was recommending was about to become impossible for
four years. In Kansas, army posts now had better things to do
than arrange hunting guides for wealthy visitors, even if they
could have got there. The railways of both North and South had
more important priorities than laying on private carriages for

British gentlemen, or even converting kennel vans for visiting hounds.

MORE RAILWAY TRACK continued to be laid during the war. When St. George Gore came with his dogs and servants, in 1854, they were able to get as far as Alton, Illinois, by train, but the last twenty-five miles still had to be made by steamboat, downriver to St. Louis. Berkeley had been able to get all the way to St. Louis by rail, but no further. By 1865, though there was still no bridge across the Mississippi, the railway had continued westward from the St. Louis side. The tracks crossed the state of Missouri to Kansas City, and construction crews had just reached as far as Fort Riley, which it had taken Grantley Berkeley weeks to reach in his ambulance wagon. The trains that were hauling in a growing number of emigrants from the eastern states and abroad could also bring gentlemen of leisure again. An excursion that had been limited to the wealthiest and most dedicated was coming within reach of a wider following, keen to try out the journey Berkeley had recommended several years before.

As the new influx of upper-class tourists traveled west after the Civil War, with banker's drafts and return tickets in their pockets, they occasionally came into contact with fellow Britons, from different backgrounds, and less well funded. One Englishman who had emigrated as a young man, and was now a U.S. Army officer, met a group of his fellow countrymen who had just reached Fort Leavenworth. Arriving to find the hotel lobby heaped with guns and rifle cases, saddles sewn in canvas covers and smart baggage of unmistakably English appearance, Major J. S. Campion asked the hotel clerk what was going on. "Tell you what's up? There is a parcel of English aristocrats arrived, who are going to kill all the game in the country. They have brought their dogs, their weapons and their mountebanks with them, and

they have got a kit of everything in the universal world that is of
no earthly use in this country. They are in No. 8 and there is nothing good enough for them in this 'blarsted' hotel!"[49]

When the major went up to the room to introduce himself
and offer help, he was curtly rebuffed. The visitors who had just
stepped off the train from the East could not deal with a stranger,
about whose social status they knew nothing, who might be out
to cheat them. Campion was embarrassed by the rudeness of his
fellow countrymen and the effect it had on frontier Americans.
"To them their looks were strange, their accents ridiculous, many
of their expressions hardly intelligible, their technical and slang
phrases enigmas, their nobby servants 'mountebanks.' . . . [The
Americans] would ask me what *really* was their standing in the
'Old Country.' I should have to say they belonged to the Upper
Class."[50]

One redoubtable female English traveler, Isabella Bird,
described another encounter. She was spending the night in a
Colorado cabin when a local hunting guide came in from a camp
nearby, with the young Englishman who had hired him. She
immediately recognized the type, in spite of his rough buckskins:

This gentleman was lording it in true caricature fashion, with
a Lord Dundreary drawl and a general execration of everything; while I sat in the chimney corner, speculating on the
reason why so many of the upper class of my countrymen—
"High Toners," as they are called out here—make themselves
so ludicrously absurd. They neither know how to hold their
tongues or to carry their personal pretensions. An American
is nationally assumptive, an Englishman personally so. He
took no notice of me till something passed which showed him I
was English, when his manner at once changed into courtesy,
and his drawl was shortened by a half. He took pains to let me
know that he was an officer in the Guards, of good family, on
four months leave, which he was spending in slaying buffalo

and elk, and also that he had a profound contempt for everything American. I cannot think why Englishmen put on these
broad, mouthing tones and give so many personal details.[51]

Just a few visitors managed to work out the way to avoid fric-
tion. Another Guards officer, Captain Trench Townshend, who
went hunting from a U.S. Army post in Nebraska, warned British
travelers that "equality" had to be the watchword: "The assumption of the slightest tone of superiority or command to the American who is socially inferior, is immediately resented by a display
of obstinacy, sulkiness, or insolence, while the same man, treated
as your equal, will probably be obliging and polite. At hotels, railway stations, etc, one need not feel surprised if he hears himself
addressed and spoken of as a 'man' or a 'person,' while the waiter,
porter, etc will be termed a 'gentleman.' . . ."[52] But many believed
the Americans were impossibly prejudiced, however they behaved.
Sir Edward Sullivan was dismayed by the rabid anglophobia he
found, whether in St. Louis or smaller towns along the Mississippi or the Missouri, and blamed the press. "The information
vouchsafed on European matters very often displays the grossest
ignorance; and it is owing to their bitter articles against the old
country (which they delight to describe as a bloodstained country, where an iron-heeled aristocracy is continually trampling
up to their knees in the life-blood of a crushed peasantry!) that
such bad feeling continues to exist throughout the Western States
against England."[53] From the American point of view it was still
a seasonal affliction. Most of the "high toners" and "top shelfers"
came in the summer and fall, and then they would be gone again,
on the schedule Berkeley had recommended.

FOR THOSE WHO did not want to join the ranks of tourists with
guns, and still retained a romantic belief in a distant, unspoiled

wilderness, images of the Far West landscape and its fauna were still being brought across the Atlantic. The vogue for rolling panoramas had passed, but a new generation of artists were reaching the country that Alfred Jacob Miller, Karl Bodmer, and George Catlin had traveled over. In 1865, the American painter William Hays showed paintings from a journey up the Missouri to the Yellowstone, including a large and exquisitely detailed rendering of a *Bison Bull at Bay*, at Thomas McLean's Gallery in the Haymarket. Three years later, at the same gallery, Albert Bierstadt's enormous *Storm in the Rocky Mountains* was put on view.

The German-born Bierstadt was by then the most successful American artist, in terms of his output and earnings, with his reputation resting on his luminist paintings of American scenery. His series of "grand paintings" of the Rocky Mountains and California, made in the course of three trips, depicted the Far West in magnificent, idealized terms and the largest became one-off attractions in themselves, so well publicized that visitors would pay to see them. *Storm in the Rocky Mountains* had been shown in New York with a wigwam and part of the artist's own collection of Indian objects. Bierstadt's older rival, Frederic Church, had already shown his most dramatic pictures, including his *Niagara Falls*, in London. When Bierstadt followed him, lords and ladies flocked to the gallery, and he opened a studio and sold pictures to British patrons. He met Dickens and Tennyson, Landseer and Frith, the Duke of Argyll, William Gladstone, and the Prince of Wales.

It only remained for the Queen to give her blessing, too. On December 24, 1868, Victoria was staying in her palace on the Isle of Wight, for the Christmas holiday. Earlier in the week, two tall wooden packing cases had been sent down from London, taken across the Solent, and delivered to Osborne House. Albert Bierstadt followed, to supervise the unpacking and display. At noon, Bierstadt and his wife were presented to the Queen and members of the royal family in the drawing room. He showed them his magnum opus, *Storm in the Rocky Mountains*, twelve feet across, and the slightly smaller *The Rocky Mountains*, a scene of towering peaks, with radiant light, a waterfall, primeval trees and vines, and in the foreground a small group of Indians butchering a grizzly bear. Bierstadt's images, locked in the age of innocence, gave a misleading picture. Already questions of ownership and legality in the Far West, and the future of America's public lands, were starting to cloud the Edenic vision.

PART II

Staking a Claim

6

Private Paradise

What! An English "Milord," to lay claim to all the most
valuable land of Estes Park, that he and a few of his for-
eign bobs and nabobs, counts and no-accounts might have
a convenient place to hunt and fish? . . . the idea seems too
preposterous.

—*DENVER TRIBUNE*, 1874

On a bright crisp day in December 1872, the Earl of Dunraven and two titled friends, with Sandie Campbell, a hunting guide he had brought from Scotland, reached the top of the first ridge of the Rocky Mountain front, fifty miles north of Denver. They had been climbing up from the flat prairie land below for many hours, with a train of mules carrying their supplies, and a wagon loaded with guns and ammunition. By the time they reached the highest ridge, they had lost sight of the Great Plains, stretching behind them to the east, across Colorado and Kansas and all the way to the Missouri River. But when the Dunraven party looked directly west, a new vista opened up, under the intense milky blue sky. A long valley two or three miles wide lay below them, backed by a half circle of craggy snow-topped mountains, with Longs Peak rising to the left. Further ranges stretched away in the distance,

toward the Continental Divide and the Pacific. This was the fabled
hunting ground the British peer had been told about.

Clear in the cold dry air, they saw brown grassland broken by
stands of aspen and ponderosa pines, dusted with snow, with iced-
over streams glinting in the sunlight. As they followed a steep
and icy track down into the bowl known locally as Estes Park,
the hired men had to hold back the heavy wagon with ropes. Dunraven found the forests swarming with game. Staying in a cabin
that belonged to Griff Evans, a reclusive Welsh hunter who was
the park's only resident, they spent three weeks killing big-horned
mountain sheep, elk, and deer.

To the American mule handlers and wagon drivers who were
part of his traveling retinue, Lord Dunraven was as puzzling and
exotic a figure as most of the British aristocrats who had preceded
him west, from the time that Captain Stewart first rode alongside
a fur trade caravan in the early 1830s. Dunraven owned estates
in Wales and Ireland. Already wealthy from the agricultural rents
on his 40,000 acres, his income was now rising rapidly because
coal had been found under the family land in South Wales. By
1872, twenty-two colliery companies were paying him royalties of
£37,000 a year, and he was free to spend on an epic scale.

The earl had made three previous visits to the United States,
but he found this remote mountain area unlike anything he had
seen before. The hunting and scenery were so exceptional that he
decided to buy Estes Park, to reserve it for himself. The procedure for acquiring fresh federal land was complicated, and hedged
about with rules to favor the small settler, but land agents and
lawyers assured him that assembling a private hunting preserve
would be quite possible. In the summer of 1873 he came back
to Colorado, to start the process. Dunraven's move was, at that
stage, the most extensive foreign land purchase the territory had
ever known, and the advance to owning prime sections of the Far
West, rather than simply visiting, marked a further ratcheting up
of aristocratic involvement.

When Dunraven first saw his Colorado Shangri-La he was thirty-one, and had been in control of the family's burgeoning fortunes for just a year, after the death of his father. Until he became the fourth earl, he had carried the title of Viscount Adare. Growing up at the family's mansion near Limerick in the west of Ireland, he heard stories of bears and wolves at firsthand from Captain John Palliser, a family friend who came across from Waterford to visit. The grizzly bear slayer played Indians with the boy among the rhododendrons, and put up wigwams beside the small salmon river that rushed over a weir in front of the house and on through the deer park to join the Shannon. Adare Manor had been rebuilt by his grandfather in the Gothic Revival style, heavily embellished with marble and stained glass. Chimneypieces, staircases, and paneling were designed by Augustus Pugin. In the long library the young Adare could find well-bound copies of the major accounts of western exploration and travel, among them *The Journals of Lewis and Clark*, Ross Cox's *Columbia River*, and the Jesuit Father De Smet's *Oregon Missions and Travels in the Rocky Mountains*, as well as the books of the English travelers, including Murray and Palliser. But what he enjoyed reading most, at home and at school, were adventure stories set in the Far West.

Novels about the American frontier had moved well beyond James Fenimore Cooper, both geographically and in literary style. Having seen the massive sales achieved by Cooper and Washington Irving, not only in English but translated into almost all the European languages, other American writers came galloping in. As they competed to supply the ravenous demand for western stories, they shifted the focus beyond the Kansas and Nebraska territories, and set tales against the parched scrub and stony canyons of the Southwest. Most early western novels contained standard ingredients, and a cast that included plains travelers, scouts, scheming half-breeds, outlaws, and Indians. The "good" Indians were handsome, noble, and even saintly, while the hideously scarred "bad" Indians liked to roast their white captives over open fires, slice off their skin in strips, or use them as human targets. The narratives were equally predictable. Most amounted to little more than a series of loosely linked "desperate adventures," in which crafty ambushes were followed by firefights, desperate chases, captivity, inventive tortures, extraordinary rescues or escapes, and rapid and rough retribution.

European authors, acknowledging that their fellow countrymen were more excited by the Far West than by any other part of the world, began to write "westerns" of their own in German, French, Italian, Norwegian, even Hungarian, following the same formula. Gustave Aimard, the "French Fenimore Cooper," was able to move his pen so quickly that he could scratch out manuscripts for his Paris publishers at a rate of one a month. He achieved huge sales from the 1850s: *Les Pirates des prairies* and *Les Trappeurs de l'Arkansas* were followed by *La Loi de Lynch*. Translated into English, his stories sold hundreds of thousands of copies in cheap railway bookstall editions in the United States and Britain. Writing in a villa in Potsdam, Balduin Möllhausen earned the matching sobriquet as the "German Fenimore Cooper," starting with *The Half-Breed* in 1861. The British master of the western story, almost as prolific as Aimard, was Captain Mayne Reid, who had been educated in Ireland and then spent eight years in America. He sailed up the Mississippi from New Orleans and hunted in the Kansas Territory; then after a spell as a journalist in Philadelphia and New York, he volunteered for the U.S. Army in the short campaign against Mexico. His war experiences gave him the background for *The Rifle Rangers*, published in 1850, by which time he had returned to England.

Reid's ability to write quick-fire, action-packed prose was confirmed when his second book, *The Scalp Hunters* (1851), proved a runaway success. Because his short, vigorous paragraphs were so much easier to read than Cooper, his publisher advised him to concentrate on younger readers. In a short space of time he rattled out *The Desert Home, The Boy Hunters, Osceola, the Seminole, The White Chief, The Hunter's Feast,* and *The Headless Horseman.* The flamboyant Reid, whose rank of captain was in some doubt, wore a monocle, lemon yellow gloves, and suits in loud check patterns, and used his earnings to construct a sprawling Mexican-style hacienda, "The Ranche," near Gerrard's Cross in Buckinghamshire. New titles appeared throughout the 1850s and 1860s, and though he also based stories in India, Africa, the West Indies, and South America, he was always happiest among the Pawnees, the Apaches, and the Comanches. His gentler and more literary contemporary Robert Ballantyne, author of the children's classic *Coral Island,* felt obliged to follow him into the same territory with a number of fanciful yarns set in the American and Canadian West, including *The Prairie Chief* and *The Dog Crusoe: A Tale of the Western Prairies,* in which a faithful Newfoundland canine, with wondrous qualities of intelligence and courage, helps three young hunters on a mission of peace to the Indians.

The story of Reid's *Sculp Hunters* had a more conventional trajectory, following a wealthy Englishman as he took a steamboat up the river to St. Louis and joined a party of traders heading along the Santa Fe Trail from Independence. Critics carped that Reid's novels lacked plots, but between the strung-together incidents and the narrow escapes he made prairie life seem almost irresistible and showed how travelers could be gripped by it. Near the start of *The Scalp Hunters,* Reid picked up on a term and a diagnosis by then in common use. His traveler has spent several days crossing the prairie, and is approaching the Arkansas River: "What with the wild gallops by day, and the wilder tales by the night watch-fires, I became intoxicated with the romance of my new life. I had caught the 'prairie fever!' So my companions told me, laughing! I did not understand them then. I knew what they meant afterwards. The prairie fever! Yes. I was just then in the process of being inoculated by that strange disease. It grew upon me apace. . . ."

Responding to the prairie effect, Mayne Reid's hero finds himself undergoing a transformation:

> My strength increased both physically and intellectually. I experienced a buoyancy of spirits and a vigour of body I had never known before. I felt a pleasure in action. My blood seemed to rush warmer and swifter through my veins; and I fancied my eyes reached to a more distant vision. I could look boldly upon the sun, without quivering in my gaze. Had I imbibed a portion of the divine essence that lives, and moves, and has its being in those vast solitudes? Who can answer this?
>
> The prairie fever! I feel it now! While I am penning these memories, my fingers twitch to grasp the reins—my knees quiver to press the sides of my noble horse, and wildly wander over the verdant billows of the prairie sea."[1]

A whole new generation of boys were inspired by this, as their fathers had been excited by *Last of the Mohicans*, and Cooper was still being read as well.

Viscount Adare, the future 4th Earl of Dunraven, was ten when *The Scalp Hunters* appeared, and at the end of each year through the 1850s the latest Mayne Reid was always on the publisher's "Christmas list for boys." Adare read them all voraciously. He was independent and active, shooting rabbits on his father's estates, and sailing small boats from Garinish Island, off the coast of Kerry. After Oxford, he joined the 1st Life Guards. When he traveled to the United States for the first time, in 1869, the scenes that had imprinted themselves during his childhood were as compelling as ever, and he went with every intention of shooting big game and crossing the Rockies. "I was young," he wrote, ". . . not yet twenty-eight years of age; and my boyish brain-cells were stored to bursting with tales of Red Indians, and grizzly bears, caballeros and haciendas, prairies and buffaloes, Texans and Mexicans, cowboys and voyageurs.

. . . I was in search of such sports as, under the circumstances, were to be found."[2]

Circumstances were against him on his first trip, because this was also his honeymoon. His bride, Florence, daughter of Lord Charles Lennox Kerr, was more interested in making a leisurely circuit of east coast society than heading for the backwoods. The couple went to Philadelphia, Washington, Virginia, and then upper New York State. Dunraven managed to get to Cooperstown and Otsego Lake, to see the landscape that inspired *Last of the Mohicans*, before they reached the summer resort of Saratoga Springs. Then they moved on to Newport, Rhode Island, where British aristocrats were always well received. After this, Dunraven had planned to break off and go west for some shooting, but they dallied for too long with the super-rich, and were further delayed when he was ill for several weeks.

When they finally left New York, in early October, the Dunravens hooked themselves onto a party led by the transatlantic cable promoter Cyrus Field, who was taking a group of wealthy friends to see the sights of frontier America, now that the railway made it possible to do this in such comfort. Traveling west on the Kansas Pacific route from Kansas City, they saw the new wheat fields and the ripening heads of Indian corn, and occasional signs of habitation. "Very curious are these small settlements, some of them consisting of only two or three mud, or rather adobe, houses, or a few wooden shanties . . . ," wrote Dunraven. "They look as if providence had been carrying a box of toy houses, and had dropped the lid and spilt the contents on the earth. The houses have all come down right-end-uppermost, it is true, but otherwise they show no evidence of design; they are scattered around in every conceivable direction, dumped down anywhere, apparently without any particular motive or reason for being so situated."[3] At that time the line reached only as far as Sheridan, Kansas, and they continued by Concord coach for the last 250 miles, over the Colorado border to Denver.

Like most first-time visitors, they were struck by the dramatic beauty of Denver's position, with the Rocky Mountain range looming up on the western skyline only fourteen miles away. The brash, lively town had been settled ten years earlier, on a roll of the prairie beside the South Platte, and was growing rich with the mining boom. New buildings in brick and stone were going up for banks and stores, replacing the first cabins and wooden frame buildings, and shade trees were being planted along the grid of streets. The population had reached 5,000. There was no time for the hunting trip Dunraven had been looking forward to before the winter set in. But having glimpsed the high country, and heard all the talk of big game at Charpiot's Hotel, he was determined to come back the following summer. The earl would continue to return to the West, sometimes making several visits a year, for the next sixteen years.

Though he was to attract as much American opprobrium as any British blue blood, Dunraven was more open-minded and progressive than some of the aristocrats who had come before him. Though sport was still the main concern in his well-provided-for life, he could be analytical about what he enjoyed, and his tastes were modern. He belonged to London's slightly bohemian Savage Club, whose members included writers, actors, and musicians, and he played the banjo at smoking concerts. He put money into a new theater, the Opera Comique, off the Strand. He dabbled in spiritualism, and was fascinated by psychic phenomena and poltergeists. For a time he fell into the thrall of the fashionable Scottish medium David Dunglas Home, and maintained that at one séance he had seen a grand piano levitated several inches off the floor and heard a spirit play "The Last Rose of Summer" on an unmanned accordion.

Dunraven wrote fluently, producing a stream of articles and books about travel and hunting. It was a sign of his more enlightened attitude that on his second trip to America he again took his wife, Lady Florence, out to the prairies with him, to what other aristocrats had hitherto thought of as an exclusively male preserve. At that stage there was no thought of buying land, and he planned a foray of just a few weeks. Their path was eased, in the traditional manner for the grandest British visitors, by high-level introductions. In Chicago, Dunraven met the Civil War hero General Philip Sheridan, now in command of the Missouri Department of the U.S. Army, charged with policing the Plains Indians, increasingly warlike as their plight became more desperate. Sheridan referred him to the officer in command at Fort McPherson, the army post built to protect travelers on the Oregon and California trails, and keep watch on the Sioux and the Cheyenne in western Nebraska.

Getting to the departure point for a prairie hunt had never been less onerous. The first transcontinental railway had been completed in the previous year, and the Union Pacific's track ran in a straight line west from Omaha to pick up the wide, sandy, shifting Platte River and follow the route across the plains taken by the fur trade mule trains and Captain Stewart, and the emigrants in their slow Conestoga wagons. The Dunravens, with the earl's doctor, George Kingsley, made the journey from the Missouri to the station that served Fort McPherson in less than twenty-four hours, in the stuffy comfort of a Pullman palace car, lined with wooden marquetry, mirrors, and etched glass in ormolu frames, with tasseled and brocaded seats that converted into sleeping berths at night. Dunraven described the moment of arrival at the small halt:

We found ourselves, when we stepped on to the platform, plunged suddenly into the wild and woolly West. For a few moments only the place was all alive with bustle and confusion. The train represented everything that was civilized; all the luxuries that could be carried in a train were to be found on board of it; the people were all clothed in fashionable dresses; it was like a slice out of one of the Eastern cities

set down bodily in the midst of a perfect wilderness. In a few
seconds it was gone, civilization vanished with it, the station
relapsed into its normal condition of despoliation, and we were
almost alone in the heart of the desert.[4]

While they were still standing on the platform and their baggage and guns were being loaded onto an army wagon that would
take them across to the fort on the other side of the North Platte,
two horsemen cantered up in the Nebraska evening, and threw
their reins over a post. They turned out to be William Cody, the
guide General Sheridan had recommended, and his assistant
John Omohondro, also known as "Texas Jack." Cody was already
referred to as "Buffalo Bill." "I had never seen two more picturesque figures. Both were tall, well built, active-looking men, with
singularly handsome features . . . ," wrote Dunraven. "Jack, tall
and lithe, with light brown close-cropped hair, clear laughing honest blue eyes, and a soft winning smile might have sat as a model
for a typical modern Anglo-Saxon. . . ."[5] In his view, Buffalo Bill
and Texas Jack were "the finest specimens of their race" to be
found anywhere.

Luckily, Cody's experience with British gentlemen on the plains
had been happier than that of some of the other hunting guides.
Before Dunraven, he had been retained by a genial knight from
Dorset, Sir John Watts Garland, who was as flexible and sympathetic as the Honorable Grantley Berkeley of Gloucestershire had
proved rigid and arrogant. Sir John had agreed on the virtue of
the "unicorn" western saddle that Berkeley had so despised, and
had appeared almost democratic. According to Cody, "When he
went out with a party he roughed it like the rest of us, slept in
the open on his blanket, took his turn at camp duty, and rode his
own horse in the races which we often got up for our amusement."[6]
Cody already had a reputation beyond Fort McPherson, and his
exploits were being recounted in magazine articles and dime novels. But it was Texas Jack whom Dunraven took to most, and he

would continue to engage Jack as a guide for years to come, not just in Nebraska but in Colorado, Montana, and Canada.

The 5th Cavalry at Fort McPherson received the Dunravens hospitably, and offered the earl an escort of soldiers to protect him from Indians. "The next morning, after paying some visits and making some preliminary arrangements for a hunt, I wandered off a little distance and sat down on the trunk of a fallen tree, and tried to realize that I was in the middle of these prairies that, thanks to Captain Mayne Reid, had haunted my boyish dreams. . . ." Dunraven's first response to the landscape was not the immediate rapture so many of his predecessors had felt, and not what he expected. Rather, "I was oppressed by the vastness of the country, the stillness and the boundlessness of the plains seemed to press like a weight upon my spirit. . . ." He blamed his feeling of melancholia on the heat, the eerie silence, and the monotonous gray-brown coloring of the dry grass and tired stands of cottonwood at the end of summer. After a few days he recovered. "It was with a feeling almost of exultation that I at last found myself riding on the boundless prairie, the tall flagstaff and the wooden houses of the fort fading in the distance, and before me nothing but the illimitable wilderness."[7]

The size of the game was specially important to Dunraven, and he hoped to find wapiti, or what in the United States were called elk, the largest member of the deer family. The party intercepted them on the third day out. Dr. Kingsley, who had served as personal physician to the Marquis of Aylesbury, the Duke of Norfolk, and the Duke of Sutherland, and had been brought along out of Dunraven's concern that his illness of the previous summer might reoccur, was almost overcome with excitement. "This elk running is perfectly magnificent . . . ," he wrote back to his wife. "We ride among the wild sand hills till we find a herd, and then gallop after them like maniacs, cutting them off till we get in the midst of them, when we shoot all that we can."[8]

Going after elk from a horse was held to be more exciting than

pursuing buffalo, which hurtled along in a straight line, whereas
the elk liked to dart and weave and run round in circles. Dunraven described his triumphs, as animal after animal fell to his
Express rifle: "I stuck to my deer, though he doubled and turned
in all directions, and at last by a lucky shot turned him over like
a rabbit, a fact which I announced by a yell which I should think
must have been heard in the settlements." If such moments had
been described many times before, he was not as tough as some,
and showed signs of emotional fragility. He was the first to admit
to instances of severe post-Nimrod depression. He confessed that
after one run, he was

> utterly and completely lost as far as finding my way back to
> camp was concerned, and I began all at once to feel a sense
> of dismalness creep over me. A sudden reaction set in after
> the great excitement I had enjoyed. Only a few seconds before
> I had been careering at full gallop over the prairie, shout-
> ing from sheer exuberance of spirits, every nerve in a state
> of intense excitation, the blood coursing madly through every
> artery and vein, every muscle and sinew strained to the utter-
> most, bestriding an animal in an equal state of excitement,
> and pursuing a herd of living creatures, all instinct with life
> and violent movement. In a second it was all gone . . . there
> was not a living creature to be seen, and the oppressive silence
> was unbroken by the faintest sound. I looked all around the
> horizon; not a sign of life; everything seemed dull, dead, quiet,
> unutterably sad and melancholy. The change was very strange,
> the revulsion of feeling very violent and not agreeable.[9]

Dunraven climbed to the top of a sandhill, waited till he saw
another of his party in the distance, then slowly rode back to
rejoin him.

They hunted buffalo with Cody, as well as elk, but Dunraven did
not care for it, sharing Captain Ruxton's revisionist opinion that

the lumbering beasts were an overrated and unworthy quarry—
"It is exciting . . . but it is scarcely sport."[10] His companion Dr.
Kingsley agreed. "It is a thing to do once; but for sport, No, Sir!"
The doctor was even more dismissive about the slack and lazy
practice of shooting them from the ground. "As for stalking a single buffalo, I would as soon stalk an old woman, stone deaf and
parcel blind, picking up sticks to boil her kettle with. . . ."[11]

Though Dunraven made several more visits to Nebraska and
Fort McPherson, he had by then hunted in Montana and Colorado, and found he was happiest further west, in the Rockies. "The
prairie is the place to go if you want a big bag, but for true sport
commend me to the forest and the hills. To me at least there is
infinitely more charm in stalking wapiti among the mountains, in
the magnificent scenery to be found there, than in running them
on the plains. . . ." He considered that picking a handsome wapiti
stag, and creeping up to him, was as fine an activity as could be
found anywhere in the world: "it is like deerstalking in Scotland,
with everything in grand proportions, mountains many thousand
feet in height, instead of hills of a few hundred, and a magnificent
animal weighing 600 or 800 pounds instead of a comparatively
small deer which would not turn the scale at twenty stone."[12]

It was a sign of changing times and attitudes that Dunraven
felt the need to justify the natural instincts of the British aristocrat and present them in the best possible light. He maintained,
to his readers at home, that hunting was not a barbarous, blood-
thirsty pursuit but a science, requiring years of study and hard
work: "Every good hunter will agree with me that it is not the
killing of the animal that gives pleasure. The charm lies in overcoming difficulties—in matching your natural intelligence and
acquired knowledge and skill against the instinct, cunning, intellect and reason the animal you are endeavouring to outwit. . . ."
More than ten years before Theodore Roosevelt wrote *The Wilderness Hunter*, Dunraven made the wider environmental and philosophical case for hunting, and the virtues of the free, self-reliant

adventurous life. But he was more defensive than Roosevelt, whom he met several times. "It is the fact of overcoming, not the act of killing, that brightens the hunter's eye, and renders his occupation so charming. The hunter's craft gives health, its sur- roundings are beautiful, it calls forth some of the best qualities of man, it is full of fascination. . . . It is most annoying that every- thing that is pleasant is all wrong."[13]

Though he did not share the respect that the earlier grandees had felt for the Indians, he was quite aware of the cost as well as the benefit of civilization, and the paradox of progress: "This is the sequence—hunting, cattle-tending, sheep-herding, fresh air, good water, lovely scenery, wholesome excitement, healthy lives, and—barbarism; agriculture, manufactures, great cities, hideous country, poisoned water, impure air, dirt, disease, and civiliza- tion. It is difficult sometimes to know exactly what to say when preaching civilization to a savage."[14]

Dunraven continued to spent a large part of each year trying to outwit antelope, black and grizzly bears, mountain sheep, and moose, up and down the Rockies. Some British visitors, whose manner had made for difficulties, put it about that their American hired help were rough and disagreeable. Dunraven, with more emotional intelligence, defended the guides and packers stoutly: "to a stranger who knows how to behave they are, as far as my experience goes, most civil and obliging. If a man is civil to them, they will be civil to him. . . . Of course if a man gives himself airs he must expect to pay for it."[15]

In 1874, Dunraven went up to the Montana Territory and the higher reaches of the Yellowstone River to see the spectacular scenery and natural wonders that had just been protected by the creation of the first National Park, and to hunt over country that remained very hard to reach. The northern Pacific line was not yet built. He took Dr. Kingsley; his cousin Captain Wynne; his Scottish gillie Sandie Campbell; Valentine Bromley, a London artist hired to record the trip with paintings and sketches; and

View of St. Louis, Missouri, looking across the Mississippi River from the east bank, at the time when the first British aristocrats were reaching the city, in the early 1830s. Painting by Leon Pomarade.

Breakfast at Sunrise. The slow journey across the prairies to the Rockies could take the fur trade caravans eight weeks. In 1837 Sir William Drummond Stewart hired his own artist, Alfred Jacob Miller, to record the daily routine.

Attack by the Crows. Sir William Drummond Stewart and his hunter, Antoine Clement, face up to a band of Indians who went on to rob his party of their horses, supplies, and arms. Miller's picture was based on Stewart's account of the 1833 incident, in which he had been lucky to escape with his life.

Sir William Drummond Stewart, who spent seven years traveling and hunting in the Far West. Portrait by Henry Inman. Joslyn Art Museum.

Two of a set of buffalo chairs, specially carved in mahogany to the order of Sir William for use at Murthly, his castle in Perthshire, Scotland.

THE LAST

OF

THE MOHICANS;

A NARRATIVE OF 1757.

"Mislike me not, for my complexion,
The shadowed livery of the burnished sun."

BY THE AUTHOR OF "THE PILOT,"
"THE SPY," &c.

REVISED, CORRECTED,
AND ILLUSTRATED WITH A NEW INTRODUCTION, ETC.
BY THE AUTHOR.

LONDON:
HENRY COLBURN AND RICHARD BENTLEY,
NEW BURLINGTON STREET;
BELL AND BRADFUTE, EDINBURGH;
AND CUMMING, DUBLIN.
1832.

THE PRAIRIE:

A TALE.

Mark his condition and the event ; then
Tell me if this be a brother.   Tempest.

BY J. F. COOPER.

REVISED, CORRECTED,
AND ILLUSTRATED WITH A NEW INTRODUCTION, NOTES, ETC.
BY THE AUTHOR.

LONDON:
HENRY COLBURN AND RICHARD BENTLEY,
NEW BURLINGTON STREET:
BELL AND BRADFUTE, EDINBURGH;
CUMMING, DUBLIN; AND
GALIGNANI, PARIS.
1832.

The "Leatherstocking" stories of James Fenimore Cooper, in particular
The Last of the Mohicans, helped fire British interest in the American
frontier. In *The Prairie,* Cooper moved his Natty Bumppo character a
thousand miles west, from the forests of New York to the prairies

A procession of Snake Indians ride toward Sir William Drummond Stewart
(right, on a white horse) as they greet him at the 1837 fur trade rendezvous,
in the valley of the Green River. Miller's huge painting *Cavalcade* was completed when he came back from the Rockies.

The Egyptian Hall, on Piccadilly, where a series of western American attractions were staged in the 1830s and '40s and were received by Londoners with mounting enthusiasm.

The American artist George Catlin brought his exhibition of Indian pictures and artifacts across the Atlantic in 1840.

Banvard's immense picture had to compete with a rival journey up the Mississippi showing at a gallery in Leicester Square.

Queen Victoria (left foreground) watches Ojibbeway Indians perform a war dance at Windsor Castle in 1843. George Catlin, with hand outstretched, provides a commentary. Sketch by Catlin.

Another American artist shows the Queen and her family more scenes from the west in 1849. John Banvard displays his "moving panorama" in the same hall where the Indians had danced.

The Honorable Grantley Berkeley wrote a self-glorifying account of a brief hunting trip to Kansas in 1859, made for *The Field*.

THE BISON'S CHARGE.

THE VANQUISHED FOE. (Page 293).

Rejecting the standard western design, Berkeley put a light English saddle on his horse. Though Americans mocked some of his claims, the book brought many more "buffalo tourists" across the Atlantic.

A SWELL SPORT ON A BUFFALO HUNT.
Aw - I say ! Don't see any Buffalo !

A SWELL SPORT STAMPEDED.
By Jove - I say ! Was that an Earthquake ?

An American response to British upper-class buffalo hunters, from the popular illustrator Thomas Worth, in a pair of 1882 lithographic prints published by Currier and Ives, New York.

THE
BOY'S OWN PAPER

No. 74.—Vol. II.   SATURDAY, JUNE 12, 1880.   Price One Penny.
[ALL RIGHTS RESERVED.

BEN NORTON:
A FRONTIER STORY.

BY S. S. ROBBINS, U.S.A.

CHAPTER V.

THE Indians, alarmed at the unexpected reception they had met, disappeared rapidly from sight, and the little party were at liberty to do all they could for the dying man. It was now broad daylight. They piled together whatever they had that would make a bed, his wife sitting by him with his head raised upon her arm, and the rough frontiersmen, used to sudden and cruel deaths, standing around him, with husked and tender faces, waiting for the end.

"Is there no one here who can pray for me?" said the faltering voice. "'Now I ay me—' No, not that; that's my

"So close that one shied, and hollowed as it caught sight of him."

The buffalo were almost gone from the plains by 1880, but continued to stampede in the pages of magazines for young readers.

William Close, a well-connected banker's son and Cambridge oarsman, whose belief in American land values led him to start a British colony in Iowa.

Frederick Close, William's younger brother, was a role model for other colonists. He found time for football, athletics, and horse racing, and introduced polo.

SUPPER WITH THE HERDER.

A *Harper's* cartoon from 1880 notes a new and fashionable presence on the range.

COLONISING IN IOWA, U.S.

(*A Hint to the Younger Sons of our Aristocracy, and eke to the Daughters thereof.*)

Lady Maria. "HOW LATE YOU ARE, BOYS! YOUR BATHS ARE READY, AND I'VE MENDED YOUR DRESS TROUSERS, JACK. SO LOOK SHARP AND CLEAN YOURSELVES, AND THEN YOU CAN LAY THE CLOTH, AND KEEP AN EYE ON THE MUTTON WHILE EMILY AND I ARE DRESSING FOR DINNER."

Lord John. "ALL RIGHT. HOW MANY ARE WE TO LAY FOR?"

Lady Emily. "EIGHT. THE TALBOTS ARE COMING, AND MAJOR CECIL IS GOING TO BRING THE DUKE OF STILTON, WHO'S STOP-PING WITH HIM."

A year after the American *Harper's*, the British magazine *Punch* makes fun of the same aristocratic influx in a cartoon that appeared in November 1881.

Young members of the short-lived British colony at Runnymede, near Harper, Kansas, pose in their western working clothes.

Murray Faulkner, who farmed at Runnymede.

Yours Sincerely
Murrae Faulkner
Feb. 25th 1890

Paul MacGregor, who had come out in a group of gentleman settlers.

A summer afternoon on the prairie in Harper County, southeast Kansas, in the late 1880s. With a tennis club, a steeplechase course, and a full program of sport and social activities, farming took second place.

Moreton Frewen, most ambitious of the British ranchers in Wyoming. For a time his fortunes rose with the cattle boom, but he overreached himself.

The Honorable Claud Anson, a younger son of the Earl of Lichfield, who put his inheritance into cattle and land.

The Cheyenne Club, in Cheyenne, Wyoming, provided a comfortable refuge for ranchers during the free range cattle boom, and many of the members were British aristocrats.

Scenes from the annual roundup at Claud Anson's Kickapoo Ranch, near San Angelo, Texas, in the 1880s, with the chuckwagon that served the team of roundup cowboys, and the branding of the season's new calves.

The Honorable William Anson (with banjo) at his ranch at Valera, Coleman County. Older brother Claud is behind him in a rocking chair, brother Frank is seated on the left. The three sons of Lord Lichfield all bought ranches in the same part of Texas.

The 4th Earl of Dunraven made many sporting trips to the Far West and invested in the cattle business. But his purchase of a private hunting preserve in the high country of Colorado met fierce opposition.

Cattle Lords Among the many senior aristocrats who put money into cattle ranches in the 1880s were (in descending order on the page, above and right) the Earl of Airlie, who bought land and set up his son in Colorado; the Earl of Wharncliffe and the Duke of Manchester, who both took large stakes in the Powder River Cattle Company in Wyoming; and the Marquess of Tweeddale, chairman of the company that owned the huge XIT Ranch in Texas.

HIS GRACE THE DUKE OF SUTHERLAND, K.G.

The immensely wealthy 3rd Duke of Sutherland, who toured the United States by private train in 1881, caricatured by *Punch*. Though he had already put money into American railway companies, his purchase of western land brought a political outcry.

Lord Dunraven paid Albert Bierstadt $15,000 to paint a picture that would remind him of Estes Park, in Colorado, which he had just bought for himself. *The Rocky Mountains, Longs Peak* showed the view from the site of Dunraven's house.

his collie dog Tweed. Texas Jack was leader and guide, and Maxwell, a Negro cook, also acted as barber.

Dunraven's first independent and sustained sortie followed in a long tradition of wealthy men's pleasure excursions, but his outfit could be smaller because there was no need for a long preliminary crossing of the prairies, and the Indians in the area were not a threat. In marked contrast to the earlier expeditions, where the carting of home comforts and luxuries into the wilderness became part of the challenge in itself, simplicity and reversion to the backwoods life was part of the appeal. There were no iron bedsteads or striped tents. They traveled light, trapper style, with a small column of horses and mules, taking only flour, sugar, coffee, and basic supplies, and expecting to procure their own meat on the way. They wrapped and tied their own packs, collected their own wood, and wore deerskin trousers and flannel shirts rather than gentlemen's shooting clothes.

They visited the Crow Indians, who had reluctantly accepted the fate Washington had decided for them, on their reservation. Dunraven described the territory they crossed on their way up to the Yellowstone country, with its jagged peaks, deep canyons, waterfalls, and geyser basins. He entirely supported the creation of the National Park, accepting that if the federal government had not stepped in, the sights would have been pounced upon by speculators and "the beauties of Nature, disposed of to the highest bidder." He had been shocked by the commercialization he had seen at Niagara, where all the viewpoints had been bought up, so that tourists had to pay to see the falls. "Nothing is more revolting to our instincts, more disgraceful to our civilization, than the system of trafficking in the charms with which nature is so beautifully endowed."[16]

In his book *The Great Divide*, illustrated by Bromley, Dunraven recorded the atmosphere of the jaunt, and adventures and mishaps, which at times reads like *Three Men in a Boat*. Running to escape from a grizzly bear, Dr. Kingsley was "treed." Happily,

said the earl, "your grizzly . . . is no gymnast, and from the security of a treetop a man can laugh his adversary to scorn."

Their trip was characterized by a peculiarly English style of
banter, born of private school and the officers' mess. While making
their way through high-altitude pine forests, Wynne "enlivened
the road with humorous stories; and many a song, composed and
sung by some campfire in the Crimea, or in some far-away bivouac
of India, rang through the forest and awakened the echoes."[17] The
men kept up their spirits composing light ditties that would have
been normal at one of the Savage Club's musical evenings, or the
Opera Comique, but were new to Texas Jack and Maxwell the
cook. After many days of appalling weather, with torrential rain,
the horses losing their footing and floundering, they sang dolefully, to the tune of "Ten Thousand Miles Away":

It snows, it blows, and rains, and then begins to freeze;
All sodden is the ground, and all dripping are the trees;
The hill tops are all crowded in impenetrable fog,
The creeks they are all flooded , and the valley is a bog.
I have wet breeches on my legs, a wet shirt on my back,
I've lost my hat and spectacles, and busted my shupack;
The horses have stampeded, the mules are gone astray;,
My own dog snarled and bit me, and then he ran away.
My tent is full of holes, and my bedding it is damp;
The ground is quite a puddle, it's a miserable camp;
The fires wont burn, but are betwixt and likewise are between,
Half flame, half smoke are they, for the wood is much too green.[18]

When it was all over, the tribulations and discomforts were far
outweighed by pleasanter memories and the thrills of the chase.
Dunraven chided his stay-at-home contemporaries in London,
suggesting it would do them good to come and taste the bracing
western life. "Think of it, ye fashionables, ye toilers of the season,
who pass laborious days panting in the dusty jam of a London

summer, and spend perspiring nights on a staircase, inhaling
your fellow-creatures, absorbing fat dowagers, breathing men and
women!"[19]

Once back home himself, evening parties aside, Dunraven
became increasingly involved in politics and Irish affairs. He was
a director of a bank and a railway company in addition to his coal
mines, and he backed a new shipping line that would shorten the
transatlantic journey by sailing from southwest Wales rather than
Liverpool. In addition to Adare Manor he kept up a London house
off Park Lane; Kenry House, a small estate at Kingston in Surrey;
and Dunraven Castle, on the coast of Glamorgan in South Wales.
But as the earl traveled between London, Cardiff, Liverpool, the
Shelbourne Hotel in Dublin, and Limerick on private and political
business, the Far West was seldom out of his thoughts. He compared his urge to go back to the instincts of a salmon which had to
return to the sea: "Towards the end of August or September, any
man who has once been in the woods will begin to feel stirring
within him a restless craving for the forest— an intense desire to
escape from civilization, a yearning to kick off his boots, and with
them all the restraints, social and material, of ordinary life; and
to revel once again in the luxury of moccasins, loose garments,
absolute freedom of mind and body. . . ."[20]

To Americans, the extension of the frontier into and across the
Rockies was another chapter of a work in progress. Whether they
were prospecting for minerals across difficult country, standing
knee-deep in icy streams to wash gravel for specks of gold, fell-
ing timber on steep hillsides for railway ties, or building trestle
bridges over gorges, the mountains and forests were a place of
risk, hard labor, and exertion. Meanwhile, British aristocrats continued to see them in purely recreational terms. The 4th Earl of
Dunraven was aware of his good fortune.

It is very pleasant to lie comfortably stretched out with nothing to do but to gaze with idle pleasure and complete content

upon grand and varied scenery . . . mountain, valley, cliff, and glade are so mingled, and are so constantly changing with light and shade, that one could look for hours without a wish to move. The mind goes half asleep, and wonders lazily whether its body is really there in the heart of the Rocky Mountains leading a hunter's life, or whether it is all a dream—a dream of schoolboy days which seemed at one time so little likely to be realized, and yet which is at length fulfilled.[21]

Though he hunted in New Mexico, Nebraska, Wyoming, Montana, and in Canada, the earl quickly concluded there was nowhere to match the region he had first visited in 1869, near the end of his honeymoon. Colorado was seen as a place that was exceptionally blessed, with its wealth from gold and silver, fine conditions for agriculture, invigorating climate, and good communications. By 1872, Denver was a crossing point for five railway lines. When Isabella Bird came through on her way back from the Pacific in 1873, she found the city a bustling place that had moved beyond its initial frontier rawness and noted that "one no longer sees men dangling to the lamp-posts when one looks out in the morning!" Though Denver was still lined with drinking saloons for miners and ranch hands, it had good shops and fair hotels. In the crowded streets she saw a mix of "men of the Plains with belts and revolvers, in great blue coats, relics of the war; teamsters in leathern suits; horsemen in fur coats and caps . . . rich English sporting tourists, clean, comely and supercilious looking; and hundreds of Indians on their small ponies. . . ."[22]

Colorado's boosters referred to it as "the Switzerland of America," and in an article in *The Nineteenth Century*, the Earl of Dunraven's own checklist of the features that made the territory so attractive included the enhanced quality of the sunrises, sunsets, and rainbows, the brilliancy of the stars in the night sky, and the wonderful winter weather. Heavy snowstorms blew up suddenly but cleared just as rapidly, to be followed by calm days of warm sunshine that melted the snow quickly and left the ground clear. He wrote even more expressively about the summer, when the quivering aspens bent over banks bright with flowers, "the air is scented with the sweet-smelling sap of the pines, an occasional humming bird whirrs among the shrubs, trout leap in the creeks, insects buzz in the air; all nature is active and exuberant with life." Like so many others, he appreciated the high altitude and the dry air. "The climate is health giving—unsurpassed anywhere—giving to the jaded spirit, the unstrung nerves and weakened body a stimulant, a tone, and a vigour. . . ."[23]

As these rhapsodic accounts were published, tourists arrived by rail from the East and overseas. Ornate wooden hotels, creaking noisily and smelling of pine, were built to accommodate them in scenic spots served by the railway. It was even suggested that married couples might try a light camping break:

Colorado, to camp-out in during the summer, is little short of paradise. . . . When one considers that Pueblo or Denver is only seventeen days from Liverpool, the wonder is that it is not a more general resort of health and pleasure seekers. Horses, mules and wagons are very cheap; and with a wagon and a pony, a tent and blankets, a few cooking utensils, a good English No. 12 shot gun, a Winchester rifle, and a couple of fishing rods, a man and his wife might have three months of the most delightful wandering amongst grand and silent nature, undisturbed by any of the ills or dangers that flesh is climatically or financially heir to, for £250.[24]

Visitors were drawn not just by the grandeur of the Front range itself, but by the special quality of the country that lay just behind it. On the western side of the range a series of upland bowls were cradled between folds of the mountains. They were too wide and extended to properly be called valleys, but not level enough to be plateaux. The broad green basins, with sides made irregular by spurs from the mountains, contained open pastures and rich stands of timber, and were known as "the parks." In a region in which nature could be seen at its most savage, with skylines of snow and granite, vertiginous slopes strewn with boulders, roaring rivers, and deep forests, Colorado's natural parks appeared as softer. European visitors could imagine they had been artificially laid out by some eighteenth-century landscape gardener, with artfully positioned clumps of trees and distant views of water. North Park, Middle Park, South Park, the San Luis Park, and innumerable smaller equivalents all stood at altitudes of between 9,000 and 10,000 feet above sea level, 4,000 feet higher than the prairie at Denver. The South Park, the "Bayou Salado," provided an idyllic camp for Captain Ruxton for several months, and for the Honorable Charles Fitzwilliam. Sir George Gore and Sir William Drummond Stewart both hunted through the Middle Park.

What had changed by the 1870s was that wealthy British were coming not just to shoot or camp but to buy their own stake in this favored area, and Dunraven's decision to buy Estes Park was an extension of a trend. On the plains around Denver and further south there were many new ranches and horse farms, owned by British incomers attracted by the climate and the prospects, and invalids came for their health. A Harley Street doctor opened a hotel and spa at Menetou. A whole settlement grew around Colorado Springs, known as "little London," and the property sales were uncontroversial and largely welcome. On one level, Dunraven's well-publicized purchase seemed a shrewd and timely move, made just at the moment that interest in Colorado was rising, along with land prices.

In 1876 a British journalist, Nugent Townshend, who had himself bought land in Kansas and wrote regularly for *The Field*, extolled the beauty of one of the smaller upland bowls near the Sangre Grande Mountains. "What a spot for a residence this fine natural park would make!" he reported; ". . . glades, dells, smooth sloping lawns, thickets, clumps, and single trees are scattered

around about, now thickly, now thinly, here enclosing 20 acres,
there 1,000. If any man wants to plant with taste, let him study
nature here; not one foot of this land is taken up, it is all to be had
for the asking by naturalized citizens." Townshend thought the
parks had little future for agriculture, since the grass was poor
for cattle compared with the prairies below. Yet their value for
sport, and health, was so exceptional that "the wonder is that only
Lord Dunraven has, from the eastern world, picked up 'for a song'
a park in the western hemisphere which laughs to scorn the beauties of home ones." Using a term normally applied to the principal
country mansion of a landed aristocrat, Townshend referred to
Estes Park as "the charming and picturesque seat of the Earl of
Dunraven. . . ."[25] In other despatches *The Field*, always in touch
with its readers' interests, began regular reports on the Far West
as a place for possible settlement, not just for hunting.

By 1876, the year that the United States was celebrating its
Centonnial in Philadelphia, Dunraven was ready to seal his purchase of the park with a grand gesture. He called on the man then
acknowledged to be the master of great American landscapes,
Albert Bierstadt, whose paintings of the Rockies had been exhibited in London and seen by Queen Victoria, to come and paint
it for him. Dunraven had met Bierstadt in New York, where the
artist courted the rich and powerful who might buy his pictures.
The earl had been invited out to Bierstadt's newly built château
on the Hudson, at Irvington, bought with the fortune he had made
selling pictures to some of the wealthiest industrialists of the day.
The two men went moose hunting in Canada together. At the end
of the year, Dunraven gave a commission to Bierstadt, and a price
of $15,000 was agreed for a picture of Estes Park, slightly less
than the rate the artist was used to commanding, but still a huge
sum for the time.

Dunraven insisted on a realistic view, without the picturesque rearrangements and enhancements on nature that marked
Bierstadt's other western pictures, and the two men went out to

Denver so the painter could make preliminary sketches. In fine winter weather, almost windless under a typically cloudless sky, they rode and hunted in the park, and compared various viewpoints from which the picture could be painted. They chose a spot on high ground close to Fish Creek, south of the cabins owned by the first settler, Griff Evans, at the eastern end of the park. Bierstadt came back again the following summer, to make final sketches and notes. The picture that resulted, *The Rocky Mountains, Longs Peak*, was finished that December and shown briefly in New York at the Century Club, and then in Boston, before being shipped to London. The canvas, over eight feet across and five feet high, was exhibited at the Royal Academy in 1878, before it was sent to Adare Manor. Dunraven bought several other smaller landscapes from Bierstadt, and already had pictures of the Crow Indians painted by his Yellowstone protégé Valentine Bromley.

Dunraven could keep his western paintings privately, for his own enjoyment, on his own terms, but he had more difficulty with the real thing. He quickly discovered that the pace of change was moving even faster than he thought, and Estes Park's reputation was already too well known for him to be able to close it off as he had hoped. Too many others wanted to see it, or hunt through it. Griff Evans continued to rent out cabins at Fish Creek, for $8 a week including meals and the use of a horse. Isabella Bird was one of those who came up, staying for a month in the autumn of 1873, when the purchase was still going through. "In this glorious upper world . . . ," she wrote, "with the mountain pines behind and the clear lake in front, in the 'blue hollow at the foot of Longs Peak,' at a height of 7,500 feet, where the hoarfrost crisps the grass every night of the year, I have found far more than I ever dared to hope for."[26]

Dunraven had a house built for himself, close to the viewpoint where Bierstadt had set up his easel, but his stays did not give him the solitude and exclusive idyll he had hoped for. When he went out riding or hunting, the earl met a growing number of people coming down the steep track into the park to prospect for minerals, hunt, or trap. New squatters arrived and put up shanties on land he thought was already his. Rather than fight a losing battle to keep the park entirely to himself, he acknowledged the situation, and tried to control development on his own terms. He financed the construction of a wooden hotel, where his own guests could stay, as well as paying visitors. He set up a London-based company to run the estate as a business, brought in a sawmill, and started erecting fences so that cattle could be grazed.

Dunraven's purchase would have aroused less attention in other parts of the territory, but the status of Estes Park, as the pristine "blue hollow," of unique character, made the purchase controversial. Dunraven had praised the protection given to the upper Yellowstone country to save it from speculators, but seemed to make no link with what looked like his own exploitation of "the beauties of nature" in the park. He was not as haughty and overbearing as other peers, but he had to live with the legacy left by the others, and what really led him into trouble was the method he used to acquire the land.

At the very start, the Colorado newspapers treated the earl with the gentle mockery reserved for those they regarded as foppish Europeans. A paragraph in the "Brief Items" of the *Denver Tribune* would announce that " 'Mi Lud' Dunraven and Dr. Kingsley have registered at Charpiots,"[27] or, a little later, that "The Earl of Dunraven's luggage has arrived in Denver. He has only a thousand pounds of it, and some of the trunks are said to be almost as large as the boots of the city editor of the News."[28] An encounter with a mountain lion could be made slightly comical. "The Earl of Dunraven and party . . . have been cutting up high jinks at Estes Park and enjoying all sorts of hairs breadth escapes." They had killed "any number of 'Beasties' of various sorts and the Earl had a pitch battle with a mountain lion not so long ago that came very near to causing much weeping and wailing at Dunraven castle."[29]

But the good-humored tolerance was soon to be replaced by angry denunciation.

THE BACKGROUND STORY of how the earl had acquired his private preserve first surfaced in a small-town paper near to the park, which revealed the trickery that had been used: "We are credibly informed that the late reported purchase of 6,000 acres of land in Estes Park, embracing all the most valuable portion of that grand domain, by the Earl of Dunraven, is one of the most barefaced land steals of this land stealing age."[30] The indignant report was apparently placed by rival claimants to the land, jealous of the earl's coup, who knew how it had all been done because they might well have used the same techniques themselves.

Anyone wanting to buy federal land could either purchase it under the Preemption Act, or enter a claim under the newer Homestead Act. With preemption, they could buy up to 160 acres at a low price of $1.25 per acre, if they swore before witnesses that they had squatted on it for fourteen months. Under the Homestead Act of 1862, they were given rights if they undertook to occupy new land that had not already been preempted. They could work it for five years, "prove up," and get the full title for free; or, provided they made basic improvements, could secure the title after only six months, for $1.25 an acre. Both types of claim were restricted to U.S citizens, or those who had started the process of naturalization, and the object was to give new land to bona fide settlers and farmers rather than absentees or speculators. In practice, the government land offices were overwhelmed with claimants, and had no effective means of checking the situation on the ground. The whole process was open to manipulation, bribery, and fraud. Anyone who wanted to assemble more than 160 acres, for whatever purpose, could call on sharp intermediaries and lawyers who knew how to get around the system.

Dunraven turned to Theodore Whyte, the son of a British Army officer—who had emigrated to Colorado, worked in the mining business, and then become a land agent—to organize the purchase of the sections he wanted. He put Griff Evans, the genuine inhabitant who kept the log house and cabins on Fish Creek, on his payroll to smooth the operation. Dispensing small bribes, Whyte and Evans first organized a band of local men to petition for a government survey, swearing they were "legitimate settlers," already on the land or intending to homestead. When this had been done, and the land was surveyed and divided into sections, in the early summer of 1874 many of the same characters were brought in to the chaotic scrum of the federal Land Office on Fifteenth Avenue in Denver to file their claims.

Whyte's repertory company, drawn from saloons in Longmont and Denver, and from drifters hanging around nearby ranches, knew what was required and had probably done it before. They were happy to sign whatever papers were put in front of them in return for the promised cash reward. Several were not who they said they were, and used false names, but were ready to act as witnesses for each other. The Land Office had no time to be fussy, and through either negligence or connivance, thirty-one claims were granted. None of the men were genuine squatters, none planned to settle in the way that they swore, and few had even been to the park. Whyte filled another technical requirement by putting down "claim shanties" on many of the sections, just a few logs laid out in a square on the ground, as an indication that improvements were being made.

The payoff was made through separate and secret legal agreements, drawn up immediately after the filings. Whyte handed his false claimants sums of between $700 and $2,000 to pay the government for the preempted land, and then transfer the deeds on their 160 acres to him, adding a commission for themselves. He, in turn, shifted the land on to the Estes Park Company. In the space of a few days, for a layout of $38,000 cabled to a Denver bank, over 6,000 acres were secured for Dunraven. He had effective control over many more. When genuine settlers filed as well, and acquired land not on the original schedule, Whyte tried to buy them out to add more acres. In future years those who refused could find themselves locked in a battle with what was referred to as "the English company," which ran cattle over their land, or put up fences to block their access to water.

The most personal attack on Dunraven came from the *Denver Tribune*, from a correspondent calling himself "Veritas," who had been up to the park. The encounter he described was almost certainly fabricated, and the characterization ran on familiar lines:

While standing here, surrounded by all these beauties, and feeling they were a part of my inheritance, a wealthy gentleman, in a broad English accent, with whom I had been conversing said: "Yaas—we shall allow all the campers and tourists that are a mind to come in the park this year, you know. Next year, however, we propose to have all the cattle out, the blarsted heifers, and shall then reserve the park for our hunting and fishing, you know. Of course we caan't let common people come in then, you know, blast 'em."

I heard, but could hardly realize the impudence and audacity of my noble associate. What! An English "Milord," to lay claim to all the most valuable land of Estes Park. . . . All the American pioneers and frontiersmen, too, to be excluded by these dem foin foreigners, the idea seems too preposterous. And yet "My Lord" thought he had his property right and that all the valuable portion of Estes Park was his.[31]

Once the charges of perjury had been laid, the Land Office launched an inquiry, and the U.S. District Attorney in Denver set up a grand jury to investigate. Though witnesses testified that there had been only three or four people living in the park at the time of the survey, not thirty-one, and though summonses for false swearing were issued, they were never served because the original claimants had disappeared. The case ran into the ground; the indictments were stopped; and Dunraven kept the land titles.

Despite the fact that the federal case was not pursued, public outrage continued to grow. Rival buyers, who had been outmaneuvered by Whyte and Griffiths and had lodged the original complaint, cried foul play. A more high-minded argument, of exceptional national interest on Yellowstone lines, was made as well: "The question then arises whether the people of Colorado will permit one of the richest and most attractive portions of the Territory to be set apart for the exclusive benefit and behoof of a few English aristocrats, or whether the Government itself shall keep its title to the park, pass stringent laws relating to the fish and game, and so have this broad and lovely domain kept as a National 'Institution,' of a general benefit to the people of Colorado."[32] The earl continued to be vilified in the newspapers and grew weary of it all. Though he remained the owner of the hotel and the land he left it increasingly to his partner Whyte, and a succession of managers, and stopped subsidizing the operation with funds from home. His hunting lodge was no longer the isolated retreat it had once been, and the cattle-ranching operation was expanded. More squatters arrived, and the wapiti, bear, deer, and other game were driven back into distant, harder-to-reach ranges.

Dunraven's diaries were all lost when one of his yachts, *Valkyrie II*, sank after a collision in the Clyde; but near the end of his life he recalled his Colorado days in a few brief pages of his mellifluous autobiography. "Folks were drifting in, prospecting, fossicking, pre-empting, making claims; so we prepared for civilization. . . ." They had improved the road, built the hotel, hired a Chinese cook, and done well for a while, but it had not lasted. "People came in disputing claims, kicking up rows; exorbitant land taxes got into arrears; we were in constant litigation. The show could not be managed from home and we were in danger of being frozen out.

So we sold for what we could get and cleared out, and I have never been there since."[33] This was a very compressed version of events. He made his last visit around 1882, but did not sell up till 1908.

Dunraven's was one of the first of many aristocratic land deals, coming just as the cattle-ranching boom was about to begin. The earl's purchase of a 6,000-acre pleasure ground proved an early gift for radical politicians and newspaper editors, at a time when the whole question of how public lands were released, and to whom, was a burning issue. There were many American "land grabbers," and Washington was accused of favoring large corporations and the railway companies at the expense of the little man. The idea of "foreign nobs and nabobs, counts and no-accounts" being able to get round the rules as well, while hardworking frontiersmen were denied their due, became an additional strand among many grievances threaded into the entire land question. Dunraven, depicted as a drawling "Milord," featured in all the scare reports of foreign takeover that were to emerge in the next few years, and the size of his holding was consistently exaggerated. Within a few years a committee of the U.S. Congress was confidently asserting that he owned 60,000 acres in the new state of Colorado, in a rogues' gallery of grasping lords.

7

A Place for the Boys

*They are, I understand, young gentlemen of high birth
and some means. The peculiarly English passion for land-
holding, and going forth shooting and to shoot, led them
into this strange enterprise.*

—GRACE GREENWOOD, 1873[1]

hundred years after the Declaration of Independence, the
number of passengers crossing the Atlantic to the former
colony was greater than ever. Most were still poor emigrants in
steerage class, trying to escape from extreme poverty, or skilled
workingmen with a craft to sell, hoping to better themselves. But
by 1876, a significant number of well-to-do Britons were coming
over as tourists. The United States, with its different society, continued to fascinate the mother country, and in an age when great
international expositions represented the most compelling attractions that could be mounted, thousands came specially for that
year's Centennial fair in Philadelphia. The exhibition was larger
than any of its predecessors held in London, Paris, and Vienna,
and the British travel agent Thomas Cook judged it "a scene such
as the world never before saw, nor is likely to be seen again."[2]

Held in Fairmount Park on high ground on the western side of
the Schuylkill River, a trolley ride from Chestnut Street and the

old Statehouse where the Declaration of Independence had been signed, the Centennial was heavily promoted in Britain. After spending four or five days at the exhibition, many traveled on to see other parts of the country, including the Far West and California, on Cook's tours that lasted up to three months. The cheapest return excursion from London to Philadelphia could be had for just over £20.

In the flag-decked, iron-framed halls, which stretched for over half a mile, the country's new manufacturing might was on view, with avenues of gleaming railway engines and lines of black-enameled lathes, shuddering printing presses and hissing pumps. The machinery awed and alarmed British businessmen, who could see how rapidly the United States was emerging as a major rival. But it was the farm displays, from the latest reapers, hay loaders, and threshing machines to the pavilions in which individual states advertised their bountiful harvests, that impressed the aristocrats and country gentlemen who made their way there. Colorado and Kansas shared a soaring, cathedral-like pavilion, in the plan of a cross. From under the central dome hung a facsimile of Philadelphia's Liberty Bell, formed entirely from ears of corn, with the bell's clapper supplied by a six-foot-long gourd. While Colorado displayed gold quartz and silver ore, Kansas asserted its extraordinary fertility with sheaves of wheat six and a half feet high, and stalks of corn standing seventeen feet. In the fanned arrangements of produce, the brimming sacks of oats and barley, the glass vials of rich black earth, and the steeply angled lines charting record yields, visitors saw an updated vision of the American prairies. The perception of a wild natural landscape had been completely replaced by what promoters now called "the golden west."

The proud displays at the Centennial Exposition came just as cheap American wheat was starting to be shipped to Britain. The realization that American farming was more mechanized, with a seemingly boundless expanse of new land and a climate that favored good harvests, coincided with gloom and depression in the more constricted, damp, and long-worked British countryside. Farm prices were falling, and there had been several years of poor weather. Most British landowners, stolidly blinkered, believed the cycle would right itself, and expected their tenants and laborers to soak up any pain meanwhile. A few, more imaginative souls believed there could be opportunities in American land itself, from transferring their capital and buying property to hold and rent, or even moving to the United States to farm. There was now a new and additional reason for upper-class interest in the western United States. As well as continuing to come for hunting, shooting, and the renowned prairie air, there could be an economic motivation as well. By the time of the 1876 exhibition one wealthy Briton seemed to be showing the way, and was already known for his belief in large-scale Kansas farming. George Grant spent several weeks in Philadelphia distributing prospectuses for his land scheme, speaking to British visitors and trying to publicize his "colony," pitched at a new sort of immigrant.

THE PUBLICITY DRIVE to attract settlers to Kansas had begun in the late 1860s, not just in the eastern United States but through agents and advertising in Britain, Scandinavia, and much of the rest of Europe. In a campaign of sustained and expert puffery, railway companies and state officials sang the glories of a veritable rectangle of plenty, 400 miles across by over 200 miles deep, now crossed by a railway linking New York and San Francisco. The state was said to have the ideal "in-between" climate, not too far north for the worst winters, not too far south to be impossibly torpid. "All the choicest gifts which nature bestows, in land, to make a country desirable for homes, for the production of wealth, and all the comforts of life are found here," claimed the *Kansas Pilot*.[3]

It was more than just a place to farm. Propagandists claimed the state offered a unique refuge for the human spirit and inspiration for the soul. Lawrence Burch, author of *Kansas As It Is*, maintained that prairie farming brought a sense of well-being and contentment that sounded very similar to the sublime if transient satisfaction British sportsmen had experienced when they came to visit, but secured permanently. "It is the royal freedom of the camp on the boundless plains, under genial, radiant skies, as against the petty tyranny of society and the empty glamour of the drawing room. . . . Here is health and amplitude, gratified sense and restfulness of soul, unknown to the older ways and places of human living." All this could easily be had, if only people would realize how much was still available to be taken up. "The heart aches as you tramp from county to county over the vast region of Kansas, and behold millions of acres of the richest lands in the world lying idle and uncultivated, that requires only to be tilled by the hand of the husbandman to produce immense crops."[4] The glowing generalizations blurred the very different characteristics of eastern Kansas, more welcoming and fertile, where most of the settlement had taken place so far, and the drier, treeless expanses to the west.

George Grant had made his fortune as a silk merchant in London, and then turned himself into a gentleman farmer, with a large estate in Scotland. Enterprising and energetic, he was considering putting some of his money into American land. After touring the United States, he had first seen the high plains of western Kansas in the spring of 1872, and was spotted as a likely prospect by the Kansas Pacific Railroad. The company owned 6 million acres, in a twenty-mile-wide strip that ran on either side of its line across the state. Granted as an inducement for building the track, the land followed a checkerboard pattern, alternating with square sections retained by the federal government for homesteading, and the company needed to sell it off as fast as it could. The snag was that much of the route lay across the country once

dismissed as "the great American desert," so the railroad was trying to change this perception and redeem the barren reputation
of the high plains. The Kansas Pacific ran its own experimental
farms to explore how crops could be grown in challenging combi-
nations of soil, rainfall, and temperature, and tried out different
species of trees. Even if the precipitation seemed low, the hopeful
theory was that the climate would grow wetter once the virgin
land was plowed. In a virtuous circle, less of the sun's heat would
be reflected, and new vegetation would make the atmosphere
more humid, to create a new and even more perfect climate—or
so the thinking went.

Company agents showed Grant what they had available around
Fort Hays, in Ellis County. He saw it in late May, in the weeks
of the year when the land looked at its very best. The days wore
bright and clear after spring rains, and the gently rolling expanse
of green gamma grass ran off into the distance, with patches of
wildflowers. The country was broken by a few shallow valleys,
through which clear streams flowed. Grant was so impressed by
what he saw, and the possibilities for rearing sheep and cattle,
and so convinced by the Kansas Pacific agents' talk of new "dry
farming" methods for cereals, that he bought 25,000 acres. He
planned a large grazing operation of his own, and would persuade
English and Scotsmen with means to come and establish farms
alongside him.

On one level it was just another shrewd investment, by a man
with a proven record for good timing. Grant paid $2 an acre and
believed he could sell much of it on at a profit. But his purchase
was also an impulsive, emotional move, driven by a touch of prairie fever. He was excited by what he had seen, convinced that
this was country where he and others could not only prosper but
lead healthy and fulfilling lives. On his return, he placed small
but enticing advertisements in the London and Edinburgh newspapers, worked on his own friends and associates, and sent out
brochures which claimed "a Second Eden" was to be found in Ellis

County. "Those green prairies, rolling like gentle swells in the ocean, starred and gemmed with flowers, and threaded with dark belts of timber which marked the windings of the streams are a joy forever."[5]

"Colonies" were already an established way of selling and settling the prairies. Land grant railway companies encouraged them, since it was more profitable to sell large acreages to one collective group than small lots to many individual settlers, and they believed new arrivals would have a greater chance of success if they faced the challenges of opening up new country together. Kansas already had colonies of workingmen from Massachusetts and Ohio, Brooklyn and Pittsburgh, and black colonies from Kentucky. Danes, Swedes, Bohemians, and Mennonites from southern Russia arrived together. Idealists set up communes for utopian living, and temperance groups came to live without alcohol. George Grant proposed a colony that would be defined not by language, religion, or country of origin but by class and capital. Hoping to interest the scions of British noble families, and the sons of the gentry, he planned to restrict sales to lots of 640 acres, or a whole square-mile section, and made it clear that more than £2,000 should be allowed, for breaking the land, buying livestock, and building. His colony would be called "Victoria."

In February 1873, Grant drove from the railway station at Dumfries, in the Scottish borders, to see Lord Herries, at Terregles House in Nithsdale. With snow on the ground and foxhunting canceled, he was able to spend much of the day talking with Herries by the fireside. He explained the venture he was planning, and spoke of the beauties of western Kansas, the plentiful water, the rich chocolate brown soil, and the conditions for both cereal farming and stock rearing. The 13th Lord Herries was just the sort of aristocrat Grant needed to convince. A devout Roman Catholic, he had thirteen children—six sons and seven daughter—to provide for. The expense of marrying off his daughters had been reduced after four of them chose to become nuns.

His eldest son, Marmaduke, would inherit his title and run the family estates in Scotland and Yorkshire. One son had died. That still left four boys to shepherd into adult life, and the meeting with Grant was to discuss the future of his fifth son, Walter, who was asking for money to buy a farm on the prairies. Perhaps more brothers would wish to follow.

Herries was impressed by Grant's plausibility and knowledge of farming, and agreed his son could go. Two months later, Walter and thirty other young men from good families joined Grant in Glasgow, where they boarded the steamship *Alabama*. They had read Captain Mayne Reid, and the familiar stories of the frontier, the hunting, and the clashes between Indians and settlers added to the sense of adventure. Lord Herries wrote in his diary: "My dearest boy Walter leaves for America. May everything prosper with him and may the Angels of Heaven protect him."[6]

Along with the first party of settlers, Grant also took a nucleus of farm livestock of good quality, obtained from Scottish breeders, including four bulls, a number of purebred cows, thirty sheep, and several draft horses. They sailed to New Orleans, shifted to a river steamer, and went up to St. Louis, where they transferred the beasts and baggage to the railway. When the party reached a halt in Ellis County, 570 miles from St. Louis, they found a wooden warehouse, erected by the Kansas Pacific as a temporary depot and sleeping quarters, waiting for them. It was the only building for ten miles around, in an almost treeless expanse. Until recently this had been buffalo country, and Grant's land adjoined the site of the original Fort Hays, once commanded by General Custer, where Buffalo Bill had served as a scout, before the post moved a few miles to the west.

If their first impression of the Second Eden was a disappointment, the settlers did their best to share Grant's dream. He envisaged a new town just south of the railway to be called Victoria, and he renamed Big Creek, which ran from west to east five miles to the south, the Victoria River. The founding party was

soon joined by others. Most bought plots from Grant, while others homesteaded on the adjoining government sections. The Honorable Walter Maxwell chose land fronting onto Big Creek, and
sent his father an itemized breakdown of what he needed, starting with 1,289 acres at $4 an acre, or £1,280; £400 for a house;
and £200 for cows. After setting down other sums for furniture,
servants, and sheep, he ended: "Estimated cost required £2190."[7]
On receipt of this note, Lord Herries telegraphed a further £2,000
to the account Walter had opened at the First National Bank in
Kansas City on his way west, and would send another £1,800 over
the next two years. Meanwhile, he continued to pay Walter his
regular allowance of £200 a year.

Trains from the East brought in the breeds of sheep Grant
thought most suitable, including Cotswold, Lincoln, and Leicester ewes, and fifty-nine rams. Stationary steam engines wound
steel hawsers, tugging heavy breaking plows up wide strips of
grassland that were to be planted with wheat or barley. When
the matted prairie was turned over it was left, so the grass could
rot before cross-plowing, leaving the ground ready for sowing the
following year. No rain fell for months at a time, and the temperature was regularly over 100° F., going as high as 115°. Young
Walter Maxwell had never farmed before, and after a few weeks
he was already wearying of it. He wrote home, on his family's
crested notepaper, that "two days after tomorrow I will go on this
hunt. As I have had no real pleasure trips this summer I deserve
it, and the plans for my house will be done by the time I return.
Yesterday was terrifically hot with a regular gale, 105 in the
shade. . . . Today I have been simply pouring with perspiration
since early this morning. My shirt is wet through and I have to
go and change."[8]

Other immigrants to western Kansas, in their first year,
would have expected to live in a dugout cut in the side of a bluff,
or a sod hut of earth bricks made from plow furrows, with a roof
of grass. Grant's gentleman settlers ordered in builders from

Hays and as far as Topeka to construct solid villas, in the English style, with gardens and hedges. An architect came from London to lay out the town and design Grant's own farm buildings. The Kansas Pacific company, desperately keen for the enterprise to succeed because it could lead to more sales, contributed a two-story station and hotel, with a cupola. Grant moved into a house high on a hill south of Big Creek, built in rusticated blocks of a golden limestone easily quarried from outcrops on the prairie. The shaded porch faced north, to avoid the scorchingly hot wind that blasted up from the south in the summer. From the back windows he could see his private domain stretching away for four or five miles, with cattle and sheep grazing, toward a thin line of treetops rising from the bottomland, where the Smoky Hill River looped its way eastwards.

As with all land schemes of the time, the key to success was to generate a rush of interest and maintain momentum, to keep the buyers coming in. Grant knew this, and talked up his results. Kansas papers, with a vested interest in their state's success, reprinted the figures he gave out for the growing size of his flocks and herds, and yields he was getting from his crops, unquestioningly. They referred to him as Sir George Grant, and always overstated the number of acres he owned. Though he had bought more land after the first tranche, to reach 60,000 acres, he was said to have 100,000 acres, then 250,000. One of his own pamphlets claimed his estate ran to 560,000 acres. Taking this figure as gospel, the *New York Times* judged that Grant "now owns probably the largest tract of land ever owned by any one individual in this country."[9] The *St. Louis Republican* went even further. Sir George's farm was "larger than any Dukedom in Europe, and no doubt, the largest farm in the world."[10] Unlike Dunraven in Estes Park, there was no objection to British ownership at the time, and the legal titles were sound; but reports of this immense dukedom would be remembered, and added to the general charge sheet of British "aristocratic greed" to be produced later.

The Episcopalian Bishop of Kansas traveled west from Topeka
to agree on the site for a new church, and give Victoria his blessing. "I spent the day with Mr. George Grant, driving with him over
a part of his farm which embraces a large part of the County—
a principality in extent—and seeing the flocks, herds and other
stock of this immense estate."[11] Money was raised for a church,
which was built in the same local limestone, with donations solic-
ited from England.

Grant gave interviews about his scientific approach to farming,
as he crossed Texas and Cherokee cattle with coal black Aberdeen
Angus bulls from Scotland, though journalists were usually more
interested in the breeding and status of the settlers themselves.
The *New York Tribune* reported that farms had been bought by a
type of person who would not normally go into business: "Mr. Grant
declares that in the colony in Victoria young men of culture and
education will find a field of usefulness which they would not attain
in their original homes. Their money would here yield a good interest and they would be surrounded by a community whose culture
and refinement would make the society congenial."[12] "This colony
differs in every respect from other colonies founded in the United
States," declared the *St. Louis Democrat*; ". . . most of the settlers
being persons of fair fortunes who are seeking a healthy climate
and country life."[13] A Massachusetts woman who met Grant on a
train showed how he appeared to native-born Americans: "He is a
strikingly aristocratic looking personage and Victoria is an aristocratic enterprise, its constitution providing that no member shall
own less than a square mile of land. . . ."[14]

It was part of Grant's recruiting pitch to make comparisons
between going to Victoria, and possible alternatives for genteel
settlement in other parts of the United States or elsewhere. A
British journalist, who had not been out to see it but accepted
Grant's own account of his community, described the social
advantages of Victoria: "Every objection which offends so greatly
the man of refinement in the colonization of Australia and other

distant settlements is here avoided, and instead of being driven
to solitude or to association with the lower class from the mother
country, he is surrounded by all the arts and graces of life . . .
instead of the slovenly shanty of the Australian squatter or the
log hut of the American backwoodsman, handsome stone houses
are erected, and the farms present every token of prosperity."[15]

The Honorable Walter Maxwell completed his house, and paid
for high-walled stone shelters to be built to protect his sheep from
winter snowstorms and prairie wolves. He went back to Scotland
and his family for the winter, and returned with thoroughbred
riding horses. His neighbors with frontage on Big Creek, and on
the river's North Fork, which passed under the railway track at
Victoria, included Captain Prescott, son of Sir George Prescott
of Theobald's Park in Hertfordshire, and Henry Smithes, from a
London wine merchant's family. Smithes built a dam across Big
Creek to create an ornamental lake, and ordered a boat, powered
by a small steam engine, to be used for picnic trips. The boat
arrived, and was christened *The Jolly West*, but the stone dam
was knocked aside by the spring floods, and the steamer sank.
Foxhunting, the essential pastime and passion of the British
countryside, proved impossible because there were no foxes, but
the settlers formed a Hunt Club nevertheless, with huntsman and
horn, and chased antelope and coyote with dogs, wearing the correct red hunting coats and black bowler hats.

Though they managed to mount a Hunt Ball at the Ellis
County Courthouse in Hays in the spring of 1877, it proved difficult to combine the lifestyle of a refined country gentleman, as the
British defined it, with the first stage of true pioneering. There
were never more than two hundred settlers, and they were dispersed over too wide an area. Victoria was hardly a village as
yet, just a few sheds and a cattleyard, and the colonists shared
no focus except for George Grant himself. In the first years, they
suffered from the biblical scourge of which all Kansas farmers
lived in perpetual fear, and that the boosters said little about:

the sudden arrival of cloud after cloud of all-devouring grasshoppers, or locusts. Percy Ebbutt, an Englishman farming in central Kansas. described how the insects could appear out of a clear sky and fall like snow, forming drifts as they dropped down in ever-increasing numbers. The inch-long creatures, each with white underbelly, antennae, distinct mouth, thorax, and six legs, clustered together like swarming bees. "They alighted on houses, people, animals, fences, crops, covering everything, while the ground was strewn several inches thick, so that it was impossible to walk about without killing dozens at each step, while it was a hard job to keep them brushed off hands and face."[16]

Wave after wave fell for several days, munching their way through any kind of vegetation: "They began on the green corn and garden crops and made a clean sweep. In the morning the corn was waving in all its beauty . . . in the evening nothing remained but the bare upright stalks, which were rapidly blackening under the influence of their bites and through which one could see all over the field. Flowers, leaves, silk, corn, ears, all had vanished down their rapacious maws."[17] They cleared the fruit off trees, the leaves off the new hedges. The Victoria settlers lost almost all their first crops, and the insects came back the following year. Even before the grasshopper attacks, which struck in August, they were suffering from a severe drought. The trees and gardens the colonists had planted withered in the baking summer heat. In the early years they were stoic and resilient, following Grant's leadership, and he persuaded most of them to stick it out. It was believed the grasshoppers would exhaust themselves and were a part of a cycle that would pass.

With their financial reserves, Grant's colonists were in a better position to survive the setbacks than some of the others who had answered the Kansas Pacific summons. A growing number of immigrants, from very different backgrounds, were arriving to homestead land on the interleaved government sections. They included several thousand German-speaking Russians from the

Volga region, who came into Hays for their supplies in ragged sheepskin coats and shapeless felt boots. The influx had one benefit for the Victoria colonists, who could now find people to do their heavy manual work for them. They found they could get their land plowed, stone quarried, or dams built for a wage that far undercut the going rate until then, and they paid the hardworking Russian women 25 cents a day for their labor.

When more realistic accounts of the "Second Eden" reached home, and Grant found he was not attracting a sufficient number of noblemen's sons, or anyone else's offspring, to take up the acreage he was holding, he appointed a New York agent and tried to interest wealthy easterners as well. Among those he signed up were Richard Gunther, whose uncle had been the mayor of New York, and Walter Shields, heir to a Brooklyn fortune. The 1876 Centennial Exposition was another opportunity to lure more settlers. As well as handing out his Victoria pamphlet, Grant took part in the livestock championships held under the Centennial banner, in a 25-acre showground to the south of the main exhibition. The long rows of stables and pens contained horses, cattle, bulls, and pigs entered by farmers from all over the United States. Grant brought some of the finest purebred sheep from his Ellis County flock, several Angus cattle that had originally come from Queen Victoria's herd at Windsor, and his short-horn bull Royal George. He won no medals, but the animals served as a further advertisement for what the British were thought to be contributing to Kansas.

In 1876, Victoria was the most ambitious and best publicized British "colony" in the United States. If it was the first to aspire to a country gentleman's lifestyle in an American setting, advertise the availability of educated company and good sport, it failed to live up to expectations. It became clear that on his visit in 1872 George Grant had seen the Second Eden at its very lushest, in the early summer when the prairies were particularly green after an unusually wet spring, and that in the following years the weather resumed a more typical pattern. Even the most tenacious young colonists, who had recovered from the first years of grasshopper blight, lost heart. For a while Walter Maxwell put on a brave face in his letters, alternating his accounts of antelope hunts and cricket matches with requests for more money, since his spending far exceeded any return he was making from farming.

Grant's own stock raising was more successful. With 11,000 sheep, his belief in the viability of the colony remained unshaken. But in 1879 he was taken ill and died, and was buried beside the small Episcopalian church he had paid to have built, south of the Kansas Pacific tracks. With no one to boost Victoria or maintain his messianic vision, the British started to move on. Walter Maxwell returned to Europe and went to study at a seminary in Rome. Within a few years the land was taken over by the poor but practical German-Russian immigrants whose expectations were far lower, and who were ready to live in the kind of huts and shanties they had been accustomed to beside the Volga. Victoria was renamed, and became Herzog.

IF VICTORIA WAS a speculative venture, it was also a response to a peculiarly British social problem, of which the need to find an outlet for the Honorable Walter Maxwell, the fifth of six brothers, was just one illustration. Shared by many upper-class households, it could be summed up in the question: "What shall we do with our boys?" Editorial writers pondered the dilemma, clergymen preached about it, and the public figure who fretted most of all was the untiring Thomas Hughes, author, lawyer, social reformer, sometime Member of Parliament, and author of *Tom Brown's School Days*.

"Go through any English county . . . ," Hughes wrote, "and you will scarcely find a family which does not own one or more cadets, of fair average abilities, good character . . . and strong bodies, who

are entirely at a loose end, not knowing what in the world to turn
their hands to."[18] The problem had been made worse, according
to Hughes, by the growing number of private boarding schools—
the so-called public schools—to which the British upper classes
dispatched their sons for character building and a traditional
education. Ancient establishments like Eton and Winchester had
been joined by newer schools, including Marlborough and Radley,
Malvern and Wellington, all placing the same emphasis on the
classics, cricket, and muscular Christianity, rather than science
or mathematics. They were turning out legions of young men each
year, minted in the same mold, but what were the boys to do when
they left?

Business was largely closed to them because of the general
snobbery toward "trade." While the eldest sons could take over
family estates, it was difficult to find employment for younger
brothers. Becoming a lawyer or doctor demanded high academic
standards, and the professions were already overcrowded. It was
no longer possible to buy them a commission in the army, after
recent reforms, and it was harder to enter the Church or the Civil
Service. "The need of finding something to which they can turn
their hands gets more pressing,"[19] said Hughes. "What outlet of a
satisfactory kind can be found for the swarming manhood of the
English gentry and middle class?"[20]

Hughes's own answer was that they should be encouraged to
swarm to the United States, where there was much more room
for them, and they could flourish more easily. Two of his neph-
ews had gone to Texas to ranch, and he knew America, where he
was a popular lecturer after the success of *Tom Brown's School
Days*. In 1879, he led a scheme for another British "colony," very
different from Victoria. If Grant's proposition offered a bracing
life of refined independence in the wide open spaces of the prairies, Hughes's solution was a community run on smaller, more
protected and idealistic lines. If Grant's operation was in the Far
West, on empty land which could be grazed immediately, or broken

by the plow, the Hughes colony was well to east of the Mississippi, on an earlier frontier, in the forests of eastern Tennessee. Like Victoria, the location was linked to the developing railway system. A new line running from Cincinnati down to Chattanooga and the South made a tract of country on the Cumberland plateau suddenly accessible.

The Tennessee plan originated with a group of Boston investors, who wanted to buy a large parcel of land that could be sold off for farms. Hughes took the scheme over, with much help from American friends and backers, and 40,000 acres were acquired for a colony that would incorporate his ideas about the dignity of manual labor, and the need for cooperation and mutual support as well as enterprise. It was to be a social experiment, where the sons of British gentlemen could learn to farm and lead a "manly, outdoor life," or take up carpentry or handicrafts among their friends and equals, "a place where what we have been calling the English public school spirit . . . shall be recognized and prevail."[21] He named the new community "Rugby," after his own alma mater.

A seven-mile dirt road was built up to the village from Sedgemoor, the nearest train station, nine hours south of Cincinnati, with talk of a narrow-gauge railway spur to come. Believing it essential to have a physical core that settlers could identify with from the start, the land company made a heavy initial outlay on public buildings. Rugby soon had a wooden Gothic church with an imported organ, a fifty-room hotel called the Tabard after Chaucer's inn at Southwark, a smaller boardinghouse, a co-operative store, a school, and a handsome public library with 5,000 books donated by well-wishers, set in clearings among the trees. Settlers who bought lots in the village built neat frame cottages along the sandy avenues, with picket fences, that might have graced an Indian hill station. The cool breezes and views across the mountains, and smell of pine needles, gave the feeling of a resort, at least in the summer. Hummingbirds flitted among the dogwood and magnolias. A visiting British headmaster acknowledged "a charming and invigorating climate . . . great natural beauty; a place cheerful and well cared for, and a society which happily combines refinement with simplicity."[22] A New Yorker was struck by the strong English tone: "Upon the hotel plaza in the evening discussions were of blooded horses and blooded cattle and blooded dogs. And strange as it may seem, representatives of such stock are to be found down there in the backwoods. Valuable dogs are especially numerous. . . ."[23]

Unlike Victoria, the scheme at Rugby was not aimed at those sons whose fathers could dole out several thousand pounds to set up large farms, but at men with allowances of £150 or £200 a year but little capital. They could buy land from the company on a hire purchase basis over several years. It was part of the Hughes idea that wellborn Englishmen should be able to practice trades and crafts that would be beneath them at home, and a visiting journalist found one young aristocrat "making bread in the washbowl from an entirely original recipe in which flour, baking powder, and saleratus entered as equal components."[24] When Thomas Hughes made his first visit, for the formal opening, he was happy to be met at the station by five young Anglo-Saxons—from Eton, Harrow, Wellington, and Rugby—brimming with good health, dressed in battered straw or felt hats, flannel shirts, weather-stained breeches, gaiters, and boots. The Episcopalian Bishop of Tennessee led the inaugural service, and in his own address Hughes said the aim was to create "a community of gentlemen and ladies" who would pull together. They sang "Jerusalem the Golden," and the service ended with "God Save the Queen." The New York publisher J. W. Harper described the settlement as the start of Britain's second period of colonization in America. If it succeeded, then British gentlemen would see "the superiority of the United States as a place of residence over Australia, the Cape of Good Hope, or Canada."[25]

Over a hundred young Britons moved to Rugby and slotted into a companionable expatriate life, which included cricket, croquet, rugby, and football. The village had an archery range, tennis, an amateur dramatic society, and a monthly magazine to publish the colonists' poetry. An old Etonian wrote back to his school, appealing for more young men to come out and join them. "As for the tennis club, whist etc, and the rest . . . you will see that we have what is known as a 'bully time' on this continent."[26]

Just as the Volga Germans had never seen anything like the Victoria colonists, the scattered denizens of the Tennessee mountains were puzzled by the enclave set down beside them. Poor whites and Negroes, living in tar-paper shacks, burning back the brush for subsistence farming and keeping a few pigs to root under the trees, saw the passenger wagon passing up and down the Rugby road, filled with nonchalant young Britons. They heard the *thwack* of bat on ball, and wondered at the way these aliens spent their time. A railway engineer from Cincinnati thought the colonists far too genteel for the work that needed to be done: "A community of labourers and not a society of gentlemen is what is required . . . to make the colony successful."[27]

The colonists were accused of loafing, and spending too much time on the tennis court, but the odds were stacked against them. Before anyone could farm, the primeval forest had to be cleared, trees felled, and roots grubbed out and burned. The soil, once exposed, was found to be thin and sandy. The winter was colder and wetter than expected, turning the roads into sludge. Verses in *The Rugbeian* demonstrated colonist resolve:

> *Rain, drizzle, sleet, plash, drip, drop, swish*
> *Our wagons sink below the nave,*
> *(some call it hub). We really wish*
> *The weather bureau would behave.*
>
> *But spite of all the rain and snow,*
> *On paper we'll our feelings vent.*
> *We'll work and laugh at earthly woe*
> *Nor for the weather care a cent.*[28]

This was neither cereal or cattle country and there was no infallible staple crop. The most industrious tried to grow melons, potatoes, peanuts, tomatoes, and tobacco. They planted out fruit trees, and grazed sheep, but after only eighteen months a returning visitor was discouraging. "They are not farmers nor the sons of farmers, and they are poorly prepared, both by education and disposition, for the hard life and slow accumulations of the frontiersman."[29]

As the community began to falter, it became clear that Rugby was the impractical dream of a sanctimonious if kindhearted man. The ethos Hughes encouraged was too idealistic, almost communistic, in its reliance on mutual help and its rejection of the profit motive. At the same time the colony company, the philanthropic-sounding Board of Aid for Land Ownership, was accused of misrepresenting the quality of the land, and using the genial Hughes as a front for a hard-nosed property scheme. Rugby did not attract enterprising types who wanted to farm on a large scale. The ban on the sale of alcohol did not help. Above all, Hughes had put down his colony in the wrong place, ignoring the proven appeal of the prairies. At a time when young men were hearing the rallying call to go west to the new lands, it seemed an anomaly to be setting up in a backwater of the post–Civil War South, rather than on the main transcontinental axis. *Harper's Weekly* said that even residents of Tennessee were "surprised" at the effort to develop the unpromising area, when there was clear land, with better prospects, in Iowa, Kansas, or Colorado.[30] A scheme was briefly mooted to move the whole enterprise to better land in Minnesota, but nothing came of it.

The immediate reason for the failure of the colony was an outbreak of typhoid, when the water supply at the Tabard was contaminated by a carelessly placed cesspit, dug close to the hotel well. Twenty cases were identified, seven young Englishmen died, and the village's claim to an invigorating and healthy climate was permanently tainted. Many of the colonists fled to avoid the epidemic, and in the months that followed others gave up the struggle against the carpet of oaks, hemlock, spruce, and pine that covered the hills. By the end of 1881, the population was down to sixty, from a peak of three hundred.

Though it had been said that the opening of Rugby marked the start of Britain's "second colonization of America," no one ever accused the colonists of an unwelcome takeover, or felt threatened, or seemed to feel anything other than pity for them. Some of the more energetic now headed west to try their luck in Iowa or Kansas, where the air was known to be more bracing, and many of their contemporaries from school or university were already establishing themselves out on the prairie.

8

"Hail Britannia!"

*Our great advantage is having no Americans on either
farm. We both of us have good homes, good food, and English gentlemen to associate with, and what could you wish
for more?*

—WALTER COWAN, Le Mars, 1883[1]

In late August 1877 a herd of eighty steers were being driven
along a dirt road in western Iowa, toward the farm that two
young Englishmen had bought in the very new settlement of Denison. The operation did not go smoothly. The cloud of dust they
were kicking up made it impossible to see the front of the strag-
gling column from the rear. The fields on either side were planted
with Indian corn, or what the British knew as maize, there were
no fences, and the cattle kept straying off the track to feed on
the leaves or ruminate among the tall stalks, higher than a man.
Some wandered deep into the forest of corn and were lost under
the green canopy. The brothers, covered with grime from the trail,
rode backward and forward trying to get the steers under control,
shouting and cursing with increasing desperation.

Frederick Close, the younger man, had purchased the animals
to fatten, and had the better grasp of how to move them along. His
elder brother, William, who had been at school at Wellington and

just come down from Cambridge, had never taken cattle across
country before. When he tried to use his brand-new stock whip,
he cast it back as he would have used a hunting whip with a pack
of British foxhounds. The leather tail looped behind him and
cracked forward with a sound like a pistol shot, narrowly miss-
ing his horse's head. On the second attempt the rawhide hit the
animal's neck and flank, and the horse reared and nearly bucked
him off. On the next attempt he tried whirling the thong round
his head several times, as he had seen the drivers do. The heavy,
twelve-foot thong circled back and cut him across his face.

William wrote a self-deprecating, dude's account of his efforts:
"Ah! didn't it sting . . . I felt as if my face had been cut in two.
I shall now always have a certain amount of sympathy for cattle when I lash them." The painful initiation was discouraging.
"Of all the most horrid, dirty, tedious and slow occupations, cattle driving is the worst . . . the dust! It got into our noses, eyes,
mouths, ears and every mortal place it could. We were from 12 to
13 hours in the saddle, and pretty well tired. There is remarkably
little romance in driving cattle and a great deal of weariness and
dirt."[2]

The two Close brothers, sons of a wealthy London banker, were
the forerunners of hundreds of other well-educated young Englishmen who would follow them to the same part of Iowa over
the next few years. Most would have the same kind of difficulties when they first tried to handle livestock, husk corn, or make
fences, but only the Closes would make such a financial success of
it. They had caught the American land bug at the right time, and
picked an area where good land could still be bought at reasonable
prices. They were shrewd enough to use their family money and
connections to buy tens of thousands of acres for themselves, and
then to persuade their kith and kin to follow them. Iowa welcomed
them, at least at the start.

WILLIAM CLOSE'S INTEREST in American farming, and land values, sprang directly from the Centennial Exposition. At Cambridge he had been captain of the University Boat Club, and rowing took him to Philadelphia in the summer of 1876, to an international regatta on the Schuylkill River. He arrived with a four-man crew from Trinity College, and they won their first race, thrashing up the smooth brown water at a faster strike rate than any other boat in the heats. On the second day, they were wiped out. With several of the crew suffering from what appeared to be dysentery brought on by contaminated drinking water, they lost to a humbler boat from Seneca Lake, New York. "We would have won if I had not been obliged to stop rowing by reason of diarrhoea coming on in the middle of the race," explained Close. "These beastly Yankees are crowing over us."[3] If the rowing was a disaster, the visit to Philadelphia had a fortuitous result. The impact that the agricultural displays made on the young Britons when they toured the Centennial Exhibition in Fairmount Park, and a chance meeting with an American land speculator, led to the creation of the largest class based British colony in the West, more long lasting and successful than either Victoria or Rugby.

William Close was considering what he would do after Cambridge. His younger brother Frederick had come out to Virginia after leaving school, to try farming, and the regatta provided a chance for the brothers to meet up and travel, with the possibility of buying American land. They hardly knew where to start, except for the general enjoinder to go west, but while taking a weekend away from the heat of Philadelphia, at a hotel on an Atlantic beach, William met an Illinois businessman who had made a fortune buying and selling land in the Midwest. Rather than Kansas, Daniel Paullin steered him toward Iowa, where conditions would have more in common with British farming, and which was closer to the big city markets. Since Paullin was trying to set up his own two sons with farmland, and since his daughter Mary liked the young Englishman, he suggested they take a trip, to see what was available.

In October 1876, the two Close brothers, with another member of the Trinity crew, and Paullin's son Henry, then at Harvard, crossed the Mississippi into Iowa and went beyond Des Moines, the capital. In the soft sunlight of an Indian summer, they hired a wagon and team and explored the western side of the state. William sent back letters in the form of a journal, to be circulated around his family. "This drive took us Englishmen through the first Prairie land with which we had any near acquaintance, and we were very much struck with it. I know nothing like it in Europe . . . rolling prairie, hardly any level land, but none of the hills rising to much above 100 feet above the level of the larger creeks."[4] The grass was a dry reddish-brown, and the only contrast came from the pale yellow of the Indian corn stalks, and the occasional patch of dark brown, almost black, newly broken land. Though much of the land had been plowed in the previous few years, there were still hundreds of thousands of empty acres for sale, held by the railway companies, or by speculators who had bought and held it but not broken it, in anticipation of rising values.

The two brothers were so taken by what they saw, and by the go-ahead and optimistic attitude they found in the smallest village, that they decided to move to Iowa to farm and try to make money from land that seemed to be undervalued when compared with other regions. The following year they came back, in early June, when the prairies were covered with a bright carpet of new grass. By August, they had bought their first 2,500 acres, in Crawford County. From the start they wanted to be landlords, and to invest in land for resale or for rent. But they also wanted to farm in their own right, and bought pigs and drove in their first cattle to fatten. Setting up house in Denison, with a population of nine hundred, the two brothers managed to avoid the mistakes so many of the sporting tourists were guilty of. They joined in, took part in the Fourth of July picnic and church socials, and William taught at Sunday School. Nevertheless, the Iowans assumed these were the aristocrats of old. "When we first arrived in Denison Fred and I received a note from one of the ladies asking us to come to some party and it was addressed 'The Lords the Brothers Close.' We thought it was for fun and replied in the same style, but we happened to find out that she really thought we were lords, and that it was likewise the prevailing idea in Denison."[5]

One season's experience convinced the two brothers that what they had suspected was correct, that the area had somehow been overlooked because of earlier grasshopper plagues, and that farming in America could be a great deal more profitable than in Britain, where produce prices were falling and the dire saga of foreclosures and bankruptcies continued. Bringing in a third brother, James, they began to plan their own land investment company, partly funded by the family bank. With the aim of being long-term landlords they would finance the plowing of virgin land on a large scale, erect cabins, and then let to small farmers on a crop-sharing basis, in what they described as their "break and rent" formula. They would also buy and sell land to farmers with capital, and act as land agents, putting buyers and sellers together. To further raise values and make the area distinctive, they would attract Britons of their own sort to join them, and create a British community on a sounder and more realistic footing than Grant's Victoria, 300 miles to the southwest in Kansas.

William Close took the lead. He was not a blue-blooded aristocrat, though he moved in smart social circles, and he was more interested in team sports and athletics than in hunting and fishing. Unlike so many of his generation, he did not disdain business. His true blue sporting record and charm were matched by an entrepreneurial streak, and in Iowa he found a chance to use it, on a scheme that appealed to him. His American commitment was the more serious because he was now engaged to Mary Paullin, the daughter of his mentor.

In the early summer of 1878, as the weather grew warmer, they crisscrossed northeast Iowa, driving on dirt roads that rose and dipped across the prairies, until they found what they wanted, well to the north of Denison and nearer the Missouri, in Plymouth County. William Close was elated. "We came upon what may turn out to be the lands we are in quest of near Sioux City, pronounced sue, a lively little town of some 6,000 inhabitants situated near the junction of the Big Sioux River with the Missouri, and a better course for a regatta than the Big Sioux I never saw, a wide calm straight stretch of river 20 feet deep. It made me long to scull over it."[6]

The parcel of land was unbroken, owned by a New Yorker who had kept it back but now needed to sell. "The lands I am speaking of made my mouth water as we drove over them. Nothing could be finer; gently undulating, just enough to carry the surplus water away and prevent any swamps, perfectly watered lands, too, abundant springs in all directions, splendid dark rich soil." The top layer of soil was between five and ten feet deep, and even the subsoil would raise crops. He quoted another Briton as saying that "many farmers in England would fill their pockets with it and roll in it for delight."[7] They agreed to pay $2.40 an acre, and arranged for the funds to be sent from London.

The "colony" that grew up from the Closes' purchase in Iowa was never a separate and freestanding imperial implant in the sense of Victoria, Rugby—or Runnymede, yet to come in Kansas. It came into being attached to the apron strings of a young community called Le Mars, then at the same stage as thousands of other small towns in the Midwest and West. The area had first been settled by farmers from the New England states, and by German and Swedish immigrants. The town was founded in 1869, and in the first years its fortunes were governed by the same volatile mix of weather patterns, farm prices, transport routes, and freight rates as all its neighbors. Set to the east of a belt of cottonwood, Le Mars grew rapidly when it became the meeting point of two railway lines, which ran on together to the river port of Sioux City. One track came in from the northeast and Minneapolis; the other crossed the state from the east, the most direct route from Chicago.

The wide, unpaved Main Street was lined with the irregular two-story facades of grocery and dry goods stores, harnessmakers, blacksmiths, and seed suppliers. On either side of the main axis, a grid of eight avenues and streets had been pegged out, and new timber-boarded houses were starting to fill in the empty blocks in the section of the town that sloped up a gentle hillside from the business district. As the center for an increasingly busy farming county, the town had a population of 2,000, a courthouse, five grain elevators, and two flour mills. At the end of 1878, the *Le Mars Liberal* broke the news of the transforming land deal. The Close brothers of England had purchased 16,000 acres in the county, and were negotiating for 50,000 more.

The massive investment was an immediate boost for local pride, greeted with the headline "Hail Britannia!" The *Le Mars Sentinel* anticipated that "our county will receive an important addition of sturdy, thrifty, well-to-do, law abiding immigrants that will add materially to our growth and prosperity." People expected their own prospects would be lifted by the incoming tide, and their hopes were born out. The town's European-sounding name, which had nothing to do with France but was a composite of the initials of its six founders, became known not just in Iowa and neighboring parts of Minnesota but all over the eastern states and overseas. For nearly twenty years, the identity of Le Mars was intertwined with the ethos, attitude to work, interests, and recreations of the British upper classes, including their concern with class itself.

By the time the purchase was made public, William Close was back in England making plans to bring in the right type of settlers, while Frederick and James stayed in Iowa. Fully aware of the ongoing "What shall we do with our boys?" debate,

William's recruitment drive was more precisely targeted than
George Grant's efforts to sell the high plains of western Kansas,
and less airy than Thomas Hughes's offering of Rugby, launched
at almost the same time. He opened an office, wrote magazine
articles, sent letters to the papers, and used his connections to
the full. In Cambridge, he was a member of the wealthiest and
smartest college, whose handsome sets of rooms were filled with
the sons of aristocratic families. He was known throughout the
wider university as a sporting hero, who had rowed in three boat
races against Oxford, and continued to coach the Cambridge crew
on the towpath. In 1879, every student at the university received
a thirty-two-page promotional pamphlet from the gilded athlete,
suggesting their future might lie in Plymouth County, Iowa. He
posted the same brochure to every clergyman in the Church of
England, many of them worried about the prospects for their sons.
In straightforward language, Close set out the type he was looking for. His intention was to establish "a colony of English people
of the better class, and thus combine Western farming with some
English society."[8] So this might not be the place for artisans or
mechanics or laborers, who would be better off looking elsewhere.

The Close pamphlet made much of Iowa's natural blessings,
which included some of the best land in the country: "The new-
comer has no clearing at all to do. He has simply to plough up the
virgin sod to a depth not exceeding 2½ inches, and has no stones,
rocks etc to contend with in his ploughing."[9] It gave convincing
detail, from the cost of plows and harrows to the market price for
hogs, at that time 2d. a pound. Close stressed the good character
of the existing inhabitants, among whom this wedge of English
society was to be inserted. He had considered other areas before
settling on Plymouth County, but found problems of attitude, or
too much "loafing about at the saloon doors." In Missouri, for
example, the land was magnificent but the state was "cursed with
a most wretched and shiftless population."[10] In Iowa, British gentlemen could expect to find a kindred people, thrifty, law-abiding,

and industrious. He reassured his readers that, happily, the dangerous and untrustworthy Indians were gone. Bundling together two further prejudices, he was pleased to note that the Northwest was "entirely free from 'coloured gentlemen' and low Irish. Life and property are perfectly secure."[11]

Prospective colonists were given careful advice on how much money was needed, how to get out to Iowa, and what to expect when they got there: £500 was essential; £1,000 would be better. The cost of travel through to Le Mars would be between £15 and £19 when taking first class on the ship and train. It would be best to arrive in the spring, ready for breaking and plowing in April. They could expect "capital shooting," for prairie hens, quail, wild duck, and deer. Among the words of caution, they should note that domestic servants were scarce, and "are treated better than in England and are looked upon more in the light of helps than servants."[12] Those with no experience were advised to board on established farms as pupils for a while, and be trained on the job. When they were ready, the Close Brothers company would act as agent to find and purchase farms for them, and get them going.

The takeup was immediate and unprecedented. For a time Close was receiving up to fifty letters of inquiry a day. Part of it was a response to the pervasive gloom about British trade and economic prospects at the end of the 1870s. But Close was also, like Grant, tapping into the long-standing fascination with the prairies, and the more recent hope that the culture and traditional pursuits of the British countryside could somehow be transferred to them. In theory, similar schemes for collective upper-class immigration would have been feasible in New Zealand, Australia, or Southern Africa, but they were much further away, and never carried the same mystique. The day of wealthy emigration to the Canadian prairies was yet to come.

A steady flow of Britons were soon following the Pied Piper's call, and when they reached Plymouth County, their first impressions were reassuring. The gently undulating landscape reminded them of home, a flatter version of the Wiltshire Downs, or Leicestershire without the hedges and stone walls. In this familiar-looking countryside, it was possible to believe that they could, once properly established, live in the manner and style they hoped for. The local practice was for farms to be known simply by their owners' names, but the newcomers tried to raise the tone by giving their spreads proper identities, as they would have done at home. Neatly lettered signs appeared along the straight section roads, at points where rougher tracks led off toward a house and a cluster of outbuildings. They recalled the English countryside: Gypsy Hill Farm, Carlton Farm, Westbourne Farm, Prestledge Farm; or evoked Ireland, Wales, or Scotland: Dromore Farm, Snowdon, Troscoed, Garrickdale, Inchinnoch, Cairlogie.

Though they bought land over a wide area, up to twenty-five miles out from Le Mars, spreading into neighboring counties, the British converged on the town to buy groceries and farm supplies, to meet each other, and to get some relief from the isolation of farm life. On Main Street, lined with buggies and farm wagons that were mud-spattered in spring and autumn and coated with dust in summer, groups of well-turned-out Englishmen hailed old friends from school or college, or distant cousins, in booming voices. To accommodate new arrivals and their families, the Close company bought the Commercial Hotel and changed the name to the more aspirational Albion House. For a lower nightly rate, visitors could put up at the House of Lords, a British-run tavern that served Bass ales and Guinness. Other saloons appealing to the British included the House of Commons and the Windsor Castle. If some of the older Le Mars residents took against the slightly imperious way in which the newcomers made themselves quickly at home, they could also see how they were benefiting, if only on paper, as property values rocketed upwards. Mr. O. A. Moore had homesteaded land two miles north of Le Mars in 1869, and built a farmhouse on a spot which had the highest elevation for many miles around, with views up and down the shallow Floyd

Valley. He had planted a sizable grove of trees, by now well established, and bought more land. His neighbors were excited when they learned he had sold his 280 acres to the Honorable Reynolds Moreton, fifth son of the Earl of Ducie, for the fabulous price of $34 an acre.

Moreton, a forty-four-year-old retired naval captain, ordered the construction of a seventeen-room house with a mansard roof and bay windows, and two large hay barns, with new corncribs, cattleyards, and pigpens. He moved in with his wife, Margaret, three sons, two daughters, and four Irish servants. From the start the Closes thought it important to have experienced older men, like Moreton, to bring stability and balance, and the captain became a leader in the colony, running his farm with the brisk efficiency he had brought to Her Majesty's warships. He added to his land until he had nearly 1,000 acres, dug wells, erected a windmill, and prospected for coal.

The incomers were a cross-section of the Victorian upper class, young men just out of private school or university, younger sons of aristocrats and clergy, retired army officers, and men who had tried other careers but now wanted something more adventurous. They arrived expecting a healthy prairie life, and fresh start, but in a familiar social framework. Robert Maxtone Graham, second son of a Scottish laird, brought up at Cultoquhey House in Perthshire, came in the very early days, and took to it so well that he wrote a testimonial for the Close pamphlet. The Honorable Frank Sugden, son of a clergyman and grandson of Lord St. Leonards, came after he had tried sheep raising in Minnesota. Alfred Lascelles, a younger son in a family of eleven children, and a grandson of the Earl of Harewood, came straight after Oxford, with his university friend Matthew, the second son of Sir Charles Smith-Dodsworth. Gerald Garnett, son of a Lancashire landowner, and a keen cricketer and horseman, arrived after school at Cheltenham. Walter and James Cowan had both been at Winchester, and headed for Iowa after failing to get army commissions as their elder brother had done. Walter was twenty-four, James nineteen.

The Honorable Eric Rollo, son of Lord Rollo, was joined by his younger brother Herbert. The Honorable Ronald and Cecil Jervis were sons of a viscount. Admiral Sir Arthur Farquar, who had thirteen children, bought 1,100 acres only six miles west of Le Mars, named it "Cairlogie Farm," and set up four of his sons—Albert, James, Mowbray, and William—with a spinster aunt to keep an eye on them. The size and quality of the houses the British colonists built were themselves objects of wonder. Newly arrived German or Swedish farmers would reckon to spend $200 or $300 for a two-room farmhouse, to an almost standard design. Captain Moreton's mansion cost $20,000, and included a fine walnut staircase. Arthur Gee's cost $17,000. The English put in bathrooms, and powerful furnaces blasting heat up from the basement through the winter. As the community grew, more brought wives and families. Several married while they were in Le Mars, to the sisters or cousins of their friends, and a few to Iowa girls. At the peak, around 1883, there were reckoned to be between five hundred and six hundred of them. There was nowhere else like it in the United States.

A sense of how the rest of Le Mars saw the influx, and the impression the new arrivals made, comes from a newspaper account of the station in the spring of 1881: "A rare sight indeed is the Le Mars depot on the arrival of fresh accessions to the English colony. The newcomers confound all our knowledge and established traditions of immigrants, for immigrants they are. They descend from the recesses of the Pullman palace cars dressed in the latest London and Paris styles, with Oxford hats, bright linen shining on their bosoms, gold repeater ticking in the depths of their fashionably cut vest pockets. . . ." The women were equally well dressed, with coquettish bonnets on their heads, fresh-faced, beaming with ruddy health. The children were clean and well cared for, "and nowhere among young or old is there a hint of travel-stained weariness or poverty."[13]

They brought nannies for the children, gun dogs, and spaniels. One family was clocked in with eighty-two pieces of luggage. Far from mocking or sneering, the *Sentinel* reaction was one of admiration and respect: "They are by no means as dainty as they seem. In a day or two the men are seen on the streets in the plainest of corduroy suits, with knee-britches and leather leggings. Great strong, hardy looking fellows they are, with plenty of muscle and snap. . . . The question will be asked, What kind of settlers for a new country do these dainty and wealthy looking persons make? And the answer is, the best in the world."[14]

For those established for some time, the young farm pupils provided a free source of labor. Captain Moreton relied on a changing crew of well-connected apprentices to do his work for him, before they moved up in the pecking order to buy their own farms. Other ex-officers who took in trainees included Colonel James Fenton, Captain Cooper, and Captain Bridson. The pupils, referred to as "pups," received no wages, and many paid an initial premium. Frank Baker, son of a gentleman farmer, signed indenture papers and paid out £100 to work for the Closes' own farm for a period of a year, plus another £50 for his board. He was only in Le Mars for two hours before Frederick collected him and drove him twenty-two miles to the Close farm at Quorn. "They make us work pretty hard here . . . ," Frank wrote to his parents, "and as they are behind hand because the winter was very long, there is a great deal to do."[15]

In the first few weeks he helped with sheep-dipping, and the range of farm chores. "We had one day branding cattle, rather fun, but you get kicked pretty well all over, and up to your knees in mud." One of the few who already knew about farming, because his father ran 600 acres in Kent, Frank was unimpressed by the Closes' claim to "training," and wished he had not been signed up. "There is really nothing to learn about the sort of farming required here. They just scratch the land and stick in a crop and put the same thing in again next year. They only grow Indian corn, oats and millet on this farm. They say wheat does not pay, in fact only sheep and cattle and hogs, and sheep best of all."[16] Baker's own hopes of buying a place for himself ended early, in tragedy. He died after contracting typhoid, after only six weeks at Le Mars, and was buried in the local cemetery.

Most of the single young men were doing manual labor for the first time in their lives, and it took a while for the soft-handed sons of aristocrats, squires, and parsons to get used to long days wielding shovels or brooms, axes or hay rakes. Walter Cowan described the routine in a letter to his sister Lillias: "We turn out at 5.30 and go out to what we call 'chaws.' 'Chaws' means feeding the beasts, milking, and cleaning out the sheds. . . . I clean out and feed my four horses, groom them and harness the ones that are going to work. Then I feed the pigs and come in for breakfast."[17] He spent the main part of the day cutting fenceposts, plowing, or carting hay. Before they finished at 7 p.m., there were cattle to bring in and hogs to be fed again. Walter was determined to stick to it: "A very few days of this kind of life lets a fellow understand what it really is and I am certain it will suit me."[18] A few months later, he assured his parents, "We are both in perfect health and hardest possible 'training,' regular boat race form. No amount of physical exertion seems to have any effect on us now that we have got into our present condition . . . in England I could never have bound sheaves in harvest time from early morn till dewy eve without collapsing but I am fully capable of doing that now."[19]

Captain Moreton, who believed no British young gentleman could work hard on an American farmer's diet of beans and bacon, fed his boys generously, with beef and potatoes, pies and puddings. They slept at the top of the house, in a long dormitory, as they had at their boarding schools, and in the evening played cards, chess, or cribbage together, or sang round the captain's piano. Before they bought their own property, the Cowans were on separate farms, a few miles apart. James went to Mr. Price, forty-two, who had been a master at Cheltenham. Walter Cowan stayed with Jack Watson, who had managed to pull off what other genteel settlers would acknowledge as the ultimate arrangement, importing his old nanny. "I am sure I will be comfortable as he keeps a Scottish housekeeper who used to be his nurse. She is a regular old family servant and was so devoted to him and his brother that she came out with them when they left home."[20] On Walter's twenty-fifth birthday, she produced a rhubarb tart with his initials on the crust. "You have no idea of the sumptuous way in which we live. Mrs. McPhail is really a boss cook and is able to make so many tasty little dishes."[21]

In their own small preserve of Englishness, the naive young Cowans hoped they could enjoy all the fulfillment and adventure of the prairie life without too much contact with the natives. In another letter home Walter told his mother why they were so satisfied with the arrangements so far: "Our great advantage is having no Americans on either farm. We both of us have good homes, good food, and English gentlemen to associate with, and what could you wish for more?"[22]

Though they could enjoy a microcosm of English society, and keep up standards in the kitchen, there was nothing they could do about the very un-British weather. New arrivals soon discovered that the extremes had been played down in the Close pamphlets. The summer heat was fiercer than represented and the winters colder. James wrote that "Last Friday and yesterday were two of the hottest days I have ever been out in. The thermometer on Friday morning standing at 105f and I was working in the sun all day."[23] Tornados scythed in regularly from the west and southwest. "English people can have no idea of what storms are like out here. They are a regular terror. Thunder and lightning are terribly severe, but the wind and hail storms are what we are all so afraid of. A man never knows at what moment his buildings, crops and stock may be all dashed to pieces, so you may imagine that seeing a storm coming may be anxious work."[24]

Hailstorms, during which stones as large as cricket balls pelted from the clouds, were terrifying. The bombardment of ice, starting with almost no notice, could decimate standing crops, and kill or concuss hens, geese, and cattle. One July afternoon during his first summer, Walter was driving a wagon home when the sky darkened suddenly and he heard a roaring sound. He whipped the team on as fast as he could, along a road already puddled and mired from earlier rain, toward the nearest farm. "When about ¼ mile from the house the stones fell thicker and thicker and one caught me on my knuckles and made me drop my reins." He managed to grab them with his other hand, and raced into the yard just as the storm arrived in earnest. "I stopped at the stable door and tried to unharness my horses but it was no good, I simply could not stand the hail any longer. Three big stones caught me nearly simultaneously on the head, one of which cut my head pretty badly. Another came whack on my knee and lamed me for a while."[25]

None of this discouraged the two Cowan brothers. After six months they found land they could afford, though it was twenty miles west of Le Mars where the more attractive rolling country ended in a bluff, overlooking a belt of low-lying land along the Big Sioux River. On the far side, the flat, drier Dakota Territory stretched westwards. They persuaded their father to put aside his worry that the boys might lose the family capital from storms or floods, and send the money they were asking for. They bought 600 acres of rich, fertile, pasture running beside the river, and tried to get a house, barns, and sheds built before winter started in earnest. By November the cold was setting in, and the two put on a cheerful face. Walter wrote that "Tonight it is milder again, only 20 degrees of frost. We have moved into the house now, but of course everything is upside down and it will be sometime before we get settled. It is most comical how everything gets frozen, even the very ink I am writing with had to be melted on the stove before I could begin writing."[26]

By the following summer, the corn was planted and they had bought their first pigs, and they congratulated themselves on how clean and well ordered the farm was. "Yankees as a rule are terribly untidy and seem not to have the smallest sense of neatness . . . plenty of people have told us that ours is the neatest farm they have seen!"[27] They found an English couple to help them, though Mrs. Taylor's cooking was no match for Mrs. McPhail's. The ingenuous James continued to grumble about his American neighbors, who were not only untidy and untrustworthy to deal with but did not treat God's creatures properly: "A Yankee looks upon a horse or any animal simply as a machine out of which to get as much profit as possible at the smallest possible cost and trouble and also something that is meant to be ill used. The way some of them treat their horses is simply atrocious and makes me so savage at some times that I can hardly control myself."[28]

The progress of Le Mars was closely followed in Britain. The proprietor of *The Times*, John Walter, passed through in the course of an American tour and was full of admiration. *The Field* ran a long piece under the heading MR. CLOSE'S COLONY IN IOWA, suggesting this corner of the prairies was under English upper-class occupation. "On a Saturday afternoon the streets of Le Mars are full of English ladies and English gentlemen, of English children and English babies. There is but little provincial about it—it is a metropolitan picnic in a provincial town; for all the young fellows have the air of the public school, the university or the United Service about them, and so discomfort is laughed at, inconvenience chaffed at, and hardship ignored."[29]

Nugent Townshend, tireless western correspondent for *The Field*, was taken through the country around Le Mars in a light buggy, driven by Hugh Hornby, the twenty-two-year-old son of Sir Edward Hornby. He found an Arcadian scene: "The small grain was nearly all in sheaf that day, and tall green Indian corn waved in the warm prairie breeze. English farmhouses dot the hillsides near and far; a few poplar-like cottonwood trees grow well as shade and shelter for these homesteads. . . ." Their first stop was at Captain Moreton's exemplary Dromore Farm, where

"Lord Hobart was mowing, assisted by two of Lord St. Vincent's sons, and the Hon. Captain was feeding a threshing machine. It was hot but everyone looked happy. . . ." Again, a picnic atmosphere could be detected, and the twenty-two "pups," doing all the farmwork, were "clear eyed, bronzed and muscular, in the highest health and spirits. How much more sensible and useful lives they live here than they would live at home!" It was August, and calling at a succession of British farms, they spun across fields where the grass came up to the knees of the two fast-trotting horses. Invited to dinner with Charles and Harry Eller, Townshend was delighted to find "English servants, English cooking, and thorough English neatness."[30]

New York's *Harper's* magazine, so interested in Rugby, Tennessee, that it had run two long articles on the Hughes settlement the previous autumn, sent a reporter out to Iowa to see the latest example of British colonization. "The young men who make up this community are, for the most part, graduates of Oxford and Cambridge. On one farm I met two tall and handsome young farmers whose Uncle had been a distinguished member of parliament. The last time I had seen them had been in a London drawing room. . . ."[31] Poultney Bigelow, the writer, seemed as impressed by the milieu as any gushing society columnist. He dropped the names of young aristocrats, the sons of judges and admirals, and a few with more rarefied claims to fame: "Another young farmer whom I noticed on horseback with top-boots, flannel shirt, sombrero, and belt knife, was pointed out to me as the grandson of the author of *'Paley's Theology.'* He was attending a cattle auction. . . ." These enterprising youths "had all been attracted here by their love of a free, active life, and the knowledge that they would enter a society congenial to their tastes and early associations."[32]

The rugged example set by "young England" led some to fear that America's own privileged youths were lagging behind. *Century* magazine, also in New York, published a letter asking: "Why should not the men of Harvard, Yale, Princeton, Columbia, and the other colleges of the East, organize colonies in the West, and, while making homes and careers for themselves assist in building up this new country?" The editor agreed there was potential, but the east coast youngsters had to examine themselves carefully. "It would be a grievous mistake to suppose that a change of longitude alone insures success. Idleness, incompetency, and a nerveless, drifting disposition, have no better chance in Montana than Massachusetts."[33]

The British around Le Mars were soon constructing a coexistent world, in which almost all their particular requirements, appetites, and interests were catered for. To provide for their spiritual needs, they imported the Reverend Herbert Cunningham, an English clergyman and a classical scholar of Brasenose College, Oxford. With his help, they raised money to build their own Episcopalian church, in a traditional Gothic style, though constructed of painted wooden boards, with stained glass and a small spire, where they sang the Anglican hymns they had grown up with, and followed the English prayer book. Captain Moreton was a lay reader. Le Mars was said to be the only church in the country where prayers were offered for Queen Victoria as head of state.

Even before the church was completed, the colonists set up another essential, their own gentleman's club, with an entrance fee of $25 and a similarly high annual subscription. Membership was limited to British men of the right background, to be vetted by the committee, for a careful distinction was made between "British gentlemen residents" and "British residents." After an inaugural meeting, held at Captain Moreton's, they found premises in a new brick building, at the junction of Main Street and Third Avenue, across from the Plymouth County Bank. There were similarly masculine retreats all over the British Empire, and though Le Mars was not technically part of this, the Prairie Club followed the standard formula. With heavy furnishings, soon impregnated with pipe and cigar smoke, the club had a room for billiards, a reading room with the London papers and periodicals, a club room, bar, and kitchen, and limited sleeping accommodation. A Le Mars paper, allowed to view the sanctum, called it "a paradise of luxury, ease and comfort." The man from *The Field* also approved. "I maintain that, at any rate abroad, nothing so keeps up the *esprit de corps* of Englishmen as a club of their own. Nothing creates so strong a moral control over the actions of new arrivals as the opinion of a club of their fellow-countrymen."[34]

The club became the main meeting place for the most active and gregarious members of the colony. Regular concert parties included comic turns, songs, and recitals; and "The Prairie Minstrels," a group of members on banjo, bones, tambourine, and triangle, entertained with a medley of popular tunes. The British soon had their own choir, and amateur dramatics. The Reverend Cunningham started a chess club. Fancy dress dances, then so popular back at home, catered to the need to put on extravagant, bizarre, or humorous clothes, and colonists turned out as clowns, sailors, bandits, or pantomime villains. In a sign of how quickly the recent Sioux inhabitants had ceased to be taken seriously, three colonists came to one party dressed as Red Indians.

Each Thursday, the *Le Mars Sentinel* reminded its readers of the fairy tale that was under way, and held forth about their town's miraculous advance. In less than twenty years, Le Mars had moved from bleak prairie, over which the red man roamed, to become "the crowning gem in the bright galaxy of fair Iowa's cities." A regular column of terse jottings gave a kaleidoscopic sense of this progress:

—*Clarke, the new dry goods man, is having a fine run of business.*

—*Wilcox has raised his hardware store and made a sidewalk to grade.*

—*There was a slim attendance at the Temperance meeting on last Sunday night.*

—*Baptist oyster supper on Wednesday.*

—*The English boys are to play a big game of football on the 19th.*

In the gist of these listings, as in real life, it was the focus on outdoor sport and horseflesh that distinguished the British from everyone else. When they were not attending to their businesses, or farming, other citizens of Le Mars devoted themselves to the onward and upward process of civic improvement. They pressed the county for bridges to replace the fords across the roads, campaigned for gutters and drains to reduce the great mire of mud that filled the streets in the fall, established a fire department, and looked forward to a waterworks and gaslights. But the British, whose capital and buying power contributed much to the town, seemed to view their farms as duties that had to be attended to as quickly as possible, and conserved the best of their energies and efforts for recreation and hunting.

The town's two newspapers, grateful for column-filling ballast of any kind, carried dense reports of rugby football matches. The Le Mars home team played another English side from Akron and West Fork. "After the drop out F. Close got away with the ball and made a rare run passing to Waddilove, who nearly got in but was well tackled by J. D. Chiene within 20 feet of the goal line. A splendid rush by the Le Mars forwards led by Farquar and Colledge made matters better. . . ."[35]

They held tennis championships and athletics meetings, and started a cricket club, leveling a pitch near the brickyards. Captain Moreton served as president. "A game of cricket will be played by two picked English teams," noted the *Sentinel*, ". . . and this will be the first ever played in Le Mars, and in the Northwest as far as we know. It is looked forward to by our citizens with interest."[36] Cricket teams were formed in surrounding small towns, and Le Mars played visitors from the city of St. Paul. They learned ice hockey to occupy themselves in the winter. The Floyd River was too narrow and serpentine for rowing, and the

Big Sioux, eyed up by William Close, had other disadvantages. But rowers could be accommodated on Spirit Lake, eighty miles to the north across the Minnesota border, which became a small summer outpost. The most dedicated Le Mars oarsmen went up to practice and race, and the Honorable Ronald Jervis, the future Lord St. Vincent, won the single sculls in 1884.

As ever, it was horses—for hunting, racing, and polo—that aroused the most passion and gave the greatest opportunities for spending and display. "They have the very best ground for fox hunting in the world," warbled Poultney Bigelow, ". . . a rolling prairie with a creek here and there. Every colonist makes it his chief care, after buying his farm, to breed a good hunter for the steeplechases. . . ."[37] The racing began modestly in 1880, and the first spring meeting held on Captain Laing's farm had the feel of an English country point-to-point. The course circled round a patch of higher ground, which gave a vantage point from which spectators could watch the horses taking the rough fences. Close Brothers presented a $50 prize for the principal contest, the mile-and-a-half Le Mars Cup. The following year, the occasion had escalated into something altogether bigger. Better horses, including valuable thoroughbreds from England, were entered. An improved location was found, a new wooden grandstand was erected, and more prize money, bookmakers, beer tents, and stalls made for a festive atmosphere.

These refinements and fripperies were some way from the wild, dangerous, shaggy races that Captain Stewart had run across the natural meadows at the Green River rendezvous fifty years earlier. As the buggies from the farms drove into the raceground, the Le Mars Cornet Band played, and riders wearing brightly colored silk shirts and caps moved through the crowds, the town could persuade itself that here was something close to Derby Day at Epsom. "The whole made up a panorama of life, activity and sportive energy never before seen in this region. Conspicuous everywhere was the omnipresent Englishman, to whom a horse race is the sum total of human enjoyment," said the *Sentinel*.[38] The appreciative American crowds seemed to accept that British rules applied. All but two of the six races were restricted to English-owned horses, or horses ridden by Englishmen. One race, the Hail Columbia Stakes, was reserved for American-owned horses, but only two could be found to take part. Few American farmers were willing to fritter their time on sport when there was so much farmwork to be done, or to spend money on horseflesh that could otherwise be spent on livestock, or a new reaper.

The June Derby, and another meeting in October, became regular dates in the Le Mars calendar, with special excursion trains and press coverage as far away as Chicago. The English races enhanced the town's reputation, marking it out from others of the same size, so that it became "a city of the first class rather than the third," as one proud local put it. When Frederick Close went on to introduce the game of polo, which had only just arrived among the millionaires of Newport and New York, the special status of Le Mars was confirmed once again. He formed a polo league with clubs in Sioux City, Sibley, and Denison. At Cairlogie Farm, the four Farquar brothers—a team in themselves—bought nimble Indian ponies, built log stables, and practiced on a flattish paddock across a small creek from the farm.

Though horses were all-important, Poultney Bigelow's claim that this was also the "best ground for fox hunting in the world" was fanciful. The country might have looked like Leicestershire, but Iowa foxes were rare, with so little cover, and becoming rarer. Shooting was limited to prairie chickens, rabbits, ducks, and snipe. So when all else failed, the colonists rode after a paper trail, strewn from a satchel by a rider going ahead. Further west from Le Mars, James Cowan tried hunting otters by, and in, the Big Sioux River, and wolves could still be found. "The way fellows hunt here does not take my fancy much. They track a wolf in the snow or hunt about till they see one and then run him down in a few minutes with large greyhounds. I am going to start on

an entirely different plan and hunt him with 'smell dogs' just as
one hunts a fox. I don't care what anyone says, even if you don't
kill so often, you have much better sport; and in about two years
time Mr. Cowan's Wolf Hounds will hold the foremost place in
the packs of North West Iowa and be unique in their composi-
tion."[39] Cowan's pack was never formed. In truth, there was less
to hunt than there would have been at home, where game laws
and estate keepers ensured there was always some bird or animal
to be raised. Nor was big game within easy traveling distance.
The nearest grizzly bear and wapiti were almost 500 miles away.
When they read the books of William Baillie-Grohman, or Lord
Dunraven describing campaigns in the Rockies, they seemed
almost as wondrous to the colonists in Le Mars as they would
have done when read in Sussex.

Iowa farming proved to be not as fulfilling or profitable as
they had expected, either. This was not the country for grazing
large numbers of cattle, nor was it suitable for great expanses of
waving wheat. It was best used for labor-intensive mixed farming, to grow some beans and potatoes, grass for the hay crop, and
corn that could then be used to fatten hogs and cattle. Settlers
found it hard to hire men to help them, and were locked into
the grind of plowing, harrowing, sowing cereals and beans, harvesting corn, husking, and throwing the cobs into a wagon once
the frost had come. The winters, when the farms could be cut
off for several days and the ground was deep frozen, were hard
to endure. The wealthier Englishmen, like Lord Hobart, or the
Honorable Arthur Lascelles, who inherited £60,000 while living
near Le Mars, were able to return home each November. Those
who had to stick it out, feeding the pigs and cattle and breaking
the ice round the water troughs with a crowbar, suffered from
loneliness and homesickness. Though many, including Captain
Moreton, made spectacular profits from raising pigs at the start,
prices were falling by the time the Cowans arrived, and their
animals were repeatedly struck by swine cholera. After further

setbacks and accidents, they had to ask their father to help them out and transfer more money.

In their letters home the Cowans tried to maintain the image of the West they had had before they left, and which their friends and relatives still subscribed to. James wrote to his mother that "if you can picture me in an old cloth hat, flannel shirt with rolled up sleeves open in front, pair of breeches, thick boots and spurs, with a big stock whip riding a bay mare and sweeping majestically across the boundless prairie, followed by three faithful hounds, the herd in the distance and no houses within two or three miles, you will have me as I have been for the last three weeks."[40] But they were deceiving themselves. Iowa arable farming was not about riding the range, and they began to believe they had chosen the wrong state and the wrong latitude.

Other colonists regretted their timing, and the fact that they had chosen to follow the Close brothers to Plymouth County and take up mixed farming, at the moment that the potential for ranching in the grander scenery and better climate of Colorado and Wyoming was just becoming clear. After only eighteen months in Iowa, the Cowan brothers were considering a move. In a week in which the thermometer had dropped to nearly 40° below zero, and after a three-day ice storm in which many cattle and pigs had been killed by the cold, James wrote to their father about selling the Akron farm, and homesteading or buying in the Far West:

Both Walter and I have come to see the advantage of Wyoming. You can either buy a ranch there, or take one up by declaring your intention of becoming an American citizen. . . . If you buy one you can get a good ranch for very little, say $2000 and almost all the rest of your capital can go into stock. The great advantage of all this is that living there costs almost nothing. All your meat and groceries there amount to very little. We have determined to sell out the first chance we get and mean to put the farm on the market at once. . . . Having sold out,

Westward ho! will be our watchword, as no state east of the
Rockies is free from these beastly storms and almost every
state either in or west of the Rockies has plenty of timber so
that building is cheap. . . .[41]

In the era in which a new generation of young British gentry
learned to see the West as a workplace, requiring a degree of economic activity which ate into the leisure pursuits they regarded
as their natural right, they could no longer behave quite as their
fathers had done, who had come for sport alone. It was necessary
to deal with banks and land agents, horse dealers and seed merchants. They had to live alongside Americans and other immigrants from Europe, who were less soigné, however canny, and
whose education had been very different. With the respected
Frederick Close as their example, many of the British tried hard
to enter into local life as Close did, taking part in theatricals and
choirs, and donating prizes for best vegetables at the Plymouth
County agricultural show. But in the privacy of the Prairie Club,
and in letters home, they clung to their sense of caste and identity. Many disliked western manners and forwardness, and complained that Americans could not be trusted and were always in
pursuit of the dollar.

At the same time, the Close Brothers land business went from
strength to strength, just as they had hoped it would. Values continued to rise. While Frederick was still the public face of the
colony, taking part in every possible sport—athletics, football,
cricket, racing, and polo—and attending to morale, his brother
William was steadily amassing more acres not just in Iowa but
in Minnesota and Kansas. By 1882, Close Bros. were advertising
500,000 acres for sale, with offices in Le Mars, Sibley and Pipestone, Minnesota, and were managing the assets of several other
British land companies. Their skill was to blend in with American
commercial life. If they had been true aristocrats, and genuinely
"the Lords . . . Close," this would have been more difficult.

———

THOUGH THE LE Mars gentlemen's colony received the most attention, because of its self-confident sense of identity and the astute-
ness of the Close brothers in publicizing it alongside their main
land company, there were others. In Britain, Kansas was far better known than Iowa, from the buffalo-hunting era, and thanks to
the continuing promotional efforts of the Kansas Pacific Railroad.
"Home on the Range" had just appeared as a poem in a Kansas
newspaper, and was set to music and adapted as a popular song.
It had yet to become the anthem of the Far West as a whole, but
its verses helped convey the ineffable glories claimed for Kansas,
a land of plenty, where seldom was heard a discouraging word,
and the sky was not cloudy all day.

If opening up the high plains of western Kansas had been too
much for George Grant's colonists, life was easier for those who
did not try to go so far. *The Field*'s Nugent Townshend based himself in Topeka in eastern Kansas and speculated in land to hold
and rent. A cluster of about two hundred English "capitalists"
settled around Florence, fifty miles north of Wichita, where the
mix of fields and woods in Marion County reminded them of England. In the subtle gradations of the British class system, which
few Americans could understand, these were not the "gentry" but
"gentleman farmers," who had managed to sell up in Norfolk or
Lincolnshire, and bring their cash to America. They bought land
that had been broken and farmed for a few years, rather than virgin prairie. Though no single promoter or speculator was respon-
sible, they gave each other mutual encouragement. With farming
in their blood, they prospered immediately. "From all, without an
exception, I heard the same tale of present success, and of hopeful-
ness for the future," wrote one visitor. "They speak of hard work
accomplished, of difficulties overcome, of minor losses, of satisfactory profits on the whole, and of a great future that seemed to be
opening out for them in the State of Kansas."[42] Exchange visits

took place between their British Association of Kansas and Le
Mars, with fraternal dinners at which they ate barons of beef and
roast goose, and toasted Her Majesty.

A little later, in south-central Kansas, west of Wichita, a
direct attempt to copy the Le Mars formula was made by Francis Turnley, son of a wealthy Irish landowner. Though he lacked
the resources of the Close family bank, the idea was the same:
buy land, exploit the prairie fever, offer to train gentlemen's sons
to farm, and see values increase to everyone's benefit. Turnley
envisaged a freestanding, exclusively British community, unlike
Le Mars and more similar to Victoria. His smaller creation had
a different character to Le Mars, more raffish and carefree, and
some of his settlers would never have passed muster with the
Prairie Club. Few were from Oxford or Cambridge, or the top tier
of private schools. Some were problem cases, sent into prairie exile
by their fathers, and a few came to practice trades or try running businesses, in a way Thomas Hughes would have approved
of. But as far as their American neighbors were concerned, they
were undoubtedly British gentlemen, with substantial capital, or
living on allowances from home, and their style of life impressed
and exasperated their neighbors as it had elsewhere.

Francis Turnley had spent a brief spell in the army and then
gone to Kansas to fill time, while he waited to inherit his father's
estate on the coast of County Antrim. In 1885, he bought several
thousand acres beside the slow-running Chikaskia River, nine
miles northeast of the small town of Harper, and built a farm. He
bought 2,000 black and white holstein dairy cattle, who grazed in
the fields in the summer and were fed corn in the winter. Friends
from the army and from Ireland came out to join him. The country was flatter than northwest Iowa and not so attractive, and the
summers were sultrier, but the winters were slightly less harsh.
To provide some female society, Turnley's three sisters stayed
for months at a time. There were picnics, musical evenings, and
tennis. One of Turnley's sisters, Sophia, married Captain Percy
Wood, who bred horses on his Titipoo Ranch.

What began as a lackadaisical farming venture, in congenial expatriate company, soon turned into something more ambitious. Infected by the enterprise on every side of him, and seeing the rapid rise in land prices and the continuing fascination with Kansas back home, Turnley used more of his father's money to buy additional property, to rent or sell off to Britons of his own class. His land company was centered on a new town he laid out and called "Runnymede," on land that sloped gently down to the river, with his own ranch on the far side. From England, where he went to recruit colonists, Turnley wrote back to Kansas, "Am preparing to advertise the place largely, and am satisfied that I can bring quite a large colony. Send photos as soon as possible, need them badly, and be sure and send me the 'Harper Sentinel' every week."[43]

Captain Charles Seton traveled out in a group of sixteen men, crossing on the RMS *Britannic* and bringing his savings for a house and farm. William Hooper, another former army officer, had been recruited to manage a hotel. But most of the party were younger, and coming as farm trainees. Hooper, an old acquaintance of Turnley, wrote home to his wife: "The boys Francis is bringing out seem rather a nice lot and I fancy we shall all get on well."[44] Among the youngsters who paid $500 to be indentured at Turnley's own Chikaskia Ranch was nineteen-year-old Lionel Palmer, fifth son of Sir Mark Palmer MP, coal owner, ironmaster, and founder of a shipbuilding dynasty in the northeast of England. Once they had arrived, Hooper found the heat not as bad as he feared, and even enjoyed the storms: "We had a lively thunder storm on Sunday night . . . it was a most glorious sight, and the lightning here does not appear to be nearly so dangerous as it is at home, because instead of striking down from the heavens it darts up into the clouds from the earth."[45]

Runnymede's principal street included a general store and post office, a butcher, a dairy, a billiard parlor, a blacksmith, and a three-story hotel. The Runnymede Arms was built under the direction of Captain Charles Seton, formerly of the Hampshire

Regiment, and run by the newly arrived William Hooper. Though they failed to find a permanent clergyman, they built a small Episcopal church, in the same style as Le Mars. Unlike northwest Iowa, where the "top shelfers" were spread over a wide area and tied into a larger economy, the Runnymede colony was highly concentrated, and Turnley's private fiefdom. He accepted the incomers as pupils or buyers; he was the biggest farmer; and he held the lots in the town. As well as taking premiums from the pupils, he stood to gain from almost every land transaction. He owned the general store and post office, and the major share in the hotel. But he was also making a long-term property gamble, linked to an expected new railway. A new line was planned, connecting Wichita with El Paso to the south and west. If it came through Runnymede, as he was lobbying for, the town would grow rapidly, and Turnley and the group of friends he had first settled with would make their fortunes.

As more young Britons arrived, the familiar pattern was followed. They started a tennis club, took up clay pigeon shooting, played cricket, and formed the Runnymede Wanderers Football Club. They held monthly horse races on a new track, and laid out a separate steeplechase course, with hedges and water ditches to jump. As at Le Mars, the round of fixtures and entertainments seemed endless to the local newspapers. "The 31st of October will be a great day in Runnymede. There will be athletic sports from 11 to 12, an hour rest for dinner, and then horse racing and general jollification until dark. Then after supper a dance will be given."[46] When polo was played for the first time, the *Harper Sentinel* explained the game: "There were four men on each side, all riding ponies and armed with long handled clubs something like a croquet mallet set diagonally so as to strike parallel to the ground . . . it is surprising how quickly the cowpony catches on the game, chasing the ball through all the runs, repulses and scrimmages, with apparently as much concern as he would display in separating cattle."[47]

The hunting was better than in Le Mars. The Chikaskia Hounds, with H. G. Hoblyn as Master, met on Mondays and Thursdays during the winter season, with the followers dressed in red coats. In the absence of foxes, the hounds went after coyote, as they had at Victoria. When there were no coyotes, they were reduced to rabbits. Neighboring farmers did not appreciate the British convention that riders could follow hounds wherever the scent took them, tearing over newly sown fields or growing crops. A little further away, in rougher, scrubbier country that was slashed by more small valleys, it was possible to hunt wolves. For a time Lionel Palmer had charge of a pack of twelve wolfhounds while their owner, Major Lobb, was back in England. "I have killed five wolves this season. Its rare good sport when you jump canyons 20 feet wide, which if you fall down you'r a gonner. It makes you put in the spurs pretty tight."[48]

As in Le Mars, the locals in Harper, Danville, and Norwich welcomed the effect on their land values, though the practical jokes and drinking sprees tested their patience· "If, when the Englishmen take the town next, they would leave the uncivilized American citizens a quiet corner, the latter would be everlastingly obliged."[49] They knew them as "remittance men," a term just coming into use in Australia and Canada to describe young upperclass Englishmen distributed to far corners of the empire because there was no outlet for them at home.

If Runnymede was more carefree than Victoria or Le Mars, it was largely because of the style set by its founder. Francis Turnley lacked the zeal and vision of George Grant, or the social connections, financial backing, and seriousness of William Close, but understood the type of young men he was bringing in. Runnymede made the Le Mars colonists seem hardworking drudges by comparison. Most saw their time on the prairies as a lighthearted and probably temporary adventure, subsidized by the banker's drafts they received from home. Few of the pupils actually bought their own farms; but after several years in Runnymede, the young

Lionel Palmer saw a ranch he wanted to buy, when one of the early arrivals died. He wrote to his wealthy father, who had a house off Grosvenor Square and a 4,000-acre estate at Grinkley Park in Yorkshire, asking for money. Sir Mark, whom Lionel referred to as "the Governor," thought he knew his son and refused point-blank, despite an intervention from Turnley.

In Kansas, crossed by the old overland trails that the fur trade caravans and emigrant wagons had taken to the Rockies, the prairie experience seemed more authentic, with more reminders of the recent history than in Iowa. Wichita had grown up at a crossing of the Arkansas River, one of the principal routes into Indian country from the Mississippi, followed by many of the early explorers and travelers, including Stephen Long and George Catlin. British buffalo hunters had come up the Arkansas and been guided from Fort Gibson, Kansas. Expanses of the original prairie grass were still to be found, in uneven country that had not yielded to the plow. To give a sense of the new world he had moved to, Lionel Palmer sent home a parcel of souvenirs, including an ear of Runnymede-grown corn, a cowboy's powder flask made from buffalo horn, a pair of worn Mexican spurs, an Indian pipe and slippers, and some wolf hides. "I couldn't get the Indian head dress into the bag as it is a big thing. You will have to get the hides properly tanned as I only caught them the other day."[50] Harper County was on the very southern boundary of the state, backing onto the 37° line of latitude that marked the border with Indian Territory, into which more than sixty tribes had been shifted from the east or north during the removals. When Runnymede was enjoying its brief hey-day, the border was a focus of the nation's attention, as the Indian Territory was superseded by the creation of Oklahoma, and the Cherokee strip was opened up to settlement.

Though they were technically in the corn belt, they were much closer to true cattle country and the vast ranch acreages of the South and West. While the cattle kept by Turnley and his Harper County neighbors were improved breeds, sleek and fat from being fed on rich grass and corn, meat prices were kept down by the cheaper, scrawnier longhorns being driven north from Texas to the Kansas railheads. Most came up the Chisholm Trail, only twenty miles away from Runnymede. At nearby Caldwell, terminus of the trail for several years during the 1880s before the railway was extended further south, the colonists could see the cattlepens and loading chutes, and the residual dust and stench of a cow town.

The Runnymede British settlers had been exposed to the same long tradition of western fiction, going back to the 1830s, as those who preceded them, but because they had grown up a generation later, they were more influenced by the recent changes that had taken place in the image of the Far West. The imaginations of the first boys to read Captain Mayne Reid had still been fired by the interplay between trappers, voyageurs, settlers, and Indians, and the Mexican and Indian wars. But as the West was tamed and the Indians were ground down, the new era produced its own stories. In the cheap railway novels mythologizing the life of "Wild Bill" Hickok, or Calamity Jane, a fresh cast was introduced, who lived out their lives on the cattle ranges. Stories for boys now dealt with lassoing and branding at the roundup, cattle rustlers, sheriffs, and mail coach robbers. The trappers were gone, buffalo were scarcer, and Indians were rarer, making die-hard raids. It was the cowboys, inevitably depicted as skilled horsemen—rugged, brave, and independent—who now provided the most interesting characters. They were muscular, clear-eyed, honorable and, in fiction at least, usually Anglo-Saxon.

Influenced by these role models, the Runnymede colonists tried to act out the part, if only to impress their relations at home. They sent back pictures of themselves, mounted on horseback in broad-brimmed hats and tasseled leather jackets, with bone-handled pistols in their belts. In a letter packed with bravado, Lionel Palmer told his older brother Claude, a steadier character who had entered the family shipyard in Sunderland, "This life wouldn't suit you very well, it is rough and tumble and a man has to be as careless of his life as he does others. I have been in several shooting rows in drinking saloons. I saw a cowboy shot dead as mutton for shooting a billiard ball off the table."[51]

As the remittance men lived out their fantasies, the editor of the *Harper Sentinel* made another appeal for better behavior. "There are some gentlemen who come over in the evening and amuse themselves by firing off six-shooters in Main Street. Now, my dear children, kindly refrain from making yourselves a nuisance in town."[52] Despite the closeness of the Indian Territory, the reality was that Runnymede had been established in a hardworking farming region, a place of quilting bees and church picnics. Their neighbors were sober German-Americans, who recoiled at stories of the wilder West, and were alarmed by all the posing and posturing. One Harper resident, Mrs. Mary Frances Martin, the doctor's wife, recalled, "The greatest danger was that the inexperienced youths might shoot themselves accidentally. . . ." She went to a funeral where young Englishmen from Runnymede served as pallbearers. "As they lowered the coffin their coats fell aside revealing the six-shooters they loved to wear and several families nearly fainted at the sight."[53]

At its peak, Runnymede counted over a hundred colonists; but by 1892 it was all over. Turnley lost his bet on the railway, which passed two miles away, and returned home to Northern Ireland, where he succeeded his father and became a pillar of Protestant society in Antrim. Many of the colonists went back at the same time, or drifted to other parts of Kansas, or on to Colorado or Wyoming, where it was possible to spend far more time in the saddle. Fifteen years later, Captain Seton published his recollections: "Some of us had considerable money—enough to be considered poor in England but comfortable in the United States. None of us had any financial sense. While we waited for a miracle to be performed that would transform . . . the town of Runnymede into a vast metropolis, we feasted and danced and made merry."[54]

THE COLONY AROUND Le Mars had been winding down several years earlier, as the first profits from farming fell, and the settlers finally accepted that their hope for a country life as comfortable as it might have been in Sussex or Gloucestershire was unrealistic. The enhanced forces of nature proved too much for them, when their finely built barns were blown down by tornados and crops were flattened by hailstorms. Some returned to Britain; others stayed in the United States but struck out on their own, finding that proximity to British society and mutual support was not so essential after all. They moved further west to Colorado or Wyoming, or on to the better climate of California. A few went down to Florida, to try growing oranges. A newspaper in Alton, ten miles north of Le Mars, noted that "There is no sadness in the northwest over their flight. In leaving they sunder no ties which will bleed at their departure . . . the idea of caste, of an American aristocracy, is unknown to the brawny armed settlers."[55]

The prairie fever had not ended. It was about to move up to another level, in which all the old factors—the recollection of the wilderness, the wide horizons, the outdoor life, and the limitless space—would continue to exert their appeal, but with far better financial prospects attached. The colonies had been a way for many wellborn families to export a financial liability: their sons. But from the late 1870s it began to seem that the West, while still offering the sense of freedom and release it had always done, could also make or restore their fortunes.

9

Cattle Lords

*Such a mob of Englishmen here you never saw; we are
turning the natives out here and I think we shall annex the
country before long.*

—MORETON FREWEN, Cheyenne, 1883[1]

The stockbrokers and financiers who worked in the City, London's financial district, were always susceptible to fads and fashions, and many of the nineteenth-century investment crazes were linked to the latest opportunity thought to be ripe for the picking in the United States. For a while British investors poured funds into American railway schemes, and then into companies formed to prize gold or silver from the Rockies and the California Sierras. In 1880 a new enthusiasm was pumping up, and it was the most engaging yet, because the landscape and freedoms it evoked were in such contrast to the cramped offices and courtyards, the noisy streets clogged with omnibuses and hansom cabs, around the Stock Exchange and the Bank of England. In the City, and in clubs and country houses, the talk was suddenly of beef cattle on the American prairies, their numbers and their profitability. One cattle trade insider, a farm manager from Berwickshire in Scotland who acted as a go-between for British investors, described the atmosphere he saw on one of his trips back to Britain. "The drawing room buzzed with stories of this last of bonanzas," wrote John Clay, ". . . staid old gentlemen who scarcely knew the difference betwixt a steer and a heifer discussed it over their port and nuts."² *The Times* filled almost a full page with an article about American meat production, showing how and where cattle were raised and how they were sold. As if the figures and statistics were not enough, *The Times* gave an insight into life on the ranges that would have sounded seductive to many of its readers: "The ordinary work consists in riding through plains, parks, and valleys to see that food and water are sufficient, hunting up stragglers, and on some runs providing salt." There were only two periods of really arduous hard work, which were of short duration, "when masters and men, well mounted, 'round up' for miles all the cattle they find, drive them into convenient natural gorges or corrals, brand the young ones and all that are unmarked, separate and forward strays from neighbouring ranches . . . and select animals for killing and sale."³

FROM THE MOMENT when semi-wild long-horned cattle, descendants of animals left by the Spanish colonists, were first rounded up and herded in Texas in the early nineteenth century, the breed's ability to thrive in the desert and brush country of the Southwest was seen as almost miraculous. A new trade developed when it was found that the bony, wild-eyed cattle could be taken up overland trails to Missouri or Illinois, and sold at lower prices and greater profit than the more prepossessing and plumper animals reared in the corn-growing midwestern states themselves. After the Civil War, with the industrial cities showing an insatiable hunger for cheap meat, Texas cattle were driven to new railheads that opened as the lines stretched west and south, and the loading yards of Abilene, Caldwell, then Dodge City, took their turn as the fastest route to the markets. Steam-powered, ingeniously

mechanized killing plants were built in Chicago, St. Louis, and
Kansas City, to slaughter, eviscerate, cut, process, and pack tens
of thousands of animals a day. By 1878, over a million cattle were
being unloaded at the Union Stockyards in Chicago every year.
East coast investors were soon pouring money into the business,
and the British were not far behind, at a time when the pound
sterling was the dominant world currency, and Britain had a vast
surplus of capital looking for a home.

The inspiration for many Britons, and the man who showed
them what was possible, was John Adair, a wealthy landowner
from Ireland. He had come to the United States and made a first
fortune as a broker in New York, funneling British loans to American borrowers at high interest rates. While taking a trip to hunt
buffalo, which had by then become "the thing," he saw the business promise of the new West and moved his office to Denver.
In 1876 he met the legendary cowman Charles Goodnight, who
had been one of the first to herd columns of beef cattle up from
Texas, and went into partnership with him. Adair put in $50,000
to expand a promising cattle operation Goodnight had just established in the Texas Panhandle, taking a half share.

The two went to see the ranch together, southeast of Amarillo in the Palo Duro Canyon, whose sandstone walls dropped
almost 1,000 feet below the monotonous plain, giving a sheltered
range up to fifteen miles across. Until recently the land had been
a Comanche hunting ground, but they had just been routed out by
the U.S. Army and shifted to the Indian Territory, in one of the
last Indian wars. Adair and Goodnight bought an initial 25,000
acres running along a fork of the Red River, and took down a
hundred shorthorn Durham bulls from Colorado to run with
the native Texas cattle and improve the breed. They put a fence
across the canyon to segregate their herd, focus the attentions
of the imported bulls, and keep the thousands of buffalo, who
had been able to survive in the protected canyon, off the brown
grass. They built a headquarters with rock chimneys at each end
of a log building, accommodation for the hands, a mess house, a

blacksmith shop, and a cistern to collect rainwater, and called it the JA Ranch. Adair watched the *vaqueros* heat up the branding irons to an ash gray and sear his initials onto the flanks of the purchased cattle and new calves, in clouds of pungent smoke. It seemed an altogether more wholesome and productive world than his 40,000-acre estate in Donegal, which had been a source of constant aggravation, ever since he evicted two hundred tenants to clear space for a new castle and park for himself.

Adair still liked to spend part of the year in Ireland and England, where he moved in a fast set that included the Prince of Wales. The following summer he came back for a second visit to Texas, this time bringing Moreton Frewen, a young acquaintance from the Leicestershire hunting field, to see the ranch and shoot some of the remaining buffalo, who had so far managed to survive in the canyon. It was Frewen's first transatlantic trip, and he was so captivated by the life that he determined to get into the cattle business as well. Adair and Goodnight continued to occupy more land, and soon the JA claimed 1,335,000 acres and 100,000 cattle. The steers, admired for their fine quality, were driven up to the loading yards at Dodge City and made heady profits for the partnership.

News of Adair's success, and the wealth of other cattle kings, was followed closely in Britain, where farmers, already suffering from imports of cheap wheat, now feared competition from American meat. The introduction of refrigeration on ships meant chilled American quarters of beef were being unloaded at the Liverpool and London docks, while more live cattle were coming on the hoof, to be slaughtered immediately they landed. A Chicago newspaper wrote that "The merry roast beef of England in Old England itself is giving way to American beef, which is now actually ruling the roast there."[4] Believing imports from the plains would soon ruin their home trade, many Britons came to the conclusion that if they could not beat the competition, they should at least try to profit from it.

Happily, they found they had an advantage. It was known

that anyone taking part in the cattle business needed a substantial amount of capital at the start, to cover the costs of raising
or buying animals, and holding on to them for up to four years
before they reached the optimum weight to be sold. They had to
pay the wages and expenses of the herders for the long drive to
the railheads, and the cost of railway cars, before any return was
received from the markets. Borrowing in the United States could
cost up to 16 percent interest. In Britain, investors had difficulty
getting a return of more than 4 percent on their capital, so putting
money into American cattle, either directly or through a company,
sounded lucrative as well as exotic.

Enterprising financiers rushed out prospectuses, illustrated
with finely rendered engravings of placid and corpulent cattle, to
raise money for new British ranching concerns. The pioneer was
the Prairie Cattle Company, capitalized at £200,000 and chaired
by Lord Airlie, which bought range rights and herds in northeast
New Mexico and the Texas Panhandle. Confirming its initial confidence, the Prairie paid a dividend and bonus of 20 percent in
1882, and 28 percent in 1883. Ten other British joint stock companies were formed to put money into Texas alone, including the
Matador, the Western, and the Texas Land & Cattle Company.
Most were launched from Edinburgh or Dundee, because Scots
were thought to know about grazing animals over large areas in
the hills in difficult conditions, and black Highland cattle were
traditionally driven hundreds of miles to be slaughtered. Ambitious young farmer's sons with practical experience of stock raising and droving went out from Scotland to work for western ranch
companies, or vet new acquisitions. Letters and telegrams passed
between Texas, London, Edinburgh, and Aberdeen dealing with
ranch hands' wages, the cost of barbed-wire fencing, and the selling price of "beeves," per 100 pounds, at the slaughtering plants
in Kansas City or Chicago.

American agents and brokers selling land and cattle saw the
novice British investors as an easy mark, taking advantage of

their inexperience to inflate prices or misrepresent what was being acquired. In many deals, the number of cattle was taken at a "book count," a historic figure often far higher than the number actually out on the range. When real tallies were insisted upon, the numbers could be lifted with double-counting scams; but so long as the price of cattle was rising, all this fell within the margin of expected costs.

For the aristocracy, the cattle business had an extra dimension from the beginning. To ordinary investors, the high returns were all that mattered, but for blue-blooded and landed families, who kept clear of most commercial activity, here was something they had a feeling for, which had never been true of silver or copper mining. Scottish lairds, in particular, believed they were on an inside track. The most senior peers could be persuaded to decorate the boards of ranching companies as directors, and put in their own cash. The list of those who took large stakes in companies and syndicates included Lord Aberdeen, Lord Airlie, the Duke of Argyll and his son Lord George Campbell, Lord Castletown, the Earl of Dunmore, the Earl of Ilchester, Lord Neville, the Earl of Strathmore, the Marquis of Tweeddale, and a pack of others.

Though most were simply investors, some acquired ranches for themselves or their families, and took a direct part. Lord Airlie bought a 2,000-acre Colorado ranch for his son the Honorable Lyulph Ogilvy. The monocle-wearing Lord Tweedmouth bought the 200,000-acre Rocking Chair Ranch in the eastern Panhandle, with the Earl of Aberdeen. Tweedmouth then sent one of his younger sons, Archibald Marjoribanks, off to Texas to get him out of harm's way. The twenty-two-year-old had just come down from Oxford, and when he first arrived the cowboys teased and terrified him, riding at him full tilt, yelling and firing their guns. Marjoribanks, who never adjusted to western informality and the lack of respect for titles, disliked being referred to as "Marshie." He spent over ten years at the isolated ranch headquarters in Collingsworth County, serving as assistant manager, keeping the

books, and reporting the smallest expenditure to London. But he
was insufficiently astute to notice that a gigantic fraud was in
progress, and that the manager, John Drew, was systematically
claiming Rocking Chair calves and mavericks for a private herd
in his own name. Lord Tweedmouth and his fellow owners were
puzzled that, at the end of each summer roundup, the Honorable
Archibald's reckonings showed they had far fewer cattle to sell
than they should have done, and the Rocking Chair ran at a spectacular loss.

Scattered across the sun-baked flatlands and hill country of
the Southwest, the scions of British families who tried to establish themselves had mixed success. The Earl of Lichfield sent his
fifth son, Claud Anson, to Texas almost as soon as he had finished
at Harrow. After an apprenticeship working with cattle, he paid
£1,000 to take over the Kickapoo Ranch near San Angelo, and
two of his younger brothers came to join him, later buying their
own ranches. As well as raising beef cattle, they introduced the
game of polo, and bred polo ponies. They adapted to local ways
so quickly that no one ever accused them of arrogance or snobbery, and they were soon accepted among the other Texas ranchers. Lord Delaval Beresford, the youngest son of the Marquis of
Waterford, bought a ranch and hacienda in the far Southwest, in
Mexico, just across the border from El Paso, and almost disappeared from view. Reports came back to his family that he was
living with a Negro woman known as "Lady Flo."

For the 7th Earl of Aylesford, who had hunted tigers in India,
Texas was a refuge of last resort. Fleeing London to get away from
a steamy scandal involving his wife and the Marquis of Blandford, "Sporting Joe" Aylesford arrived with his valet, his horses
and dogs, and a railway car full of baggage. He bought a ranch at
Silver Spring, south of Dallas, to start what amounted to an exile
from London society. Though he showed no capacity for ranching,
his neighbors and hands found him relentlessly hospitable, pressing beer or whiskey on his visitors. The earl drank himself into a

stupor within two years, dying at the age of thirty-eight, leaving
a small mountain of empty bottles behind his ranch.

BRITISH PARTICIPATION INCREASED still further as the cattle business moved north, and into the Rocky Mountain states and territories of Colorado, Wyoming, and Montana. In the mid-1870s a
belt of country hundreds of miles across lay waiting, stretching
up to Manitoba, the buffalo gone, the Indians no longer the danger they had once been after the surrender in May 1877 of Crazy
Horse. The discovery that Texas cattle could be driven 1,000 miles
up to these virgin grasslands, and that they would then put on
weight despite the cold winters before being shipped east to market, shifted the whole orientation of the trade. Cattle ranching
was already profitable, but now it became even more attractive to
Europeans, with an appeal that combined the landscape they had
historically been most inspired by with a farming formula that
seemed almost to be good to be true.

In Texas, where public land was owned by the state rather
than the federal government, and with land grants going back to
Spanish days, large acreages had to be bought freehold or leased,
even if cattle were also grazed on adjacent land that was still in
public hands. But on the northern high plains, where the federal
government had ruled that the newly opened country was to be
homesteaded by bona fide settlers, grazing could be had for free.
It was enough to buy or homestead the minimum 160 acres, to
secure a house, corrals, and the all-important access to water,
and cattle could then be left to wander and feed over a much wider
area on what was termed the "free range."

A series of books and articles spelled out how the free range
economics worked. Cattle could be bought cheap, for a few dollars, fattened on Uncle Sam's land with only a small cost in labor,
and eventually sold for much more. William Baillie-Grohman,

big-game hunter and friend of Lord Dunraven, marveled at the wonder of it all in the *Fortnightly Review*: "To Old World ears it sounds not only strange, but hardly credible, that you or I can today . . . pick out for our stock a good range for grazing, as yet unoccupied, drive on to it a herd of ten thousand cattle, select a suitable spot near to a convenient creek, and there build our ranche . . . and, in fact, make ourselves entirely at home, disporting ourselves as virtual owners of the land, without paying one penny for it, or outstepping any territorial or United States statute, or doing what is not perfectly lawful. There is no trouble about title, deeds, surveyors, and lawyers."[5]

The most persuasive case was made in *The Beef Bonanza; or How to Get Rich on the Plains*, by General James Brisbin, which was published in the United States but sold thousands of copies in Britain. The chapter headings conveyed the feverish tone, and included "The Money to Be Made," "Estimated Fortunes," and "Millions in Beef." Brisbin claimed the profit from cattle on the free range could be as much as 60 percent. A German aristocrat from Breslau, who had settled in Colorado, asserted that by contrast with the much-touted western mining companies, no livestock enterprise had ever failed to pay large dividends, once established. "There is not the slightest element of uncertainty in cattle raising."[6]

As more consignments of cattle were driven up the trails and onto the northern ranges, with up to 4,000 animals jostling and bumping along together in the care of a dozen men, each herd sending up a dust cloud that could be seen for many miles, a new stampede of British aristocrats and gentry rode onto the prairies. John Clay, the Scottish farmer's son who acted for many of the British buyers and companies, described the mood when he first came to western Nebraska and Wyoming: "There was a freedom, a romance, a sort of mystic halo hanging over those green, grassy, swelling divides that was impregnated, grafted into your system. . . . It was another world; the rough, ready, joyous prospect of a broader field on windswept plains. . . ."[7]

For the most elevated, including the Duke of Sutherland, the Duke of Manchester, or the Earl of Strathmore, it was an inspiring but distant world, to which they would make occasional and restorative visits. But for younger sons of noble families who possessed few skills other than riding and shooting, and titled first sons who sensed their British fortunes slipping away, raising cattle along the Rocky Mountain front seemed to offer an irresistible mix of pleasure and profit. It was believed there would be far better sport, and more congenial company, than in Texas or New Mexico, with the prospect of making money on an altogether larger scale than at colonies like Le Mars, if for a larger initial investment.

Baillie-Grohman tried to capture the special appeal.

The stockman's life out West is one offering certain attractive inducements to the English character; for not only does his vocation bring with it an infinite amount of exercise on the bright breezy Plains, in a temperate zone, in the most delightfully bracing climate in the world, but it is a life where manly sport is an ever present element. The cowboy and his horse are one. . . . If the young settler goes far enough West, shooting of the best kind can be combined with the duties of his life. Wapiti and Bighorn are often either a day's or a two day's ride, and an encounter with the dreaded grizzly roaming freely over the uplands will test his nerves. It is a tough life; indeed coming straight from his English club existence, it will at first perhaps repel him. But the roughness has its good sides, a short experience generally sufficing to weed out the effeminate and unmanly. . . .[8]

If the Runnymede colonists could only dress the part, posing beside the potted cactus in the photographer's studio, in Wyoming the life was to be had for real. Educated young Englishmen could find manly work as cowpunchers on the British ranches, and even if they lacked the funds to buy their own operation, they could put their own money into the purchase of a number of cattle, and take a financial stake in the animals they were herding. Geoffroy Millais was the third son of the most popular British painter of his day, Sir John Millais, whose Pre-Raphaelite and landscape pictures paid for a fine house in London and the rental of a sporting lodge in Perthshire. As a child, Geoffroy had sat as a model for some of his father's best known paintings. At the age of twenty-two he went to Wyoming to work on a British-owned ranch in the shadow of the Big Horn Mountains, working alongside lank, leather-faced ranch hands from Texas and New Mexico who had been in the open air since boyhood.

Letters arriving at the artist's mansion and studio at 2 Palace Gate, just south of Hyde Park, gave his parents a glimpse of a more rugged and active world:

> I have just returned from the "roundup" where I have been working hard, being in the saddle sometimes 18 hours at a time. We have breakfast at 3 every morning and are out until one o'clock riding all over the country so it is ten hours before we get our dinner, which one has scarcely time to eat before we are off again till six or seven when we come in to supper. If there are any cattle to be held over you have to get up in the night and take your turn night herding for two hours. So you can see out of 24 hours you are working practically all the time. We hardly ever spend more than one night in the same place.[9]

For the young Millais, the routine experiences of ranch life, the roundups, and trekking great distances across country in search of lost horses, were thrilling adventures. He told his Uncle George, "One wants a good horse to swim the rivers or else you get left. . . ." When his youngest brother, Johnny, was coming out from London to join him for a hunting trip, Geoffroy planned to go and collect him from a station on the transcontinental line: "It will

all be very new to him and he will have plenty of shots at antelope on the drive up, as it is very wild country. There is one day's
drive of seventy miles without striking a ranch. I have got him a
good hunter who goes by the name of Rattlesnake Jack."[10] Millais
had put some of his own money into the business. "Our cattle are
looking very well indeed, in fact fatter than any other lot in the
country. My share in the herd, from the natural increase from
calving at the same valuation I went in at, is worth about £6,800
now, or £1500 more than what I put in a year ago, which shows
what a good business it is. I should come out about £1500 to the
good in one year. The beef round up commences in a week and I
shall go down to the railway with them and see them shipped to
Chicago."[11]

In May 1885 the two Cowan brothers, tiring of their pigs and
the corn harvesting, left their Iowa property in the hands of a
hired man, and set out to Wyoming to see if they could make the
shift from arable farming. When they arrived, they finally found
the sense of well-being they had been hoping for all along. James
wrote home to his mother in Devon: "Here I am up in the Rockies
at 6350 feet above the sea. The most splendid air and scenery I
ever saw . . . not a cloud in the sky and the atmosphere is so clear
that you can see any distance. There is a snow capped range of
mountains about 12 miles off and they seem right behind us. It is
wonderful how the cattle and horses survive the winter and yet
they are just as fat as butter now with only a few poor ones."[12]

Once they had completed their reconnaissance, the brothers
planned to sell their 600 acres beside the Big Sioux River, and
put their money into stock on the free range. In the meantime,
they were taken on by a British-owned ranch near Rawlins. "I
don't like working for wages, and it would be ten times nicer to
have cattle of one's own but take it all round, provided one has a
good string of horses, I rather like the work and certainly think
it gets away with farming. If I had to work for wages, 'cow punch-
ing' is the job I would take up."[13] In Iowa, James had been deeply

xenophobic, disliking his American neighbors and utterly convinced of the comparative excellence of English food, farming
practice, and company. But in Wyoming, for whatever reasons,
the natives seemed an altogether better type. "The cowboys are
an awfully nice crowd," James told his mother; ". . . quite a lot
different from the Iowa Yankees. In fact one would hardly know
they were Yankees at all. Some of them of course are rather rough
but even these are more like an educated English labourer than
a Yankee and most of them are just as nice gentlemanly fellows
as you could wish to meet, and they have some sense of humour
which is a quality the Iowa Yankees are utterly devoid of. Altogether I expect to enjoy this summer very much and also to learn
a good deal. . . ."[14]

Not everyone could be, or even hope to be, their own master. Some remittance men chose to go native, try to conceal their
British identity altogether, and merge into the shifting pool of
Texan, Mexican, and Yankee hands who moved from ranch to
ranch. Charles Messiter came across one of them in the course
of a hunting trip. "I remember in Dakota, when out after deer,
meeting a rough looking cowboy, to whom I spoke a few words,
and then as we were both going in the same direction we rode
side by side for some time without speaking. It was a very hot
day and he suddenly said 'Wouldn't some iced champagne cup be
nice now?' And on my looking hard at him, he said 'You seem to
think I have never tasted it, but indeed I have, very often. I lived
in South Kensington once, and went about in a stove pipe hat and
a frock coat.' "[15]

The distance between the prairies and the metropolitan vanities of London was not so great as it had once seemed. A stream
of well-to-do Britons were now crossing the country on the Union
Pacific to visit California, or join a ship at San Francisco for the
fastest route from Europe to Japan. The line passed across southern Wyoming before going up through the Medicine Bow range,
and on over the Continental Divide. In 1883, Sir James Pender

and his wife, Rose, stepped off a Pullman palace car to visit a ranch he had invested in, east of Laramie, in the course of an American holiday lasting several months. The doughty Lady Pender, traveling in a thick homespun Norfolk suit and bringing a patent "Etna" alcohol stove to brew her tea, wrote up their excursion in *A Lady's Experience in the Wild West*. She dispensed tart judgments on the many features of American life that disappointed her, including the Indians. Her *Last of the Mohicans* expectations were spoiled when she saw "four 'braves' engaged in the exhilarating game of croquet" on a station platform as they passed through Indian Territory. She measured them against the standard upper-class prejudices of the time. "I was greatly disappointed with the red men . . . a great many had the lowest Irish type of features. . . ." Aside from looking Irish, she thought them physically feeble by contrast with other colonial subjects she had known, and "vastly inferior in strength to the Zulu."[16] British ladies were not noted for their philanthropy when it came to the Indians. A few years later another traveler, Lady Theodora Guest, confided: "Happily, I think, the tribes are dying out from illnesses and epidemics, and this is surely not to be regretted."[17]

The highlight for Lady Pender, as for other visitors from the East or Europe, was the twice yearly ritual of the cattle range, which had replaced the buffalo hunt as the embodiment of prairie life. "After driving a couple of hours we at last came upon the 'Round-up,' and a curious sight it was. Almost as far as the eye could see were vast herds of cattle streaming slowly along. . . ." Their manager and escort calculated there were some 20,000 animals. "The incessant bellowing sounded formidable, and the appearance of the cattle was not reassuring, for though not large their huge wide-spread horns and wild eyes made me rather glad to be in the buggy." They stopped, and watched the cowboys cutting out cattle from the large herd: "It certainly was very cleverly done. Two men rode right in amongst them till they got close to the particular beast they wanted; they then quietly forced him along till quite outside the rest, when they yelled and shouted like demons. . . . Once they had got him up to the small bunch of cattle that he belonged to, all was well, but frequently he dodged them, and in spite of their frantic galloping, their awful oaths and yells, he got back to the large herd, and all had to be done again." Giving a rare feminine perspective on the most macho procedure of the plains, Lady Pender thought more sensitive handling would have yielded better results. "I could not help thinking that were the whole thing done more quietly and gently much time might be saved, as the cowboys so terrify the wretched beasts that they become like mad things."[18]

The several different ranches who were sharing the "pool" roundup in the district each kept a camp of their own, around the battered chuckwagons that carried their provisions, cooking utensils, firewood, and bedding onto the range. The English visitors spent the night with their own outfit, from the Niobrara Ranch. "It was certainly a lovely and picturesque sight—the river glistening in the bright full moonlight, the white tents and wagons, the camp fires burning at intervals for over a mile, the background of hills looking snow-white under the moonshine, and the huge herds of cattle, with the mounted guard of cowboys in their picturesque dress, to say nothing of the herds of horses enclosed and feeding round, made up a scene I shall never forget, and which quite atoned for the discomforts and fatigues we had undergone."[19] Lady Pender confessed that later that night the lowing of the tens of thousands of cattle made her melancholy.

The Penders gained a different impression of the cowboys than that of James Cowan, or Geoffroy Millais. The young Englishmen who took part in range work were accepted by the other hands, with a certain amount of joshing. The Penders were visiting proprietors, and whether it was something in their manner, or because the Niobrara cowboys resented absentee ownership as a matter of principle, they were coolly received. The foreman and cowpunchers watched in silence as the visitors from London drove up, and offered them no help with unhitching their horses, tethering them, or fetching water. In England or Scotland, Lady Pender said, a man would have lent a hand as a matter of kindness, "but in free America, where everyone aims at independence, a man dreads an act of courtesy of this kind, lest his fellow men might imagine he was derogating from his standard of equality." When they sat on logs by the fire and tried to get the men to talk, they found them brusquely monosyllabic. "I did not like the cowboys; they impressed me as brutal and cowardly, beside being utterly devoid of manners or good feeling."[20]

Cheyenne, Wyoming, 500 miles and twenty-five hours by rail from Omaha, became the new center of the free range boom. Though due north of Denver, it was further away from the Rockies, and less dramatically positioned, with the Laramie Mountains low on the western horizon. The raw city stood out on the prairie, a crisscross of wide, treeless streets running beside the cattle-loading yards, the railway tracks, and the Union Pacific's locomotive workshops. The capital of the territory, Cheyenne was referred to by true believers as "the magic city of the plains," and hotels, law offices, and brokerages hummed with the sound of deals being struck and money being made. This was where livestock were bought and sold, ranch property changed hands, and profits were spent in new shops and saloons. From its headquarters, the Wyoming Stock Growers Association kept the brand book, set the dates of roundups in the different districts, tried to stop rustlers, and represented the cattlemen's interests with the politicians. At the low wooden railway station, passengers changed between the transcontinental line and the Kansas Pacific, running down to Denver. The wealthiest ranchers met each other at the newly established Cheyenne Club, a paneled retreat of discreet service and good food, with green leather furniture and electric light, that might have been in New York or Chicago, and where the many members from the East and Europe made for a cosmopolitan atmosphere.

One of the British blue bloods seen most frequently on the club's wide veranda was the suave Moreton Frewen, who returned to the United States in 1878, the year after his trip to Texas with the cattle king John Adair. A third son, he had been brought up at Brickwall, a half-timbered Tudor manor house at Northiam in Sussex, with formal gardens, a small deer park, and thousands of acres of prime farmland. His elder brother Edward now owned the estate, and Moreton, six foot three, handsome, energetic, and quick-witted, was left to lead the life of a young society buck. In his memoirs, he recalled how he kept himself occupied after leaving Cambridge: "I chronicle my own times and seasons. From November to April hunting in Melton, then a month's salmon fishing in Ireland and Punchestown races; May, June and July were spent in London. Then came Goodwood and Cowes; then 'grouse' somewhere and Doncaster; next a broken week or two at Newmarket and a little schooling of young Irish horses after cubs. Such as this was the determination of pleasure of tens of thousands—or really the pick of our young fellows."[21]

Moreton Frewen pursued all this so single-mindedly, keeping a stable of hunters and racehorses, betting at race meetings, and playing cards in London clubs, that by the time he was twenty-five he had burned up most of his sizable inheritance. At that moment, his visit to Adair and Goodnight's model ranch in the Palo Duro Canyon offered a shaft of revelation, and he convinced himself he could restore his wealth by cattle raising in America. The Panhandle, however, was not the landscape he had in mind. "The wild life of the ranches was, of course, immensely to my liking, but the treeless arid wastes of Texas were very far from satisfying my imagination. . . ."[22]

Frewen returned the following summer to scout for a place where ranching could be combined with the quality of sport British aristocrats traditionally expected. Many of his friends were now on the same trail. On his way out, at the Brevoort Hotel in New York, he met his friend the Earl of Dunmore, whose family had a long connection with America from before 1776, and whose uncle, Sir Charles Murray, had lived at close quarters with the Pawnee Indians. Dunmore praised the country he had been looking at in southern Wyoming and Colorado.

Before getting down to serious cattle raising, Frewen felt the need for a few months' hunting. He and his younger brother, Richard, went further north of Cheyenne, to the Big Horn range, through which Sir George Gore had cut such a swath. They shot bear and wapiti, and then made a foolhardy winter crossing of the mountains, from west to east, battling their horses through deep snow. In December 1878, they emerged from the pine forests onto the eastern edge of the range. A timbered slope fell away to the plains 3,000 feet below, near the present town of Buffalo. They looked east, and experienced a moment of discovery that matched Dunraven's first sight of Estes Park. "Never was such a view!" wrote Moreton. "Every traveller knows the immense range of the perspective in the tenuous atmosphere of these mountain solitudes. Near two hundred miles south we could see Laramie Peak. To the east was the limitless prairie, the course of Powder River showing in its broad belt of cotton woods fading out in the far distance. To northward we could see up to the Montana frontier a full two hundred miles. Not a human habitation was in sight; no cattle, nor could we make out any buffalo . . . it was all virgin prairie, just waiting for man"[23]—or, as he meant, waiting for the white man.

The blood-soaked ridge beside the Little Big Horn, where General Custer and his force had been wiped out by the Sioux and Cheyenne in 1876, was just over the Montana line. From their vantage point they could see the country where the Indians had been pursued and fought their last battles in the aftermath, and where Crazy Horse had finally surrendered only nineteen months earlier. For Moreton Frewen, confident British adventurer, this was already history. His powerful imagination came into play, and as he looked out over the Powder River basin, he believed he had found the ideal place to base a cattle empire of his own, that would match and surpass John Adair's.

Most of the free range taken into use so far had been below the Platte, on the undulating plains around Cheyenne and Laramie, and in western Nebraska and Colorado. Frewen would claim he was the first to see the promise of the country much further north, reached by a rough road that ran nearly 200 miles from the Union Pacific station at Rock Creek, up through Fort Fetterman to an army post at Fort McKinney, where the trail crossed the main fork of the Powder River. The road then continued past the site of present-day Sheridan, up to Montana. In reality, the country was not quite as empty as Frewen's aerial view suggested. Others were already coming in, squatting, putting up small cabins from which they could hunt, or homesteading to keep a few cows. But none had the same ambition as the Frewen brothers. Wyoming papers referred to them as "gentlemen of business acumen," and they were the first to preempt a sizable area of the Powder River basin for their own use and stock it with quality cattle.

With little money of his own, Moreton prevailed on brother Richard to spend the remainder of his own inheritance of £16,000 to start an enterprise they named Western Ranches Ltd. Within weeks they had picked a site on a high bank of the Middle Fork of the Powder River, just below the junction with the North Fork. They hired a foreman, bought an existing herd of 4,500 cattle that were marked with the "76" brand, and had them driven up from the Sweetwater, in the south of the territory. They ordered more cattle to be brought from Oregon. When the brothers began construction of a house, their newly hired cowpunchers realized this was to be unlike anything they had seen so far, on a baronial scale. While the ground-floor walls were built with massive pine tree trunks, chinked with mortar, in a heavy, roughhewn style, the facade of the upper floor was timber-framed, with black beams running vertically and horizontally between white boarding. The effect was Jacobean, in the same character as the black and white eaves of Brickwall, the family house in Sussex. Teams of oxen dragged heavy freight wagons—loaded with banisters and joinery, enameled baths, imported furniture, and a piano—up the stage road from Rock Creek. The vaulted Great Hall, forty feet square and double height, was large enough for twenty people to sit down to dinner. A wide staircase led up to a balustraded musician's gallery, from which doors opened to the bedrooms. Moreton Frewen called the house a "shooting box," as it might have been described on the Yorkshire moors or in a Scottish glen.

The Frewens knew they needed far more capital than they had themselves, and Moreton made several trips to England to raise it. In Sussex, London, and Leicestershire, he talked up the surefire nature of the plan with friends and acquaintances, trying to attract the £300,000 that would allow Western Ranches to expand to the size they had in mind. It was part of the scheme that potential investors could be invited to come and stay at the Powder River house, where they would be seduced by the oxygen, the great skies, and the endless grass, and accept that the proposition was irresistible. Moreton had an additional reason for completing the place to a high standard after he became engaged to a New York millionaire's daughter, and expected to bring her west to see his domain once they were married. His fiancée was Clara Jerome, eldest daughter of the Wall Street financier and racehorse owner Leonard Jerome. Her sister Jennie was already at home with the British aristocracy, having married Lord Randolph Churchill, and given birth to their first son, Winston Spencer Churchill.

Frewen wrote to Clara to say how pleased he was with the house. He was decorating the walls with stuffed heads, mounted antlers, and Indian bows and arrows. For a more homely touch, he hung a large picture of a polo match between the Royal Horse Guards and Monmouthshire, played at the Hurlingham Club in London. The chromolithograph was of an original painting by George Earl, shown at the Royal Academy. In the evening, from

the west-facing terrace, they could watch "the great purple shad-
ows stealing down over the prairie from the mountains."[24] The
last upstairs rooms were being plastered and wallpapered for her.
"So darling, why don't you come and be chatelaine next year?"[25]

In a further social refinement, the Frewens segregated the
British masters from their American men. "It is so nice now that
we have moved our manager and all the cattle hands, with all the
horses, except for about 25 for our own riding and driving, into a
ranch about fifteen miles lower down the river, and so we are now
entirely alone except for the house servants; and this I rejoice at,
on your account. I do not like the idea of you being here with a lot
of rough frontiersmen always in evidence."[26] With that resolved,
he tried to persuade Clara she would come to like their wilderness home as much as he did: "I can make you so comfortable on
the Powder River. I sometimes think you will love that life so well
that you will never wish to return to a world that though bright,
is not perfect."[27]

At a time when many British aristocrats were looking to
American heiresses to rescue their finances, the disappointment
for Frewen was that Clara's father was suspicious of the match.
Alarmed by Moreton's financial recklessness and racy past, Leonard Jerome would not come up with a dowry, and so the pressure
to make a new fortune from cattle was all the greater. "I do so
want money and I think it can be had here, I don't see how I can
fail."[28] His certainty continued to grow. "Truth to tell, necessity
did send me West but inclination and every good gift of my nature
will keep me here . . . I wish I could be here till I am so rich, that
I can do anything at home, and I know here that it is a matter
of very few years. The west is growing like a mushroom."[29] They
were married in June 1881 at a society wedding at the Grace
Church on Broadway in New York. The Honorable William Bagot,
soon to be Lord Bagot, was best man, and the guests included
Lord Stafford, heir to the Duke of Sutherland.

By then Frewen had been joined by other gentlemen ranchers,

who were setting themselves up, ten or twenty miles apart, across the Powder River Valley, and on the ranges crossed by the Tongue and the Belle Fourche rivers, as well as in the Greybull basin on the western side of the mountains. Lord St. Oswald's son James Winn was on the Nowood River. Among Frewen's closest neighbors was the Honorable Horace Plunkett, twenty-five-year-old son of Lord Dunsany, who found land that had been homesteaded closer to the Big Horns, beside a stream called Crazy Woman's Fork. With his Eton schoolfriend Alexis Roche, son of Lord Fermoy, as a partner, Plunkett took over a basic log cabin, and paddocks fenced with irregular wooden palings, and bought the previous owner's cattle. Though he had only 160 acres of his own, he was surrounded by thousands of square miles of free grazing. Many of the cattle carried Frewen's "76" brand; but as more were trailed in, even a range as vast as this began to fill up.

On the way out to Wyoming in his second year, Plunkett stopped in Le Mars to visit his old friend Captain Moreton, where he saw one of the standard sights of the British colony in Iowa, a son of an aristocratic family following a team of plow horses. He noted in his diary: "I never saw one more like a plowboy and less like an Earl. But the blood is there and such are the times in which we live. I am tempted to buy land out here. It will rise in value fast." For a while he wished he had speculated in Le Mars rather than on the open range. "But then there is no romance except plowing etc, and it is not as healthy—malaria and ague at times—and the water alkali."[30]

With no pigs or store cattle to feed, it was far easier for a gentleman cattle rancher to return home in the winter than it was for an arable farmer from Iowa. For nearly ten years, Plunkett divided his life between turreted Dunsany Castle in County Meath and the EK ranch in Wyoming. He followed the same schedule each year, with the voyage out to New York in April, arrival at the ranch, cleaning up after the winter, the hiring and firing of hands, the acquiring of new livestock. He grumbled about the physical strain of the work, and the jolting stagecoach journeys, and nights spent in bedbug-infested trail stops when he was traveling to buy cattle or do business. He also recorded what made it worthwhile. After a day on the roundup, he wrote: "Branding again. 'Hair, dust and corruption' as one cowboy described it. But the weather is heavenly."[31] Each November he returned to Ireland, to a regimen of foxhunting several times a week, parties and balls at other country houses, and dealing with the supplications of fathers who wanted to find a place for their sons in America.

Plunkett was untypically serious about the practice of ranching. With a command of double entry bookkeeping rare for Etonians of his time, he took a commercial approach and was so efficient that he was soon asked to run two other ranches for their British owners. Surprised to discover a moneymaking streak in himself, he started to buy and sell land. He explored a plan to transport and house tourists in the new Yellowstone Park. He thought of launching a stock exchange in Cheyenne, where cattle company shares could be traded with more knowledge and expertise than in New York or London. Meanwhile, his income grew.

Other British ranchers, less professional than Plunkett and less willing to learn, were dabblers by comparison. Many of them saw buying a ranch as a way to a particular quality of life, and the main attraction was that they could be close to the legendary sport that had drawn Stewart, Palliser, Dunraven, and so many others to the Rockies and the Big Horns over previous decades. It was unfortunate that one of the most arduous times of the year, when cattle had to be rounded up at the end of the summer, and the four-year-old steers gathered and sent east, coincided with the start of the hunting season; but recreation had to come first.

For every manly Briton who established himself in Wyoming, there were many more friends and relations back at home who wanted to come and visit for a few weeks. Before departing, the visitors fitted themselves out with new guns and clothing, and a few made special efforts to get into good physical shape. Before

Lord Caledon set out for Wyoming in 1880, he slept in the open air in the gardens of Caledon House, instructing his footmen to keep his blankets damp during the night. At times the British were almost tumbling over each other in the Big Horns. In 1880 Major Lovatt Wise, late of the British Army in India, arrived for a hunt. When he saw the large house on the Powder River, he wrote, "The brothers Frewen have set up a palace here in the wilderness. They have built the ranche of logs and fitted it out most comfortably. They are real good fellows and have ordered all our stores for us, and the camp outfit and have gotten us hunters and horses and everything we can want."[32]

While they were getting ready, Wise filled in time by learning to throw a lasso, and then left on an extended backwoods trip with two friends, three guides, a cook, a packer, and twenty-one horses and mules—"The weather is delicious and we are all in high spirits. . . ." With boyhood stories of the treacherous red man on his mind, Major Wise was always on his guard, and worried when he noticed a human figure a long way off, apparently watching them but trying to keep hidden behind rocks. After a further hour's march he saw the man again, on the crest of a hill, watching them stealthily. Was he an Indian scout? In fact it was Lord Rodney, straying from another British hunting group on the other side of the ridge. The twenty-four-year-old Rodney had, for his part, also mistaken Wise and his party for Indians.

Despite the growing number of hunters in the Big Horns, and the encroachment of civilization on the range below, it was still possible to find the expected thrills and dangers. Wise had a classic encounter with a grizzly bear, though at some cost to his guide. "I saw him quite close, about 8 yards off; he was sitting up, looking about him. . . . I fired and knocked him down, and the next moment, with a loud roar he came straight for us." The major managed to swing aside, nimble as a matador, as the heavy beast flashed past, but his American guide, Oliver Hanna, started running and the bear overhauled him. "I heard a fearful

scream and on reaching the brow saw the bear worrying at something—growling furiously." He managed to fire at the animal, and
drive it off. "I got Hanna back to camp, but the poor fellow was
in great pain. When we stripped him, I found his arm was badly
bitten in two places, also the thigh and calf of the leg, and he was
badly clawed on the head and neck, but nothing broken! It might
have been worse."[33] Quickly bandaging Hanna up, they carried
on hunting for several more weeks, and by the end had killed four
bear, twenty wapiti, six buffalo, and assorted wolves, antelope,
and mountain sheep. The horns and hides were sent back to Britain, though Wise was shocked at the cost of getting the trophies
packed into boxes and freighted to Rock Creek station.

In 1881 Horace Plunkett's autumn visitors at the EK included
Lord Manners, followed by Lord George Montague; the Honorable Bernard Fitzpatrick, heir to Lord Castletown; and the Earl
of Mayo. He felt distracted by all the company. "Mayo and Porter
and servant, and 14 others on business, or loafing, are crowded
together in the ranch and it is almost impossible to do any work."[34]
He dutifully bought horses and mules with them, set them up
with minders and cooks, and ordered their provisions and supplies, though the earl was imperious in his dealings with the help.
"Mayo was difficult to manage and was in constant danger of falling foul of western independence. But we outfitted them and sent
them up into the mountains."[35]

Plunkett stayed behind, working with his cowpunchers at the
roundup and branding. The boundaries between the normal level
of hospitality that the upper class were expected to extend to each
other, and providing something above and beyond this, were hard
to draw. At the EK ranch, they led to misunderstanding. "Lord
Mayo and Porter left. The settlement of the account that one is
bound to charge them gave great offence. They leave in thinking we have made money out of them. . . . We have lost about
$70 through them which is almost all we can be expected to give
to men richer than ourselves and whom we did not particularly

want."[36] Though the diligent Plunkett felt he had to receive them, he was increasingly vexed by their behavior. "The English visitors cost us a lot of money, and make themselves and us very unpopular in the country by their inability to adapt themselves to the people, and interfere much with our business."[37] Moreton Frewen was possessive about the hunting, over what was public land in the Big Horns, and worried that other well-to-do Britons might discover it. He told Clara, "I have just written a letter to 'The Field' which I hope will have the effect of keeping the shoal of cockney sportsmen away from here. I feel a proprietary right to these mountains, and 'we' will keep the game for our friends."[38]

In the months before their marriage, Frewen had tried to explain to Clara the sense of identity and purpose sport provided for Britons like himself. "I wonder darling if you will love this whole life. I think you will."[39] "You know, the sporting instinct implies a great deal more than *killing*: the love of new and wild experiences, the artistic soul, the love of untutored nature, and this sporting instinct your sex has in equal measure with ours. So darling, don't anticipate disappointment, for I am certain I can make life so happy for you here. . . ."[40] In the late summer of 1881, he was able to get her to Wyoming. Reaching the Powder River on their honeymoon, they swept into an extended shooting party with a house full of titled guests and potential investors. For a time there was discussion as to whether Clara's sister Jennie, Lady Randolph Churchill, would be coming too, in turn bringing more friends. Moreton demurred: "We will be an immense crowd as it is, and any more rifles will ruin sport, so if she suggests to you more than one pal you might be able to put her off."[41]

Among the first entries in their visitor's book were Lord Ashbrook, Sir Samuel Baker, Lord Castletown, Lord Donoughmore, the Honorable Charles Ellis, the Honorable Charles Fitzwilliam, Lord and Lady Lonsdale, and Sir Arthur Paget. In subsequent years their guests included the Earl of Onslow; Lord Hopetoun; the Earl of Dunraven; William Grenfell, the future

Lord Desborough; George Bennet, the next Lord Tankerville;
and John Brocklehurst, the future Lord Ranksborough. Clement
Finch, brother of the reprobate Lord Aylesford, came to stay, as
did Frewen's elder brother Edward, his sister Louise, friends from
Cambridge, and a few elegants from New York who had grown up
with Clara Jerome. Many brought their wives. All had to endure
the bone-shattering journey by heavy stagecoach, drawn by four
horses, from Rock Creek up to Fort Fetterman, where Frewen met
them with riding horses or an open wagon. Once they reached the
ranch, the standard of entertainment far exceeded anything that
Horace Plunkett, fifteen miles away, could possibly supply. The
Earl of Mayo, returning a couple of years later, this time bringing six dogs, stayed with Frewen not Plunkett, but made himself equally unpopular. "That crazy ass Mayo has been spoiling
everyone's sport with a lot of curs with which he has been drawing the woods and he has succeeded in scaring all the elk off the
mountains."[42]

In a territory where most were out of touch with the world
for weeks at a time, and the main subjects of concern were beef
prices, water rights, and winter storms, the comings and goings
of the British quality were a source of amusement and wonder.
Stories were inevitably talked up and enhanced, just as they had
been in St. Louis or along the Platte. Moreton Frewen was said
to be ordering fresh-cut flowers from Denver, crates of champagne
from Chicago, and iced oysters from the Atlantic coast; but it was
attitudes and manners, rather than any particular excesses, that
jarred. A widely circulated story had it that one new arrival from
England referred to his host's "cow-servants" rather than cowboys.

The British upper-class ranchers who moved to Wyoming
were still referred to as "top shelfers." Their everyday dealings
with the men who worked for them were as likely to founder on
British prejudice and American expectations based on the historic form, as they had done when the grandest sporting travelers
clashed with their guides and packers. Ranch hands were riled

when swells expected to be addressed by their titles, or asked for their horses to be saddled up and brought round to them. William Baillie-Grohman, more flexible and open-minded, endeavored to explain the concept of western equality to his kith and kin, as others had tried to do: "The West rejoices in the absence of 'nobs' and 'snobs'—worshipped lords and those that worship them . . . the qualities of a man stand on his own merits; he fails or rises by them, unabetted in either of these processes by extraneous wealth, family or condition. We can understand therefore that the air of the West is a frightfully uncongenial atmosphere for vanity and self importance."[43]

The big-game hunter and writer tried to show that American society, with its heterogeneous mix of backgrounds, nationalities, and types living alongside one another, did not fall into the neat categories they had been brought up with: "the English settler will for some time sadly miss the social laws which govern the intercourse of different classes in the old world. At first he will not like the independence of the cowboy under him, who by look and manner will let him know that the question who is the better man of the two has long been settled in his own mind. His hands will itch when some saucy 'Do it yourself' is the only answer he receives to some order concerning a matter not quite within the scope of his 'help's' duties. . . ."[44]

Indeed, the British rancher should forgo ideas of status and hierarchy altogether: "A man out west is a man, and let him be the poorest cowboy he will assert his right of perfect equality with the best of the land, betraying a stubbornness it is vain and unwise to combat." A little earlier, sporting tourists had been warned that if they appeared too imperious or arrogant their guide would have them trudging over great distances until they were exhausted, while making sure they never encountered the trophy animals they had come for. Baillie-Grohman advised that in the cattle business it was ten times as important not to appear domineering: "in no vocation is popularity more essential than in this, for let a man receive once the name of being moved by unsociable pride, and there will not be a man in the country who . . . will not then be ready and willing to spite or injure him. In no business is a man so dependent on his neighbours, so open to petty annoyances, and so helplessly exposed to vindictive injury to his property as in stock-raising out West."[45]

Frewen had a different perspective, implying that the Americans were at fault for not appreciating the qualities and values of his own class. "Oh Clara dear, how I weary sometimes at the struggle to keep on terms with these western men; our manager—a very good cattleman—has for his own sake been telling lies about us and has half the country by the ears about us; then too we have received the old jealous feeling about having the best range and the largest herd . . . we have both been so just and even generous that what feeling there is will soon subside, but I begin to believe that being a gentleman is much against one here, as in the colonies generally."[46] Frewen grew so irritated that he was tempted to fetch the horse whip: "these western men, at least some of them, are the most impracticable, aggressively independent people possible, and I often long to thrash one or two but for the want of dignity in such a proceeding."[47]

When they took their first steps in the cattle trade, the Frewens had little difficulty raising the cash needed, but their backers were soon disappointed. The high return on their money they had been led to expect failed to come through. Moreton blamed the start-up costs, but he had spent too lavishly on stables, barns, workshops, and equipment, including a twenty-two-mile private telephone line from the ranch to the nearest post and telegraph office. His timing was poor; he had bought cattle at too high a price; and debts built up. After three years, Richard pulled out of the partnership, complaining of his brother's managerial ineptness, and Moreton was forced to go back to London to raise more money. Persuasive as ever, he deftly stitched together a new, much larger enterprise to be floated on the London Stock Exchange as the Powder River Cattle Company, which would buy out his own interest, and take over the "76" cattle.

When the elderly Duke of Manchester agreed to be chairman, Frewen was relieved. "So my trouble is over, it is easy to find people to serve with a Duke!"[48] Two other lords were hired as directors. With Frewen giving assurances that meat prices could only continue to rise, since America was facing a "beef famine," and that their range had a uniquely benign climate protecting it from harsh winters, the offering raised £300,000. Within weeks, Frewen was back in Wyoming with over $1 million to spend in a cattle-buying spree on a scale Cheyenne had never seen before. He told Clara that prospects had never looked better: "I have done splendidly, 40,800 cattle for £215,000."[49] He even made a bid, briskly turned down, for Horace Plunkett's EK ranch. For the moment Frewen was a commanding figure, pronouncing on the future of the range cattle industry to journalists. After withdrawing to New York and London over the winter, he was back in April 1883, when everything seemed to be running like clockwork. "Do not stint yourself in any way darling little wifie, we are making money so fast it is no imprudence to spend freely and enjoy; I hope you have succeeded in getting a footman. Has the new carriage been finished?"[50]

Waves of British money continued to roll toward the Rocky Mountains. In addition to ranches bought privately, cattle companies were still the fashion on the London Stock Exchange and were acquiring more assets. Scottish investors bought up a group of existing ranches to form the huge Swan Land & Cattle Company in Wyoming, and the Deer Trail Cattle Company bought outfits in Colorado. The Earl of Dunraven, extending his commitment beyond Estes Park, put money into the Dakota Stock & Grazing Company, and became chairman. By the end of 1884 over thirty English and Scottish enterprises had been launched, and it was calculated that 15 percent of the western cattle industry was in British hands. In Wyoming, the share was far greater than this. Moreton Frewen, in Cheyenne, seemed to take a hubristic delight in the invasion. There were so many Englishmen in town that he boasted to Clara: "we are turning the natives out, and I think we shall annex the country before long."[51]

The idea of the golden West as an immense and inexhaustible source of wealth had completely replaced the older depiction of a savage wilderness, and the British upper classes embraced the change with gusto. The firsthand accounts of intrepid travelers and hunters, in the tradition of Palliser and Ruxton, were followed by a new rash of books which dealt with the attraction and viability of cattle ranching. In just one week in the autumn of 1884, London publishers put out four titles: *Gone to Texas*, *Cattle Fields of the Far West*, *Life and Labours in the Far, Far West*, and *Ranch Notes*. In the last of these, Reginald Aldridge, who had 7,000 cattle in the Panhandle, recommended that prospective ranchers go out with four ordinary tweed suits, two extra pairs of cord trousers "to stand the wear and tear of the saddle," a dozen flannel shirts, two pairs of lace-up boots, two pairs of Wellington boots, and a warm Ulster coat. "A revolver is by no means a necessity nowadays, but a good many cow-boys still carry them. Their favourite arm is a Colt's single action .440 calibre revolver. It is an excellent weapon, carries a big charge of powder, and shoots like a rifle if you hold it straight." Aldridge was confident about the long-term prospects: "The first question to be asked is—Will it pay? My answer to this is, that it *has* paid, and I do not see any reason why it should not continue to pay; though it is not at all likely that profits will ever again be as large as they have been in the last few years."[52]

On one of his stays at the Cheyenne Club, Horace Plunkett, the aristocratic odd man out, sensed an undercurrent. "Living at a club where one is supposed to have certain social relations with fellow members, one feels one's position among the people of the country. They don't like us naturally, and on the whole I don't like them. They are to a certain extent clannish and feel our intrusion. The feeling they would express thus—you have a social position. We have hardly any. You compare us with your 'society.' We don't compare favourably perhaps. But we are members of a greater nation than yours though you don't know it."[53]

By 1884, the mushroomlike growth showed signs of slowing. Prices for young cattle started to fall, and so many had been brought onto the range that the grass was cropped down to the roots. When they were rounded up to be shipped and sold, cattle were scrawnier and weighed less, and when they reached the stockyards in Chicago or St. Louis, buyers paid lower prices for them, pound for pound. The Powder River Cattle Company, having bought tens of thousands of animals with Moreton Frewen's new funds at the peak of the market, was in trouble. Still a believer in the free range, Frewen's proposed solution was to move their cattle north to Alberta, in Canada, a continuation of the same grassland belt, where there was still plenty of space. His directors in London would not allow it and he managed to shift only a few thousand. Other schemes, to ship young western cattle to Britain alive and fatten them on arrival, did not work out.

A hard winter in 1884–85 was followed by a rainless summer when the grass was parched and the cattle were thin even before the onset of winter. After huge losses, angry investors forced Moreton Frewen to resign, and he faced heavy personal debts of his own. In July 1885, he abandoned the ranch house by the Powder River. "It was a perfect summer morning when I left, and with quite a lump in my throat, I halted my horses on the ridge, and before passing for ever out of sight, took a long last look at the good black and white house which the river folk called 'The Castle.' It had proved the centre of a very short lived social system. . . . I never revisited the spot."[54]

As all ranchers faced the same difficulties, the measures they took to survive made them increasingly unpopular in the territory, and the British took the brunt of it. The Honorable Horace Plunkett, by now a leading figure in the Stock Growers

Association, spoke up at meetings in Cheyenne with his own ideas on how costs could be cut. He persuaded fellow ranchers, American and British, to withdraw the "grub line," the hospitable custom by which they had always given free board and lodging to itinerant ranch hands as they made their way across the country in search of work. When Plunkett became a leading proponent of a cut in cowboy pay, he found his own men at the EK turning against him: "They have been talking of shooting me all winter as I have been made the scapegoat of the attempt to reduce wages. I think I shall outlive it, but it is unpleasant being scowled at by the blackguards."[55]

Even as cattle profits fell away, new settlers were coming in, squatting or staking claims for homesteads on the same public land that was being used for free grazing. Since the acreage they wanted most was next to the streams and rivers, ranchers put up wire fences to keep the water for their herds. At the start, in the innocent days when it was said that there need be "no trouble about title, deeds, surveyors or lawyers,"[56] many of the owners of large ranches had not bothered to register land claims, but they now resorted to various ruses to keep control. More companies and owners filed for homesteading and preemption rights in the names of third parties, using false identities, as Dunraven had done in Colorado. With all these tricks, the British were only using the same devices as their American counterparts, but they were easy targets for politicians who spoke for sheepmen and small ranchers.

The wisest British heads realized that with free grazing no longer the boon it once was, the only answer was to try to purchase more in fee simple. Where there was railway grant land, they could use the familiar "intermingling" tactic—buying a latticework of sections and blocking off access to the squares of public land that lay between them with wire fences, or having their ranch hands "ride the line" to scare off interlopers. Since large holdings of land were more easily acquired in Texas and New

Mexico because of their different history, and land laws, companies turned back to the South and West. In 1885, the British-run Texas Land & Cattle Company bought 388,000 acres. The Aberdeen-based Matador secured the title to over 400,000 in Texas, and the American Pastoral bought 300,000, much of it in New Mexico.

For the individual aristocrats who had moved in, another prairie dream had been punctured. For a few years they had been able to convince themselves that it really was possible to lead a country gentleman's life, and combine sport and recreation with profitable business, while lording it over thousands of acres of parklike country belonging to the U.S. government. The scale of this ambition far outshone the earlier "colonies," and the presence was more visible. But they allowed themselves to be dazzled by the giddy promise of the free range, and their understanding of the speed at which the West was changing and the forces at work, was inadequate. Frewen had expected he might be left alone to increase his herds, in his own domain in the shadow of the Big Horns, for a decade or two, but his "short lived social system" could never have held back the tide.

In the first forty years since their appearance in the hotels of St. Louis, Kansas City, or Denver, the British nobility had played a colorful part on the sidelines in the opening of the West. Indomitable, sometimes eccentric and outrageous, they had done little real harm except to the fauna. But the scale of their investment and participation in the land and cattle boom, and the measures they adopted to preserve their interests, were leading them into a wider confrontation that marked national politics in the 1870s and '80s. It was argued that a group of rich capitalists were attempting to monopolize the use of public land in the West, just as industrial combines were trying to assert control over the railways, oil, or the mines, and break the power of labor in the East. Though the British cattle companies represented the savings of the middle-class investors as much as anyone else, the high profile of the aristocracy allowed anti-British feeling to be personalized and focused.

General Philip Sheridan had befriended and assisted many British hunters, but when he referred to Moreton Frewen as "that grasping Englishman" in a letter to Washington, he showed how American attitudes had changed. From the sporting-mad adventurer, whose manners might be irritating but who was basically benign, the visiting aristocrat was now perceived as a threatening figure, driven by money and greed.

10

"Land Grabbers"

*There is probably no other measure before Congress which
has behind it such a powerful public sentiment as have
these bills against alien ownership. American land for
American citizens, say our people.*

—WILLIAM McADOO, Washington, D.C., 1886[1]

In May 1881 a special train rumbled slowly down into western
Iowa from Minnesota, with an engine pulling two luxurious
private cars, and a kitchen and baggage van. Furnished with
every comfort of the Gilded Age, the drawing room had fresh flowers, fine porcelain, and a harmonium. The train was normally
used by American railway magnates, but for this journey it had
been lent to a British duke, the greatest landowner in Britain and
one of the richest men in Europe. The Duke of Sutherland, his son
Lord Stafford, and a small entourage had set out from New York
on a grand tour, and after Washington, Chicago, and Minneapolis, were now heading further west. A member of the party wrote
that "it is a cruise on wheels, a yachting excursion on iron rails
rolling over the land."[2] But it was more than this.

At a time when British investment in the United States was
increasing each year, the duke had come to see the country for
the first time. In Britain, he owned nearly 1.5 million acres, with

a great castle at Dunrobin in the north of Scotland, a stately
home at Trentham Hall in Staffordshire, the magnificent Stafford House in London, and a steel-hulled steam yacht lying at
Southampton. He was the largest shareholder in the biggest British railway company, and he told reporters he was coming to learn
about the American rail system, and for general sightseeing. He
did not say that he was also interested in buying American land.

As the train rolled on at a steady twenty-five miles an hour,
Sutherland could look out onto the country, with the new season's
grass growing fast, while maps were produced showing the railway grant sections still for sale. William Close had joined the
train that morning in St. Paul, hoping to persuade the duke to
put money into his new Iowa Land Company, just established, to
accumulate still more acres. They made a brief stop at Sibley, a
few miles south of the Iowa border, where carriages were brought
to the side of the train. Close took the duke on a two-hour side
trip, to see a part of his land where massed teams of heavy horses,
working alongside each other, were plowing the virgin sod. Close
was breaking 42,000 acres that summer, to be divided into small
farms for rent. Then the train steamed on, passing through Le
Mars, to Council Bluffs, and Omaha. The ducal train crossed the
high plains, when for hour after hour there was nothing to be seen
but isolated groups of cattle feeding or roaming in the immense
landscape, and then went over the Rockies to the California coast,
returning through Colorado, New Mexico, and Kansas. Sutherland's trusted secretary and financial manager, Henry Wright,
took careful notes of everyone they met and what they saw.

Though the duke did put money into Illinois and Iowa, the
advice by then was that the Midwest was no longer the shrewdest
place to invest. The western cattle boom was fully under way, but
the duke was already a little late. Using the contacts and knowledge he had gained, he went on to invest heavily in livestock and
ranches further west, in Kansas, Nebraska, and Texas. But the
locations of his purchases were less significant than the way the

railway cruise was reported. Fifty years earlier, when William Stewart had been the first aristocrat to make a much slower journey across the prairies, he had brought his own preconceptions about the fur trade characters and the Indians, and the myths ran in only one direction. By now the West was sufficiently populated to have its own reverse myths, and well-developed prejudices about the British aristocracy and what they represented.

The Duke of Sotherland's trip received huge press attention, with breathless reporting of the peer's blandest utterance, his demeanor, and his style of dress. In light of all the buildup, a few journalists expressed disappointment that he looked quite normal, without the specially erect bearing, livid countenance or absurd voice they had expected. A Cleveland paper complained that "The appearance of the Duke is very ordinary, with nothing particularly characteristic of nobility. He is rather tall, of medium build, and was dressed in a short sack-coat of drab, with black pantaloons and a Derby hat."[3] Nevertheless, most newspapers gave their readers the stereotype they would have wanted, with comical descriptions of his luggage and entourage: "The perspiring servants bustled about, frantically exclaiming 'Is Grace wants 'is 'at box,' 'My Lord wants 'is 'andbag.' "[4] At one station, crowds gathered on the platform to see the duke take breakfast. The *San Francisco Chronicle* recorded: "Through the ornamental windows of the coaches the open-eyed and expansive mouthed population of Lathrop caught glimpses of white aproned and sable hued waiters flitting with silver coffee pots. The cooking carriage was sending up a volume of smoke as large as if the Duke were arranging a barbecue for his 24,000 tenants."[5]

A RICH FOLKLORE already surrounded the activities of aristocrats in the Far West, where they were generally held to be overbearing, pompous, and selfish. But in the early 1880s two new factors

were adding to their historic reputation. One dated from the start
of serious land buying and ranching, and their use of fair means
and foul to get titles or keep others from sections of the public
domain that they had claimed as their own. The other, far more
toxic, sprang from what the English landowning class was reckoned to be doing in Ireland, and to a lesser extent in Scotland, and
the allegation that they were now bringing their deplorable and
wicked ways from across the Atlantic.

The resentment of "British gold" and the "Shylocks of Lom-
bard Street," who lent money for farm mortgages, went back many
years. The high profile that aristocratic ranchers and investors
showed in the cattle trade came just as American farmers felt
they were not sharing equally in American progress. Plains farmers, suffering from falling prices, were coming to believe that the
whole economic system was rigged against them by a government
beholden to big business, and were joining new grassroots organizations to lobby and agitate. At meetings of the Greenbackers,
the Granges, and the Farmers' Alliances, held in backcountry
chapels and barns, angry speakers made tub-thumping attacks
on grain merchants, commodity dealers, bankers, and most of all
on the railway companies, for exploiting their monopoly power to
gouge farmers with high freight charges. In the same tirades they
started to attack wealthy foreigners for taking up huge tracts of
railway grant land, and blocking Americans from their rightful
access.

Together, big corporations and "titled aliens" were accused of
filching the patrimony of the people. Radical workingmen's organizations, the urban equivalents of the farmers' movement, added to
the growing clamor. Terence Powderly told his Knights of Labor,
meeting in Cincinnati, that the threat from titled incomers, and
their greed for land, was the issue of the hour. "It is astonishing,
but true, that alien landlords own millions of acres of American
soil," said the leader of the Knights, who had adopted the title of
"Grand Master Workman" for himself. "I recognize no right in the

part of the aristocracy of the old or new worlds to own our lands. We fought to hold them once, and if it is necessary I am willing to advocate the same measures again; but I will never cease this agitation while the foot of the alien oppressor has a resting place within our boundaries."[6]

Newspapers watched out for large purchases, and swooped down on cases where the booted heel of the alien land grabber could be detected. Vote-hungry politicians, seeing how public opinion was moving, took up the land question more actively. In 1882, the U.S. Senate passed resolutions asking the Department of the Interior to look into the false claims made on behalf of the Earl of Dunraven in Colorado, and three other British companies in the West. The House Public Lands Committee named British companies which were putting up fences that blocked legitimate settlers from preempting or homesteading as they were entitled to, or denying water to smaller cattlemen. In 1884, the main political parties took up the issue at their political conventions. When the Republicans met in Chicago and adopted James Blaine as their presidential candidate, the party platform pledged that the "public lands are a heritage of the people of the United States, and should be reserved, as far as possible, for small holdings by actual settlers."[7] They promised new legislation to keep the aliens out, as did the Democrats, who blamed successive Republican administrations for allowing the abuses.

"How often have we read of the Nobility of England, Scotland, and of other of the British possessions coming over to America, pre-empting vast tracts of the public lands and fencing them in as cattle-farms with no more concern than if they were fencing in a deer-park on their ancestral possessions?" wrote Chauncey Black, a Democrat stalwart, and former Lieutenant-Governor, from Pennsylvania. He portrayed the offenders in the familiar, broad-brush strokes Americans recognized from the days of the sporting tourists: "These men come over to this country with an abundance of wealth . . . they go West with their servants, their hampers and their equipments, and with little difficulty and without discomfort pre-empt vast sections of land. . . ." As a result of this distortion of what the founding fathers had intended, "there has already grown up in portions of Kansas, Colorado, Wyoming and Dakota, a landed aristocracy composed of titled foreigners."[8] When Grover Cleveland won the election, and formed the first Democratic administration for thirty years, action seemed more likely. He ordered new measures to remove barbed-wire fencing from public land, sending a detachment of U.S. Cavalry to Wyoming to enforce the law, and ordered the cattle bosses to remove their herds from the Cherokee strip, in the Indian Territory.

The drive against foreigners was based not on the goal of "American land for Americans" alone, but on a deep suspicion of the social and economic system that would come with British ownership in particular. Whenever the land issue was aired, the term "British" was used almost interchangeably with "aristocratic." Apart from implying an immutable hierarchy Americans jibed at, "aristocratic" was taken to mean that the incomers would be *landlords*, renting to tenants on the harshest terms. The generalized assumption was misleading, though it was truer in the Midwest than in the Far West. Traditionally, at least in principle, American farmers owned their own land and tilled their own soil as free men. With the arrival of so many poor immigrants, wanting to farm as they had in the old country, but without the funds to buy, this was already changing. Not all had the stamina or the wish to homestead, and landowners, both American and British, had no qualms about providing plots for them to rent. The number of tenant farmers in the United States was escalating, and by 1885 there were reckoned to be over a half million.

Virulent anti-British feeling was standard among the American Irish, with every reason for it. Most had firsthand or close family memories of the ruthlessly imposed rent raises, the evictions, and the poverty and hunger that had forced so many to leave. As Charles Parnell's Land League continued its agitation within Ireland, and the battle over home rule proposals was fought out in the British Parliament, support for Ireland's cause was spreading far beyond the Irish-American community itself. At the same time the accusations against landowners were no longer limited to their alleged crimes at home, but were extending to cover their more recent behavior in the United States and particularly in the West. Heavily influenced by the experience of Ireland, campaigners and politicians condemned renting outright, as "un-American," and adopted the Irish Land League's condemnation of all landlords for themselves.

They presented an apocalyptic vision for the future of the United States. "It is impossible to exaggerate the gravity of the danger that threatens the Republic if the seeds of absentee landlordism, so plentifully planted by the British aristocracy, be allowed to grow and bring forth their legitimate fruits of poverty and degradation," warned the *Chicago Daily Tribune* in March 1885. "The ancestors of the men who are now stealing the fairest proportion of the public domain stole the lands of Ireland 200 years ago. . . ." By their greed they had turned a naturally rich and fertile country into a famine-scourged wasteland. "The same causes will produce the same effects on this side of the Atlantic if the American people be so foolish as to allow English land thieves to steal the public domain."[9]

The man who emerged as the archetype, who was castigated most often, was another wealthy Briton who, like the cattle king John Adair, owned land in both Ireland and America, and claimed to subsidize one through the other. Though he was not a genuine grandee, campaigners knew he would be easier to vilify if they ennobled him. He was referred to as "Lord Scully," though his disinterest in field sports was the clue that he was not quite the real thing. William Scully had inherited property in Tipperary, and after a fracas with his Irish tenants over rent arrears and evictions, had taken much of his capital off to Illinois in the 1850s, hoping to build a new domain for himself in America.

By paying cash to buy out the 160-acre "land warrants" the government had given to veterans who had fought in the Mexican War, Scully assembled a 25,000-acre tract of poorly drained prairie land near Lincoln in the center of the state, dividing it into small segments for rent. Some of Scully's first customers included Irish families driven out by the "black hunger" of the famine years, from estates like his own. He continued to add more property, and moved on to Kansas and Nebraska, where he bought large blocks of railway grant land. By the 1880s he had over 200,000 acres rented out to small farmers, mostly from Ireland, Germany, and Scandinavia.

Because of his previous form in Tipperary, where he had used firearms against one resisting tenant, the sons of Erin watched Scully closely, and accused him of bringing over the whole gamut of bad landlord practices. He insisted his tenants pay all taxes and make their own improvements. He gave one-year cash leases, with no undertakings of renewal. Rent had to be paid in advance, on January 1, before crops were sold. His land agents acted as enforcers, and tenants who did not observe their leases to the letter were thrown out. The *Chicago Daily Tribune* kept after him over several years, publishing exposés of his methods and strict terms: "his 'rules of the estate' foster the detestable 'Irish spy system' and reduce the tenants to the conditions of serfs and vagabonds."[10] Attempts were made to organize boycotts and rent strikes, with little success. His tenants were either too cowed, or having been evicted once in Europe, did not want to go through it again.

In proper absentee style, Scully visited only every two years, when he toured with his agents, carefully avoiding any direct dealings with the tenants. For the rest of the time he lived comfortably in London, in an expensive house in Holland Park, on the rental income remitted from America. The focus on "Tyrant Scully," also known as "His Royal Nibs,"[11] offered some cover for other British renting operations, from whom he drew the fire.

Richard Sykes, who had been at Rugby and pioneered the muscular Christian game of rugby football in the United States, led
a syndicate that bought 70,000 acres in the Dakota Territory. He
rented it out and established Sykeston and four other towns, with
the Duke of Sutherland as one of the investors. In Minnesota,
Iowa, and Nebraska, the Close Brothers' estate was larger than
Scully's, with 270,000 acres let out, and many more tenants, if it
was run less ruthlessly.

Finer distinctions between these landlords, who were renting
on the European model, and the aristocrat ranchers and British
cattle companies who were grazing their herds on their own land
in Texas or the Southwest, or running their own ranches on the
free range, were glossed over. A composite picture of oppression,
exploitation, and vampirelike greed emerged. All British noblemen
stood accused of bringing in feudal or illegal methods, whether it
was by renting in an extortionate way, by fencing public land,
or making false claims. They invariably employed "impudent and
lawless" agents to do their bidding and enforce their whims.

The fears were soon picked up and amplified through fiction.
A novel published in 1886 told the story of an enlightened young
aristocrat, Lord Waverland, visiting the United States with a conservative and equally fictional peer, the Duke of Melvorne. The
two characters went out to Melvorne's land in the Dakota Territory, which allowed a description of the scale of one nobleman's
spread, where "the prairie stretched away in the distance like a
mighty sea of gently undulating verdure. It was a country fresh
from the hand of nature." The Duke explained how he bought the
land from the railway company, and introduced his agent. "Thus,
riding and chatting from day to day, sometimes on horseback,
sometimes on wheels, but always in hunting suit; with game bag,
dogs and servants, and guns, we spent two weeks on the Duke's
great estate. It is in extent about twenty five miles wide by fifty
long, equalling in size . . . a medium principality in Germany, or
a small Dukedom in England."[12]

The purpose of *Waverland: A Tale of Our Coming Landlords*, by the American author Sarah Brigham, was more political than literary. It was intended as a cautionary tale, with every abuse explored in long passages of dialogue. A group of peers, including the Duke of Melvorne, a carefree Nimrod, and his friend Lord Sanders, "a dried-up little man with a dark squeezed up face," said to be modeled on Scully, discuss their plans with a disapproving U.S. Army officer visiting London. They meet at the Duke's Mayfair club. "It seems to me," said Colonel Haynes "that about the time Ireland is free from English landlords, America will be pretty well burdened with them. The thought is repulsive. . . ." Placing his hand on the American's shoulder, Brigham's Lord Sanders tells him not to get so excited, explaining, " 'We pay for the lands we get, and we have a right to buy where ever we choose. And then, we have a right to use our property as we wish. No government on earth has a right to say where I shall live or where I shall spend my money.' 'That is true,' said the Duke of Melvorne, approvingly. 'I hold large tracts of land in the United States, and I intend to own ten times as much within the next five years.' 'Hear! Hear!' cried several voices 'So will we.' " At one point the Duke boasts, "We are gaining the lands our fathers lost, without fighting any bloody battles for them."[13]

The suspicion that the purchases were all part of a British conspiracy, to reverse the outcome of 1776, was floated by real-life politicians as well. Congressman Lewis Payson of Illinois warned, "It may happen that the nation which failed to conquer us with its arms may yet prevail with its treasure."[14] The *Denver Republican* judged that British ownership of American land was "contrary to the spirit of independence."[15] A more nuanced response came from the *New York Times*, which suggested that, for all their misdeeds, the British had been taken advantage of, and that much of the fault lay with the government in Washington.

In attempting to legislate against aliens, Congress should not forget that they have been enabled to get vast tracts into their hands by the rascality of Government officers, and where an Englishman has grabbed one acre, an American has grabbed fifty. . . . The Englishmen were attracted and even invited by these American speculators and thieves. They found scoundrels in abundance who were ready to get hold of the land by fraud and collusion with Government officers and then to transfer it to their rich employers.[16]

Out in the West, where aristocrats were as self-obsessed and ill-tuned to the currents of American political life as ever, it was assumed this was simply talk and nothing would come of it. But a shiver of fear ran through the boardrooms of British ranching companies. With prices already falling, and the prairie grassland eaten down, John Clay's staid gentlemen, who had conversed about the finer differences between steers and heifers over the port and nuts a few years earlier, now agitated about what the next despatch from Washington might bring. From late 1883 onward, politicians introduced a succession of bills to Congress, as they tried to find a formula that would send the aristocrats packing. In session after session, in both the House of Representatives and the Senate, they expatiated on the evils of alien ownership, the principles at stake, the trickery and dishonesty that had been used, and their suspicion of long-term British intentions. As Congressman Payson put it, "We are at present permitting the coining of immense private fortunes in the hands of foreign nobility and gentry." The public lands should be preserved "from the encroachment of aliens whose birth and education create and foster sentiments inimical to the country from which they are attempting to derive wealth, to maintain an aristocratic splendour in their own country."[17]

The idea of a class war between the foreign lords who were said to have claimed the prairies and the rights of honest and humble settlers was a constant theme. William McAdoo of New Jersey invited his listeners to imagine an injured ex-soldier, who had lost an arm in the Civil War, going out to one of the states or territories of the West to find a home for himself and his family. But the brave veteran and amputee finds his way blocked when he is confronted by "the minions of some lisping Lord or the satraps of some capering Count." Surely, he had given his blood to secure this land, and it should be a heritage for him and his children, and "those who are yet to come from beyond the seas as citizens and settlers in good faith."[18] James Belford of Colorado asked, "Are we the servile and supple tools of foreign capitalists, or are we going to preserve the country for our own people?"[19]

In the House chamber, where two of Albert Bierstadt's epic pictures were mounted on the wall, one on each side of the Speaker's rostrum, showing historic moments of American discovery in idealized scenery, the same cast of suspects were denounced time and time again. Always included in the roll call was the Earl of Dunraven, who had his own Bierstadt painting of the wild western American landscape hanging at Adare Manor. The Duke of Sutherland had become part of the mythology too, and for McAdoo, the cross-country railway cruise of 1881 epitomized the whole scandal: "Travelling free of expense on the land grant railroads of the United States, and finding landlordism and feudalism now unpopular in the British Islands, the vulture-like claw of these hereditary land pirates and feudal barons is reaching out to take the princely inheritance of the people of the United States. . . ." The congressman, who had been born in Ireland and brought to America while still a boy, then put the duke into context, as he saw it: "And who is the Duke of Sutherland? A man whose ancestors cleared from the Highlands of Scotland over fifteen thousand people . . . with a barbarous cruelty scarcely credible, almost the entire population of his vast estate."[20]

The first specific proposal to deal with the aristocrats emerged from the House Public Lands Committee, driven by its chairman, William Oates of Alabama, who had himself lost an arm in the Civil War. Though it would not be retrospective, the committee's bill stopped aliens, resident or non-resident, from acquiring or owning any land anywhere in the United States unless they had begun the process of becoming citizens. Oates said there was a simple principle at stake: "We maintain that American soil should be owned exclusively by American citizens. . . ."[21] Senator Plumb of Kansas said the same thing in the Senate.

The consensus was that the remaining public lands were needed as a national safety valve, a place where genuine settlers could set up homes and smallholdings. Only a few defended the cattle interests and the benefits to the country of cheap beef, though one Nevada congressman was skeptical about the alternative future, and the idea that the same land could be taken up by poor farmers. "I say and reiterate that in all that vast area which this bill strikes at there is not one acre on average in a million that will grow a single bushel of potatoes," said Representative George Cassidy. "It is utterly worthless for every reason under the sun except for cattle growing."[22] His own answer was that the government should regularize the situation by leasing out public land.

Few listened to these doubters, and the Oates proposal was overwhelmingly approved by the House. But the bill was criticized in the press for being too broadly drawn, and damaging because it would exclude foreign investment from other areas, like mining and railways, where it was still appreciated. More crucially, the Judiciary committees of both houses believed the bill ran up against the rights of individual states, and was thus unconstitutional. Senators next put forward a more carefully written and narrowly focused bill, applying only to the territories, and leaving the states to make their own laws. Foreign companies would be limited to a maximum of 5,000 acres. The House would not have it, but watered down its own Alien Landlord Bill a little further the following year. No compromise seemed possible, and the promise of action was bogged down in interminable wrangles.

The single most damaging piece of evidence to emerge, which proved to be the clincher in the public mind, was a list of major foreign owners produced by Department of the Interior officials at the request of congressmen. At the start, the campaign against foreigners had been based on a mix of national chauvinism, strong Irish feelings, and fevered polemic, but the report appeared to quantify the whole situation, replacing anecdotes and folklore with precise facts and figures. Culled from Land Office records, it stated that by 1884 foreign "noblemen," most of them British, had taken up nearly 21 million acres of U.S. land. To help the public visualize what was involved, it was calculated this was equivalent to a strip of territory ten miles wide, running from the Atlantic to the Pacific coast.

The list of twenty-nine worst offending foreign owners included familiar names, as well as less known ones. The Marquis of Tweeddale was there with 1,750,000 acres, the Duke of Sutherland with 425,000, Lord Dunmore with 120,000, Lord Houghton with 60,000, and the Earl of Dunraven with 60,000. Nor was it limited to the West. Sir Edward Reid and associates were said to have 2 million acres in Florida, and another syndicate had 1,800,000 in Mississippi. In other named holdings, some with over 1 million acres, titled aristocrats were said to be the major investors. For good measure, a handful of French and German proprietors were named as well.

Some suspected the grand total of over 20 million acres was an exaggeration, and the list contained obvious mistakes. The tally of territorial tyrants credited George Grant with 35,000 acres in Kansas, though he had died eight years before and his holdings had long since been sold off. The catalogue was read into the *Congressional Record*, reprinted widely, and increased the sense of paranoia. Newspapers across the country joined the chorus. The *New York Sun* wrote that "If a man like the Duke of Sutherland wishes to be the lawful owner of a homestead in our Western Territories, let him take, like other emigrants, the proper steps to get his naturalization papers, but let him leave at home the hateful ambitions of the British landowner."[23]

The attempt to find a workable bill ran on for nearly three years, and it was not until the summer of 1886 that the House and Senate finally seemed close to reaching agreement. A revised House bill that restricted aliens from owning any land in the territories—which meant Montana, Dakota, and Wyoming—was passed, and seemed likely to be agreed by the Senate. In the oppressive humidity and heat of the Washington summer, through July and the first days of August, it ran into the ground again, with senators arguing it was too serious a matter, with wide implications, to be rushed through in the final days of a session, and should be held over yet again.

In practice, the foreign companies and noblemen had by this time appreciated that their game was up. The mere talk of legislation, in prospect for so long, combined with the fall in cattle and beef prices, had put a blight on their buying, and the frenzy was over. New companies could not be floated, and many existing British owners, already in difficulties, were selling their land back to the same Americans who had offloaded it at premium prices a few years before. Individuals who had bought land and wanted to stay began to think the unthinkable, and consider taking out citizenship to protect themselves against any future moves. Nature then took its own part, on the northern plains, even before the law had been changed.

SOME 1,500 MILES from the deliberations in Washington, D.C., the practical difficulties of the ranchers and cattle companies on the free range continued to mount. The summer of 1886 was particularly hot, and by August the range was bone-dry and the grass denuded and brown. Cattle, driven there to be fattened, were unable to put on weight. From mid-November snow started to fall, and high winds blew constantly. A quick thaw at the New Year was followed by an ice storm that covered the snow with a frozen crust, and temperatures were in the –30's F. Cattle already weakened by the conditions of the previous summer had to paw or trample through compacted ice and snow to reach the earth, where hardly a blade of grass remained. They gnawed the bark off the willows and box elder beside frozen streams and rivers, and drifted across the snowy wastes, blown by howling winds, until they were stopped by a barbed-wire fence or a gully, where they crowded together and froze to death on top of one another. Trains crossing the country were held up for hours by wild-eyed, starving animals who moved onto the plowed tracks. The blizzards and the cold were the worst in the recorded experience of either white men or Indians.

The cattle owners, away on the east coast or abroad, had no way of knowing how their hoofed assets were faring. Only three years earlier, Moreton Frewen had assured his British shareholders that they not need to worry about the "bogey" of winter losses, claiming the Powder River district had "a local exemption from snowstorms," and that he had "the utmost confidence in the security of the industry on a well selected range." [24] This was another of his miscalculations.

While winds were still blowing, and before the full impact of the calamity was known, Congress finally passed the compromise Alien Land Bill, at the end of February 1887. No alien who had not declared the intention of becoming a citizen could buy land in the territories. When corporations bought land, four fifths of the stock had to be held by American citizens, and no company could own more than 5,000 acres. In the months that followed, individual states moved quickly to pass similar laws so that large new landholdings were no longer possible. But by that time, few wanted to make them anyway. The cattle boom was over; heavy losses were expected from the winter; and the most recent and frantic manifestation of the prairie fever had been quenched. The claws of Congressman McAdoo's vulture had been pulled, but by that time they had in any case ceased grabbing.

There was no discernible reaction, or sense of outrage, among British aristocrats, always known for their imperturbability. It was far less bad than it could have been. In the first versions of the bill, they were to have been stripped of their land, but in the final version existing holdings were not affected. The Duke of Sutherland had returned to the United States at the start of 1887, spending time with anglophile society in New York and Philadelphia before going south to Charleston, where his 1,000-ton three-masted steam yacht, the *Sans Peur*, named after his family motto, was waiting for him. The duke, with a crew of twenty-five that included seamen, engineers, stewards, an Italian chef-de-cuisine, and his personal bagpiper, Aleck, left for Havana and the Caribbean. He was cruising off the Florida coast with his mistress, Mrs. Blair, when President Cleveland signed the Alien Land Act on March 3.

Epilogue: 1887

We want no caste, no upper classes, no "lower orders."
We should unite in trying to stamp out feudalism and
flunkeyism.

—COLORADO NEWSPAPER, 1887[1]

The climax of Victoria's Golden Jubilee celebrations came with a national holiday on Tuesday, June 21, 1887, when the Queen was to drive through the streets of central London. From early morning, hundreds of thousands of loyal subjects filled the pavements and parks, and every window along the route. Shortly before the cavalcade was due to leave Buckingham Palace, excited crowds in the middle section of Piccadilly spotted a familiar figure, with white beard and outsize hat, coming out onto the upper-floor balcony of a grand mansion, and broke into wild cheers. As Buffalo Bill was recognized by more people, he gave a theatrical bow, removed his hat, and waved to acknowledge the rippling applause.

A few minutes later the advance guard could be seen approaching, having come up Constitution Hill and around Hyde Park Corner. Buffalo Bill, the Sioux Indian chief "Red Shirt," and members of the "Wild West" troupe, taking time off from their own daily spectacle, were held by the pageantry and polish of old

Europe as the royal procession came toward them. Mounted Life Guards, and carriage after black-lacquered carriage filled with admirals, generals, functionaries of the royal household, Indian maharajas, and European princes, passed directly below them. More detachments of jogging cavalry were followed by the Master of the Queen's Buckhounds and the Queen's huntsmen, carrying their horns. They were followed by the closest members of the royal family, and then Victoria herself, in a black dress, with a white lace bonnet threaded through with diamonds, sitting in an open landau pulled by eight horses.

Clattering below Buffalo Bill's lookout on the corner of Arlington Street, and then past the Egyptian Hall, they went under a triumphal arch and turned down toward Whitehall. At Westminster Abbey, the cream of the British establishment were already seated, the peers in their full plumage—with coronets, crimson robes with ermine linings, white breeches, and silk stockings—for a service to commemorate the Queen's fifty years on the throne.

In another anniversary, it was also fifty years, almost to the day, since Captain William Stewart had pitched his striped tent at the 1837 trappers' rendezvous, in the flat pastures beside the Green River, at Horse Creek, and watched the Snake chief Ma-wo-ma and 2,000 braves ride past, in full feathers and regalia, firing off muskets and shouting war whoops. It was also fifty years since Sir Charles Augustus Murray, just back from eating boiled dog with the Pawnees, had shown off his Indian ponies to the young Queen at Windsor.

Bells rang from churches throughout the British Empire, and British communities in the rest of the world sent loyal messages to London. In Le Mars, Iowa, the colony filled St. George's Church, where a crimson and gold banner, "V.R. 1837–1887," hung above the altar, for a special service which ended with a "God Save the Queen" that shook the walls. With such a large number of British residents and cattle ranchers in Colorado, one of the largest commemorations was held in Denver, at the Episcopalian Cathedral

of St. John in the Wilderness, where a Service of the Royal Jubilee
was led by Dean Martyn Hart, a British clergyman who had emigrated to the United States at the age of forty-one.

The Reverend Hart processed into the nave as the choir sang
a special Jubilee hymn he had written himself. In a lengthy ser-
mon, he eulogized Victoria's purity and faithfulness as woman,
wife, mother, and empress. Expounding on the order and security
the British social system provided, and the exemplary role the
Queen and her court played at the apex of it, he regretted the
recent "carping" in the United States about the ruling class of his
home country. "I have heard much about the unconsciousness, the
selfishness, the overbearing presumption of the English aristocracy. There are black sheep in every flock, but who would describe
the whole flock by the dusky exceptions!" The dean said he knew
many titled families, and had stayed in their houses. "If you want
to find simplicity of life, perfection of manners, and absolute truth
of existence, you will find it in a degree little to be surfeited in
the very uppermost circles of English life."[2] As evidence of this,
the perfectly mannered Earl and Countess of Aberdeen passed
through Denver on Jubilee Day, and were guests of honor at a
British residents' picnic in Argo Park. They were in the midst
of a trip taking them on to the Rocking Chair Ranch in Texas,
which Aberdeen owned in partnership with his brother-in-law,
Lord Tweedmouth.

Dean Hart's effort to reclaim the reputation of the blue bloods
was coming late in the day, and there was little generosity of
spirit left in the western United States at large. Many of the aristocrats had already departed, and those who had gone from the
northern ranges were not mourned. When Moreton and Richard
Frewen had left Wyoming, a Cheyenne editor had written: "Of all
the English snobs of great pretensions who flew so high and sank
so low, probably the Frewens are the chiefs."[3]

The dean would have run into graver trouble in other cities, where honoring a foreign potentate was deemed even more

provocative. In New York the main Jubilee service and celebration could not be conducted in an Episcopalian church, so they used the Metropolitan Opera House, where a choir sang Handel's "Coronation" anthem. In Boston the equivalent event, with music, prayers, and a loyal address, was also held in a public hall. Though there were picnics, sack races, athletics contests, and fireworks for British loyalists in several cities, a counter program, mounted by Irish-Americans, gave a rival interpretation to the day. A quarter of a mile from the Opera House, at New York's Church of the Holy Innocents on 37th Street, Father John Larkin conducted a high requiem mass for the souls of 150,000 Irish who had died of starvation during the Queen's reign, over a symbolic coffin, and accused Victoria of cruel indifference to the suffering of her subjects. Further downtown, on the East Side, the Republican organization Clan-na-Gael draped the Great Hall of the Cooper Union in black mourning, and hung placards listing Irish deaths from famine, in dungeons, and on the scaffold. In Boston, 4,000 people surrounded the Faneuil Hall, "the cradle of liberty" where the breakaway of 1776 had been nurtured, objecting to its use to celebrate the long reign of George III's granddaughter. The demonstrators called it a "desecration of American soil."

Even in Denver there were protests. By appearing to bless the monarchical system from an American pulpit, the dean had sailed close to the wind, and Colorado papers carried indignant letters in the days that followed. "As Americans we are utterly and resolutely opposed to English ideas of caste," wrote one. "We do not believe in the reign of the upper-tens; we do not respect a man for his long winded titles, and we can never be led to think or call Queen Victoria 'the first lady in the world.' The extremely reverend gentleman can concede to her such sycophantic compliments as he sees fit, but we ignore such toadyism. . . . We want no caste, no upper classes, no 'lower orders.' We should unite in trying to stamp out feudalism and flunkeyism."[4]

ONE SMALL PART of American society never joined the attacks
on the British aristocracy. Among the wealthy Protestant elite
who dominated east coast business life there was continuing talk
of "hands across the sea," the need for closer bonds with the old
country, and the incontrovertible superiority of those who came
from Anglo-Saxon stock over the Slavic hordes from Europe who,
it was feared, might fill up the West and overwhelm them. Links
by marriage grew, blue bloods continued to come to Saratoga and
Newport each summer, and many seemed as at home in Manhattan as they were in Mayfair. A younger son of the Duke of
Argyll, Lord Walter Campbell, came to live in New York. While
in the Caribbean, the Duke of Sutherland was able to anchor his
yacht beside the similar vessels of cruising American plutocrats.
But among plainer and less privileged Americans, the suspicion of
the monarchical and aristocratic system was as powerful as ever,
intensified by the reports from Ireland. General Adam Badeau,
soldier and diplomat, wrote that "the existence and influence of
the institution are to a democrat, fresh from the equality and uni-
formity of social and political life in the New World, a matter of
unceasing marvel."[5]

In a potboiling study of the power and role of the British aristocracy published one year before the Jubilee, Badeau gave an
astringent account of their manners, the way they treated their
servants, and their well-known addiction to sport, based on
his observations during eleven years as U.S. consul in London.
Badeau theorized that the concentration on shooting and stalking affected their personalities, to make them uniquely insensi-
tive. "To be forever planning and inflicting death and pain, even
on animals, cannot be refining. The English nature is coarse in
itself, but sport renders it more so." His general impression of high
society matched that of earlier visitors, including James Fenimore Cooper. "Like everyone else they can be civil enough when

it is in their interest to be so. But when none of these reasons exist—interest, or preference, or necessity—they are often cold, supercilious and arrogant to a degree that is unknown in what is called good company elsewhere."[6]

Though the Alien Land Act had been passed, the wariness remained. The new law was criticized for being mild and toothless, for leaving the aristocrats' existing holdings untouched. Congressman McAdoo, still not satisfied, introduced an amending bill the following year in another attempt to make it impossible for any Englishman, or foreigner who was not yet an American citizen, to own any land anywhere in the United States and the territories. The issue was kept alive with fresh allegations that British landlords were treating their American tenants harshly, in the brutal manner they resorted to in Scotland or Ireland.

A new cause célèbre emerged in the autumn of 1887, when landlord's agents drove a wagon along dirt roads to a down-at-heel farmhouse close to the town of Primgar, Iowa, thirty miles from Le Mars, to evict a bedridden widow who had not paid her rent. According to reports, they found Mrs. Scott too ill to be able to leave on her own feet, so the men lifted the bed, with the widow still on it, out of the house and set her down on the open prairie, without shelter. It was known that the company owning the land was British, and after the first accounts had appeared, the *Chicago Daily Tribune* managed to make the connection that gave the case a still greater inflammatory value. This was not Lord Scully again, but an even bigger vulture: ". . . it appears that the merciless Highland evictor the Duke of Sutherland is the principal member of the syndicate of British landowners whose agents have been engaged in evicting American settlers from their houses in north western Iowa. This greedy aristocrat and his father cleared a whole shire in Scotland to make way for deer forests and grouse moors. His agents want to clear a whole county in Iowa in order to enrich himself and his partners."[7]

The sequence of events at Primgar may not have been quite as written up, and the duke was only one of a number of investors in the Western Land Company, but the image of the Scottish noble-man's bailiffs tossing innocent widows out onto the prairie, in the heartless way his father had expelled his crofters, gave extra edge and propaganda value. In fact, the duke's interest in western land had cooled by then. His mercurial enthusiasms had shifted and his time was taken up by schemes for new railways in the Middle East, and Siam. But in 1887 he bought one more piece of Ameri-can land, on the Gulf coast of Florida, before the state's law was changed. The purchase was made during a shore excursion from the *Sans Peur*, with the help of the Governor of Florida, and the plot amounted to less than 100 acres.

There was room to build a substantial house, surrounded by pinewoods and newly planted groves of oranges and lemons, overlooking the clear waters of what was then Lake Butler, later renamed Lake Tarpon, to serve as a semi-tropical elysium for the duke and his female companion. He was able to marry Mrs. Blair when the first duchess died, after a long illness, the following year. From then on they spent their winters at Sutherland Manor, Tarpon Springs, where the British flag flew from a tall flagpole, unbothered by the vituperation that continued from the farmers' movement and the Chicago newspapers.

In practice it was not the continuing resistance to the idea of another country's ruling class bringing its hauteur across the Atlantic, or populist-driven indignation against "landlordism," or even an act of Congress that finally halted the aristocratic inter-est in the Far West. Their turning away had more to do with the sheer unpredictability of nature itself, and the final disappear-ance of a frontier that had been receding for so long.

Buffalo Bill continued to be one of the celebrities of the age, with a dedicated following in Britain, where, on subsequent tours, he moved on from long seasons in London or Manchester, and took a traveling version of the show to over a hundred provincial cit-ies and towns. Queen Victoria asked to see the "Wild West" once more, in 1892, when Cody put on another special performance for her, this time at Windsor Castle. Stories of the West, the staple of cheap novels since the 1860s, were about to become the standard fare in fleapit cinemas. But though the legends had passed into British popular culture, the reality on the ground had changed beyond recognition, and everyone knew it. The difference between the West and Victorian Britain was not as extraordinary as it had once been, and if the horizons were as limitless as ever and the air as exhilarating, some of the "elasticity of spirit" was gone. Much of the open prairies had been fenced and divided into farms and ranches. Three newly completed railways crossed the country, with feeder lines between them. Thousands of small towns had telephone wires, jewelry shops, piano teachers, insurance agents, savings banks, and the complexities of late nineteenth-century life.

For the British cattle lords of Wyoming, Nebraska, and Montana who had not pulled out earlier, the disastrous winter of 1886–87, striking just as the legislation was going through in Washington, provided a further blow, puncturing the short-lived dream that ranching on the open range could offer endless profits from free land. When the thaw came, and cowboys rode out to look for the surviving cattle, they found piles of bones along the fences, and the riverbanks and gullies lined with carcasses. As the reports were sent back to London and Edinburgh, they showed how the herds had been decimated. The Powder River Cattle Company lost 75 percent of its stock and headed into bankruptcy. Other British-owned outfits, including the Swan, went down at the same time. The Penders' Niobrara ranching company held a final roundup and the surviving stock was sold. John Clay, who had not been at Eton or Oxford himself, but had been entrusted with the affairs of many who had, summed it up: "Three great streams of ill luck, mismanagement, greed met together—in other words, recklessness, want of foresight, and the weather, which no man can control . . . the story, with its flavour of romance, ends in hollow failure."[8] The Honorable Horace Plunkett left the EK ranch in

1888, and though he kept up some of his Wyoming interests, he returned only occasionally. On one of his trips back to Cheyenne, he noted in his diary: "Cheyenne dull and doleful. Surely the glory has departed. The cattle kings are gone and Cheyenne must settle down to the humdrum life of a farmer town. . . ."[9]

The era of long-distance ownership by foreign syndicates had ended, and the few individual ranchers who stayed learned to be less exclusive. In West Texas, the three younger sons of the Earl of Lichfield, who had grown up on the Shugburough estate in Staffordshire, stayed on running ranches south of San Angelo, raising cattle and horses. During the Boer War they acted as purchasing agents for the British government, and shipped 20,000 mounts to South Africa for army use. Claud Anson eventually went back to Britain after marrying a daughter of the Marquis of Waterford. Frank followed a little later. But the Honorable William Anson stayed on, married an American woman, and took U.S. citizenship.

In Colorado, the Earl of Airlie's son, Lord Ogilvy, continued as a rancher. In Wyoming, in the Powder River basin, a small number of aristocrats still kept a cluster of ranches at the foot of the Big Horns. All were younger sons, who had first served their time on other outfits, as Geoffroy Millais and hundreds of others had done. They were young enough to have seen the greed and mismanagement of their elders and learn from it, and their expectations were more modest. They included Frederick Bennet, son of Lord Tankerville; Malcolm and William Moncrieffe, sons of Sir Thomas Moncrieffe; and their cousin Oliver Wallop, son of the Earl of Portsmouth. Wallop had lost all his cattle in the winter of 1886 but started again, and they raised horses and polo ponies as well as beef cattle. They knew they had to move beyond the "cow-servant" stories of the Frewen era. Interviewed in Chicago in 1891, the Honorable Frederick Bennet took pains to emphasize the difference: "We have been cowboys for so long now, that it would have been very difficult to separate ourselves from the wild free life. You can bet we have no society dudes in the Powder River section where our cattle run."[10] William Moncrieffe volunteered for the Spanish-American War in 1898 as one of Theodore Roosevelt's Rough Riders, and he and Oliver Wallop later took U.S. citizenship.

"Landlordism" was not eliminated, even if fresh British capital was no longer being injected. Though the newspapers continued their campaign against Scully and now referred to him as "Viscount," the wiliest British landowner of them all continued to rent out small plots and farms and expand his domain. This was possible because he took out U.S. citizenship at the critical moment, and bought a house in Washington, D.C. The Scully lands continued in family ownership into the twentieth century. Close Brothers had extended itself beyond Iowa and bought hundreds of thousands more railway grant acres in Kansas, Colorado, and Texas. William and James had shifted the main office to Chicago, where they were both living. After the 1887 Land Act, they were unable to carry on buying land; but by that time they were concentrating on mortgages and loans to farmers, and making new investments that had nothing to do with agriculture at all. The business that had grown from William's delighted and emotional response to seeing the rolling Iowa prairie for the first time had moved on, and seemed like any other American business.

The settlements of British younger sons, dating from before the cattle boom, faded quickly. The Jubilee year marked the point at which it was finally realized that the Far West could never be part of the British Empire, even in spirit, and that the attempt to re-create a gentleman's lifestyle, whether individually or in colonies, was a fantasy. The improvements in travel that had made it possible to reach the western United States so easily were now extending to other parts of the world. Younger sons could go to western Canada, as many did after the 1880s, where they could stay under the imperial umbrella. More went to South America and Southern Africa. The colony around Le Mars lasted longest,

but three years after the Jubilee celebrations at St. George's in
Le Mars, the loss of a crucial figure seemed to mark the end of
that chapter, just as it had when George Grant died in Victoria,
Kansas.

Frederick Close, though involved in the firm with his two
brothers, had continued to run a farm in Iowa and keep his connections with Le Mars. He was thirty-five, physically fit, still
steeplechasing, and playing cricket and polo. On a Saturday
afternoon in June 1890, Close rode onto the field for a game of
polo in Sioux City, in a park beside the Missouri River, the crucial
route up which so many of the early explorers, hunters, and British grandees had traveled when this was still Indian Territory.
The Englishman was wearing the Sioux City team's colors of dark
blue cap and belt with white stripes. In a typical demonstration of
gallantry and horsemanship, he did not allow the fact that he was
playing with his left arm tied in a sling, after breaking it while
foxhunting in England during the winter, to slow him down.

Close's side was ahead by three goals when his horse cannoned
into another and he was thrown from the saddle. When he hit the
ground, he was unable to help himself up. A falling horse rolled
on him, completely crushing his chest and injuring his head. The
game was stopped, and a doctor instructed that he should not be
moved. Blankets were brought and a tent was erected over him
out on the polo field. He died at midnight.

Frederick had been the colony's most charismatic leader, the
embodiment of the belief that an island of upper-class society, sustained by British pluck and the public school spirit, could thrive
on the prairies. His funeral was a grim affair, attended by many
of the remaining Britons who made the forty-mile journey down
from Le Mars. Four Englishmen lowered him into a grave in the
Sioux City cemetery, on a high knoll overlooking the town and the
Missouri, where the steamboats belched smoke into the sky and
long trains of grimy freight cars shunted in and out of the railway
yards by the river.

The hunting was not as good as it once had been. Except for a few hundred survivors in protected pastures around Yellowstone, the buffalo were gone, even from the few last refuges, like John Adair's Palo Duro Canyon. The stream of visitors who had found such satisfaction hunting and camping in the 1860s and 1870s now gravitated to the Pacific Northwest, or Newfoundland. The Earl of Dunraven, who had once hoped to enjoy years of magnificent sport, despatching all the elk, mountain goats, wolves, and bears he could dream about, on convivial and comfortably outfitted expeditions with his closest friends in Estes Park, now spent more time fishing and shooting in the remoter parts of Canada.

The memories were kept up through the thousands of heads and horns brought back for proud display during the previous fifty years. At the American Exhibition in London in 1887, to which the "Wild West" show was intended to be an addendum, but which Buffalo Bill completely overshadowed, a whole gallery was devoted to American hunting trophies, shot by—and now loaned by—British grandees. They included antlers with record spans, and the fiercest and most formidable heads of buffalo, bear, and moose, most of them mounted and styled by Henry Ward or his son Roland, who had become the British Empire's leading taxidermists, from their address at "The Jungle," Piccadilly. They came from the Duke of Argyll, the Marquis of Lorne, the Earl of Dunraven, the wealthy big-game hunter William Baillie-Grohman, Sir John Millais, the Earl of Mayo at Palmerstown House, Lord Walsingham at Merton Hall, and from Sir Henry Seton-Karr at Kippilaw. Other galleries showed American pictures, including twelve canvases from Albert Bierstadt, who could still find British buyers, though the scenes were now endlessly recycled.

No animals or paintings were on show from Murthly Castle, and the first upper-class adventurer to make his way across the prairies and return with hunting trophies and a unique pictorial record was almost forgotten. Sir William Drummond Stewart, the original prairie romantic, whose primitivist delight in the

skies and wilderness, and belief in the nobility of the Indians, had
kept him in the Far West for seven fulfilling years, never owned
an acre of land in America and never saw the prairie fever in its
later and grosser forms. After his death in 1871, and an unseemly
row over his will and his rightful heir, most of his cache of Indian
dress and weapons, his skins and animal heads, and the unique
collection of western paintings he had commissioned were sold off
and dispersed in a two-day-long sale held at Mr. Chapman's auction rooms in Edinburgh. A few of the pictures, including the outsize *Attack of the Crows*, were reacquired by the aggrieved branch
of the family that retained Murthly Castle; but most of Alfred
Jacob Miller's pictures, of a West that had now disappeared, were
dispersed among British buyers. They would not start to make
their way back to the United States until the 1930s.

One implant from the Far West could not be removed, or sold, or
subject to litigation, and it proved to be the most long-lasting and
evocative of them all. Sir William's seedlings of Rocky Mountain
Douglas fir (*Pseodotsuga menziesii*), sent back via New Orleans
wrapped in damp sackcloth, and planted out by his estate workers
in 1839 and 1840, were now well established, though it would be
many more years before they reached their full mature height of
up to 200 feet. But visitors to Murthly could by 1887 start to get
the feeling Sir William must have hoped succeeding generations
would be able to experience. The huge, widely spaced western
American trees that now clothed stretches of hillside overlooking
the salmon lies of the river Tay gave the truest and simplest sense
of the vaulting forests and freedoms that had so inspired him in
western Wyoming. These were the trees that grew in the foothills
of the Wind River Mountains and cradled the sparkling lakes
where he had found his most contented moments, sitting round
the fire with the trappers, while the blue smoke curled upward.

Acknowledgments

The sources that I needed to write this book were on both sides of the Atlantic, and separated by great distances, but the thanks I owe to the many people who helped me are no less heartfelt for being so widely spread. In Britain I am particularly grateful to the knowledgeable and patient staff at the county record offices, who helped me track down the letters and diaries of prairie travelers and settlers, within the estate and family papers they hold. I was assisted by the Sheffield Archives, who keep the surviving Wentworth-Fitzwilliam family records from Wentworth Woodhouse as well as the Wharncliffe papers; the Northamptonshire County Record Office, with their separate holding of Fitzwilliam archives from Milton Hall; the Staffordshire Record Office, who have the Sutherland papers from Trentham; the Hull History Centre for the Herries family; and East Sussex for the Ashburnham and Frewen records. I also thank the Surrey History Centre, the Kinross-shire Record Office in Perth, the Westminster Archives, the National Archives of Scotland, the Limerick University archives, and the library of University College Dublin, as well as all the staff at the London Library.

In the United States I received invaluable help from the state historical societies, whose resources in most of the state capitals must make their hard-pressed British equivalents deeply envious. I thank the librarians of the recently rebuilt Colorado History Center in Denver, the State Historical Society of Iowa in Des

Moines and Iowa City, the Kansas Historical Society in Topeka, the showpiece Minnesota History Center in St. Paul, the venerable State Historical Society of Missouri in St. Louis, the Montana Historical Society in Billings, and the Nebraska State Historical Society in Lincoln, for access to their manuscript and oral history collections, their own proceedings and journals, and their historic newspapers.

This book was being researched during the time that the program to transfer valuable holdings of hundreds of small town newspapers onto searchable electronic databases was starting in several states. Colorado was the pioneer. I would like to pay special tribute to the unsung visionaries who saw the need for this expensive but necessary one-off exercise, and found the funds to pay for it. Though amateur genealogists may turn out be the first beneficiaries, entering simple name checks, the character-reading technology can have a turbo-boosting effect on some of the research for an endeavor like this. It allows extraordinarily thorough trawls, and can yield up references that might never have been found in years of thumbing through disintegrating bound volumes or spooling through scratched microfilm. Some of the narratives in this book—for instance, Dunraven in Colorado and Scully in Illinois—would have been much sketchier without this transformative new tool. The British Library's recent initiative, digitizing a first set of nineteenth-century provincial papers, was launched just in time to bring some last-minute additions on the British side.

I thank Mary Robinson at the McCracken Research Library of the Buffalo Bill Center in Cody for showing me the records of the 1887 British tour; John Waggener at the American Heritage Center, attached to the University of Wyoming in Laramie, for his help with Frewen, Cowan, and Millais material; and Jeff Briley at the Oklahoma Historical Society for permission to reproduce one of the society's handsomest pictures, Alfred Jacob Miller's *Cavalcade*. I thank the Yale University Library for permission to quote from the papers of James Watson Webb.

I am grateful for the advice and generous spirited help I received from Curtis Harnack, whose study of the British in northwest Iowa, *Gentlemen on the Prairie*, originally published in 1985, built on Jacob Van der Zee's much earlier *The British in Iowa*. Harnack's beautifully written book offers a sympathetic account of the colony from the perspective of a native Iowan. In Le Mars itself I owe much to Glada Koerselman and Judy Bowman of the Plymouth County Museum, for passing on their store of knowledge and for so much work on my behalf. I was also helped by Norman Barker, Malcolm Brodie, and Marlyn Renken in Brunsville, and Kristina Hager in Kingsley. In Kansas I thank Vivien Minshull-Ford, in Wichita, for sharing her own research on the Runnymede colony and for her unstinting help with several other lines of inquiry. In Harper County thanks go to Mickey Bowen and to Gilvin and Karen Walker for guiding me to the plowed prairie fields where Runnymede stood, along tracks that were deeply mired at the time. George Zepp provided insights from Rugby, Tennessee. In St. Louis I am grateful to Dave Jump for his encyclopedic knowledge of, and enthusiasm for, his city's dynamic nineteenth-century history. In New York Sarah Levitt made valuable research sorties, and Zoë Pagnamenta gave sage advice on work in progress. Additional thanks are due to Dr. M. O. Grenby, Michael Baker, Dr. Molly Warsh, Karl Sabbagh, and Jane Wyatt.

I am specially indebted to those with family links to some of the travelers, nimrods, and settlers in this book, who took such an interest in it. Rosemary Close-Brooks lent me William Close's unpublished "Prairie Journal" and photographs. Lady Vanessa Hannam and Colin Anson helped with the family history for the 2nd Earl of Lichfield and his three sons who went to Texas, and Mrs. Sarah Kerr kindly provided photographs of the Anson ranches, as did Ryland Howard from San Antonio. In the west of Ireland, near Limerick, Thady Wyndham-Quin, the 7th Earl of Dunraven (who died in 2011, before the book was completed), produced scrapbooks and albums of the 4th Earl, and Lady Dunraven showed me Adare Manor, sold by the family in 1984 and now a hotel.

In Perthshire Henry Steuart Fothringham supplied family records and the fruits of his own research into the life of Sir William Drummond Stewart, and was kind enough to read and comment on several chapters. His nephew and the present inhabitant of Murthly Castle, Henry Steuart Fothringham, showed me the improvements Sir William made to the house on his return from America, including the crimson velvet–lined dining hall, recently restored. In the parkland surrounding the house, Sir William's plantations of Rocky Mountain Douglas-firs are more impressive than ever.

At W. W. Norton I thank my editor, Star Lawrence, for his enthusiastic interest in this story and his shrewd guidance on how it could be told, and Melody Conroy and Anna Oler for taking the manuscript through the production process so smoothly. Ann Adelman was a sympathetic and constructive copyeditor, and Martin Lubikowski brought his customary clarity and intelligence to the map making. My agent, Gill Coleridge, was a true support at all times, through an interrupted gestation period, and worked successfully on my behalf, as did Melanie Jackson in New York. Finally, and more personally, I thank my godmother, the late Alison Olcott of Red Lodge, Montana, and later Billings, who first showed me the limitless horizons of Montana and Wyoming, and my wife and family for their tolerance while my mind was often elsewhere, following this particular long distance trail.

Notes

Introduction

1. Letter from Charles Wentworth-Fitzwilliam to 5th Earl sent from Cleveland, October 7 1850 Northamptonshire Record Office, Fitzwilliam Milton papers. FM(c) Bundle FV

2. Letter from Charles Wentworth-Fitzwilliam Letter to 5th Earl sent from Indian territory, on the Kansas river August 17 1851 Northamptonshire Record Office, Fitzwilliam Milton papers. FM(c) Bundle FV

3. Francis Duncan "Our Garrisons in the West", London, Chapman and Hall, 1864 p 184

4. ibid

5. Richard F.Burton, "The City of the Saints" New York Harper Bros 1862, p 1

6. ibid

7. William Baillie-Grohman "Camps in the Rockies". London, Sampson Low, 1882 p 3

Prologue

1   "Queen Victoria's Journal," 11 May 1887, Royal Archives, Windsor Castle.

2. American Exhibition, London 1887, Official Catalogue (New York & London: J. J. Garnett and B. W. Dinsmore, 1887), p. 17.

3. "Queen Victoria's Journal," 11 May 1887.

4. *Chicago Daily Tribune*, June 19, 1887.

5. *Daily News* (London), April 16, 1887.

Part I: Freedom for the Spirit

1. Encircling Vastness

1. *Poems by William Cullen Bryant* (Boston: Russell, Odiorne & Metcalf, 1834), p. 39 (first published in *The Knickerbocker* [December 1833]).

2. William Fairholme, *Journal of an Expedition to the Grand Prairies of the Missouri*, 1840 (Spokane, WA: Arthur H. Clarke, 1996), p. 46.

3. Thomas Jefferson, Inaugural address, March 4, 1801.

4. Fairholme, *Journal of an Expedition to the Grand Prairies of the Missouri*, 1840, p. 48.

5. Letter from Earl of Ashburnham to William Stewart, August 19, 1832, National Archives of Scotland, GD 121/101/1/ 21.

6. Letter from Percy Ashburnham to William Stewart, December 29, 1832, National Archives of Scotland, GD 121/101/1/24.

7. Letter from Lord Ormalie to William Stewart, November 1, 1832, National Archives of Scotland, GD 121/101/1/23.

8. Captain Basil Hall, *Travels in North America* (Edinburgh: Cadell, 1830), Vol. 2, pp. 287, 282.

9. John James Audobon, letter to his wife, Lucy, from Liverpool, August 7, 1826, in Alice Ford, ed., *The 1826 Journal of James Audobon* (Norman, OK: University of Oklahoma Press, 1967), p. 324.

10. *Eclectic Review* (London) (February 1816), p. 106.

11. Letter from James Fenimore Cooper to Mrs. Peter Jay, January 1829, in James Franklin Beard, ed., *Letters and Journals of James Fenimore Cooper* (Cambridge, MA: Belknap Press of Harvard University Press, 1960), Vol. 1, p. 356.

12. Letter from James Fenimore Cooper to Mrs. Peter Jay, January 1829, in ibid., pp. 354, 357.

13. James Fenimore Cooper, *The Prairie* (London: Henry Colburn and Richard Bentley, 1832), p. vii.

14. Ibid., p. 6.

15. Ibid., p. 389.

2. Beyond the Mississippi

1. William Drummond Stewart, *Edward Warren* (London: G. Walker, 1854), p. 113.

2. Letter from Lord Ormalie to William Stewart, November 1, 1832, National Archives of Scotland, GD 121/101/1/23.

3. Stewart, *Edward Warren*, p. 113.

4. Ibid., p. 135.

5. Dale L. Morgan and Eleanor Towles Harris, eds., *Rocky Mountain Journals of William Anderson* (Lincoln, NE: University of Nebraska Press, 1987). Anderson diary entry for June 11, 1834, p. 120.

6. Ibid., p. 1129

7. Stewart, *Edward Warren*, p. 274.

8. Ibid.

9. *Original Journal of Charles Larpenteur. My Travels to the Rocky*

Mountains Between 1833 and 1872, ed. Michael M. Casler (Chadrou, NE: Museum Association of the American Frontier, 2007), p. 4.

10. *Journal of Captain Nathaniel J. Wyeth's Expedition to the Oregon Country, 1832–1836*, ed. Don Johnson (Fairfield, WA: Ye Galleon Press,1984), p. 58.

11. Washington Irving, *Adventures of Captain Bonneville* (Paris: Baudry's European Library, 1837), p. 147.

12. Stewart, *Edward Warren*, p. 288.

13. Letter from Captain Stewart to James Watson Webb, November 15, 1835, Watson-Webb Papers, Yale University Library, 683, Series 1, Box 1, Folder 7.

14. *Quarterly of the Oregon Historical Society*, XVII (1916), "Diary of Rev. Jason Lee," July 4, 1834, p. 142.

15. W. H. Gray, *A History of Oregon*, 1792–1849 (Portland: Harris & Holman, 1870), p. 116.

16. Ibid., p. 117

17. De Witt C. Peters and W. R. C. Clark, *Life and Adventures of Kit Carson* (New York, 1858), p. 120.

18. Stewart, *Edward Warren*, p. 302.

19. Robert C. Warner, *The Fort Laramie of Alfred Jacob Miller* (Laramie, WY: University of Wyoming Publications, 1973), p. 144.

20. Marvin C. Ross, *The West of Alfred Jacob Miller* (Norman, OK: University of Oklahoma Press, 1951), pl. 37.

21. Ron Tyler, ed., *Alfred Jacob Miller: Artist on the Oregon Trail* (Fort Worth, TX: Amon Carter Museum, 1982), p. 22.

22. Ross, *The West of Alfred Jacob Miller*, pl. 147.

23. Ibid., pl. 39.

24. Tyler, ed., *Alfred Jacob Miller: Artist on the Oregon Trail*, p. 31.

25. *William H. Gray: Journal of His Journey East, 1836–1837*, ed. Donald R. Johnson (Fairfield, WA: Ye Galleon Press, 1980), entries for July 12, July 6, 1837.

26. Ross, *The West of Alfred Jacob Miller*, pl. 36.

27. Warner, *The Fort Laramie of Alfred Jacob Miller*, p. 147.

28. *New York Weekly Herald*, May 18, 1839, cited in Ross, *The West of Alfred Jacob Miller*, p. xxiii.

29. *Perth Courier*, November 7, 1839, reprinting *New York Morning Herald* dispatch of September 24, 1839.

3. Red Men and Blue Bloods

1. George Catlin, *Letters and Notes on the Manners, Customs and Condition of the North American Indians* (New York: Wiley & Putnam, 1841), p. 23.

2. Washington Irving, *A Tour on the Prairies* (London: John Murray, 1835), p. 313.

3. *The Metropolitan*, 12 (January 1835), review of *A Tour on the Prairies*, p. 411.

4. *The Literary Gazette* (1835), review of *A Tour on the Prairies*, p. 148.

5. Ralph M. Aderman, Herbert Kleinfield and Jennifer S. Banks, eds., *The Complete Works of Washington Irving* (Boston: Twayne, 1979). Vol. 24, *Letters, Volume II: 1823–1838*, Irving to Catharine Paris, September 13, 1832, p. 723.

6. Irving, *A Tour on the Prairies*, pp. 18, 29, 51.

7. *The Literary Gazette* (1835), review of *A Tour on the Prairies*, p. 148.

8. Letter from Lady Susan Hamilton, Countess of Dunmore, to A. Stewart Mackenzie MP of Seaforth, September 14, 1835, Correspondence of Mary and J. A. S. Mackenzie, Seaforth Muniments, National Archives of Scotland, GD 46/15/80.

9. Honorable Charles Augustus Murray, *Travels in North America During the Years 1834, 1835, 1836* (London: Richard Bentley, 1839), Vol. 1, p. 253.

10. Ibid., pp. 258, 277.

11. Herbert Maxwell, *The Honourable Sir Charles Murray, K.C.B. A Memoir* (London: Blackwood, 1898), p. 103.

12. Murray, *Travels in North America . . .* , Vol. 1, p. 287.

13. Ibid., p. 290.

14. Ibid., pp. 303–4.

15. Ibid., pp. 346, 368.

16. Ibid., pp. 267, 317.

17. Ibid., p. 311.

18. Ibid., pp. 307, 317.

19. Ibid., p. 319.

20. Ibid.

21. "Three weeks at court: A Diary kept at Windsor by the late Sir Charles Murray, September, 1837," *Cornhill* magazine (January 1897), p. 24.

22. Murray, *Travels in North America . . .* , Vol. 1, p. iii.

23. *Burton's Gentleman's Magazine and American Monthly Review* (October 1839), p. 227.

24. Murray, *Travels in North America During the Years 1834, 1835, 1836*, Vol. 2, p. 114.

25. Ibid., p. 64.

26. Ibid., p. 182.

27. George Catlin, *Catlin's Notes of Eight Years Travels and Residence in Europe* (London, 1848), Vol. 1, p. 4.

28. Ibid., p. vi.

29. Ibid., p. 35.

30. Ibid., p. 36.

31. Ibid., p. 37.

32. Ibid.

33. Catlin, *Letters and Notes on the Manners, Customs and Condition of the North American Indians*, p. 23.

34. Marjorie Roehm, ed., *The Letters of George Catlin and His Family* (Berkeley: University of California Press, 1966), p. 237.

35. Ibid., p. 206.

36. Catlin, *Catlin's Notes of Eight Years Travels and Residence in Europe*, Vol. 1, pp. 144, 117.

37. Ibid., p. 153.

38. Murray, *Travels in North America . . .* , Vol. 1, p. 304.

39. *Household Words: A Weekly Journal*, ed. Charles Dickens, vol. VII, June 11, 1853, p. 337.

4. Buffalo Dreams

1. John Palliser, *Solitary Rambles and Adventures of a Hunter in the Prairies* (London: John Murray, 1853), p. 111.

2. Ross, *The West of Alfred Jacob Miller*, p. xxiv.

3. Letter from A. J. Miller to Brantz Mayer, October 16, 1840, in Warner, *The Fort Laramie of Alfred Jacob Miller*, p. 155.

4. Letter from A. J. Miller to Decatur Miller, October 31, 1840, in ibid., p. 163.

5. Letter from A. J. Miller to Brantz Mayer, October 18, 1840, in ibid., p. 157.

6. Letter from A. J. Miller to Decatur Miller, July 26, 1841, in ibid., p. 180.

7. Palliser, *Solitary Rambles and Adventures of a Hunter in the Prairies*, p. 108.

8. Murray, *Travels in North America During the Years 1834, 1835, 1836*, Vol. 1, p. 370.

9. *New Orleans Daily Picayune*, December 22, 1843.

10. Diary of Mathew Field, Monday, August 7, 1843, reprinted in Matthew C. Field, *Prairie and Mountain Sketches*, ed. Kate L. Gregg and John Francis McDermott (Norman, OK: University of Oklahoma Press, 1957), p. 135.

11. Diary of Matthew Field, Tuesday, August 21, 1843, in ibid., p. 163.

12. Diary of Matthew Field, Tuesday, September 19, 1843, in ibid., p. 200.

13. Diary of Matthew Field, Wednesday, September 20, 1843, in ibid., p. 201.

14. William Clark Kennerly and Elizabeth Kennerly Russell, *Persimmon Hill* (Norman, OK: University of Oklahoma Press, 1948), p. 147.

15. Ibid., p. 148.

16. Fairholme, *Journal of an Expedition to the Grand Prairies of the Missouri, 1840*, p. 111.

17. George F. Ruxton, *Adventures in Mexico and the Rocky Mountains* (New York: Harper Bros., 1848), p. 254.

18. Honorable Grantley F. Berkeley, *The English Sportsman in the Western Prairies* (London: Hurst & Blackett, 1861), p. 263.

19. *New Orleans Daily Picayune*, February 9, 1844.

20. *New Orleans Daily Picayune*, November 28, 1843.

21. Kennerly and Russell, *Persimmon Hill*, p. 147.

22. *New Orleans Daily Picayune*, January 10, 1844.

23. Ibid.

24. *Concordia Intelligencer* (Vidalia, LA), cited in Field, *Prairie and Mountain Sketches*, p. 200.

25. Letter from Charles W. W. Fitzwilliam to 5th Earl, June 9, 1852, Sheffield Archives, WWM G77/63.

26. Letter from Charles W. W. Fitzwilliam to 5th Earl, August 18, 1852, Sheffield Archives, WWM G77/64.

27. Letter from Charles W. W. Fitzwilliam to 5th Earl sent from Fort Vancouver, December 3, 1852, Northamptonshire Record Office, Fitzwilliam Milton correspondence FM(C) Bundle FV.

28. Henry J. Coke, *A Ride Over the Rocky Mountains* (London: Richard Bentley, 1852), p. 94.

29. Ibid., p. 106.

30. Henry J. Coke, *Tracks of a Rolling Stone* (London: Smith, Elder, 1905), chap. XV1.

31. Coke, *A Ride Over the Rocky Mountains*, p. 130.

32. Ibid., p. 134.

33. Ibid., p. 169.

34. Ibid., p. 106.

35. *Blackwood's Edinburgh Magazine*, 71 (February 1852), review of Henry J. Coke's *A Ride Over the Rocky Mountains*, p. 187.

36. Murray, *Travels in North America During the Years 1834, 1835, 1836*, Vol. 2, p. 158.

37. Fairholme, *Journal of an Expedition to the Grand Prairies of the Missouri, 1840*, p. 131.

38. Murray, *Travels in North America . . .* , Vol. 1, p. 464.

39. Ibid., Vol. 2, p. 16.

40. Ibid., Vol. 1, p. 464.

41. Coke, *A Ride Over the Rocky Mountains*, pp. 105, 176.

42. *New York Daily Tribune*, June 23, 1854 (reprinting *Ohio State Journal*), cited in *Kansas Historical Quarterly*, vol. 6, no. 3 (August 1937), p. 200.

43. *Daily News* (London), September 20, 1847.

44. Francis Parkman, *The Oregon Trail* (New York: George P. Putnam, 1849), p. 392.

45. *New York Daily Tribune*, June 23, 1854, cited in *Kansas Historical Quarterly* vol. 6, no. 3 (August 1937), p. 200.

46. Ibid., p. 316.

47. *Missouri Historical Society Bulletin*, January 1966 article on Henry Chatillon by Mrs. James O'Leary, p. 137.

48. William F. Cody, "Famous Hunting Parties of the Plains," *The Cosmopolitan*, vol. 17, no. 2 (June 1894), p. 133.

49. Randolph B. Marcy, *Thirty Years of Army Life on the Border* (New York: Harper Bros., 1874), p. 402.

50. Letter from Alfred Vaughan, Indian Agent at Fort Union, to Col. Alfred Cumming, July 1856, C620 Bureau of Indian Affairs, National Archives, Washington, DC (cited in *Montana*, vol. 9, no. 2 [April 1959], p. 64).

51. Letter from M. C. Meiggs to Secretary of the Interior Robert McClelland, December 20, 1856, Central Superintendancy Letters Received, M234 Bureau of Indian Affairs, National Archives, Washington, DC (cited in ibid.).

52. Cody, "Famous Hunting Parties of the Plains," *The Cosmopolitan*, p. 32.

53. Hubert Howe Bancroft, *History of Nevada, Colorado and Wyoming* (San Francisco, 1890), p. 696.

54. *New York Times*, June 22, 1854, p. 2.

55. *The Sporting Review* (June 1839), p. 425.

56. "A Discourse Against Laziness," cited in John C. Phillips and Lewis Wess Hill, eds., *Classics of the American Shooting Field* (Boston: Houghton Mifflin, 1830), p. 21.

57. Henry William Herbert ("Frank Forester"), *Complete Manual for Young Sportsmen* (New York: Stringer & Townsend, 1857), pp. 27, 29, and 31.

58. *Frank Forester's Field Sports* (New York, 1849), Vol. 1, p. 26.

59. Herbert (Forester), *Complete Manual for Young Sportsmen*, pp. 31, 22.

60. Richard F. Burton, *The City of the Saints* (New York: Harper Bros., 1862), p. 73.

5. "Who Would Not Go A'Pleasuring!"

1. George Frederick Ruxton, *Life in the Far West* (Edinburgh: Blackwoods, 1849), p. v.

2. Banvard's program quoted in *Sharpe's London Journal*, vol. IX (London, 1849), p. 82.

3. Ibid., p. 83.

4. *The Era* (London), April 28, 1850, p. 12.

5. Ibid.

6. *The Athenaeum*, May 31, 1851, p. 575.

7. *The Literary Gazette*, January 10, 1852, p. 32.

8. Ruxton, *Adventures in Mexico and the Rocky Mountains*, p. 267.

9. Ibid., p. 285.

10. Ruxton, *Life in the Far West*, pp. 185, 187.

11. Ibid., p. 189.

12. Ibid., p. v.

13. Ibid., p. xiv.

14. Ibid., p. ix.

15. Palliser, *Solitary Rambles and Adventures of a Hunter in the Prairies*, p. 56.

16. Ibid., pp. 136, 150.

17. Ibid., p. 232.

18. Ibid., p. 222.

19. Ibid., pp. 220, 275, 120, 163, and 142.

20. *New Monthly Magazine*, 98 (London, 1853), p. 464.

21. Palliser, *Solitary Rambles and Adventures of a Hunter in the Prairies*, p. 105.

22. *Dublin University Magazine*, XLII (July 1853), p. 47.

23. Palliser, *Solitary Rambles and Adventures of a Hunter in the Prairies*, p. 233.

24. Grantley Berkeley in *The Field*, May 12, 1860, p. 354.

25. Honorable Grantley F. Berkeley, *The English Sportsman in the Western Prairies* (London: Hurst & Blackett, 1861), p. 4.

26. Ibid., p. 290.

27. Ibid., p. 246.

28. *Fraser's Magazine*, 14 (August 1836), p. 247.

29. Berkeley, *The English Sportsman in the Western Prairies*, pp. 95, 59.

30. Ibid., pp. 120, 115.

31. Ibid., pp. 116, 161.

32. Ibid., p. 429.

33. *Chicago Press and Tribune*, November 7, 1859, p. 3.

34. Berkeley, *The English Sportsman in the Western Prairies*, pp. 173, 250.

35. Ibid., pp. 44, 28.

36. Ibid., p. 240.

37. *Spirit of the Times* (New York), December 1, 1860.

38. Ibid.

39. *Spirit of the Times*, February 11, 1860.

40. Berkeley, *The English Sportsman in the Western Prairies*, p. 170.

41. Ibid., p. 177.

42. Ibid., pp. 96, 95.

43. Letter from Charles William Wentworth-Fitzwilliam to 5th Earl, December 10, 1850, Northamptonshire Record Office, Fitzwilliam Milton Correspondence FM(C) Bundle FV.

44. Letter from Charles William Wentworth-Fitzwilliam to 5th Earl, February 14, 1851, Northamptonshire Record Office, Fitzwilliam Milton Correspondence FM(C) Bundle FV.

45. Letter from Charles William Wentworth-Fitwilliam to 5th Earl, March 1851, Northamptonshire Record Office, Fitzwilliam Milton Correspondence FM(C) Bundle FV.

46. Fairholme, *Journal of an Expedition to the Grand Prairies of the Missouri, 1840*, p. 62.

47. Berkeley, *The English Sportsman in the Western Prairies*, p. 87.

48. Ruxton, *Adventures in Mexico and the Rocky Mountains*, pp. 317, 319.

49. J. S. Campion, *On the Frontier* (London: Chapman & Hall, 1878), p. 72.

50. Ibid., p. 75.

51. Isabella L. Bird, *A Lady's Life in the Rocky Mountains* (New York: G. P. Putnam, 1879), p. 206.

52. F. Trench Townshend, *Ten Thousand Miles of Travel, Sport and Adventure* (London: Hurst & Blackett, 1869), p. 125.

53. Edward Sullivan, *Rambles in North and South Americas* (London: Richard Bentley, 1852), p. 179.

Part II: Staking a Claim

6. Private Paradise

1. Captain Mayne Reid, *The Scalp Hunters* (London: Charles J. Skeet, 1851), Vol. 1, p. 33.

2. Earl of Dunraven, *Past Times and Pastimes* (London: Hodder & Stoughton, 1922), Vol. 1, p. 65.

3. Earl of Dunraven, "Wapiti-running on the Plains," *The Nineteenth Century* (October 1880), p. 593.

4. Dunraven, *Past Times and Pastimes*, p. 73.

5. Ibid., p. 74.

6. Cody, "Famous Hunting Parties of the Plains," *The Cosmopolitan*, vol. 17, no. 2 (June 1894), p. 32.

7. Dunraven, "Wapiti-running on the Plains," *The Nineteenth Century* (October 1880), pp. 597–598.

8. George Henry Kingsley, *Notes on Sport and Travel* (London: Macmillan, 1900), p. 125.

9. Dunraven, "Wapiti-running on the Plains," *The Nineteenth Century* (October 1880), pp. 604–5.

10. Earl of Dunraven, *The Great Divide* (London: Chatto & Windus, 1876), p. 7.

11. Kingsley, *Notes on Sport and Travel*, citing letter to *The Field*, p. 126.

12. Dunraven, "Wapiti-running on the Plains," *The Nineteenth Century* (October 1880), p. 608.

13. Earl of Dunraven, "A Colorado Sketch," *The Nineteenth Century* (September 1889), p. 448.

14. Ibid.

15. Dunraven, "Wapiti-running on the Plains," *The Nineteenth Century* (October 1880), p. 596.

16. Dunraven, *The Great Divide*, pp. 15, xi.

17. Ibid., pp. 6, 229.

18. Ibid., p. 177.

19. Ibid., p. 54.

20. Earl of Dunraven, "Days in the Woods," *The Nineteenth Century* (April 1880), p. 638.

21. Dunraven, "A Colorado Sketch," *The Nineteenth Century* (September 1889), p. 442.

22. Bird, *A Lady's Life in the Rocky Mountains*, p. 162.

23. Dunraven, "A Colorado Sketch," *The Nineteenth Century* (September 1889), pp. 451, 445.

24. John George Hyde and S. Nugent Townshend, *Our Indian Summer in the Far West* (London: Charles Wittington, 1889), p. 41.

25. S. Nugent Townshend, "Colorado: Its Agriculture, Stockfeeding, Scenery and Shooting," *The Field* (1879), pp. 7, 50.

26. Bird, *A Lady's Life in the Rocky Mountains*, p. 96.

27. *Denver Tribune*, December 6, 1872, p. 2.

28. *Pueblo Daily Chieftain*, June 17, 1874, p. 3.

29. *Rocky Mountain News*, June 24, 1874, p. 4.

30. *Las Animas Leader* (West Las Animas), August 28, 1874, reprinting *Larimer County Express*, August 14, 1874.

31. *Greeley Tribune*, August 26, 1874, reprinting *Denver Tribune*.

32. Ibid.

33. Earl of Dunraven, *Past Times and Pastimes*, Vol. 1, p. 143.

7. A Place for the Boys

1. Letter from Miss Grace Greenwood, August 1, 1873, *Kansas Historical Collections*, XXIX (Topeka, KS, 1943), p. 39.

2. *Cook's Excursionist and Tourist Advertiser*, August 3, 1876, p. 2.

3. Wayne Griswold, *Kansas: Her Resources and Developments, or the Kansas Pilot* (Cincinatti: Robert Clarke, 1871), p. 10.

4. L. D. Burch, *Kansas As It Is* (Chicago: C. S. Burch & Co, 1878), pp. 58, 13.

5. *Mr. Grant's Great Property in: Victoria, in Kansas* (Edinburgh, 1873), pp. 5, 9.

6. Diary of 10th Lord Herries, Constable Maxwell Papers, University of Hull Library, DDEV 51/26.

7. Ibid.

8. Letter from Walter Maxwell to his family, July 14, 1873, Constable Maxwell Papers, University of Hull Library, DDEV/50.

9. *New York Times*, January 3, 1876.

10. *Rural Carolinian*, 6 (1875), p. 579, reprinting *St. Louis Republican*.

11. *Proceedings of the 16th Annual Convention of the Protestant Episcopal Church in the Diocese of Kansas* (Topeka, 1875). Bishop Thomas Vail's address, p. 34.

12. *Chicago Daily Tribune*, reprinting *New York Tribune*, November 4, 1874, p. 8.

13. *St. Louis Democrat*, reprinted in *The Bankers Magazine*, 34 (London, 1874), p 710.

14. Letter from Miss Grace Greenwood, August 1, 1873, *Kansas Historical Collections*, XXIX (Topeka, 1943), p. 39.

15. *Freeman's Journal and Daily Commercial Advertiser* (Dublin), July 1, 1878.

16. Percy G. Ebbutt, *Emigrant Life in Kansas* (London: Swan Sonnenschein, 1886), p. 127.

17. Ibid.

18. Thomas Hughes, *Rugby Tennessee* (London: Macmillan, 1881), p. 3.

19. Ibid.

20. Ibid., p. 21.

21. Ibid., p. 25.

22. *The Cliftonian* (Bristol) (November 1882), p. 293.

23. *New York Times*, August 16, 1881.

24. *Harper's Weekly*, November 6, 1880, p. 710.

25. Ibid., p. 711.

26. Hughes, *Rugby Tennessee*, p. 128.

27. *New York Times*, November 29, 1880, p. 6.

28. *The Rugbeian* (February 1881), in *Anthology of Rugby Poetry* (Rugby, TN: Historic Rugby Press, 1997), p. 8.

29. *Chicago Daily Tribune*, June 18, 1881.

30. *Harper's Weekly*, October 16, 1880, p. 541.

8. "Hail Britannia!"

1. Letter from Walter Cowan to his mother, April 10, 1883, James and Walter Cowan Papers, American Heritage Center, University of Wyoming, Laramie (hereinafter AHC, UW).

2. William B. Close's "Prairie Journal." Letter from Denison, August 20, 1877. MS courtesy of Rosemary Close-Brooks.

3. Close's "Prairie Journal." Letter from Philadelphia, August 31, 1876.

4. Close's "Prairie Journal." Letter from Iowa, November 1876.

5. Close's "Prairie Journal." Letter from Des Moines, January 10, 1878.

6. Close's "Prairie Journal." Letter from Des Moines, August 1, 1878.

7. Ibid.

8. William B. Close pamphlet *Farming in Northwest Iowa* (January 1880), cited in Jacob Van der Zee, *The British in Iowa* (Iowa City: State Historical Society of Iowa, 1922), p. 79.

9. James B. Close and William B. Close, *Stock Raising and Sheep Farming in North Western Iowa* (Manchester, 1879), p. 21.

10. Jacob Van der Zee, *The British in Iowa* (Iowa City: Iowa State Historical Society, 1922), p. 61, citing *Land and Water* (November 1879).

11. Close and Close, *Stock Raising and Sheep Farming in North Western Iowa*, p. 28.

12. Ibid., p. 13.

13. *Le Mars Sentinel*, April 7, 1881.

14. Ibid.

15. Frank Baker, letter to his mother, Frances Baker, May 12, 1881. MS courtesy of Michael Baker.

16. Frank Baker, letter to his father, Thomas Baker, May 24, 1881. MS courtesy of Michael Baker.

17. Walter Cowan letter, April 22, 1883, James and Walter Cowan Papers, AHC, UW.

18. Walter Cowan letter, April 15, 1883, James and Walter Cowan Papers, AHC, UW.

19. Walter Cowan letter, July 27, 1884, James and Walter Cowan Papers, AHC, UW.

20. Walter Cowan, letter to his mother, April 10, 1883, James and Walter Cowan Papers, AHC, UW.

21. Walter Cowan letter, August 6, 1883, James and Walter Cowan Papers, AHC, UW.

22. Walter Cowan, letter to his mother, April 10, 1883, Cowan Papers, AHC, UW.

23. James Cowan letter, July 22, 1883, James and Walter Cowan Papers, AHC, UW.

24. Ibid.

25. Ibid..

26. Walter Cowan letter, November 16, 1883, James and Walter Cowan Papers, AHC, UW.

27. Walter Cowan letter, October 12, 1884, James and Walter Cowan Papers, AHC, UW.

28. James Cowan letter, August 8, 1884, James and Walter Cowan Papers, AHC, UW.

29. *The Field*, October 15, 1881, p. 555.

30. Ibid., p. 556.

31. Poultney Bigelow in *Harper's New Monthly Magazine*, 62 (April 1881), p. 764.

32. Ibid.

33. *Century* magazine, XXV (December 1882), p. 301.

34. *The Field*, October 15, 1881, p. 554.

35. *Le Mars Sentinel*, April 12, 1883.

36. *Le Mars Sentinel*, June 28, 1881.

37. Bigelow in *Harper's New Monthly Magazine*, 62 (April 1881), p. 764.

38. *Le Mars Sentinel*, July 6, 1881 (cited by Jacob Van der Zee; original lost).

39. James Cowan, letter to his mother, January 20, 1884, James and Walter Cowan Papers, AHC, UW.

40. James Cowan, letter to his mother, June 5, 1883, James and Walter Cowan Papers, AHC, UW.

41. James Cowan, letter to his father, January 20, 1886, and James Cowan, letter to his mother, June 5, 1883, James and Walter Cowan Papers, AHC, UW.

42. Dr. Litton Forbes in *The Field*, October 15, 1881, p. 555.

43. Letter from Francis Turnley to Robert Watmough, June 1890, cited in *Kansas Historical Quarterly*, vol. XLI, no. 2 (Summer 1975), p. 194.

44. Letter from William Hooper to his wife, June 18, 1889, Kansas State Historical Society, Topeka.

45. Ibid.

46. *Norwich News*, October 29, 1890, cited in "An English Runnymede in Kansas," *Kansas Historical Quarterly*, vol. XLI, no. 2 (Summer 1975), p. 214.

47. *Harper Sentinel*, April 10, 1891.

48. Lionel Palmer, letter to his brother Claude, March 17, 1892. Collection found by Virginia Hooper, Kansas Historical Society, Topeka.

49. *Harper Graphic*, August 28, 1891, cited in "An English Runnymede in Kansas," *Kansas Historical Quarterly*, vol. XLI, no. 2 (Summer 1975), p. 201.

50. Lionel Palmer, letter to Claude Palmer, March 17, 1892. Collection found by Virginia Hooper, Kansas Historical Society, Topeka.

51. Lionel Palmer, letter to Claude Palmer, November 15, 1891. Collection found by Virginia Hooper, Kansas Historical Society, Topeka.

52. *Harper Sentinel*, August 15, 1889, cited in "An English Runnymede in Kansas," *Kansas Historical Quarterly*, vol. XLI, no. 1 (Spring 1975), p. 37.

53. Virginia S. Hooper and Agnes Nye, "They Had a Good Time While It Lasted," MS, Kansas Historical Society, Topeka, p. 12.

54. Capt. Charles Seton, article in *Kansas City Star*, reprinted in *Collections of the Kansas State Historical Society, 1911–1912*, Vol. XII (Topeka, 1912), p. 467.

55. *Alton Review*, August 31, 1883.

9. Cattle Lords

1. Letter from Moreton Frewen to Clara Jerome, May 9, 1883, Frewen Papers, AHC, UW.

2. John Clay, *My Life on the Range* (Norman, OK: University of Oklahoma Press, 1962), p. 128.

3. *The Times* (London), April 6, 1880, p. 4.

4. *Chicago Times*, March 12, 1880, cited in F. L. Paxson, "The Cow Country," *American Historical Review*, XXII (1916), p. 74.

5. *Fortnightly Review* (London), XXXIV (1880), p. 441.

6. Baron Walter von Richthofen, *Cattle Raising on the Plains of North America* (New York: D. Appleton, 1885), p. 54.

7. Clay, *My Life on the Range*, p. 5.

8. William Baillie-Grohman, *Camps in the Rockies* (London, 1882), p. 320.

9. Letter from Geoffroy Millais to his mother, June 2, 1885, Millais Papers, AHC, UW.

10. Letter from Geoffroy Millais to his uncle George, July 31, 1886, Millais Papers, AHC, UW.

11. Letter from Geoffroy Millais to his mother, August 22, 1884, Millais Papers, AHC, UW.

12. Letter from James Cowan to his mother, May 25, 1885, James and Walter Cowan Papers, AHC, UW.

13. Letter from James Cowan to his brother Henry, August 14, 1885, James and Walter Cowan Papers, AHC, UW.

14. Letter from James Cowan to his mother, May 25, 1885, James and Walter Cowan Papers, AHC, UW.

15. Charles Alston Messiter, *Sport and Adventure Among the North American Indians* (London: R. H. Porter, 1890), p. 275.

16. Rose Pender, *A Lady's Experience in the Wild West* (London: G. Tucker, 1888), p.17.

17. Lady Theodora Guest, *A Roundtrip to North America* (London, 1895), p. 86.

18. Pender, *A Lady's Experience in the Wild West*, pp. 77, 80.

19. Ibid., p. 79.

20. Ibid., pp. 78–79.

21. Moreton Frewen, *Melton Mowbray and Other Memories* (London: Herbert Jenkins, 1924), p. 98.

22. Ibid., p. 143.

23. Ibid., p. 166

24. Letter from Moreton Frewen to Clara Jerome, July 17, 1880, Frewen Papers, AHC, UW.

25. Letter from Moreton Frewen to Clara Jerome, May 1, 1880, Frewen Papers, AHC, UW.

26. Ibid.

27. Letter from Moreton Frewen to Clara Jerome, May 7, 1880, Frewen Papers, AHC, UW.

28. Letter from Moreton Frewen to Clara Jerome, May 6, 1880, Frewen Papers, AHC, UW.

29. Cited by Rico in *Antipode*, vol. 30, no. 2 (April 1998), Frewen Papers, AHC, UW.

30. Diaries of Sir Horace Plunkett, 1881–1932, E. P. Microform Ltd., 1977, by permission of the Irish Co-operative Organization Society, Dublin, entry for May 14, 1881.

31. Ibid., entry for August 30, 1881.

32. "Diary of Major Wise," *Annals of Wyoming*, vol. 12, no. 2 (April 1940), p. 80.

33. Ibid., p. 102.

34. Diaries of Sir Horace Plunkett, 1881–1931, entry for October 23, 1881.

35. Ibid., entry for August 9, 1881.

36. Ibid., entry for October 25, 1881.

37. Ibid., entry for October 11, 1881.

38. Letter from Moreton Frewen to Clara Jerome, July 7, 1880, Frewen Papers, AHC, UW.

39. Letter from Moreton Frewen to Clara Jerome, August 14, 1880, Frewen Papers, AHC, UW.

40. Letter from Moreton Frewen to Clara Jerome, September 21, 1880, Frewen Papers, AHC, UW.

41. Letter from Moreton Frewen to Clara Jerome, March 13, 1881, Frewen Papers, AHC, UW.

42. Letter from Moreton Frewen to Clara Jerome, October 1, 1883, Frewen Papers, AHC, UW.

43. Baillie-Grohman, *Camps in the Rockies*, p. 30.

44. Ibid., p. 363.

45. Ibid., p. 364.

46. Letter from Moreton Frewen to Clara Jerome, May 2, 1881, Frewen Papers, AHC, UW.

47. Letter from Moreton Frewen to Clara Jerome, February 20, 1881, Frewen Papers, AHC, UW.

48. Letter from Moreton Frewen to Clara Jerome, July 15, 1882, Frewen Papers, AHC, UW.

49. Letter from Moreton Frewen to Clara Jerome, September 18, 1882, Frewen Papers, AHC, UW.

50. Letter from Moreton Frewen to Clara Jerome, May 4, 1883, Frewen Papers, AHC, UW.

51. Letter from Moreton Frewen to Clara Jerome, May 9, 1883, Frewen Papers, AHC, UW.

52. Reginald Aldridge, *Ranch Notes in Kansas, Colorado, the Indian Territory and Northern Texas* (London: Longmans, Green & Co., 1884), p. 223.

53. Diaries of Sir Horace Plunkett, 1881–1931, entry for July 21, 1881.

54. Frewen, *Melton Mowbray and Other Memories*, p. 224.

55. Diaries of Sir Horace Plunkett, 1881–1931, entry for June 18, 1886.

56. *Fortnightly Review*, XXXIV (1880), p. 441.

10. "Land Grabbers"

1. Congressman William McAdoo, *Congressional Record*, 49th Congress, May 11, 1886, p. 4380.

2. William Howard Russell, *Hesperothen—Notes from the West* (London: Sampson Low, 1882), Vol. 1, p. 203.

3. *Cleveland Leader*, May 10, 1880.

4. *Cleveland Penny Press*, May 11, 1880.

5. *San Francisco Chronicle*, June 8, 1880.

6. T. V. Powderly, *Thirty Years of Labor* (Columbus, OH, 1889), p. 341.

7. George D. Ellis, *Platforms of the Two Great Political Parties, 1856–1928* (Washington, DC: Government Printing Office, 1932).

8. Chauncey F. Black, *The Lives of Grover Cleveland and Thos. A. Hendricks* (Philadelphia: Thayer, Merriam, & Co., 1884), p. 284.

9. *Chicago Daily Tribune*, March 23, 1885, p. 9.

10. *Chicago Daily Tribune*, January 25, 1886, p. 1.

11. *Marion, Kansas, Register*, March 2, 1887.

12. Sarah M. Brigham, *Waverland: A Tale of Our Coming Landlords* (Chicago: Chicago Stereotype Works, 1886), pp. 13–14.

13. Ibid., pp. 14, 9.

14. Congressman Lewis Payson, *Congressional Record*, 49th Congress, July 31, 1886, p. 7831.

15. *Denver Republican*, February 5, 1887.

16. *New York Times*, January 24, 1885.

17. Congressman Lewis Payson, *Congressional Record*, 49th Congress, July 31, 1886, pp. 7830–31.

18. Congressman William McAdoo, *Congressional Record*, 48th Congress, June 3, 1884, p. 4782.

19. Congressman James Belford, ibid., p. 4778.

20. Congressman William McAdoo, *Congressional Record*, 49th Congress, February 21, 1887, p. 2041.

21. Cited in *The Times* (London), January 23, 1885.

22. Congressman George Cassidy, *Congressional Record*, 48th Congress, June 3, 1884, p. 4776.

23. *New York Sun*, May 22, 1886.

24. Moreton Frewen, *Free Grazing: A Report to the Shareholders of the Powder River Cattle Company* (London, 1883), p. 8.

Epilogue

1. *Castle Rock Journal* (Colorado), July 1, 1887.

2. *Denver Republican*, June 20, 1887.

3. *Cheyenne Daily Sun*, October 13, 1887.

4. *Castle Rock Journal*, July 1, 1887.

5. Adam Badeau, *Aristocracy in England* (New York: Harper Bros., 1886), p. 5.

6. Ibid., pp. 253, 149.

7. *Chicago Daily Tribune*, October 9, 1887.

8. Clay, *My Life on the Range*, pp. 172, 174.

9. Diary of Sir Horace Plunkett, 1881–1932, E. P. Microform Ltd., 1977, by permission of the Irish Co-operative Organization Society, Dublin, entry for December 3, 1889.

10. *Cheyenne Daily Sun*, May 7, 1891.

Credits

1. Leon Pomarede, *View of St. Louis*, ca. 1832–35. Oil on canvas, 29 x 30 inches. Courtesy of Crystal Bridges Museum of American Art, Bentonville, Arkansas. Photograph by Dwight Primiano.

2. Alfred Jacob Miller, *Breakfast at Sunrise*, ca. 1856–60, American, 37.1940.52. Watercolor on paper, 10½ x 13⅜ inches. Courtesy of the Walters Art Museum, Baltimore, Maryland

3. Alfred Jacob Miller, *An Attack by Crows on the Whites on the Bighorn River East of the Rocky Mountains*, 1841. Oil on canvas, 70¼ x 105¾ inches. Private collection. Photograph courtesy of Steven Rich, the Rich Gallery, London.

4. Henry Inman, *Portrait of Sir William Drummond Stewart*, 1844. Oil on canvas, 30 x 25 inches. Courtesy of Joslyn Art Museum, Omaha, Nebraska. Museum purchase, 1963.617

5. Unknown Scottish maker, pair of buffalo chairs, ca. 1842. Mahogany with rosewood. Museum of the American West, Autry National Center, Los Angeles, 91.41.1 and 91.41.2.

6. Frontispiece from James Fenimore Cooper, *The Last of the Mohicans*.

7. Frontispiece from James Fenimore Cooper, *The Prairie*.

8. Alfred Jacob Miller, *Cavalcade (Indian Grand Parade)*, 1839. Oil on canvas, 60 x 96 inches. Courtesy of State Museum, Oklahoma Historical Society, Oklahoma City. Gift of E. W. Marland (1935).

9. Engraving of a drawing by Thomas Shepherd, Egyptian Hall, Piccadilly, published 1828. Courtesy of City of Westminster Archives Centre, London.

10. Handbill advertising Catlin's Gallery of North American Indians, Egyptian Hall. 1840. Courtesy of City of Westminster Archives Centre, London.

11. Engraving from George Catlin, *Catlin's Notes of Eight Years' Travels and Residence in Europe*, London, 1848.

12. John Banvard showing his "three mile picture" of a Mississippi River journey to Queen Victoria, 1849. Engraving from unidentified source, in Banvard papers. By courtesy of Minnesota Historical Society, St. Paul.

13. Handbill advertising Banvard's panorama, Egyptian Hall, 1849. Courtesy of City of Westminster Archives Centre, London.

14. Frontispiece from the Honorable Grantley F. Berkeley, *The English Sportsman in the Western Prairies*, Hurst and Blackett, London, 1861.

15. Illustration from the Honorable Grantley F. Berkeley, *The English Sportsman in the Western Prairies*, Hurst and Blackett, London 1861.

16. Illustration from the Honorable Grantley F. Berkeley, *The English Sportsman in the Western Prairies*, Hurst and Blackett, London, 1861.

17. "Ubique," illustration from Parker Gillmore, *Accessible Field Sports: The Experiences of a Sportsman in North America*, Chapman and Hall, London, 1869.

18. "Close Quarters," illustration from Parker Gillmore, *Accessible Field Sports: The Experiences of a Sportsman in North America*, Chapman and Hall, London, 1869.

19. Thomas Worth, *A Swell Sport on a Buffalo Hunt*, color lithograph, 1882. Published by Currier and Ives, New York. American Antiquarian Society, Worcester, Massachussetts / The Bridgeman Art Library.

20. Thomas Worth, *A Swell Sport Stampeded*, color lithograph, 1882. Published by Currier and Ives. American Antiquarian Society, Worcester, Massachussetts / The Bridgeman Art Library.

21. Frontispiece from Captain Mayne Reid, *The Scalphunters*, Charles Skeet, London, 1851.

22. Frontispiece from Captain Mayne Reid, *The Lone Ranche*, Chapman and Hall, London, 1872.

23. Illustration from *The Boy's Own Paper*, London, June 12, 1880.

24. William Close, photograph, ca. 1875. Courtesy of Rosemary Close-Brooks.

25. Frederick Close, photograph, ca. 1878. Courtesy of Rosemary Close-Brooks.

26. Cartoon from *Harper's Weekly*, New York, January 1880.

27. Cartoon from *Punch*, London, November 12, 1881.

28. Original photograph in the Harper Historical Society's Old Runnymede Church, Harper, Kansas.

29. Original photograph in the Harper Historical Society's Old Runnymede Church, Harper, Kansas.

30. Original photograph in the Harper Historical Society's Old Runnymede Church, Harper, Kansas.

31. Original photograph in the Harper Historical Society's Old Runnymede Church, Harper, Kansas.

32. Original photograph in the Harper Historical Society's Old Runnymede Church, Harper, Kansas.

33. Photograph from Moreton Frewen Collection, American Heritage Center, University of Wyoming, Laramie.

34.   Photograph of the Honorable Claud Anson from family album. Courtesy of Mrs. Sarah Kerr.

35.   Photograph of Cheyenne Club from the Wyoming, Cheyenne, Cheyenne Club file, American Heritage Center, University of Wyoming, Laramie.

36.   Photograph of Kickapoo Ranch from family album. Courtesy of Mrs. Sarah Kerr.

37.   Photograph of William Anson ranch at Valera from family collection. Courtesy of Ryland Howard.

38.   Photograph of the 4th Earl of Dunraven. Courtesy of History Colorado, Denver. Denver Post Historical Collection, Scan 10026882.

39.   Photograph of the 5th Earl of Airlie, 1861, by Camille Silvy. © National Portrait Gallery, London, ref. Ax7439.

40.   Watercolor caricature of Edward Montagu Stuart Granville Montagu-Stuart-Wortley-Mackenzie, 1st Earl of Wharncliffe, by Carlo Pellegrini, published in *Vanity Fair*, London, 1875. © National Portrait Gallery, London, ref. NPG 4699.

41.   Watercolor caricature of William Drogo Montagu, 7th Duke of Manchester, by Sir Leslie Ward, published in *Vanity Fair*, London, 1878. © National Portrait Gallery, London, ref. NPG 2585.

42.   Watercolor caricature of William Montagu Hay, 10th Marquess of Tweeddale, by Carlo Pellegrini, published in *Vanity Fair*, London, 1874. © National Portrait Gallery, London, ref. NPG 4750.

43.   Caricature of George Granville William Sutherland-Leveson-Gower, 3rd Duke of Sutherland, from *Punch*, London, July 9, 1881.

44.   Albert Bierstadt, *The Rocky Mountains, Longs Peak*, 1877. Oil on canvas, 96 x 60 inches. Courtesy of the Denver Public Library. Western History Collection, Z-88849.

Index

Page numbers in *italics* refer to maps.

Aberdeen, Countess of, 284
Aberdeen, Earl of, 235, 284
Aberdeen, Scotland, 234
Abilene, Tex., 231
Aborigines, Australian, 80
Absaroka (Crow lands), 38
*Account of the History, Manners
    and Customs of the Indian
    Nations* (Heckenwelder), 26
Adair, John, 232–33, 246, 248, 271,
    293
Adare Manor, 149, 163, 168, 276
Adirondacks, 111
*Adventures in Mexico and the Rocky
    Mountains* (Ruxton), 117,
    137–38
Africa (steamship), 126
African-Americans, 203
    slavery and, 81, 98, 136–38
Africans, British and, 80
Ah-Quee-wee-zaintz, 79
Aimard, Gustave, 150
Airlie, Lord, 234, 235
Alabama (steamship), 181
Albert, Prince Consort, 75, 79
Alberta, Canada, 261
Albion House, 204
Aldridge, Reginald, 260
Alien Land Act (1887), 280, 287, 291
Alien Landlord Bill, 277
Althorpe, Lord, 23
Alton, Ill., 139
Alton, Iowa, 229
Altowan (Stewart), 40, 59

Amarillo, Tex., 232
American Board of Commissioners
    for Foreign Missions, 44
American Exhibition (London,
    1887), 2, 293
American Fur Company, 39, 124
American Pastoral Company, 263
American Revolution, xv, 19
Americans, British disdain for, xv,
    19, 128–29, 131–32
American Turf Register, 109
American West:
    changing British perception of,
        116–17
    changing nature of, xvii, 47, 163,
        242, 288, 289
    emigrants in, xii, xiii, 86–87, 88,
        95, 102, 138, 139, 155, 186–87,
        200, 206, 228, 262
    equality in, 68 69, 98, 141, 245,
        257
    in fiction, 149–52
    as hunter's paradise, 116, 117,
        121, 148, 163–64
    land controversies in, 174
    romantic appeal of, xvi–xvii,
        20–21, 116
American wilderness:
    in Cooper's novels, 21–23
    in philosophical debates, 20–21
Anderson, William, 32, 33
anglophobia, 141, 264, 270, 284
Anglo-Saxon races, supposed
    superiority of, 4, 111

Anson, Claud, 236, 290
Anson, Frank, 236, 290
Anson, William, 236, 290
antelope, 45–46, 85, 122, 241, 254
Antelope Hills, 33
Antrim, 228
Apaches, 118
Apollo Gallery, 53–54
Approaching a Herd of Buffalo
    (Miller), 85
Arapahos, 94
Argyll, Duke of, 142, 235, 293
aristocrats, British:
    American opinions of, xv, 17,
        106–7, 128, 139–40, 141, 154,
        206, 225, 228, 256–57, 260–61,
        267, 277–78, 284, 285, 286–87;
        see also anglophobia
    anti-business prejudice of, 189
    as cattlemen, *see* cattle ranching,
        British in
    class and social hierarchy as
        preoccupation of, xiv, xv, 97–98,
        201, 220, 221
    "colonies" of, *see* "colonies," of
        British gentlemen
    conflict between American
        values and, xiv
    critical accounts of, 106–7, 256,
        267
    democracy feared by, 19
    as farmers, 177, 184, 187–88,
        193, 196, 205, 207–8, 210–12,
        218–19, 220
    as landlords, 100, 101–2, 233,
        268, 270–74, 287–88, 291
    land reform and, xiii
    Native American dress and
        weapons collected by, 7
    Native Americans idealized by,
        xvi, 60–61, 75
    as obsessed with hunting and
        sports, xv, 12, 18, 109, 111,
        116, 121, 159, 175, 215, 216–17,
        224, 239, 246, 252–55, 286; *see
        also* buffalo (American bison),
        hunting of; hunting; *specific
        sports*
    press coverage of, 107, 141, 147,
        267, 274–75, 278, 284, 287
    public land controversy and, xv,
        xvii, 7, 170–74, 175, 262–64,
        268–79, 287
    and rise of middle class, xiii
    sense of identity of, 17
    servants of, on western trips,
        95–96, 98–99, 127
    snobbery and prejudice of, xv,
        15–16, 140–41, 242, 243, 244–
        45, 255, 256–58, 267, 284
    total U.S. land owned by, 278
    younger sons of, xiii, xiv, 188–
        89, 201–2, 229, 239, 290, 291
    see also "gentry"
Arkansas River, 57, 98, 117, 226
Army, U.S., 7th Cavalry of, 4
art:
    American West in, xi
    Native Americans in, xi
Ashburnham, Earl of, 15, 16, 17,
    18, 38
Ashburnham, Percy, 15–16
Athenaeum, 117
Atkinson, Fort, 94, 112
Attack of the Crows (Miller), 84,
    294
Audubon, John James, 20, 88
Australia, 80
Aylesford, 7th Earl of, 236–37
azaleas, 56

Badeau, Adam, 286
Bagot, Lord, 250
Baillie-Grohman, William, xvii,
    218, 237–38, 239, 257–58,
    293
Baker, Frank, 207–8
Balkans, 17
Ballantyne, Robert, 151
Bank of England, 230
Bannocks, 35
Banvard, John, 114–15
Bayou Salado (South Park), 117–18,
    122, 166
bears, xiii, 37, 85, 111, 123, 161–
    62, 173, 218, 239, 247, 253–54,
    293
    in Catlin's travelling exhibition,
        71–73
Beaufort, Duke of, 5

Beauly Firth, 100–101
beaver pelts, 28–29
Beef Bonanza, The; or How to Get Rich on the Plains (Brisbin), 238
Beirut, 17
Belford, James, 276
Belle Fourche River, 251
Bellevue, Nebr., 43
Bennet, Frederick, 290–91
Beresford, Lord Charles, 5
Beresford, Lord Delaval, 236
Berkeley, Grantley, *xviii*, 126–36, 138
    dogs owned by, 129, 130
    as martinet, 131–32
    press savaging of, 133–35
    snobbery and prejudice of, 128–29, 130–31, 137, 156
    western trip of, 126–28, 130–35, 139
Berkeley Castle, 129
Berthold, Fort, 124
Biddle, Nicholas, 20
Bierstadt, Albert, 142–43, 276, 293
    Dunraven and, 167–68
    Native American artifacts collected by, 142
    Queen Victoria's meeting with, 142–43
Big Creek, 181, 182, 183, 185
Bigelow, Poultney, 212, 216, 217
Big Horn Mountains, 104, 240, 247, 251, 252, 253, 255, 263, 290
Big Horn River, 122
bighorn (mountain) sheep, xiii, 85, 122, 148, 239, 264
Big Horn Valley, 38
Big Sioux River, 200, 210, 216, 241
Bird, Isabella, 140–41, 164, 168
birds, shooting of, 108, 109, 111, 122
Birds of America (Audubon), 88
bison:
    American, *see* buffalo
    European, 85
Bison Bull at Bay (Hays), 142
Bitterroot Mountains, 12
Black, Chauncey, 269–70
Blackfeet, 41, 76, 106
Blackhawks, 76
Blackwood's Magazine, 120

Blaine, James, 269
Blair, Mrs., 281, 288
Blandford, Marquis of, 236
"Bleeding Kansas," 138
Board of Aid for Land Ownership, 193
Bodmer, Karl, 48, 142
Boer War, 290
Boston, Mass., Victoria's Golden Jubilee celebrated in, 285
Breadalbane, Earl of, 16, 18, 53, 125, 127
Breadalbane, Lady, 84
Brickwall, 246, 249
Bridger, Jim, 36, 46, 50, 104
Bridson, Captain, 207
Brigham, Sarah, 273–74
Bright, John, 132
Brisbin, James, 238
Britain:
    aristocrats, *see* aristocrats, British
    economy of, 203
    interest in Native Americans in, xvi, 6, 80
    political reform in, 132
    public schools in, 189
    social hierarchy in, xiv
    travelers and explorers from, xv–xvi, *xviii*, 19–20
Britannic (steamship), 223
British Association of Kansas, 222
British Empire, xvi, 283, 291
Bromfield, George, 127
Bromley, Valentine, 160, 161, 168
Brown, Capability, 15
Brown, John, 136
Bruce, Lord, 5
Brunsville, Iowa, xi–xii
Brussels, 79
Bryant, William Cullen, 11, 25–26
buffalo (American bison), 29
    description of, 85–86
    hunting of, xiii, 3, 31–32, 83, 86, 90–92, 96, 98, 102, 111, 118, 121, 122, 158–59, 221, 226, 254
    meat of, 91–92
    Miller's pictures of, 85
    Native American dependence on, 86

buffalo (*continued*)
  near-extermination of, xvii, 293
  shipped to Scotland by Stewart,
    53, 55, 125
Buffalo Bill's "Wild West," in
  London, 1–7, 71
Bumppo, Natty (char.), 22, 24, 134
Burch, Lawrence, 178
Burr (Catlin's nephew), 76
Burton, Richard, 111–12
  in American West, xvii
Butchering a Wounded Buffalo
  (Miller), 85

Cage, Charles, 100, 101–2
Cairlogie Farm, 217
Calamity Jane, 227
Caldwell, Kans., 227, 231
Caledon, Lord, 252–53
California, 20, 86, 115, 142, 229,
  242, 266
  gold rush in, 95, 230
Calthorpe (Coke's friend), 95, 96
Cambridge, Duke of, 4
Cambridge University, 196, 197,
  202
Campbell, Lord George, 235
Campbell, Robert, 29–30, 31, 33,
  34, 38, 43, 46, 127, 130, 131
Campbell, Sandy, 147, 160
Campion, J. S., 139–40
Canada, 26, 124, 291, 293
  U.S. border with, 116
Canadian River, 57
Cape Colony, 80
Carson, Kit, 36, 40, 46
Cascade Mountains, 41
Cassidy, George, 277
Castletown, Lord, 235
Cathedral of St. John in the
  Wilderness, 283–84
Catlin, George, 48, 56, 67, 81, 114,
  142, 226
  Indian Gallery of, 71–80, 83,
    113
  Murray and, 67, 71, 72, 73, 74,
    78–79
  Museum of Mankind proposed
    by, 76

  Native American portraits by,
    72–73, 81, 117
  Native Americans idealized by,
    75, 81–82, 94
  Ojibbeways and, 77–80, 82,
    125–26
Catskills, 111
cattle:
  Angus, 184, 187
  Durham, 232
  long-horned, 231
cattle ranching:
  boom in, 174, 246, 263, 280
  capital requirements of, 233–34,
    249
  free range system in, 237–38,
    241, 246, 248, 251, 261, 262,
    263, 273, 279
  prices and, 227, 259, 261, 279
  and winter of 1886–87, 279–80,
    289, 290
  see also specific states and
    territories
cattle ranching, British in, xiii,
  xvii, *xx*, 7, 181, 184, 187, 195–
  96, 207, 230, 232–64, 266, 273,
  284, 289–91
  as easy marks for fraud, 234–35,
    236
  joint stock companies and, 234–
    35, 290
  in public land controversy, xv,
    262–63, 275
  and winter of 1886–87, 289, 290
Cayuse, 44
Centennial Exposition
  (Philadelphia, 1876), 167, 175–
  76, 187, 197
Century, 212–13
Century Club, 168
Champlain, Lake, 22
Charleston, S.C., 281
Charpiot's Hotel, 154
Chatillon, Henry, 104
Chattanooga, Tenn., 190
Chearnley, John and William, 93
Cherokee strip, 226, 270
Chesapeake Bay, 111
Cheyenne, 64, 155, 247

Cheyenne, Wyo., 245–46, 247, 248, 290
Cheyenne Club, 245–46, 260
Chicago, Ill., 155, 201, 217, 232
Chicago Daily Tribune, 271, 287
Chickasaws, 69
Chikaskia Ranch, 223
Chikaskia River, 222
Chisholm Trail, 227
chuckwagons, 244
Church, Frederic, 142
Churchill, Lady Jennie, 249, 255
Churchill, Lord Randolph, 5, 249
Churchill, Winston Spencer, 249
Church of England, xii, 202
Cincinnati, Ohio, 127, 190
City (London district), 230
civilization, savagery vs., 21, 81, 160
Civil War, U.S., 138–39, 231, 276
Clan-na-Gael, 285
Clark, Jefferson, 87–88
Clark, William, 14–15
class:
  British preoccupation with, xiv, xv, 97–98, 201, 220, 221, 285
class warfare, 275–76
Clay, John, 230–31, 238, 275, 289
Clement, Antoine, 51, 84, 87
Cleveland, Grover, 270, 281
Close, Frederick, 195–96, 197–201, 217, 220
  death and funeral of, 292
Close, James, 199, 201, 291
Close, Mary Paullin, 198, 199
Close, William, 195–96, 198–200, 220, 266, 291
  as entrepreneur, 199
  Le Mars colony recruiting by, 201–3
  as rower, 197, 200, 202, 216
Close Brothers, 203, 216, 220, 273, 291
Close farm, 207–8
coal mining, 94, 148, 163
Cobden, Richard, 132
Cody, William "Buffalo Bill," 3, 4, 181, 282–83, 288–89
  British aristocracy and, 5
  Dunraven and, 7, 156, 158

on Gore, 104–5
"Wild West" show of, 1–7, 71, 282–83, 288–89, 293
Coke, Henry, xv, *xviii,* 94–97, 99
Collingsworth County, Tex., 235
"colonies," of British gentlemen, xi–xii, *xx,* 177, 197, 229, 239, 291–92
  see also specific colonies
Colorado, 20, 104, 107, 159, 164, 174, 176, 219, 228, 229, 247, 266, 270, 291
  cattle ranching in, 235, 237, 248, 259, 290
  Dunraven's description of, 164–65
Colorado Springs, Colo., 166
Columbia, N.C., 136–37
Columbia River, 12, 41, 97
Columbia River (Cox), 149
Comanches, 80, 118, 232
Comeragh House, 120
Complete Manual for Young Sportsmen (Forester), 110–11
Congress, U.S., 174
  and public land controversy, 265, 275
  see also House of Representatives, U.S.; Senate, U.S.
Congressional Record, 278
Continental Divide, 12, 33, 148, 242
Cook, Thomas, 175, 176
Cooper, Captain, 207
Cooper, James Fenimore, 6, 21–22, 24–27, 57, 60, 75, 80, 96, 134, 149, 152
  on British aristocrats, 286–87
  European trips of, 22–24
Cooperstown, N.Y., 22, 153
Cooper Union, 285
Coral Island (Ballantyne), 151
Corbie (Stewart's valet), 87
Corps of Discovery, *see* Lewis and Clark expedition
cotton, 138
Council Bluffs, Iowa, 266
Council Grove, Kans., 127

Cowan, James, 205–6, 208–9, 210–
11, 217–19, 241–42, 244
Cowan, Lillias, 208
Cowan, Walter, 195, 205–6, 208–9,
210–11, 218–19, 241–42
cowboys, in fiction, 227
Cox, Ross, 149
Crawford, Fort, 69
Crawford County, Iowa, 198
Crazy Horse, 237, 247
Crazy Woman's Fork, 251
Creeks, 59
cricket, 215, 224, 292
Crows, 38, 50, 75, 76, 105, 161,
168
Stewart attacked by, 39–40, 84
Cuba, 42
Cumberland plateau, 190
Cumming, Alfred, 99–100, 105
Cunningham, Herbert, 213, 214
Custer, George, 4, 181, 247
cypresses, 56

Daily Picayune (New Orleans), 88
Dakotas, 102
Dakota Stock & Grazing Company,
259
Dakota Territory, 210, 270, 273
Damascus, 17
Danville, Kans., 225
deer, 85, 111, 122, 148, 173
Deerslayer, The (Cooper), 96
Deer Trail Cattle Company, 259
Delaware (tribe), 51
democracy, British aristocrats' view
of, 19
Denison, Iowa, 195, 198–99, 200,
217
Denver, Colo., 20, 147, 153–54, 164,
232, 245
Land Office in, 171, 172–73
Victoria's Golden Jubilee
celebrated in, 283–84, 285
Denver Republican, 274
Denver Tribune, 147, 169, 172
Derby, Edward Stanley, Earl of,
22–23
De Smet, Father, 149

Des Moines, Iowa, 198
Devonshire, Duke of, 23
Dickens, Charles, 82, 142
Dodge City, Kans., 231, 233
Dog Crusoe, The (Ballantyne), 151
dogs, 100, 103, 129, 130
Donegal, 233
Douglas fir, 53, 56, 89, 294
Drew, John, 236
Dromore Farm, 211–12
drought, 182, 186
Duncan, Francis, xvi, xvii
Dundee, Scotland, 234
Dunmore, Countess of, 60
Dunmore, Earl of, 235, 246–47,
278
Dunmore House, 99
Dunraven, 4th Earl of:
Bierstadt and, 168–69
Buffalo Bill and, 7, 156, 158
in cattle ranching, 259
childhood of, 149, 152
Colorado described by, 164–65
1869 western trip of, 152–54
1872 western trip of, 147–48,
247
1874 western trip of, 160–63
Estes Park bought by, 147, 148,
166, 167–74, 183, 262, 269,
276, 293
hunting as passion of, 148, 154,
157–60, 164, 218, 252, 293
political and commercial affairs
of, 163
press and, 147, 169–70, 172,
173
second western trip of, 154–59
total U.S. land owned by, 278
wealth of, 148
Dunraven, Lady Florence, 153–57
Dunraven Castle, 163
Dunrobin Castle, 266
Dunsany Castle, 251
Durham, Lord, 95

eagles, 123
Earl, George, 249
East St. Louis, Mo., 127

Edinburgh, 41, 234
Edward VII, 4, 5, 6–7, 142, 233
Edward Warren (Stewart), 30–31, 40, 46–47
Egyptian Hall, 70–71, 72–73, 76, 77, 79, 113, 283
EK Ranch, 251, 254, 259, 262, 289–90
elk, *see* wapiti
Eller, Charles and Harry, 212
Ellis County, Kans., 179–80
El Paso, Tex., 224
emigrants, in American West, xii, xiii, 86–87, 88, 95, 102, 138, 139, 155, 186–87, 200, 206, 228, 262
equality:
    as American value, xiv, 98, 141, 245, 257
    Murray on, 68–69
Estes Park:
    Dunraven's purchase of, 147–48, 166, 167–74, 183, 247, 269, 276, 293
    squatters in, 169, 173
Estes Park Company, 171–72
Eton, 189
Europeans, travel by, 19
Evans, Griff, 148, 168, 171

Fairholme, William, 12, 91, 98, 120, 137
Fairmount Park (Philadelphia), 175, 197
Fancuil Hall, 285
Farmers' Alliances, 268
farming, in U.S.:
    British upper classes and, 177, 184, 187–88, 193, 196, 205, 207–8, 210–12, 218–19, 220
    mortgages and, 268
    tenant, 268, 270–74, 287–88
    vs. Britain, 176–77, 199, 200
Farquar, Arthur, 206
Farquar brothers, 206, 217
Far West, The (boat), 42
Fenton, James, 207
Fetterman, Fort, 248, 256

fiction:
    American West in, 149–52, 227
    American wilderness in, 21–23
    landlordism in, 273–74
    Native Americans in, xvi, 26
Field, Cyrus, 153
Field, Matthew, 88, 89, 90, 92
Field, The, 126, 128, 130, 136, 166, 211, 214, 221
Field Sports of the United States (Forester), 110
financiers, British, cattle business and, 230–31, 234–35, 258–59
Finch, Clement, 256
Fish and Fishing of the United States (Forester), 110–11
Fish Creek, 168, 171
Fishing on the Grand River (Miller), 84–85
Fitzpatrick, Bernard, 254
Fitzpatrick, Thomas, 38–40, 43, 44, 49
Fitzwilliam, Charles, *see* Wentworth-Fitzwilliam, Charles
Fitzwilliam, Earl, xiv, 93, 126
Flatheads, 35
Florence, Kans., 221
Florida, 106, 229, 278, 281, 288
Floyd River, 215
Floyd Valley, 204–5
Forester, Frank (pseud.), 110–11
Fort Atkinson, 94, 112
Fort Berthold, 124
Fort Crawford, 69
Fort Fetterman, 248, 256
Fort Gibson, 226
Fort Hays, 179, 181
Fort Laramie, 88, 93, 97, 104, 112
Fort Leavenworth, 60, 63, 103, 112, 139
Fort McHenry, 19
Fort McKinney, 248
Fort McPherson, 7, 155, 156–57, 159
Fortnightly Review, 238
Fort Riley, 127–28, 132–33, 139
Fort Union, 121

Fort Vancouver, 41
Fox (Outragami), 69
foxhunting, 108–9, 129, 185, 216,
    217, 252
free range system, 237–38, 241,
    245, 248, 251, 261, 262, 263,
    279
Frémont, John, 87, 116
Frewen, Clara Jerome, 249–50,
    255, 256, 259, 260
Frewen, Edward, 246, 256
Frewen, Louise, 256
Frewen, Moreton, 230, 233, 246–
    51, 253, 255–56, 258, 260, 263,
    264, 280, 284
  in Powder River Cattle
    Company, 259, 261
  wedding of Clara and, 250
  in Western Ranches Ltd., 248–
    49, 258
Frewen, Richard, 247, 248, 253,
    258, 284
Frith, William Powell, 142
frontier, westward advancement of,
    see westward expansion
fur trade, 28–29, 42, 47, 118–20,
    267
  annual rendezvous of, 34–37,
    38, 41, 43–44, 47, 48, 65, 84,
    86, 89–90, 283, 294
  caravans of, 29–33, 43, 49, 86,
    155
  collapse of, 86

Garland, John Watts, 156
Garnett, Gerald, 205
Gee, Arthur, 206
General View of the Indian Camp
    (Miller), 53
gentlemen farmers, 221
"gentry," xiii, 221
George, Lake, 22
German immigrants, 200, 206, 228
Gibson, Fort, 226
Gish-e-gas-e-ghe, 79
Gladstone, William, 4, 142
Glens Falls, N.Y., 22
gold rush, 95, 117, 230

Goodnight, Charles, 232, 246
Gore, St. George, xviii, 112, 129
  as absentee landlord, 100
  dogs owned by, 100, 103
  1854–57 western trip of,
    99–100, 102–6, 127, 139, 166,
    247
  field sports as obsession of,
    100–101
  political controversy
    surrounding, 105–6
Gower, Lord Ronald, 5, 7
Grand American Hall, 115
Granges, 268
Grant, George, 177, 179–88, 202,
    203, 221, 278, 292
  background of, 178
  livestock raised by, 181, 184,
    187, 188
  press and, 183, 184
  and scientific approach to
    farming, 184
  see also Victoria colony
Grandtully, 17th Laird and 5th
    Baronet of, 14
Grandtully, John Stewart, 18th
    Laird and 6th Baronet of,
    17–18, 27, 47–48, 52
Grandtully, 19th Laird and 7th
    Baronet of, see Stewart,
    William Drummond
grasshopper invasions, 185–86,
    199
Gray, William, 44–46, 47, 51
Great Divide, The (Dunraven),
    161–62
Great Famine, 101, 285
Great Migration, xii, 86–87, 88
Great Plains, Cooper's descriptions
    of, 24–25
Great Reform Act of 1832, 132
Great Salt Lake, 41, 116
Greenbackers, 268
Green (Susquadee) River, 33, 47,
    89
  rendezvous at, 34–37, 38, 41,
    43–44, 47, 50–52, 65, 84,
    89–90, 283, 294

Greenwood, Grace, 175
Greenwood, William, 98
Greeting the Snake Indians
    (Miller), 59
Gros Ventre, 38
Gunther, Richard, 187

Half-Breed, The (Möllhausen), 150
Hall, Basil, 16, 19, 68
Hampton, Wade, 136–37
Hanna, Oliver, 253–54
hare coursing, 100, 101–2
Harper, J. W., 191
Harper, Kans., 222, 225
Harper County, Kans., xi, 226
Harper Sentinel, 224, 228
Harpers Ferry, Va., 136
Harper's Weekly, 193, 212
Harris, Moses "Black," 36
Hart, Martyn, 284, 285
Havana, 42
Ha-won-je-tah, 74
Hays, Fort, 179, 181
Hays, Kans., 185, 187
Hays, William, 142
Heckenwelder, John, 26
Hee-ohks-te-kin, 74
Herbert, William, 109–11
Herries, Lord, 180 81, 182
Herzog, Kans., 188
Hickok, "Wild Bill," 227
Hobart, Lord, 212, 218
Holkham Hall, 95
Holland, Lord, 23
Holmes, George, 35–36, 39
Home, David Dunglas, 154
"Home on the Range," 221
Homestead Act (1862), 170
homesteaders and small settlers,
    xv, 182, 262, 269
Hooper, William, 223, 224
Hornby, Hugh, 211
Horse Creek, 34, 89, 283
horse racing, 34–35, 43, 90, 216–
    17, 246
"Hottentot Venus," 77
Houghton, Lord, 278
Household Cavalry, 50

House of Commons, 17
    "pocket" seats in, 18
House of Lords, 17, 18, 23
House of Lords (tavern), 204
House of Representatives, U.S.:
    Judiciary Committee of, 277
    and public land controversy, 269,
        275, 276–77, 279, 287
    Public Lands Committee of, 269,
        276–77
    see also Congress, U.S.; Senate,
        U.S.
Hudson's Bay Company, 41
Hughes, Thomas, 188–89, 222
    Rugby colony of, *xxi,* 191–94,
        200, 202, 212
hunting, xiii, *xviii,* 93, 225, 293
    American attitude toward, 109,
        111–12
    British obsession with, xv, 14,
        18, 109, 111, 116, 121, 159, 175,
        216, 239, 246, 252–55
    by Dunraven, 148, 154, 157–60,
        164, 218, 252
    by Gore, 99–106, 247
    see also buffalo (American
        bison), hunting of; *specific
        sports*
Hunting of the Buffalo, The
    (Miller), 53, 59, 85
Hunting the Argali (Miller), 84–85
Hunting the Grizzly Bear (Miller),
    84–85

Ilchester, Earl of, 235
Illinois, 231, 271–72
Independence, Mo., 30, 86, 115
Indian Affairs Department, U.S.,
    105
Indian Agents, 105
Indians, *see* Native Americans
Indian Territory, xiv, 13, 30, 57, 60,
    100, 112, 226, 228, 232, 270,
    292
Interior Department, U.S., 269,
    278
Iowa, 195, 196, 197–98, 218–19,
    265, 273, 291

Iowa Land Company, 266
Iowas, 79
Ireland, 148, 149, 252
    British landlords in, 100, 101–2,
        233, 268, 270–71, 287
    Great Famine in, 101, 285
    political unrest in, xiii, 101–2,
        163, 270–71, 286
Irish, 243
Irish-Americans, 203, 270–71, 278
Irving, Washington, 40, 57–58, 60,
    75, 80, 149
Irvington, N.Y., 167

Jackson, Andrew, 132
JA Ranch, 232–33, 246
Jefferson, Thomas, 12, 15
Jerome, Clara, see Frewen, Clara
    Jerome
Jerome, Leonard, 249, 250
Jervis, Cecil, 206
Jervis, Ronald, Lord St. Vincent,
    206, 216
John (Murray's valet), 99
Johnson, Henry, 98
Jolly West, The (boat), 185
Journals of Lewis and Clark, The,
    149
June Derby, 217

Kansas, 138, 150, 176, 221, 266
    British in, 221–22, 270, 272,
        278, 291
    see also Runnymede colony;
        Victoria colony
    settlers in, 177–78, 182, 186–87
Kansas, Episcopalian Bishop of,
    184
Kansas As It Is (Burch), 178
Kansas City, Mo., 30, 127, 134, 139,
    232
Kansas Pacific Railroad, 153, 183,
    186, 221, 245
    land grant sales of, 178–79
Kansas Pilot, 177
Kansas River, 31, 127
Kennerly, William, 90–91
Kenry House, 163

Kensington, 2
Kent, Duchess of, 75
Kerry, Lord, 24
Kickapoo Ranch, 236
Kickapoos, 69
Kingsley, George, 155, 157, 159,
    160
Kippilaw, 293
Knights of Labor, 268–69
Ko-man-i-kin-o-haw, 74

Lady's Experience in the Wild West,
    A (Pender), 243
land-grab controversy, see public
    lands, controversy over
land grants, of railroads, 178–79,
    180, 198, 262, 268, 272, 291
Land League, 270–71
landlordism:
    in fiction, 273–74
    in Ireland, 100, 101–2, 233, 268,
        270–71
    in U.S., 270, 271–73, 287–88,
        291
Land Office, U.S., 171, 172–73
land reform, xiii
Landseer, Edwin, 142
land speculation, 198, 221
land warrants, 272
Lansdowne, Lord, 23
Laramie, Fort, 88, 93, 97, 104,
    112
Laramie, Wyo., 248
Laramie Mountains, 245, 247
Larkin, John, 285
Larpenteur, Charles, 30, 37
Lascelles, Alfred, 205, 218
Last of the Mohicans, The (Cooper),
    22–23, 24, 96, 117, 152, 153,
    243
Leavenworth, Fort, 60, 63, 103,
    112, 139
Lee, Jason, 43–44
Leeds, Duke of, 125
Le Mars, Iowa, 200–201, 214–15,
    220, 266, 287
    St. George's Church in, xii, 213,
        283, 292

Le Mars, Iowa, British colony at,
    xii, *xxi,* 197, 200, 204–21, 222,
    229, 239, 251, 291–92
    farm pupils at, 207–8
    horse racing and polo at, 216–17
    recruiting for, 201–3
    Victoria's Golden Jubilee
        celebrated by, 283
    weather and, 209–10, 219
Le Mars Cup, 216
Le Mars Liberal, 201
Le Mars Sentinel, 201, 207, 214–15,
    216–17
*Letters and Notes on the Manners,
    Customs and Condition of
    the North American Indians*
    (Catlin), 56, 75, 80
Lewis, Meriwether, 14–15
Lewis and Clark expedition, 12, 13,
    14–15, 20, 21, 26
Lexington, Mo., 29–30
Lichfield, Earl of, 236, 290
Life in the Far West (Ruxton), 113,
    118–20
Lincoln, Ill., 272
Literary Gazette, 117
Little Bighorn, Battle of the, 4, 247
Lobb, Major, 225
locust swarms, 185–86, 199
Logiealmond, 52, 87
Loi de Lynch, La (Aimard), 150
London, 234
    American Exhibition in, 2, 293
    Buffalo Bill's "Wild West" in,
        1–7, 71, 282–83, 293
    western panoramas in, 70–71
London Stock Exchange, 230,
    258–59
Long, Major, 92
Long, Stephen, 20, 26, 226
Longs Peak, 147, 168
Lorne, Marquis of, 5, 7, 293
Louisiana Purchase, 12

Mackenzie, Alexander, 26, 103
Mah-to-toh-pa, 73–74
Manchester, Duke of, 239, 259
Mandans, 73–74, 76, 80, 81

"manifest destiny," 116
    see also westward expansion
Manners, Lord, 254
Mansfield, Lord, 18
Maoris, 80
Marcy, Randolph, 105, 133
Marion County, Kans., 221
Marjoribanks, Archibald, 235–36
Markhead (trapper), 40
Martin, Mary Frances, 228
Matador Land & Cattle Company,
    263
Ma-wo-ma, 50, 283
Maximilian, Prince of Wied-
    Neuwied, 48
Maxtone Graham, Robert, 205
Maxwell (Dunraven's cook), 161, 162
Maxwell, Marmaduke, 181
Maxwell, Walter, 181, 182, 185, 188
Mayo, Earl of, 254–55, 256, 293
McAdoo, William, 265, 275–76,
    280, 287
McClelland, Robert, 105–6
McHenry, Fort, 19
McKinney, Fort, 248
McPhail, Mrs., 209, 211
McPherson, Fort, 7, 155, 156–57, 159
Medicine Bow range, 242
Meek, Joe, 36
Melbourne, Lord, 67
Memphis, Tenn., 114
Menetou, Colo., 166
Menomenees, 69
Merton Hall, 293
Messiter, Charles, 242
Methodist missionaries, 43–44
Mexico, 100, 125, 236
    U.S. war with, 116, 117, 150, 272
middle class, rise of, xiii
Middle Park, 166
Millais, Geoffroy, 240–41, 244, 290
Millais, John, 240, 293
Millais, Johnny, 240–41
Miller, Alfred Jacob, 53, 88, 116,
    142
    at Murthly, 83–85
    New York gallery exhibition of,
        53–54

Miller, Alfred Jacob (*continued*)
paintings hung at Murthly, 54,
59, 84–85, 294
on Stewart, 52, 54–55
in Stewart's 1837 western trip,
48–52
Milton, Lord, 94
Minneapolis, Minn., 201
Minnesota, 265, 273
missionaries, 43–44, 47, 86
Mississippi, 278
Mississippi River, 13, 20, 69, 113–
14, 150, 198, 226, 292
Missouri (state), 12, 96, 138, 139,
231
as slave state, 136
Missouri River, xiv, 13, 29, 38, 67,
103, 114, 121, 124, 127, 142,
200
Great Bend of, 30
Great Falls of, 13
Missouri Territory, 15
Möllhausen, Balduin, 150
Moncrieffe, Malcolm, 290
Moncrieffe, William, 290, 291
Montague, Lord George, 254
Montana Territory, 39, 159, 160,
247
cattle ranching in, 237, 289
Moore, O. A., 204–5
Moray Firth, 100–101
Moreton, Margaret, 205
Moreton, Reynolds, 205, 206, 207,
208, 211–12, 213, 215, 218, 251
Mormons, 116
mountain men, *see* trappers
mountain (bighorn) sheep, xiii, 85,
122, 148, 239, 254
Murray, Charles, *xviii*, 41–42,
59–60, 80, 81, 85, 91, 94, 98,
118, 149, 283
as amateur ethnologist, 64–65
Catlin and, 67, 71, 72, 73, 74,
78–79
in disillusionment about Pawnee
character, 62–63, 81
on equality, 68–69
Indian ponies acquired by,
67–68

on Native American dependence
on buffalo, 86
Pawnee brave described by,
65–66
in Queen Victoria's household,
67–68, 74, 78–79
western trip of, 60–70, 86, 99,
247
on white impact on Native
Americans, 69–70
Murthly Castle, 14, 17, 27, 47, 52,
54, 293, 294
Museum of Mankind, Catlin's
proposal for, 76

Natchez, Miss., 69
Native Americans:
in art, xi
in attacks on trappers, 38
British fascination with, xvi, 6,
80, 267
buffalo as essential to lifestyle
of, 86
in Buffalo Bill's "Wild West," 2,
4, 5
Catlin's portraits of, 72–73, 81
disease and, 81
in England, 77–80
in fiction, xvi, 26
forced resettlement of, xvii, 58,
80, 116, 226
idealization of, xvi, 60–61, 75,
81–82, 94
Irving's description of, 58–59
at trappers' rendezvous, 35, 50,
51, 65, 84
as victims of "civilization," 21,
81, 160
white interactions with, 12–13,
38, 69–70, 80–81, 203
women, trappers and, 34, 51,
84
Nebraska, 138, 141, 159, 272, 273
cattle ranching in, 238, 248,
266, 289
Neville, Lord, 235
Newfoundland, 293
New Mexico, 40, 234, 262–63, 266
New Orleans, La., 42, 43, 48, 181

New York, N.Y., 281
   Victoria's Golden Jubilee
      celebrated in, 285
New York Times, 107, 183, 274–75
New York Tribune, 184
New Zealand, 80
Nez Perce, 35, 74
Niagara Falls, 161
Niagara Falls (Church), 142
Nib-nab-be-qua, 79
Nineteenth Century, 164
Niobrara Ranch, 244, 289
North Platte River, 32, 90, 156
Norwich, Kans., 225
Nowood River, 251

Oakley, Annie, 3
Oakley Hunt, 129
Oates, William, 276–77
Ogila-sa (Red Shirt), 4, 5
Ogilvy, Lyulph, 235, 290
Oglalas, 50
Ohio & Mississippi Railroad, 127
Ojibbeways, 77–80, 82, 125–26
Oklahoma, 226
Omaha, Nebr., 266
Omohondro, John "Texas Jack,"
      156–57, 161, 162
One of the Sources of the Colorado
      (Miller), 53
Opera Comique, 162
Oregon, xvii, 37, 41, 47, 86, 93, 95,
      248
*Oregon Missions and Travels in the
      Rocky Mountains* (De Smet), 149
Oregon settlement (1846), 116
Oregon Trail, *xviii,* 86, 87, 104, 155
Oregon Trail, The (Parkman), 102,
      117
Ormalie, Lord, 16, 18, 29
Osages, 59
Ossington, Lord, 22
Otsego Lake, 153
Outragami (Fox), 69

Pacific Northwest, 293
   U.S.-Canadian border in, 116
Pacific Ocean, 12, 20, 41
pack trains, 29–33, 43, 49, 86, 155

Palliser, John, *xviii,* 83, 91, 117,
      120–25, 127, 149, 252, 260
   hunting trophies of, 123–24
Palmer, Claude, 227
Palmer, Lionel, 223, 225–26, 227–28
Palmer, Mark, 223, 226
Palmerston House, 293
Palo Duro Canyon, 232, 246, 293
Panacks, 97
panoramas, 70–71
   rolling, 113–16, 117, 142
Paris, 26, 79
Parkman, Francis, 102, 104, 117
Parnell, Charles, 270
Pathfinder, The (Cooper), 96
Pattana-quotto-weebe, 79
Paullin, Daniel, 197–98
Paullin, Henry, 198
Pawnees, 25, 32, 42, 81
   Murray's stay with, 60–67, 69,
      86, 247, 288
Payson, Lewis, 274, 275
Pender, James, 242–45, 289
Pender, Rose, 242–45, 289
Perthshire, Scotland, 14, 54, 56,
      83, 101
Philadelphia, Pa., 281
   Centennial Exposition in, 167,
      175–76, 187, 197
Pierre's Hole, 38
Pike, Zebulon, 25
Pike's Peak, 94
pine trees, 89
Pioneers, The (Cooper), 22
Pipestone, Minn., 220
Pirates des prairies, Les (Aimard),
      150
plantation owners, as American
      aristocracy, 16–17
Planter's House, 87, 103
Platte River, 20, 31–32, 43, 88, 93,
      124, 155, 248
Plumb, Senator, 277
Plunkett, Horace, 251–52, 254–55,
      256, 259, 260–62, 289–90
Plymouth County, Iowa, xii, 200,
      202, 203–4, 219
politicians, public land controversy
      and, 262, 269, 287

polo, xii, 216, 217, 224, 236, 292
populist politics, xv
Portrait of a Chief of the Snake Nation (Miller), 53
Portrait of an Arikara Squaw (Miller), 53, 59
Powderly, Terence, 268–69
Powder River, 38, 104, 247, 248, 251, 253, 261, 280, 290–91
Powder River Cattle Company, 259, 261, 289
Powtawatomies, 69
Prairie, The (Cooper), 24–25, 26, 57
Prairie Cattle Company, 234
Prairie Chief, The (Ballantyne), 151
Prairie Club, 213–14, 220, 222
"Prairies, The" (Bryant), 11, 25–26
Prairie Traveller, The (Marcy), 105
preempting, 170, 269–70
Preemption Act, 170
Presbyterian missionaries, 44
Prescott, Captain, 185
Primgar, Iowa, 287–88
primogeniture, xiv
progress, paradox of, 21, 81, 160
Pshan-shaw, 74
public lands, controversy over:
  British and, xv, xvii, 7, 170–74, 175, 262–64, 268–79, 287
  cattle ranching and, xv, 262–63
  wealthy Americans and, 174
public schools, British, 189
Pugin, Augustus, 149

rabies, 36
racism, 243
railroads, xvii, 126, 138–39, 153, 200–201, 224, 230
  land grant sales of, 178–79, 180, 198, 262, 268, 272, 291
  transcontinental, 116, 155, 177, 289
Ranch Notes (Aldridge), 260
Rawlins, Wyo., 241
Red Shirt (Ogila-sa), 4, 5, 282
Reid, Edward, 278
Reid, Mayne, ix, xvi, 150–52, 157, 181, 227

"remittance men," 225, 228, 242
rhododendrons, 56
Rifle Rangers, The (Reid), 150
Riley, Fort, 127–28, 132–33, 139
Rio Grande, 117
Roche, Alexis, 251
Rock Creek, Wyo., 248, 249, 254, 256
Rocking Chair Ranch, 235–36, 284
Rocky Mountain Douglas firs, 53, 56, 89, 294
Rocky Mountain Fur Company, 38, 40
  pack train of, 29–34
Rocky Mountains, 12–13, 28, 32, 48–49, 94, 104, 114, 117, 124, 142, 154, 159, 160, 164, 230, 252, 266
  Front range of, 147, 165
  "parks" (basins) of, 165–67
  see also specific parks
Rocky Mountains, Longs Peak, The (Bierstadt), 168
Rocky Mountains, The (Bierstadt), 143
Rodney, Lord, 253
Rollo, Eric and Herbert, 206
Romantic era, xvi, 81
Roosevelt, Theodore, 159–60, 291
Roscius, 71–72
Rough Riders, 291
Royal Academy, 168
Royal Geographical Society, 75, 124
Royal Geological Society, 75–76
Royal Institution, 75–76
Rugbeian, The, 192
Rugby colony, *xxi,* 191–94, 200, 202, 212
rugby football, 215, 273
Runnymede Arms, 223–24
Runnymede colony, xi, *xxi,* 200, 223–28, 239
Runnymede Wanderers Football Club, 224
Russian immigrants, in Kansas, 186–87
Ruxton, George, *xviii,* 91, 113, 117–20, 121, 122, 124, 125, 127, 137–38, 158–59, 166, 260

St. George's Church, xii, 213, 283, 292

St. Louis, Mo., 11–12, 13–14, 26, 57, 60, 93, 95, 99, 105, 106, 114, 124, 130, 136, 139, 181, 232
Stewart in, 14–15, 17, 41, 42, 48, 49, 52–53, 87

St. Louis Democrat, 184

St. Louis Republican, 183

St. Vincent, Ronald Jervis, Lord, 206, 216

Salt Lake City, Utah, 116

San Angelo, Tex., 236, 290

San Francisco, Calif., 20, 242

San Francisco Chronicle, 267

Sangre Grande Mountains, 166

Sanitsarish, 61, 62, 63, 64–65

San Luis Park, 166

Sans Peur, 281

Santa Fe, N.Mex., 20, 86, 100

Santa Fe Trail, *xviii,* 86, 127, 155

Saratoga Springs, N.Y., 22, 153

Savage Club, 154, 162

Scalp Hunters, The (Reid), ix, 150, 151–52

Schuylkill River, 175, 197

Scotland, 234, 266, 268, 287

Scott, Mrs., 287

Scott, Walter, 21

Scully, William, 271–72, 291

Sedgemoor, Tenn., 190

Senate, U.S.:
Judiciary Committee of, 277
public land controversy and, 269, 275, 277, 279
see also Congress, U.S.; House of Representatives, U.S.

Seton, Charles, 223–24, 228

Seton-Karr, Henry, 293

Shawnees, 115

sheep ranching, xv, 182, 183, 185, 187, 188, 207

Sheridan, Kans., 153

Sheridan, Philip, 155, 156, 264

Sheridan, Wyo., 248

Shields, Walter, 187

Shim-a-co-che, 50

Shon-ga-ton-ga-chesh-en-day, 74

Shoshone (Snakes), 35, 50, 51, 54, 283

Sibley, Iowa, 217, 220, 266

Sierra Nevada Mountains, 117

Sillen, Herr, 43, 45

Sioux, 4, 25, 74, 106, 155, 214, 247

Sioux City, Iowa, 200, 201, 217, 292

slavery, 81, 98, 136–38

smallpox, 81

Smith, John Rowson, 115

Smith-Dodsworth, Matthew, 205

Smithes, Henry, 185

Smithsonian Institution, 80

Smoky Hill River, 183

Snake River, 33, 97

Snakes (Shoshone), 35, 50, 51, 54, 283

snobbery:
of Berkeley, 128–29, 130–31, 137, 156
of British aristocrats, xv, 15–16, 140–41, 242, 243, 244–45, 255, 256–58

Solitary Rambles and Adventures of a Hunter in the Prairies (Palliser), 83, 120

Sonnambula, La (Bellini), 89

South America, 291

Southern Africa, 291

South Park (Bayou Salado), 117–18, 122, 166

South Pass, 32–33, 43, 48, 50, 89, 124

South Platte River, 154

Spalding, Eliza, 44, 47

Spanish-American War, 291

Spencer, Lord and Lady, 23

Spirit of the Times, 109, 133

Sporting Review, The, 108

sports:
British obsession with, xv, 12, 18, 109, 111, 215, 216–17, 224, 246, 286
in U.S., 108–12
see also specific sports

spruce trees, 56, 89

Spy, The (Cooper), 21

Stafford, Lord, 250, 265

Stafford House, 7, 266
"Star-Spangled Banner, The," 19
State of Nebraska (steamship), 5
steamboats, 13
steeplechases, 108, 216
Stewart, Archibald, 47
Stewart, Christina, 27
Stewart, George, 273
Stewart, John, 18th Laird of
    Grandtully, 17–18, 27, 47–48, 52
Stewart, William Drummond, *xviii,*
    102, 112, 122, 131, 136, 155,
    166, 252, 293–94
  background of, 14
  becomes Laird of Grandtully, 52
  buffalo shipped to Scotland by,
    53, 56, 125
  Crow attack and, 39–40, 84
  dispersal of collection, 294
  in 1833–35 western trip, 14–15,
    18, 28–41, 43, 116, 148, 267
  in 1836 western trip, 43–47
  in 1837 western trip, 48–52, 283
  in 1843 western trip, 87–93
  Fourth of July celebration of,
    91–92
  Gray's description of, 44–46
  at Green River rendezvous,
    34–37, 41, 43, 47, 50–52, 65,
    89–90, 216, 283, 294
  Miller and, 48–52, 83–85, 294
  Native American artifacts
    collected by, 53, 254
  novels by, 30–31, 40, 46–47, 59,
    75, 118
  in return to Scotland, 54–55
  satirization of, 92–93
  as seasoned traveler, 17
  specimen collecting by, 29,
    52–53, 56
Storm in the Rocky Mountains
    (Bierstadt), 142–43
Strathmore, Earl of, 235, 239
Sublette, William, 29–30, 46, 87,
    131
Sugden, Frank, 205
Sullivan, Edward, 141
Sussex, Duke of, 74–75
Sutherland, Duchess of, 74

Sutherland, 3rd Duke of, 7, 239,
    265–66, 273, 276, 278, 281,
    287–88
Sutherland Manor, 288
Swan Land & Cattle Company, 259,
    289
Swedish immigrants, 200, 206
Sweetwater River, 32, 90, 124, 248
Sykes, Richard, 273
Sykeston, N.Dak., 273

Taos, N.Mex., 40
Tarpon Springs, Fla., 288
Taunton, Lord, 22
Taylor, Mrs., 211
Taymouth Castle, 16, 84, 125
Tay River, 56, 84, 294
Teck, Duke of, 5
tenant farmers, 268, 270–74, 287–88
Tennessee, 190
Tennyson, Alfred, Lord, 142
Teton range, 33, 38
Texas, 227
  annexation of, 116
  cattle ranching in, 231, 232–33,
    260, 262–63, 266, 273, 290
  land ownership in, 237, 262–63,
    291
  Panhandle of, 232, 234, 235,
    246, 260
Texas Land & Cattle Company, 263
Thomas McLean's Gallery, 142
Times (London), 211, 231
Tipperary, 271
Tom (Stewart's servant), 87
Tom Brown's School Days (Hughes),
    188, 189
Tongue River, 38, 39, 251
Topeka, Kans., 221
Tour of the Prairies, A (Irving), 57–58
Townshend, Nugent, 166–67, 211–
    12, 221
Townshend, Trench, 141
trappers, 29, 41
  annual rendezvous of, 34–37, 38,
    41, 43–44, 47, 48, 50–52, 65,
    84, 86, 89–90, 283, 294
  Native Americans in attacks on,
    38

Trapper's Bride, The (Miller), 84
Trappers Camp (Miller), 53
Trappeurs de l'Arkansas, Les
    (Aimard), 150
travel:
    British fondness for, xv–xvi, *xviii*
    by Europeans, 19–20
Travels in North America (Hall), 19
Travels in North America (Murray),
    68–70
Trentham Hall, 266
Trinity College, 197, 198
Trollope, Mrs., xiv, 16, 68
Turkey, 17
Turnley, Francis, 222–23, 225–26,
    228
Turtle Mountain range, 123
Tweeddale, Marquis of, 235, 278
Tweedmouth, Lord, 235, 236, 284
typhoid, 193, 208

Union, Fort, 121
Union Pacific Railroad, 155, 242,
    245, 248
Union Stockyards, 232
United Kingdom, *see* Britain
United States:
    British complaints about, xiv
    British curiosity about flora and
      fauna of, 20
    British landlords in, 270, 271–
      73, 287–88, 291
    British tourists in, 175–76
    Canada's border with, 116
    Centennial celebration of, 167,
      175–76, 187, 197
    democracy in, 19
    emigration to, 175
    in Mexican War, 116, 117, 150,
      272
    slavery in, 81, 98, 136–38
    sport in, 108–12
    total land holdings of British in,
      278
    westward expansion of, xiii
upper class, American:
    British aristocrats welcomed by,
      286
    sport and, 108–12

Valkyrie II (yacht), 173
Vancouver, Fort, 41
Vandalia (steamship), 53
Victoria, Queen, xii, 6, 75, 213
    Banvard's panorama viewed by,
      115
    Bierstadt's meeting with, 142–43
    Buffalo Bill's "Wild West" viewed
      by, 4, 288–89
    Catlin and Ojibbeways in
      meeting with, 78–79
    Golden Jubilee of, 1, 282–85,
      291–92
    journal of, 1, 4
    Murray in household of, 67–68,
      74, 78
Victoria colony, *xxi*, 177, 179–88,
    191, 199, 200, 202, 221, 292
    drought and, 182, 186
    grasshopper blight and, 185–86
    Hunt Club at, 185
    livestock at, 181, 183, 184, 185,
      187
Victoria River, 181
Virginia, plantations in, 17

Wales, 148
Wallop, Oliver, 290, 291
Walsingham, Lord, 293
Walter, John, 211
wapiti (elk), xiii, 122, 148, 157–58,
    159, 173, 218, 239, 247, 254, 293
Ward, Henry, 126, 293
Ward, Roland, 293
War of 1812, 19
Washington, D.C., British burning
    of, 19
Wassells, Major, 127
Waterloo, Battle of, 14
Waterloo Chamber, 79, 115
Watson, Jack, 208–9
*Waverland: A Tale of Our Coming
    Landlords* (Brigham), 273–74
Webb, James Watson, 14, 41, 53
Wentworth-Fitzwilliam, Charles,
    xvi, 117–18, 136–37
    1852 western trip of, 93–94, 166
Wentworth Woodhouse, 93–94
West, *see* American West

Western Land Company, 288
Western Ranches Ltd., 248–49, 258
Westport (Kansas City), Mo., 49, 86
westward expansion, xii, xiii, 86–87, 88, 95, 102, 138, 139, 155, 163, 288
wheat, U.S. exports of, 176
whites:
    Native American interaction with, 12–13, 38, 69–70, 80–81
    Native Americans as victims of, 81
Whitman, Marcus, 44, 47
Whitman, Narcissa, 44, 47
Whyte, Theodore, 171
Wichita, Kans., 221, 224, 226
Wilderness Hunter, The (Roosevelt), 159
Winchester, 189
Wind River Mountains, 32–33, 47, 87, 89, 122, 294
Windsor Castle, 67, 78–79, 115, 289
Windsor Park, 67

Winn, James, 251
Winnebagos, 69
Wise, Lovatt, 253–54
wolves, 35–36, 37, 121, 122–23, 254, 293
Wood, Percy, 222
Wood, Sophia Turnley, 222
workingmen's organizations, 268
Wright, Henry, 266
Wyeth, Nathaniel, 37
Wynne, Captain, 160, 162
Wyoming Stock Growers Association, 245, 261–62
Wyoming Territory, 34, 107, 219, 228, 229, 242, 247, 270, 294
    cattle ranching in, 237, 238, 239–40, 241, 248–52, 258–62, 284, 289, 290–91

Yellow Bear, 94
Yellowstone National Park, 160, 161, 169, 252
Yellowstone River, 114, 122, 123, 124, 142, 160
Yellowstone Valley, 33, 37
Young, Brigham, 116